Policy Innovation and Maintaining Influential Local Governments

Onur Kulaç
Pamukkale University, Turkey

Çiğdem Akman
Süleyman Demirel University, Turkey

IGI Global
Scientific Publishing
Publishing Tomorrow's Research Today

Vice President of Editorial | Melissa Wagner
Director of Acquisitions | Mikaela Felty
Director of Book Development | Jocelynn Hessler
Production Manager | Mike Brehm
Cover Design | Jose Rosado

Published in the United States of America by
IGI Global Scientific Publishing
701 East Chocolate Avenue
Hershey, PA, 17033, USA
Tel: 717-533-8845
Fax: 717-533-7115
Website: https://www.igi-global.com E-mail: cust@igi-global.com

Library of Congress Cataloging-in-Publication Data

Names: Kulaç, Onur, 1984- editor | Akman, Çiğdem editor
Title: Policy innovation and maintaining influential local governments / edited by Onur Kulaç, Çiğdem Akman.
Description: Hershey, PA : IGI Global Scientific Publishing, [2026] | Includes bibliographical references and index. | Summary: "To understand the complexities of local governance globally, it is essential to examine the structures of countries with diverse local government systems, analyze their policy processes, and compare their approaches. In doing so, the role of policy innovation and the influence of local governments in shaping effective governance can be better appreciated"-- Provided by publisher.
Identifiers: LCCN 2025003745 (print) | LCCN 2025003746 (ebook) | ISBN 9798337304526 hardcover | ISBN 9798337304533 paperback | ISBN 9798337304540 ebook
Subjects: LCSH: Local government--Case studies | Public administration--Case studies
Classification: LCC JS78 .P5125 2025 (print) | LCC JS78 (ebook) | DDC 320.8--dc23/eng/20250415
LC record available at https://lccn.loc.gov/2025003745
LC ebook record available at https://lccn.loc.gov/2025003746

British Cataloguing in Publication Data
A Cataloguing in Publication record for this book is available from the British Library.

Table of Contents

Detailed Table of Contents

demonstrates that structured participation strengthens governance, providing valuable lessons for other countries. By institutionalizing citizen engagement and decentralizing decision-making, local governments can create more inclusive, transparent, and responsive democratic processes.

Today, digitalization in public administration has become a critical transformation area in terms of increasing the quality of service delivery and ensuring citizen satisfaction. In this context, municipalities are in a restructuring process based on the effective use of digital technologies in local governments. E-municipality applications provide citizens with fast, easy and time-independent access to public services; while also contributing to the more efficient use of public resources. This transformation is not only a technological investment; it also requires a participatory, transparent and solution-oriented change in management mentality. In this study, the basic dynamics of digital transformation in municipalities, the functionality of e-municipality applications and the current challenges encountered will be examined; good practice examples and strategic suggestions will be addressed specifically for Pamukkale Municipality, and a number of suggestions will be put forward to increase the effectiveness of local municipal services.

Local governments in France are structured in a tripartite system consisting of "municipal", "departmental", and "regional" administrations. Since French local governments are founded on the principle of centralization, they operate under strict supervision from the central government. The aim of this study is to reveal the transformation caused by migration in France and to evaluate the effects of local migration governance on migrants. In line with this aim, the study examines the migration policies of local government units in France and reveals the current state of migrant welfare at the local level. First, the concept of migration governance and policy is addressed. Second, it discusses what has been done regarding migration management in France. Lastly, it explains the migration policy of local governments in France, evaluates the condition of migrants, and discusses these issues. The study employs the method of document analysis.

Local government leaders can promote transformative progress to foster change in their communities through policies. Cities in the United States are affected by complex and interconnected issues related to land use, transportation, waste management, and housing that have evolved to fulfill residents' needs. The housing good practices identified include overlay zones, adaptive reuse, and form-based code. The transportation good practices discussed are complete streets and leveraging ride sharing. In the case of waste management, the good practices are mandatory recycling and compositing ordinances and youth educational programs. Each of the good practices is associated with ethical considerations. Policy changes often result in inequitable outcomes, which can cause ethical concerns. There is a need for future researchers to assess the ethical considerations associated with the identified good practice policies. In essence, good practice policies positively impact local government functions concerning land use, transportation, waste management, and housing.

The current research will examine the innovative aspects of municipal services for refugees in Lithuania and Croatia.. The scientific literature constantly debates the most effective social refugee integration structure or systems. The central government provided social integration services for the local government. In some cases, municipalities took the initiative and started some services in partnership with NGOs. So not only was the process top-down, but often the local communities or local authorities were proactive. There have certainly been more proactive initiatives to welcome Ukrainians compared to refugees from other countries of origin. This would allow us to discuss how a reactive response to crises allows for the improvement of municipal services and the transfer of impacts. On the other hand, it will allow us to ask why some successful solutions were short-lived and what factors (lack of resources, bureaucratic machinery, the logic of short-term crises) led to this.

This study examines the evolution of maslikhats in Kazakhstan, focusing on their role in governance and recent electoral reforms. Maslikhats, established as local representative bodies, have undergone significant changes to enhance their authority and political participation. The 2022 constitutional amendments introduced a mixed electoral system, allowing for both party-affiliated and independent candidates, which aimed to increase political competition and local self-governance. However, challenges remain, including financial and structural limitations that restrict their autonomy. The findings highlight the impact of these reforms on political dynamics, representation, and the effectiveness of local governance, emphasizing the need for further decentralization and institutional strengthening.

This study examines the role of urban areas in developing sustainable food systems. Current global challenges, including the rapid increase in urban populations, climate change, food security issues, and food waste, involve the development of sustainable food policies by local governments. This paper analyzes the Milan Urban Food Policy Pact (MUFPP) as a key initiative in the development of sustainable food systems and policies and evaluates the suggested approaches created at both global and local levels. It investigates the actions taken by the member cities of MUFPP concerning sustainable food production, distribution, and consumption and examines the impact of these actions. This study analyzes Türkiye's sustainable food policies, national strategies, and MUFPP member municipalities' projects. By examining Mezitli, Istanbul, Nilufer, Balıkesir, Efeler, Eregli, and Muratpasa it reveals the current state of sustainable food policies. The study highlights local government efforts, successful practices, and future improvement plans.

Laws ensuring equal access to rights for individuals with disabilities are a crucial component of social policy. While central governments are responsible for policy formulation, local governments, particularly municipalities, play a key role in implementing these policies effectively. By creating more accessible physical and social environments, municipalities contribute significantly to improving the quality of life for individuals with disabilities. Within the framework of "social municipalism," they develop and enforce inclusive policies that promote social integration. This study examines the role and effectiveness of municipalities in Turkey in developing and implementing social policies for individuals with disabilities. It explores the challenges they encounter in this process and the strategies they employ to overcome them. Through a comprehensive analysis, the study assesses municipalities' contributions, the difficulties they face, and potential solutions to enhance the inclusion of individuals with disabilities in society.

Preface

In today's world, the growing significance of decentralization policies, rapid population growth, and the trend towards urban living underscore more than ever the necessity of public service delivery by administrative units closest to the citizens. In this context, local governments are being brought to the forefront, and a process is underway where decentralization policies gain importance for the strengthening of these local entities. Many countries worldwide are undertaking reform efforts to transfer more authority, responsibility, and resources to local government units, which are deemed better equipped to respond to local needs within the framework of decentralization policies. As a result of the reforms implemented by countries, local governments have taken on different forms and begun to perform diverse functions. Beyond fulfilling their traditional roles, local governments have evolved into democratic institutions possessing their own decision-making bodies, preparing their own budgets, conducting international relations activities, engaging in multi-actor decision-making processes, delivering public services more effectively and efficiently, adopting more flexible organizational structures, utilizing alternative service delivery methods, demanding autonomy in borrowing and taxation, increasing citizen participation, and adhering to principles of accountability and transparency. However, these definitions can vary significantly from one country to another. An examination of country practices and policies clearly reveals that there is no single, uniform model of local government worldwide. The reasons for this include whether countries have unitary or federal state structures, their unique political, economic, socio-cultural, and social experiences and characteristics, and differences in their levels of decentralization. In this sense, it is necessary to examine the structures of countries with different local government systems, analyze local policy processes, and consider them comparatively.

The examination of countries' local government structures from different perspectives and making comparisons based on various practices are highly important for comparative public administration. Furthermore, including good practice examples from countries' local government systems can enable their transfer to other nations through reform transfer. Many countries are inclined to follow and transfer good practices in public service delivery. Therefore, the best local government practices and policy experiences of different countries play functional roles in shaping nations' public service provision. In line with different public administration understandings learned through policy and reform transfer, countries can undertake reform studies in their own local government systems and achieve significant gains. As will be understood, many countries worldwide have implemented reforms to effectively deliver increasing and diversifying public services, leading to significant changes in local government systems and practices.

This book project also aims to present how developments in the local government systems and policies of different countries have occurred, their impacts, contributions, and good practice examples. The book will be one of the pioneering works in this field, as it deeply addresses the effects of changes in local government policies and offers an opportunity for comparison. Most importantly, the detailed examination of their respective local government structures by academics from different countries featured in the book will fill a fundamental void in this field and also provide an opportunity for comparison. The book is highly important for researchers, students, and practitioners in providing information about countries' local government policies, structures, characteristics, and practices, and in making comparisons between countries. Academics can benefit from this book as a textbook or supplementary resource in their courses.

OVERVIEW OF CHAPTERS

Chapter 1: Diffusion of Policy Innovations in Migrant Local Governance: A Case Study of the Philippines and an Origin Province

This chapter showcases the case of migrant local governance by an origin country, that which was adopted by a province and its jurisdiction localities, under the lens of the Diffusion of Policy Innovations theory by Berry and Berry (1990). This chapter presents the case of the Philippines then zooms in to the province of Ilocos Norte (northwestern Philippines) and how its provincial and local government units have embraced influential national-level policy innovations on migration management. This policy innovation diffusion-cum-adoption locally has led to over-a-decade-long period of providing frontline services to overseas workers and their families. This Philippine case highlights possibilities for other origin countries of overseas migrants to diffuse migration management policy innovations locally so that migrant frontline services provision becomes a national-to-local affair that is built on coordination.

Chapter 2: Policy Innovation in Local Governance Direct Elections of Rural Mayors in Kazakhstan for Decentralization

The purpose of this study is to assess the importance of direct elections of rural mayors (akims) for local governance and community development in rural districts of Kazakhstan. The study focuses on residents' perceptions and a comparative analysis of settlements where elections have taken place and those where they have not. Ili district is taken as a case. The study is based on survey data and structured interviews. The results show that in localities where direct elections have already taken place, citizens perceive them positively and believe that they contribute to increasing their participation in local governance. The study concludes that Kazakhstan is in the process of gradually democratising its local government system, as evidenced by the introduction of direct elections of akims. This study adds to the existing literature by analysing public perceptions of the reform and its impact on rural districts.

Chapter 3: Digitalization in Citizen Participation and Effects on Local Governments

Citizen participation refers to the ability of citizens to influence political decisions that impact their lives, forming a core aspect of democracy. While some argue that citizens lack the time, information, and motivation to engage in every public sector decision, others suggest that increased participation fosters knowledge, expertise, and community engagement. The role of public administrators in this process remains debated. However, with technological and social changes, new participation mechanisms have emerged. In particular, the rise of Information and Communication Technologies in the 2000s has transformed interactions between individuals, organizations, and governments, introducing concepts such as electronic participation. This study examines electronic citizen participation in local governments by presenting a theoretical framework, explaining participation in local governance, and analyzing practical examples. Finally, the benefits and challenges of citizen participation in local governance are evaluated.

Chapter 4: Promoting Inclusive Governance through Citizen Participation: The Case of Switzerland's Local Decision-Making Processes

Citizen participation in local decision-making varies from formal mechanisms like public consultations and referenda to informal tools such as petitions and social media engagement. Switzerland stands out as a model of direct democracy, where popular initiatives allow citizens to propose legislation, and referenda enable them to approve or reject laws. Its decentralized governance grants local authorities autonomy, fostering strong public engagement. Participatory budgeting and digital democracy further enhance inclusivity, ensuring decisions reflect community needs. These mechanisms increase trust, accountability, and democratic legitimacy by directly involving citizens in shaping policies and public services. Switzerland's experience demonstrates that structured participation strengthens governance, providing valuable lessons for other countries. By institutionalizing citizen engagement and decentralizing decision-making, local governments can create more inclusive, transparent, and responsive democratic processes.

Chapter 5: Digital Transformation and e-Municipality Applications in Municipalities in the Case of Pamukkale Municipality

Today, digitalization in public administration has become a critical transformation area in terms of increasing the quality of service delivery and ensuring citizen satisfaction. In this context, municipalities are in a restructuring process based on the effective use of digital technologies in local governments. E-municipality applications provide citizens with fast, easy and time-independent access to public services; while also contributing to the more efficient use of public resources. This transformation is not only a technological investment; it also requires a participatory, transparent and solution-oriented change in management mentality. In this study, the basic dynamics of digital transformation in municipalities, the functionality of e-municipality applications and the current challenges encountered will be examined; good practice examples and strategic suggestions will be addressed specifically for Pamukkale Municipality, and a number of suggestions will be put forward to increase the effectiveness of local municipal services.

Chapter 6: Migration Policies of Local Governments in France

Local governments in France are structured in a tripartite system consisting of "municipal", "departmental", and "regional" administrations. Since French local governments are founded on the principle of centralization, they operate under strict supervision from the central government. The aim of this study is to reveal the transformation caused by migration in France and to evaluate the effects of local migration governance on migrants. In line with this aim, the study examines the migration policies of local government units in France and reveals the current state of migrant welfare at the local level. First, the concept of migration governance and policy is addressed. Second, it discusses what has been done regarding migration management in France. Lastly, it explains the migration policy of local governments in France, evaluates the condition of migrants, and discusses these issues. The study employs the method of document analysis.

Chapter 7: Good Practice Policies Examples in America's Local Governments and their Ethical Considerations

Local government leaders can promote transformative progress to foster change in their communities through policies. Cities in the United States are affected by complex and interconnected issues related to land use, transportation, waste management, and housing that have evolved to fulfill residents' needs. The housing good practices identified include overlay zones, adaptive reuse, and form-based code. The transportation good practices discussed are complete streets and leveraging ride sharing. In the case of waste management, the good practices are mandatory recycling and compositing ordinances and youth educational programs. Each of the good practices is associated with ethical considerations. Policy changes often result in inequitable outcomes, which can cause ethical concerns. There is a need for future researchers to assess the ethical considerations associated with the identified good practice policies. In essence, good practice policies positively impact local government functions concerning land use, transportation, waste management, and housing.

Chapter 8: Innovation in Improving Local Refugee Integration Systems and the Roles of Lithuanian and Croatian Municipalities

The current research will examine the innovative aspects of municipal services for refugees in Lithuania and Croatia.. The scientific literature constantly debates the most effective social refugee integration structure or systems. The central government provided social integration services for the local government. In some cases, municipalities took the initiative and started some services in partnership with NGOs. So not only was the process top-down, but often the local communities or local authorities were proactive. There have certainly been more proactive initiatives to welcome Ukrainians compared to refugees from other countries of origin. This would allow us to discuss how a reactive response to crises allows for the improvement of municipal services and the transfer of impacts. On the other hand, it will allow us to ask why some successful solutions were short-lived and what factors (lack of resources, bureaucratic machinery, the logic of short-term crises) led to this.

Chapter 9: Maslikhats in Kazakhstan in the Context of Electoral Reforms and Governance Evolution

This study examines the evolution of maslikhats in Kazakhstan, focusing on their role in governance and recent electoral reforms. Maslikhats, established as local representative bodies, have undergone significant changes to enhance their authority and political participation. The 2022 constitutional amendments introduced a mixed electoral system, allowing for both party-affiliated and independent candidates, which aimed to increase political competition and local self-governance. However, challenges remain, including financial and structural limitations that restrict their autonomy. The findings highlight the impact of these reforms on political dynamics, representation, and the effectiveness of local governance, emphasizing the need for further decentralization and institutional strengthening.

Chapter 10: Sustainable Food Policies in Cities Milan Urban Food Policy Pact and Practices from Türkiye

This study examines the role of urban areas in developing sustainable food systems. Current global challenges, including the rapid increase in urban populations, climate change, food security issues, and food waste, involve the development of sustainable food policies by local governments. This paper analyzes the Milan Urban Food Policy Pact (MUFPP) as a key initiative in the development of sustainable food systems and policies and evaluates the suggested approaches created at both global and local levels. It investigates the actions taken by the member cities of MUFPP concerning sustainable food production, distribution, and consumption and examines the impact of these actions. This study analyzes Türkiye's sustainable food policies, national strategies, and MUFPP member municipalities' projects. By examining Mezitli, Istanbul, Nilufer, Balikesir, Efeler, Eregli, and Muratpasa it reveals the current state of sustainable food policies. The study highlights local government efforts, successful practices, and future improvement plans.

Chapter 11: Municipalities and Disability Policies in Türkiye: Roles, Challenges, and Social Municipalism

Laws ensuring equal access to rights for individuals with disabilities are a crucial component of social policy. While central governments are responsible for policy formulation, local governments, particularly municipalities, play a key role in implementing these policies effectively. By creating more accessible physical and social environments, municipalities contribute significantly to improving the quality of life for individuals with disabilities. Within the framework of "social municipalism," they develop and enforce inclusive policies that promote social integration. This study examines the role and effectiveness of municipalities in Turkey in developing and implementing social policies for individuals with disabilities. It explores the challenges they encounter in this process and the strategies they employ to overcome them. Through a comprehensive analysis, the study assesses municipalities' contributions, the difficulties they face, and potential solutions to enhance the inclusion of individuals with disabilities in society.

This book will be particularly useful for students in master's or doctoral theses, as each chapter will address the local government structure of a different country. The analyses discussed in this book will likely contribute to the future studies of relevant researchers. Practitioners and policymakers will benefit from this book, and it will be an opportunity for them to follow good practice examples and draw promising lessons. Furthermore, considering the country practices planned to be included in the book by the editors, the local government structures, duties, functioning, and practices of all countries will be analyzed from a comparative perspective. This book in your hands has been designed precisely to address this need. Its primary aim is to comprehensively present the transformations in the local government systems and policies of different countries, the impacts of these transformations, their contributions, and outstanding examples of good practices. The book is shaped by contributions from expert academics, each detailing their own country's local government structure, functions, operations, and current practices. Through this, it offers an opportunity to analyze from a comparative perspective how local governments in different geographies have evolved, what challenges they have faced, and what successes they have achieved. This book aims to fill a fundamental void in this area by bringing together diverse country experiences and providing readers with a rich basis for comparison. It serves as a valuable resource for researchers, students, and practitioners by offering up-to-date and in-depth information on the local government policies, structures, characteristics, and practices of various countries. Academics can use this work as a textbook or supplementary resource, while postgraduate students will be able to benefit from each chapter individually for their thesis research. Practitioners and policymakers, on the other hand, will be able to shed light on their own reform processes by following good practice examples and lessons learned from different countries. Different public administration approaches learned through policy and reform transfer will guide countries in developing their own local government systems and achieving significant gains. This book, by deeply addressing the impacts of changes in local government policies and offering an opportunity for international comparison, aspires to be one of the pioneering works in its field. As editors, we hope that the practices included in the book of the country will offer readers a broad perspective and help them better understand the complex world of local governments.

Chapter 1
Diffusion of Policy Innovations in Migrant Local Governance:
A Case Study of the Philippines and an Origin Province

Jeremaiah Opiniano
https://orcid.org/0000-0003-3847-9494
University of Santo Tomas, Manila, Philippines

Elizabeth Marfel F Gagni
https://orcid.org/0000-0002-3925-2040
Mariano Marcos State University, Batac City, Philippines

Melissa Garabiles
https://orcid.org/0009-0009-2249-0331
De La Salle University, Manila, Philippines

Ana Marie Faith Corpuz
https://orcid.org/0009-0005-7367-6313
Mariano Marcos State University, Batac City, Philippines

Violeta Alonzo
https://orcid.org/0000-0002-6967-8448
Mariano Marcos State University, Batac City, Philippines

ABSTRACT

This chapter showcases the case of migrant local governance by an origin country, that which was adopted by a province and its jurisdiction localities, under the lens of

DOI: 10.4018/979-8-3373-0452-6.ch001

the Diffusion of Policy Innovations theory by Berry and Berry (1990). This chapter presents the case of the Philippines then zooms in to the province of Ilocos Norte (northwestern Philippines) and how its provincial and local government units have embraced influential national-level policy innovations on migration management. This policy innovation diffusion-cum-adoption locally has led to over-a-decade-long period of providing frontline services to overseas workers and their families. This Philippine case highlights possibilities for other origin countries of overseas migrants to diffuse migration management policy innovations locally so that migrant frontline services provision becomes a national-to-local affair that is built on coordination.

INTRODUCTION

Overseas migrants make up a critical social sector in their origin countries. Migrants send exponential earnings that uplift the socio-economic welfare of their families and, by extension, the origin country and the communities where they came from (Opiniano & Ang, 2024). Migrants' birthplace communities thus carry a stake in serving their needs, especially since foreign remittances provide spill-over economic benefits (Taylor et al., 1996) out of migrant families' spending, entrepreneurship, savings and investments. Migrant workers' rights, welfare, safety and health conditions abroad matter for these communities of origin (Garabiles et al., 2024).

How do local stakeholders respond to the welfare needs of their overseas migrant townmates especially when they face vulnerable situations abroad? In practice, some local governments in migrants' origin countries remain clueless about serving migrants (Nijenhuis, 2009). Research has documented the various approaches (including "innovations") of local governments in *migrant receiving countries*, to integrate overseas migrants and address their needs (e.g., Lacroix & Desille, 2018; Joint Migration and Development Initiative, 2012). Globally, since the mid-2010s, local authorities in both origin and receiving countries have committed to launch migrant-oriented programs (Lacroix & Desille, 2018). An example here is a periodic conference called the *Mayoral Forum on Human Mobility, Migration and Development*, which has formulated the *Mayors Mechanism* in 2018 (www.mayorsmechanism.org) that formally links local authorities to initiatives formulated in annual editions of the Global Forum on Migration and Development (GFMD).

However, research on the role of local governments in *origin countries* for overseas migrants is slow to keep pace with global initiatives. This development is troubling since it may leave behind origin countries' local authorities in global migration-and-development efforts, especially when their efforts are being assessed. Yet in practice, origin communities in some countries had catered to overseas migrants (Riallant, 2017). The recent COVID-19 pandemic also highlighted the role of local governments in origin countries since returnee migrant workers went back to their birthplace communities, thus requiring coordination and eventual migrants' rights and social protection services (UN ECLAC, 2020; Khishtovani, 2020).

The scant empirical literature on *migrant local governance* by origin countries does not discount the fact that practices have been prevailing in several origin countries. Such is why in some of these countries, when the COVID-19 pandemic led to droves of return migrations to origin countries and communities, local governments had to be readily respond. Seeing migration governance getting localized, with influence from national-level government agencies, is an undocumented example of *policy innovation diffusion* that some origin countries have established and now try to further institutionalize.

This Chapter thus examines how an origin country, the Philippines, has diffused national-level migration governance locally leading to sustained migrant local governance as a frontline policy and programmatic effort for overseas migrants and their families. The Philippines provides an interesting case of migrant local governance, with the country long remarked to be a model among origin countries in managing overseas human mobility (International Organization for Migration, 2005; Martin et al., 2004). Yet the growing number and geographic dispersion of temporary and permanent migrants across the decades saw national migration agencies realizing that local governments play critical roles in serving overseas migrants. When overseas Filipino workers (OFWs) or temporary migrants face vulnerable situations in host countries, receive services there ("first mile"), and get ready to return home, local governments and cooperating stakeholders provide the "last mile" of social protection services.

We use the Diffusion of Policy Innovations framework (Berry & Berry, 1999) to analyze the case of the Philippines and a province —Ilocos Norte— and its jurisdiction local governments. Primary data for this paper were gathered at the height of the COVID-19 pandemic, but the policy innovation diffusion will be explained given documentary data. The recent fieldwork saw researchers confront local surges of SARS-CoV-2 by conducting online and face-to-face *key informant interviews* (with 22 returnee OFWs and 10 local stakeholders) and *documentary data collection and analysis* (N=72 sets of documents, including local policy documents) —both done over a 15-month period (September 2020 to March 2022).

In the end, this Chapter will illustrate and analyze the policy innovation diffusion of migrant local governance that benefits and serves (distressed) overseas workers and their families. The first part of this Chapter will explain the Diffusion of Policy Innovations framework and its applicability to local governments. What follows is a global discussion of migrant local governance, emphasizing the milieu and perspective of origin countries' local governments. Authors will then elucidate the diffusion of the Philippines' migration governance approach as a policy in local governments, and then applying such in Ilocos Norte; some evaluative insights of the case will also be provided. The Chapter will end with analysis of the attributes of migrant local governance as a diffused policy innovation, with the Philippine case possibly providing policy lessons to other origin countries of international migrants.

THEORETICAL BACKGROUND

Theoretical Framework: Diffusion of Policy Innovations

This Chapter anchors itself on the *Diffusion of Policy Innovations* framework, developed by Francis S. Berry and William D. Berry in 1990. Inspired by the Diffusion of Innovations theory by communication theorist and sociologist Everett Rogers (1995; 2004), the Diffusion of Policy Innovations speaks of how policies and policy innovations get adopted by others. Innovation here speaks of a process to adopt, reinvent and create new ideas, objects and approaches (Walker et al., 2011). Meanwhile, Rogers (1995) says diffusion covers how an innovation gets communicated in a social system. When applied to the policy sciences, the Diffusion of Policy Innovations pertains to the adoption of policies —either by states or by differing tiers of government— depending on policies' necessity, viability, and promise to expand its reach and benefits (Walker et al., 2011).

In the policy making field, the effort begins with defining genuine needs and determining issues affecting identified stakeholders. What follows these tasks is strategizing how the identified needs and concerns are addressed. When the policy innovation is ready for roll out, policy makers and innovators then have to persuade other policy makers that such innovation yields high impact at optimum scale. It is in convincing other governmental actors where the policy innovation is diffused. The adoption can happen under these possible contexts (in Walker et al., 2011):

1. The problem or crisis warrants changing existing circumstances in resolving such, with serious crisis likely increasing policy adoption.
2. Innovation adoption may be influenced by a state's comfort or discomfort with existing policies.
3. Since adopting a policy innovation entails costs, fiscal viability may determine its adoption.
4. Finally, adoption also depends on the target adopting party's attitudes toward change as well as their level of experience. Community readiness and receptiveness also matter.

Taking cue from Rogers (2004), Makse and Volden (2011) identified five attributes when a policy innovation is diffused. *Relative advantage* speaks the benefits and costs of adopting that innovation, and how likely that innovation helps the adopting party improve the effectiveness of addressing the problem being targeted. *Compatibility* matters when the innovation runs consistent with the adopting party's values, past experiences and needs. *Complexity* covers how a policy innovation is challenging to understand and to use. *Observability* is an attribute wherein the policy innovation becomes visible to others that have yet to adopt it. Finally, *trialability* talks about the pilot, limited adoption of such innovation and, when successful, seeing future replication elsewhere.

The Diffusion of Policy Innovations framework provides the suitable theoretical anchor to analyze the transmission of a national-level effort to manage international migration. The authors assert that migration management efforts become more expansive and possibly more effective when diffused to local levels, and when such diffusion gets backstop national and regional-level support.

Migrant local governance

"International migration and local governance" has been a research and policy theme largely skewed towards destination countries which receive foreigners and initiate measures to integrate them (see Lacroix & Desille, 2018). The development prevails while international migration remains an issue in both origin and destination countries. A turn occurred in the previous decade to see the place of local governance in migration-and-development concerns: Multilateral organizations asserted local authorities play key roles in ensuring a destination country's smooth integration of migrants and refugees (Riallant, 2017). Primarily being discussed are the roles of *cities* in migration management as migrants flock to jobs in income-rich urban centers (Lacroix & Desille, 2018).

Being left behind in the global discussions, however, are local governments in origin countries. Even a recent systematic review within the public administration discipline yielded studies whose topics cover the countries of destination (Yeo & Huang, 2020). Yet transnationalism sees international migrants link their economic and social lives and conditions with their families, kin and networks in birthplace communities (e.g., Morocco, in Gazzotti, 2018; Mali, in Coulibaly & Lima, 2018). It is at these origin communities where local residents visibly feel the positive and negative consequences of international migration (Ulceluse, 2021). Positive consequences include remittances, businesses that have opened and investments that were placed, and improved economic conditions by families; negative outcomes include disruptions in family relationships, visible community-level inequality and absence of needed local labor (Gregorio & Opiniano, 2011).

Thus, migrant local governance in *origin countries* covers the near entirety of addressing various migration-and-development issues (including migrant social protection provision, especially for aggrieved migrants). Such coverage helps ensure that migrants' welfare and rights are respected abroad, which in turn would allow them to transfer their resources to benefit their families and, by extension, their communities of origin (Asis, 2011; Ulceluse, 2021). These realizations may all the more warrant to link local administrative processes with policy lenses so that localized services for emigrants puts these origin communities (especially in rural areas) at the frontline.

The national, local policy questions that necessitate 'diffusion'

From the perspective of origin countries, we continually wonder why local governance "is largely missing in current debates on migration and development" (Tacoli, 2010: 6). Migrant local governance for origin countries, however, may not operate without coordination from national authorities as national agencies deal with migration stakeholders in the countries of destination. Origin countries may have realized that handling the affairs and needs of overseas migrants warrants broader approaches that involve governance actors within and outside the public sector, and that span varied communities (Riallant, 2017). It is therefore necessary to investigate how local governments of migrants' home countries address the outcomes of migration locally.

Answers to these questions warrant further research from origin countries, which is glaringly few. A comparative case study (Nijehuis, 2009) of 12 municipalities in Bolivia showed that only a few local governments have projects helping migrants and migrant families. Nijenhuis (2009: 12), thus concluding that "embedding" international migration into local governance "is still in its infancy". A policy mapping analysis in Indonesia showed that local regulations (*perda*) mostly covered general employment, but less on migrant worker protection in the country's *kabupaten* (or regency, an administrative division that falls under a province) (Bachtiar, 2011). Findings also point to how other stakeholders such as nongovernment organizations (NGOs) and private recruitment agencies involve themselves. Bachtiar (2011) notably points out the reflection that a grey area for overseas employment is "whether it should be centralized or decentralized" (p. 34), especially since central government faces difficulties in dealing with migrant worker concerns that surface in the origin *kabupaten*.

We can perhaps say that on the one hand, international migration remains centered on national-level efforts together with migrants' host countries —possibly leaving out the local communities (and ergo, their local authorities) where overseas migrants came from. On the other hand, we may have yet to see an empirical case of an origin country rolling out a national-level policy commitment to her overseas migrants that goes down to local communities.

Interestingly, a multilateral organization is promoting migration governance as a national *and a local* policy response. Being referred to here is the localized adoption of the national-level Migration Governance Indicators (MGI), done by the International Organization for Migration (IOM) in 2016. The Local MGI is an index that lumps together 94 national and 80 local indicators that cover six dimensions of migration governance: migrants' rights; whole-of-government approach; partnerships; the socio-economic well-being of migrants; the mobility dimension of crises; and ensuring safe, orderly and regular migration (International Organization for Migration, 2022). The Local MGI has already covered 51 local authorities in 29 countries (https://www.migrationdataportal.org/overviews/mgi/local-mgi).

The MGI represented an attempt to measure and benchmark countries' and local authorities' efforts for international migrants (Robinson, 2020), and whether these efforts provide opportunities to expand local actions for international migrants. A sample of Local MGI assessments in identified origin communities (cities, municipalities) reveals some "bets practices": in La Palma municipality in El Salvador, a fresh ordinance mandated the provision of community-level responses for its townmates abroad; and in Kankan region, Guinea, local authorities provide reintegration support to returnee migrants and seek the involvement of the Kankan diaspora for the region's development (IOM, 2024). However, the MGI and its localized version is not explicitly shown here as a diffused a policy innovation but simply as an inventory of efforts—both done and not done— by a local community for its constituent overseas migrants.

Albeit inadvertently, these few empirical studies do not project a policy mindset of having a national migration governance policy rolled out to a country's local tiers of government. We even think that localized efforts do not operate in a vacuum, and these efforts may largely be attributed to efforts by national governments to manage international migration and its development consequences to families, communities and a country. Migration governance emerges therefore *as a national-to local policy continuum*. Migration governance thus becomes a diffused policy innovation by the Philippines that predated multilateral organizations' initiatives (e.g., the MGI), even if serving the overseas migrant clientele is never an easy affair to handle locally.

It is in this respect that authors wish to answer the following research questions: 1) *What policy-oriented attributes can be seen in the Philippines' efforts of diffusing policy innovations on migration management to local governments?* 2) *How does a Philippine province of origin, Ilocos Norte, diffused and institutionalized migrant local governance and service the socio-economic needs of (distressed) overseas workers? What challenges face local authorities with already-institutionalized migrant local governance efforts like that of Ilocos Norte?* Looking at migrant local governance from the Diffusion of Policy Innovations framework (Berry & Berry, 1999) can help explain how origin countries localize migration management and institutionalize this approach.

FINDINGS

A. Diffusing migration governance locally as a policy 'innovation'

The Philippines has decades of institutionalizing national-level migration management efforts, covering pre-departure, on-site (in the host country) and return migration. Since the country's 1974 Labor Code first regulated overseas employment, the Philippines had set up varied government agencies and programs to serve migrant workers and their families. National laws had provided mandates for the government agencies directly involved in migration management (e.g., the Department of Labor and Employment [DOLE], the Department of Foreign Affairs [DFA] and its embassies and consulates, the former Philippine Overseas Employment Administration [POEA], the Overseas Workers Welfare Administration [OWWA], and the Commission on Filipinos Overseas [CFO]). Currently, the Department of Migrant Workers (or DMW, created by a national law in 2022) spearheads the Philippines' migration governance efforts.

While overseas migration remains largely a national affair (Asis, 2011), these national agencies have deputized their regional and provincial offices to implement national programs for overseas workers (Lao, 2013). DMW then adopted the long-standing approach and started forming its regional offices. This migration governance-related development is where the interaction between provincial, city and municipal governments and the regional-level agencies of these migration agencies begins. That interaction prevails even if migration management is not directed in a landmark law on Philippine decentralization: the 1991 Local Government Code (Republic Act 7160). Noticeably also, many of these Philippine LGUs rely on the national government for the programs and services for OFWs and their families (Asis, 2011).

Roots of migration local governance. The influence of the Philippines' overseas migration phenomenon all but warranted a government response to confront the positive and negative outcomes of overseas human mobility. Even if there are no updated national stock estimates of overseas Filipinos after the 2013 stock estimate of 10.2 million (CFO, 2013), deployments of a sub-set of these overseas Filipinos —migrant workers or temporary migrants, covering both newly-hired and re-hired workers— have breached over a million land- and sea-based workers since 2016.

Filipinos are found in almost all 193 countries and territories, and in many skilled and less-skilled occupations (especially domestic work, caregiving and nursing jobs). The feminization of migrant work is evident in the Philippine case, as many concerns on migrant workers' welfare affect women (especially domestic workers).

A National Migration Survey (NMS) shows that about 12 percent of the country's households has a family member working or residing abroad (Philippine Statistics Authority, 2020). At the same time, cash remittances from overseas Filipinos over the last 50 years (1975 to 2024) have reached over-US$ 560 billion (Bangko Sental ng Pilipinas, 2025). On average, cash remittances from overseas Filipinos contribute nine percent to the country's gross domestic product. Since many migrant households reside in rural areas and inevitably receive foreign remittances (Opiniano & Ang, 2016), rural communities do receive direct and indirect socio-economic benefits and costs from international migration (Taylor et al., 1996).

First attribute of diffused policy innovation: Overarching national laws. The Philippines had its share of unfortunate incidents affecting her women migrant workers that warranted national policy responses. After the March 1995 execution of domestic worker Ms. Flor Contemplacion in Singapore (alleged for the death of a Singaporean baby and a fellow Filipino female domestic worker), the Philippine legislature enacted Republic Act 8042 into law and ratified the 1990 United Nations Convention for the Protection of the Rights of All Migrant Workers and Members of their Families.

To this day, Republic Act 8042 remains the cornerstone Philippine policy on migration management that is more enforceable legally than the migration-related provisions of the 1974 Labor Code of the Philippines (Presidential Decree 442). Even if some of RA 8042's provisions were updated and amended some 14 years later (into Republic Act 10022, in 2009), this "Migrant Workers and Overseas Filipinos Act of 1995" has been the basis of all national-level policies by the migration management agencies.

Section 20 of RA 8042 (Republic of the Philippines, 1995) includes local government units (LGUs) as among the relevant stakeholders for a mandated Shared Government Information System on Migration (SGISM). Section 23 cemented the place of LGUs in the overall migration management effort. The LGU (in Section 23-c) is tasked to help "in the fight against illegal recruitment" together with the relevant national-level migration agencies, especially through hosting PEOS (pre-employment orientation seminars), and operating OFW kiosks or desks locally. Later on, through RA 10022 (Republic of the Philippines, 2011), LGUs' place in migration management were cemented through Sections 20 (the SGISM provision), 23 (the roles of government agencies), 11 (closure orders to illegal recruitment agencies), and more importantly the elaborate Rule XII titled "The Role of LGUs." Rule XII mandated LGUs to launch aggressive anti-illegal recruitment campaigns, host PEOS, establish OFW desks or kiosks, and maintain a database of OFWs residing locally.

Administratively, and even before RA 8042 got enacted, the former POEA worked on what it calls the "decentralization" of its services so that the agency's services "to bring vital overseas jobs (and) services to the people in the countryside" (POEA, 1990: 24). Realizing the rise of illegal recruitment, POEA collaborate with local government units to launch anti-illegal recruitment campaigns (POEA, 1993; 1995) after the agency had opened regional extension units (REUs) or regional offices in 1990. Separate unpublished policy documents from POEA show that since the year 2000, POEA and OWWA have been forging memoranda of agreement (MOA) with LGUs nationwide (POEA, n.d. - a; POEA, n.d. – b).

While at the time no memoranda of understanding were forged with LGUs, POEA thinks that its decentralization program will lead to decreases in the national agency's "work pressure" (POEA, 1991: 24). The MOAs (POEA, 2009; 2012) with local governments followed in the new millennium when the anti-illegal recruitment campaigns and pre-employment orientation seminars (PEOS) of POEA intensified locally. This administrative measure by POEA contributed inadvertently to the diffusion of migrant local governance as a policy innovation.

Second attribute: Forming migrant desks through policy improvisation. Amid RA 8042, there is no overarching republic act that mandates migrant local governance. RA 7160 (Republic of the Philippines, 1991) speaks of overall local governance that reflects decentralization, but with some national-level functions devolved to LGUs (health, education, agricultural development). Employment was not among the devolved national functions, and overseas migration (in the ambit of overseas employment) was then under the DOLE. To localize DOLE's employment-related mandates, Republic Act 8759 (or the Public Employment Service Office Act in 1999) led to the formation of these public employment service offices (PESOs) (Tana, 2004). PESOs were then mandated to operate OFW Desks and operationalize migration-related duties: regulate local recruitment for overseas (and local) jobs; conduct pre-employment orientation and counseling; and provide economic reintegration services to returnee migrants. The PESO, particularly its "OFW Desk," becomes the focal point for a local government's involvement in the migrant sector (Regional Development Council – CALABARZON, 2016). At the same time, PESOs' OFW Desks have become the diffused "policy innovation" that national-level migration policy measures have mandated.

Third attribute: Civil society groups' influence on national policy. Civil society organizations within the migrant sector have long rolled out programs that target local communities and their migrant workers. The Kanlungan Centre Foundation Inc. (founded in 1989) was formed as a migrant crisis center that provides direct social services and policy interventions to women migrant workers in vulnerable situations abroad. In the 1990s, this pioneer migrant CSO ran a local economic development (LED) project that began in Naguilian municipality, La Union province (western side of Luzon island) (see KCFI's website, http://kanlungancentre.blogspot.com/).

Also during the mid-1990s, the CSOs Unlad Kabayan Migrant Services Foundation (or Unlad Kabayan, which is Filipino for "progress, compatriot") and Atikha Overseas Workers and Communities Initiative rolled out economic reintegration and migrant investment programs for OFWs and their families. Unlad Kabayan (see www.unladkabayan.org) pioneered a migrant savings and alternative investment (MSAI) program as a reintegration strategy that provides business advisory services to OFWs currently abroad and returnee migrant workers. Also founded in 1996 was the CSO Atikha (see www.atikha.org) that sought to address the social costs of migration on OFW families through family counseling, financial education and investment advisory, coalition building and localizing migration-and-development efforts in province-based cities and municipalities. The work of these CSOs has influenced the approaches of OWWA (and then DOLE, OWWA's mother agency prior to DMW) on migrant reintegration and later localizing migration management.

Fourth attribute: Stakeholder buy-in. Efforts to localize migration governance have spurred multilateral pilot projects, run by the IOM and a Joint Migration-and-Development Initiative (JMDI) under the United Nations family. Meanwhile, OWWA and the former POEA got emboldened to reach out to LGUs by forging memoranda of agreement with these local authorities come the new millennium (POEA, n.d.-a, n.d.-b). These MOAs dovetail with OWWA's program since 1983 of forming what is called OFW Family Circles (Borja, 1999). And since RA 8042 had laid out various measures and programs for the OFW sector, local measures led to the launching of programs such as migrant resource centers or MRCs, migration-and-development local plans (International Labor Organization, 2012), and local councils for migrants (Regional Development Council – CALABARZON, 2016).

Final attribute: Institutionalization at national and local levels (even under a new migration management era). Republic Act 11641 created the DMW, as its agency became fully functional on February 3, 2022. Republic Act 11641 then made OWWA (a welfare fund for migrant workers) an attached agency of the DMW. This department merged seven frontline agencies involved in migrant assistance: POEA; the DOLE's International Labor Affairs Bureau (ILAB) and the Philippine Overseas Labor Offices (POLOs); OWWA's National Reintegration Center for OFWs (NRCO); the DFA's Office of the Undersecretary for Migrant Workers Affairs (OUMWA); the National Maritime Polytechnic (NMP); and the Office of the Social Welfare Attaché (OSWA) under the Department of Social Welfare and Development (DSWD).

With DMW assuming all these agencies' functions, DMW now leads in rolling out programs and policies to empower and protect OFWs and returning migrant workers while ensuring safe, orderly and regular migration (Department of Migrant Workers, n.d.; Republic of the Philippines, 2021). As for the involvement of local governments in the DMW, RA 11641 included LGUs as part of the department's sectoral councils (Section 13) and in implementing full-cycle reintegration for returnees (Section 17) (Republic of the Philippines, 2021). Yet as the years have progressed, the DMW had broadened LGU involvement given the previous experiences of POEA, OWWA, and other relevant migration agencies.

We can illustrate current-day Philippine migration governance in a manner that harnesses national-to-transnational efforts but seeing local governments remaining connected to migration-related structures (*seeFigure 1*). We can see here that DMW and its attached agency OWWA directly work with local governments in aspects such as employment facilitation, recruitment regulation, and assisting returning OFWs. Meanwhile, other Philippine-based national government agencies outside of the migration management can directly work with local governments. Examples include the DSWD and the Department of Health (DOH). Thus, the Philippines has been exercising a whole-of-government approach for the overseas migrant sector's needs under current and previous migration management agencies —naturally fusing the involvement of local governments especially since these OFWs (and even permanent migrants) come from local communities.

Figure 1. The Philippines' whole-of-government approach in migration management

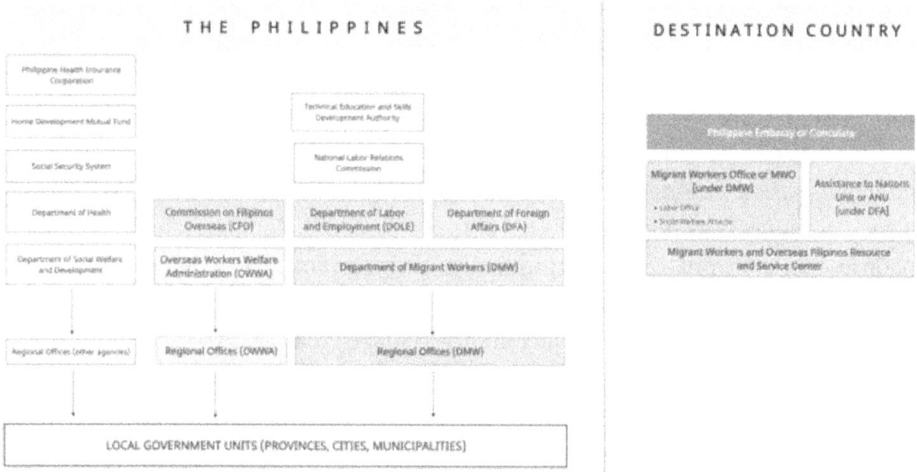

B. Institutionalizing a diffused policy innovation: Migrant local governance in Ilocos Norte

One of this Chapter's aims is to present the efforts of Ilocos Norte province for its migrant worker provincemates. Ilocos Norte has been the subject of previous decades of studies on overseas emigration (e.g. Pertierra, 1992) since the first recorded overseas Filipinos in the 20th century were sugar plantation workers who went to Hawaii, USA starting in 1906.

Ilocos Norte, a largely agricultural economy, is found some 508 kms. northeast of the Philippine capital Manila. After the Hawaii migration of sugar workers (Pertierra, 1992), migrations for both overseas permanent settlement and overseas work followed in succeeding decades. Aggregated data on temporary and permanent migrants and Filipinos who married foreign spouses and went abroad show that Ilocos Norte has an estimated 119,199 overseas migrants (*seeTable 1*). Out of that total, some 50.6 percent are temporary migrants or migrant workers (land- and sea-based migrant workers). Ilocos Norte had more female land-based migrant workers and more male sea-based workers.

The capital and seat of political power is Laoag City, where an international airport is located; the neighboring municipality San Nicolas houses the province's only shopping mall while Batac City hosts the province's state university. These three communities matter since they host 51.23 percent of all businesses (N=15,745) registered in the province's two cities and 21 municipalities as of 2017 [document DN066IN], thus driving increased local incomes and possibly desires by resident families to work and settle overseas.

Table 1. Overseas workers from Ilocos Norte province: Size and those assisted due to welfare cases and the pandemic

A. Overseas migrants from Ilocos Norte	**Overseas workers (as of 2019)**	**Emigrants (1988-2015)**	**Filipino spouses and other partners of foreign nationals (2005-2015)**
Provincial total	60,714	56,506	2,779
B. Gender of overseas workers from Ilocos Norte	**Data as of 2019**		
	Male	**Female**	**Not stated**
Land-based migrant workers	18,998	36,083	928
Sea-based migrant workers	4,547	64	94
C. Number of welfare cases / requests[1] for assistance	**Total cases**	**Resolved cases**	**Resolution rate (%)**
2016	52	50	96.2

continued on following page

Table 1. Continued

A. Overseas migrants from Ilocos Norte	Overseas workers (as of 2019)	Emigrants (1988-2015)	Filipino spouses and other partners of foreign nationals (2005-2015)
2017	63	59	93.7
2018	88	67	76.1
2019	109	76	69.7
2020	90	50	55.6
Total / Average	402	302	75.1

[1] – Though not broken down, the nature of the cases includes the following: medical repatriation, mistreatment, physical abuse, sexual abuse/rape, absconding, unpaid/delayed salaries, tax refunds, finished contract, missing whereabouts, work-related problems, non-support and non-communication to family left behind, contract violations, family emergency demands, imprisonment, need for blood money (in Middle East countries), and legal assistance.

Source: Overseas Workers Welfare Administration (OWWA) – Central Office and Regional Welfare Office 1

That observation being said, the nearer a municipality is to Laoag, Batac and San Nicolas, the more the number of migrant workers (*seeFigure 2* [DN070IN]). Vintar town, the province's largest place by land area (and found beside Laoag City), emerges as among the top three sources of land- and sea-based migrant workers. In all 23 communities, female land-based migrant workers outnumber males; male sea-based workers were overwhelmingly more than female counterparts.

From this brief international migration profile of Ilocos Norte, we now present three historical phases of the diffusion of migrant governance locally as a policy innovation.

Initial institutionalization (pre-2015). International migration has seeped into daily life among residents and was easily spotted by local officials (both elected and appointed). A former governor notes that Ilocanos abroad remit a lot of money[1], leading to the rise of the tourism and services sectors [D069IN]). This development prompted the provincial government to initiate an ordinance (2008) providing benefits and privileges to Ilocanos abroad investing in their hometowns [D071IN]. Even a national government agency (CFO) made Ilocos Norte a beneficiary of a remittance investing-for-entrepreneurship program that benefitted some 70 migrant worker / migrant family borrowers from 2013 to 2015 [D067IN].

Come the onset of the new millennium, OWWA and POEA forged memoranda of agreement (MOAs) with LGUs nationwide (POEA, n.d. - a; POEA, n.d. – a). These agreements saw LGUs operate OFW desks so that these agencies' services (e.g., anti-illegal recruitment campaign for POEA, welfare and benefit programs for OWWA) reach these localities [D025IN; D029IN]. These MOAs saw all of Ilocos Norte's LGUs (including the provincial government) set up their OFW Desks (*see-Table 2*). At that time, and to this day, "migrant desk officers" come from either a municipal or city government's social welfare and development office (SWDO) or the PESO (through its PESO manager) [D057IN].

Table 2. The landscape of migrant local governance in Ilocos Norte

Municipality and city	Seal of Good Local Governance (SGLG) awards received, 2015-2019 [1]	Total registered OFWs (land-based and sea-based) [2]	Memoranda of agreement (MOA) forged related to OFWs, by government agency [3]					Operational OFW Desk in the LGU [3]	Number of OFW family circle organizations [3]
			OWWA	POEA	TESDA	LGU	DOLE		
Adams	--	209	✓			✓	✓	✓	1
Bacarra	2017 to 2019	3,292	✓	✓	✓	✓	✓	✓	1
Badoc	--	2,695	✓			✓	✓	✓	1
Bangui	2017 & 2019	1,708	✓			✓	✓	✓	1
Banna	2015 to 2017, 2019	1,047	✓			✓	✓	✓	--
Batac City	2016 to 2017, 2019	6,311	✓			✓	✓	✓	4
Burgos	2019	977	✓			✓	✓	✓	1
Carasi	2015	128	✓			✓	✓	✓	1
Currimao	2018 to 2019	1,022	✓			✓	✓	✓	2
Dingras	--	3,459	✓			✓	✓	✓	1
Dumalneg	--	155	✓			✓	✓	✓	1
Laoag City	2015 & 2017	10,707	✓			✓	✓	✓	9
Marcos	2016 to 2017	1,507	✓			✓	✓	✓	1
Nueva Era	2016 to 2017	628	✓			✓	✓	✓	1
Pagudpud	--	2,172	✓			✓	✓	✓	1
Paoay	2017 to 2018	2,529	✓			✓	✓	✓	1
Pasuquin	2015	2,728	✓			✓	✓	✓	1
Piddig	2018	2,508	✓			✓	✓	✓	1
Pinili	2015	1,524	✓			✓	✓	✓	2
San Nicolas	2016, 2018 to 2019	3,084	✓			✓	✓	✓	2
Sarrat	--	2,819	✓			✓	✓	✓	1
Solsona	--	2,377	✓			✓	✓	✓	1
Vintar	2017	4,388	✓			✓	✓	✓	3

continued on following page

Table 2. Continued

Municipality and city	Seal of Good Local Governance (SGLG) awards received, 2015-2019 [1]	Total registered OFWs (land-based and sea-based) [2]	Memoranda of agreement (MOA) forged related to OFWs, by government agency [3]					Operational OFW Desk in the LGU [3]	Number of OFW family circle organizations [3]
			OWWA	POEA	TESDA	LGU	DOLE		
Ilocos Norte	2015 to 2016	60,714	✓	✓	✓	✓	✓	✓	1

Sources:

1 – Department of the Interior and Local Government (DILG), in https://www.dilg.gov.ph/reports-and-resources/seal-of-good-local-governance/12/

2 – Membership Processing Center (MPC), Overseas Workers Welfare Administration (OWWA) Central Office

3 – OWWA Regional Welfare Office (RWO) 1

Legend: OWWA – Overseas Workers Welfare Administration; POEA – Philippine Overseas Employment Administration;

TESDA – Technical Education and Skills Development Authority; LGU – Local government unit; DOLE – Department of Labor and Employment

These MDOs, however, are "designated" civil servants —meaning there is no official plantilla item for them that makes these MDOs do dedicated work for their localities' OFW desks [D067IN]. As for the provincial government, its MDO co-ordinates the work of the city and municipal MDOs —later becoming a province-wide MDO network that coordinates OFW welfare cases with each other and with the OWWA Provincial Office [D025IN; D029IN]. The early days of the provincial MDO saw it lodged under the provincial gender office, and then to an office that monitor's the province's compliance with the former Millennium Development Goals (MDGs) [informant LS10IN]. These developments occur as OWWA's provincial and regional offices provide services to distressed OFWs, such as those returning to the origin community because of the 2006 civil strife in Libya.

During this institutionalization period also, the national government started opening one-stop service centers for OFWs (OSSCOs) across major Philippine regions [D052IN]. For the Ilocos Region, the OSSCO was set up at Ilocos Norte's only shopping mall: Robinsons Ilocos (in San Nicolas municipality) [D042IN]. The 20 OSSCOs that house representatives of 16 national government agencies provide frontline documentary services for Filipinos planning to or who are about to work abroad, shortening documentary processing times [D052IN].

As these developments happen, OWWA continues to download the agency's programs (including some cash aid and livelihood grants) to its regional and provincial offices, to OFW Family Circles, and to individual OFWs [D04IN; D09IN; D018IN; D022IN; D023IN]. Meanwhile, the Province of Ilocos Norte Federation of OFWs (PINFO) was formed [LS06IN]. OWWA's regional office is located at San Fernando City, La Union province (some 217 kms. south of Laoag City), and some OFWs in Ilocos Norte go there to process some documentary requirements for OWWA services [D030IN; D032IN]. Note that other offices in LGUs, like the SWDOs and public attorney's offices (PAOs), also serve OFWs and their families [LS01IN & LS09IN].

Further institutionalization (2015-2019). The OWWA Regional Office continued its coordination efforts with provincial welfare officers in the four provinces forming the Ilocos Region: Pangasinan, La Union, Ilocos Sur and Ilocos Norte [D06IN; D07IN]. With directives from OWWA's national office, the Ilocos Norte provincial office continued providing social welfare assistance to distressed OFWs like those who returned from Libya (2015), Saudi Arabia (2016 and 2017) and Kuwait (2018) [D09IN; D11IN; D028IN; D030INL D035IN]. As for settling labor-related cases by these returnee workers, OWWA and POEA coordinated to operationalize an administrative approach to settle domestic and overseas labor issues and conflicts, called the Single-Entry Approach (SEnA) [D041IN]. The regional and provincial OWWA desks also served as single entry assistance desks (SEADs) [D021IN, D033IN & D040IN].

OWWA national and an attached agency, the NRCO, also coordinated with the former's regional and provincial offices [D024IN]. The aim is to reinforce the delivery of OWWA programs (e.g., cash aid, livelihood grants, start-up entrepreneurship kits, educational assistance and scholarships for technical and university education, even typhoon financial aid) for displaced returnees, for returning migrant teachers, for individual OFW families, OFW Family Circles, among others.

Around 2016, a civil servant from the DOLE's Ilocos Norte Office dabbled into programming and developed an online Case Management System [D055IN; D034IN]. This CMS allows MDOs and OWWA Ilocos Norte to refer, document and monitor welfare cases that come to the province's migrant desk officer and to OWWA's provincial personnel [D057IN]. OWWA's Ilocos regional office eventually adopted the CMS and made it region-wide [D055IN]. What followed were training activities to use the CMS [documents D07IN, D056IN & D057IN; informants LS03IN, LS04IN & LS08IN].

OWWA's Ilocos Regional Office realized that the region's MDOs and OFW Family Circles have reached sufficient numbers [D061IN; D062IN], making the said regional office organize annual capacity-building activities for both stakeholder groups. Be it annual general assemblies like an MDO Congress [D27IN] or periodic, topic-specific training workshops (e.g., on psychosocial support [D08IN)], these capacity building activities became occasions to circulate information on existing and new nationwide programs for OFWs and their families.

In 2018, OWWA Ilocos Norte was housed inside the provincial office of DOLE (near the Laoag City public market). Meanwhile, the province's MDO is housed at the provincial capitol right at the heart of Laoag City, some 200 meters from the public market. In response, the provincial MDO provided a dedicated room for OWWA Ilocos Norte personnel so that both offices easily coordinate when OFWs and their families and family circle groups need help [informants LS08IN & LS10IN; document D056IN]. Duty bearers thus were able to provide quick responses to OFWs' needs —delivered even in an "informal matter" so as to ease the anxieties of assisting clients [LS10IN].

A corollary development is the work of PINFO: regular meetings and special events have been staged during the 2015-2019 period [informants LS06IN & LS07IN]. Further cementing their roles for OFWs, top performing MDOs and OFW Family Circle groups get awarded by the OWWA regional office [D03IN, D019IN; D026IN]. Interestingly, the provincial MDO is lodged at the Office of Barangay Affairs (OBA). OFW affairs thus become a community matter since individual families are affected. Says a respondent:

> *"We have access to barangays, so we can ask 'what barangay did your wife went?' So, if he knows, we will call the barangay (officials). It is us (provincial MDO) who will assist them and set the time and day of their meeting... Because when we are informed by OWWA, our office is the one who is there (as) there is an assumption that we are linked to the barangay." [LS10IN]*

Pandemic era (2020-2022), and post-pandemic. During the COVID-19 pandemic, the province has already put in place its network of MDOs; its army of OFW Family Circle groups and their trained leaders; the physical, proximate coordination between the provincial MDO and the OWWA; the online CMS; the OSSCO; and the OWWA regional office's now-stable coordination with its provincial office, the MDOs and the OFW Family Circles. These backdrops greeted returnee OFWs who returned home because of COVID-19 and the economic recessions in host countries.

The national government, through the Inter-Agency Task Force on Emerging and infectious Diseases (IATF), handled regulations and public health protocols (IATF, 2020a). For overseas Filipinos, government already saw the need for repatriation as early as February 2020 (Opiniano, 2021). DFA, OWWA, the Department of Health (DOH) and the Bureau of Quarantine (BOQ), among other agencies, already deployed their personnel to handle the return migration, quarantine and transport to origin communities by returnee OFWs (IATF, 2020b). The "last mile" of this return journey by OFWs is where the local governments-OWWA collaboration was operationalized in Ilocos Norte.

OWWA's national office downloaded to the regional offices its usual cash aid or benefits [D048IN]. Meanwhile, DOLE (with help from OWWA) handed out one-time cash aid (P10,000 or US$200) to affected OFWs, either returnees or who stayed overseas but whose incomes were slashed [D049IN]. Two years of this pandemic saw over-540,000 OFWs receiving this cash aid; pandemic year 1 reports from OWWA show that around 14,097 OFWs from Ilocos Region got this P10,000 cash aid [D048IN]. Apart from this pandemic-related cash aid, other OWWA programs were rolled out nationwide —grants to returning women OFWs; educational subsidies and scholarships for OFW children; cash aid and business kits for returnees displaced from work abroad (a separate program from DOLE's P10,000 cash aid); training grants for vocational-technical education; and entrepreneurial loans and livelihood grants for OFW Family Circles [D073IN].

LGUs also provided actions for affected provincemates. The provincial PESO, for one, received nearly a million pesos (US$40,000) for local entrepreneurs and returnee OFWs to receive business packages (free entrepreneurial training, a bicycle, a pushcart and P2,000 [US$40] start-up capital to jumpstart street food ventures) [D047IN]. A city government, for its part, bankrolled the quarantine of its returnee OFW residents in a local hotel [D047IN]. OWWA's program to transport returnee OFWs to origin communities saw the agency bring home 8,128 OFWs to Ilocos Norte during the first two years of the pandemic (*seeFigures 2 and 3*).

Figure 2. Male and female overseas workers in Ilocos Norte's cities and municipalities

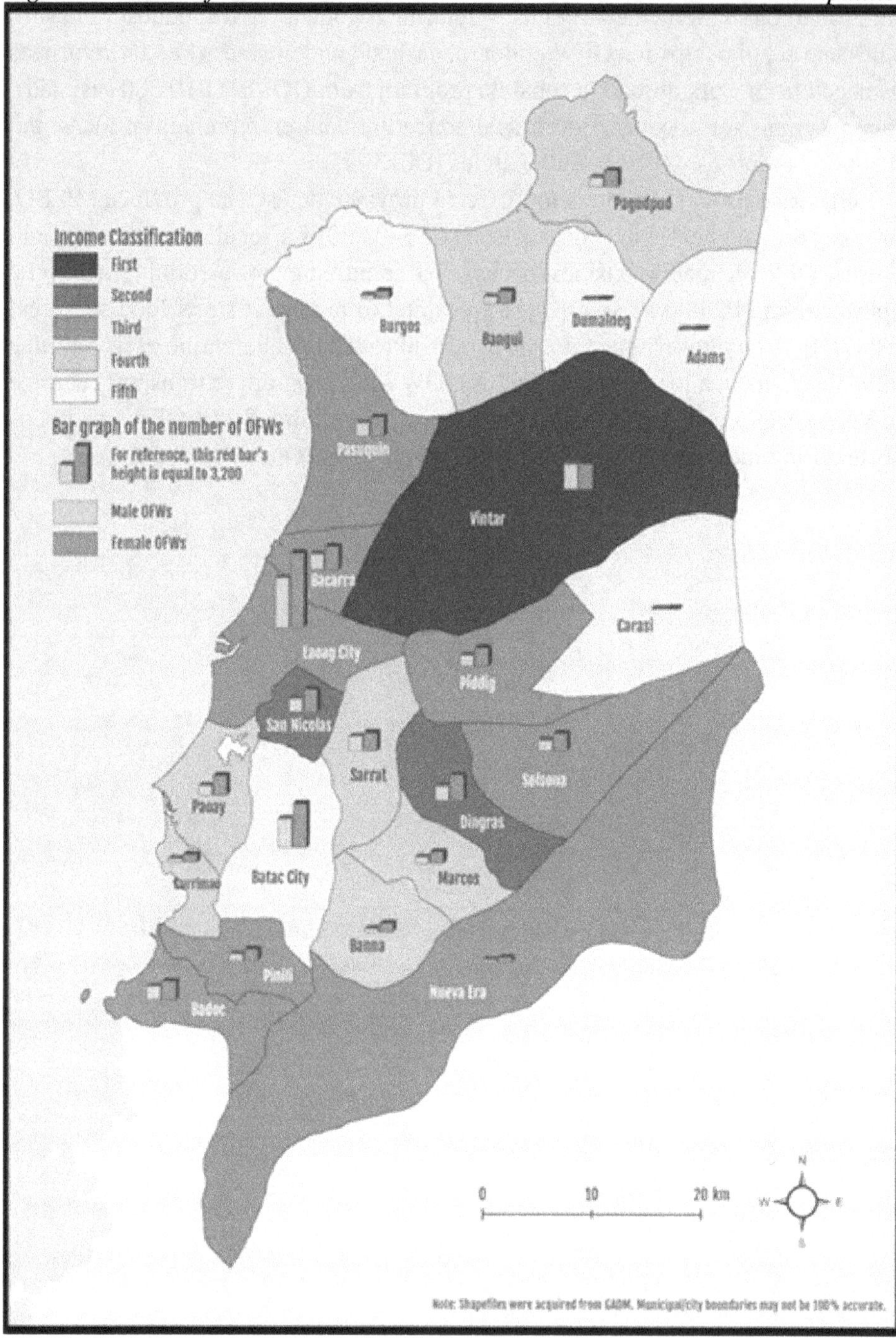

Figure 3. Total number of returnee OFWs from the Philippines' Region 1 (Ilocos Region) assisted in the first two years of the pandemic – per province

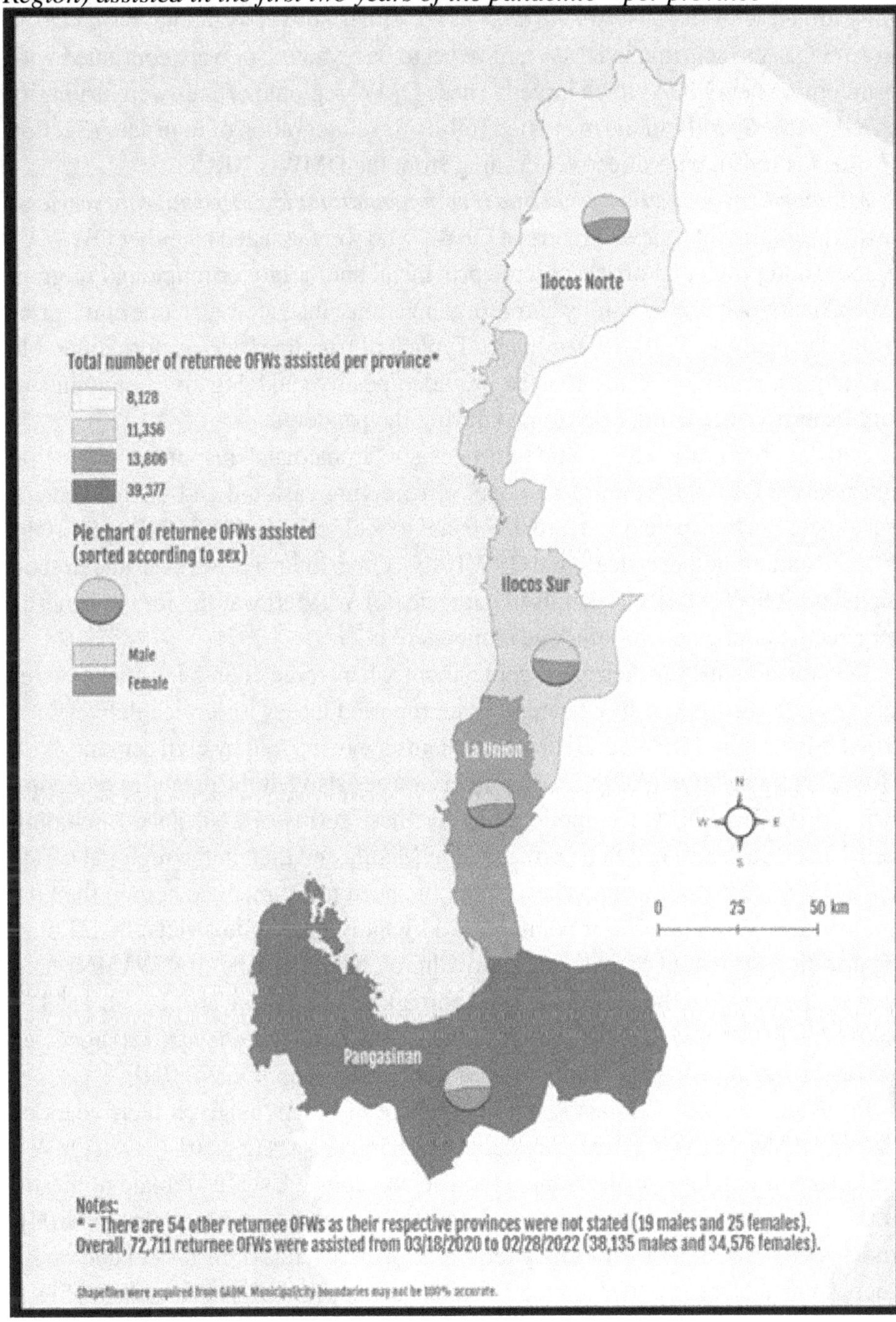

In the post-pandemic era, the Department of Migrant Workers just set up its regional offices in late-2023; OWWA's regional offices remain. Therefore, partnerships forged with LGUs (*refer toTable 1*) are either not yet available, have ceased (given POEA's inclusion in DMW), have yet to be revisited, or were continued with forthcoming new MOAs to be forged. These DMW regional offices were primarily tasked to locally roll-out the mandated full-cycle reintegration of returnees (Section 17 of RA 11649), with directives coming from the DMW's NRCO.

Management-related concerns and recommendations localized migrant services. Researchers had interviewed returnee OFWs who were assisted by either OWWA's regional and provincial offices; by the provincial and/or city or municipal migrant desk officers, or by OFW Family Circle organizations. Interviewees came home prior to and during the COVID-19 pandemic. Typical of frontline services for vulnerable populations, returnee OFWs assisted provided positive and negative comments to duty bearers —occurring prior to and during the pandemic.

Satisfactions arose when some returnees got "immediate" responses and action [interviewee OFW04IN] up to the level of receiving cash aid and other forms of assistance. Such responsive efforts led some to feel relief [OFW05IN], calm [OFW04IN] and strengthened feelings [OFW10IN]. Other interviewees even understood the delays [OFW18IN] and exercised patience [OFW19IN] waiting for the benefits to be handed out given voluminous numbers of clients.

Dissatisfactions, for their part, came about when some clients felt the slow responses [OFW10IN] of duty bearers. Even reported lapses in service delivery led to bad impressions [OFW10IN] or when clients are being told by civil servants "We will just call you" [OFW07IN]. Some interviewees also felt the delays in receiving cash aid [OFW12IN] since applications for these forms of assistance (including the P10,000 cash aid) had to be processed in Manila and then in the regional office [OFW03IN]. Since some interviewees felt the need for immediate help in the host country, and were grateful for being helped by individual compatriots, by Filipino organizations (migrant "advocates" and Church-based groups) [OFW13IN], and even by the media in the Philippines and abroad. Seeking these host country stakeholders' help came when the embassy or consulate abroad, or the national agencies in Manila, are slow in responding to their appeals for help [OFW08IN].

Provincial duty bearers also have their share of reactions given their years of serving OFWs. Many welfare cases stem from family issues (e.g., unlocated OFW), workplace or employer maltreatment, and sexual abuse. Usually, female domestic workers and irregular (or undocumented) OFWs are the ones seeking help [LS08IN]. And even if some of their cases may require legal assistance or SEnA-related assistance, some returnees prefer to receive financial support [OFW07IN; OFW15IN]. These duty bearers obviously felt the stresses of frontline work [LS08IN] while others wished that OFWs assisted will be grateful for the help received [LS06IN].

Other stakeholders noticed that OFWs may not be mindful of the "negative consequences" of going abroad [LS09IN] given the focus on the eventual earnings. For example, returnees assisted may not be mindful of the provisions contained in work contracts [LS09IN]. Others think the willingness of the OFW client to be helped is where the success of the intervention rests [LS01IN].

The years of assisting OFWs led many interviewees to specially recommend something in unison: have a dedicated OFW Desk per LGU. A month after the first declared lockdown in the Philippines, a surprising development came: the Department of the Interior and Local Government (DILG) released Memorandum Circular 2020-075 calling for the establishment of the "DILG OFW Desk and the designation of the OFW Desk Officer". This memorandum responded to an IATF order to assist returnee OFWs from their quarantine, entry and eventual to their origin communities. The already-established OFW desks in Ilocos Norte had made it easy for migrant desk officers of the province to submit monitoring reports that the DILG requires.

Other recommendations were put forward. Returnees recommended: a) More swift action in the services and programs being offered and downloaded locally; b) Alertness to requests for help; posting updates to OFWs' requests for assistance; c) Equal treatment to all those requesting help; d) Available information on programs and services; and e) Guides in accessing online information and documentary requirements. Stakeholders, for their part, called for formal collaboration between among offices and stakeholders directly and indirectly involved for OFWs, and maximizing the services of other LGU offices that are *not* the LGU's designated OFW desks.

Yet a striking insight from the interviews with both stakeholders and the returnees is that OFWs are considered a community matter. For example, village or barangay captains can directly intervene in OFW concerns and refer cases to the provincial MDO (which is under the Office of Barangay Affairs since the OFW "is part of barangay affairs" [LS10IN]). Other offices even treat OFWs not as a separate client but as "a head of the family" like non-OFW residents [LS01IN]. Even some returnees claimed to directly approach their mayors [OFW13IN] and their issues being "a barangay matter" [OFW16IN]. Some returnees were even hopeful that their municipality or city will help them [OFW07IN] through a dedicated program for them [OFW22IN].

DISCUSSION AND CONCLUSION

This case study research featured the more-than-a-decade work of a Philippine province on *migrant local governance* that included efforts during the COVID-19 pandemic. The work of Ilocos Norte is a by-product of a diffused policy innovation from national-level migration management agencies, referred to here as *migrant local governance*. Global actors in migration-and-development have recognized the Philippines to be a model of migration management among origin countries (Martin et al., 2004; IOM, 2005) owing to an elaborate bureaucracy and national laws that set into motion the influence of Filipinos' international migration phenomenon on Philippine local governance.

Key informant interviews and documentary analyses enabled researchers to surface a running historical, case study account of migrant local governance, which was linked to a national "history" of how local governments were invited to be involved in overall migration management. The study responds to knowledge gaps that migrant local governance is largely a host country affair —unwittingly leaving out origin countries in the global study of migrant local governance (e.g., Basa & Villamil, 2009; Gazzotti, 2018; Coulibaly & Lima, 2018).

The work of Ilocos Norte shows the national-to-local migration governance effort that has institutionalized migrant local governance in this province, in coordination with national migration agencies. This institutionalization served the end-goal of the Diffusion of Policy Innovations framework (Berry & Berry, 1990): upscale the policy innovation and extend the reach of such innovation. Pragmatically, the major outcome here is that OFWs and their families directly get help from their local authorities. Local governments here then become partners with relevant migration management agencies at the national level.

Let us now use the Diffusion of Policy Innovation framework (Berry & Berry, 1990) to analyze the approach of the Philippine migration management bureaucracy to diffuse such migration management for a policy innovation. International migration continues to yield crisis situations wrought by labor conditions abroad, by political situations in the host country, by natural events, etc. Handling these crises and ensuring OFWs' welfare all but prompted the diffusion of migrant local governance as the policy innovation, with LGUs coordinating with the national and regional offices of the migration agencies. Ilocos Norte provides a case in point.

Because of the dwarfing social influence of Filipinos' international migration (as evidenced by the millions who went abroad), national migration agencies' efforts to collaborate with LGUs reveals both comfort in working with them, and discomfort with the absence of an overarching law that cements and eventually funds LGU involvement with OFWs in their geographic communities. The case of Ilocos Norte's LGUs shows that the OFW Desk is assigned to not just the PESO but to the SWDO of the LGU. Yet serving the OFW sector locally has made OFWs one of the target clients, but not a dedicated client that leads to a funded, dedicated OFW desk with an assigned personnel. OFWs or overseas Filipinos from a geographic community are not the only vulnerable sector being served by these local authorities. Nevertheless, the diffusion of migration management as a policy innovation locally was marked by the conduct of work-around measures such as networking with fellow local stakeholders (especially OFW Family Circle groups), and support from OWWA. In a sense, LGUs and the national and regional offices of migration agencies exert cost-effective measures to somewhat offset the demanded resources of running an OFW Desk, such as using some public funds and sweat equity from involved local stakeholders.

As evidenced in Ilocos Norte LGUs' involvement with the OFW sector through their OFW desks, it took over a decade to initiate, bolster and eventually sustain attitudes of local stakeholders towards helping the OFW sector. No wonder that these LGUs' OFW desks and the OFW Family Circle groups in the province, with support from OWWA's regional office, have helped Ilocos Norte become ready to assist vulnerable OFWs and their families (especially during COVID-19).

Rogers (2004) said diffused policy innovations carry five "attributes". Let us dovetail Rogers' five attributes to the Philippines-to-Ilocos Norte case. In terms of *relative advantage*, the diffused policy innovation that is migrant local governance became a cost-advantageous measure even if, frankly, LGUs are co-shouldering the tasks of national migration agencies. An example is anti-illegal recruitment, which the former POEA had long "decentralized" such a task through coordination with local government units (POEA, 1990). All that the former regulating agency for overseas employment wanted was "to bring overseas employment, (and) services to people in the countryside" (p. 24) —so as to "decrease work-pressure" (p. 25). It was over the years that this specific national-local collaboration expanded into broader frontline social protection services for the OFW sector, which Ilocos Norte currently does.

The migrant local governance policy diffusion effort easily satisfied Rogers' other policy attributes of *compatibility, observability* and *trialability*. Since the national agencies, then led by the POEA, had been forging memoranda of agreement left-and-right with LGUs nationwide, in a sense national-to-local collaboration related to migration was easily bought in. Even Ilocos Norte's LGUs worked with OWWA to produce "localized innovations:" an electronic case management system for distressed workers, a province-wide networked referral system, and local government-local civil society engagement.

However, interviewees do note the *complexity* of the migrant local governance effort from a policy standpoint. Since the PESO Act of 1999 did not mandate LGUs to allocate personnel plantilla items for PESO managers, or to even allot funds for OFW desks, efforts to serve localities' OFWs and their families become a best-effort affair. Such situation led to another form of complexity: localities' OFWs, returnees and migrant families are already expecting efficient, responsive frontline services for them. These services are, quite frankly, sourced from meager local funds, from available support from OWWA regional offices, and from local stakeholders' sweat equity. No wonder satisfactions and dissatisfactions emerged from OFW clients who were interviewed.

Therefore, the current-day institutionalization of migrant local governance requires newer forms of policy innovation. At the level of national migration agencies, officials can lobby national legislators to enact an overarching law mandating and funding migrant local governance. Locally, progressive local governments can enact ordinances that mandate the formation of OFW desks, migration-and-development councils, allocate local funds for migrant social protection services, and stage projects that harness foreign remittances for local development. Other localities have been doing migration-and-development initiatives (ILO, 2012; Ducanes, 2012; Regional Development Council – CALABARZON, 2016). Other local stakeholders can be tapped for this effort, like associations of provincemates abroad, CSOs, and individual returnee migrants.

Other origin communities of migrants' home countries may find the Ilocos Norte and Philippine situations unique since the country has the established migration-related offices and policies. Nevertheless, migrant origin countries can operationalize migrant local governance systems in the context of their nations' existing state-run offices for migrants. We account of course the contexts of other origin countries in terms of the social importance of international migration, and the level of that country's policy development on international migration. Nevertheless, a progressive migrant-origin country's efforts to expand the outreach for her overseas migrants easily makes a diffused policy innovation like migrant local governance a receptive local policy measure.

Ulculuse (2021) conceptualized various ways that origin countries' local governments serve migrants. Yet documented experiences from various origin countries remain few, thus warranting experiences like that of the Philippines to be put together through cross-country research (similar to the Local MGI). This set of evidence matters so that origin countries' local governments can assert their work through venues such as the Mayors Mechanism, and the annual Global Forum on Migration and Development.

Origin countries' local governments provide "last mile" migrant services for distressed overseas migrants, hoping that trust gained locally leads to harnessing the resources of overseas migrants for local development. As for the Philippines, its decades-old approach to migration management expanded through "decentralization," through migrant local governance. Other origin countries and origin communities may handle their own overseas migrants differently given varying politico-administrative structures by national governments and local authorities. May lessons from one origin community that this paper had surfaced motivate other local authorities in origin countries to roll out innovative local governance for overseas migrants.

FUNDING DECLARATION

This research received support from the "Human Rights Grants in Aid Program" of the Philippine Commission on Human Rights. The Philippine nonprofit Institute for Migration and Development Issues (IMDI) also provided some financial assistance.

REFERENCES

Asis, M. M. (Ed.). (2011). *Minding the gap: Migration, development and governance in the Philippines*. Scalabrini Migration Center.

Bachtiar, P. P. (2011) The governance of Indonesian overseas employment in the context of decentralisation. Discussion Papers Series 2011-25, December 2011. Philippine Institute of Development Studies (PIDS). Retrieved from https://www.pids.gov.ph/publication/discussion-papers/the-governance-of-indonesian-overseas-employment-in-the-context-of-decentralization

Basa, C., & Villamil, L. (2009) Migration, local development and governance in two small towns: Two examples from the Philippines. Working Paper Series on Rural-Urban Interactions and Livelihood Strategies (no. 17), September 2009. International Institute for Environment and Development (IIED). Retrieved from https://www.iied.org/10576iied

Berry, F., & Berry, W. (1990). State lottery adoptions as policy innovations: An event history analysis. *The American Political Science Review*, *84*(2), 395–415. DOI: 10.2307/1963526

Coulibaly, H., & Lima, S. (2018). Decentralisation and territorialisation of migratory resources in Mali: Towards which local and transnational governance? In Lacroix, T., & Desille, A. (Eds.), *International Migrations and Local Governance: A Global Perspective* (pp. 97–110). Palgrave MacMillan. DOI: 10.1007/978-3-319-65996-1_6

Department of Migrant Workers. (n.d.). About DMW. Agency website. https://dmw.gov.ph/about-dmw

Ducanes, G. (2012). *Situation Analysis of Outbound and Return Migration and Local Institutional Mechanisms to Support Migrants in La Union, Ilocos Sur and Nueva Ecija*. International Labor Organization.

Garabiles, M., Gagni, E. M., Corpuz, A. M. F., Alonzo, V., & Opiniano, J. (2024). Mapping and evaluating the localized migrant assistance services in Ilocos Norte, Philippines: An asset-based and multi-stakeholder approach. *Journal of Social Service Research*, *50*(6), 1058–1074. DOI: 10.1080/01488376.2024.2393411

Gazzotti, L. (2018). Local governance, civil society and migrants' support to local development: Perspectives from Morocco. In Lacroix, T., & Desille, A. (Eds.), *International migrations and local governance: A global perspective* (pp. 79–96). Palgrave MacMillan. DOI: 10.1007/978-3-319-65996-1_5

Gregorio, M.C.C. & Opiniano, J. (2011). Harvests and hardships: Analyzing overseas migration and Philippine rural development. Institute for Migration and Development Issues (IMDI) and the Philippine Partnerships for the Development of Human Resources in Rural Areas (PhilDHRRA).

International Organization for Migration. (2005). [Costs and benefits of international migration. IOM.]. *World Migration Report*, •••, 2005.

IOM. (2024). *The Migration Governance Indicators success stories 2024*. IOM.

Joint Migration and Development Initiative. (2012). *Mapping local authorities' practices in the area of migration and development: A territorial approach to local strategies, initiatives and needs.* JMDI. https://www.local2030.org/library/190/Mapping-Local-Authorities-Practices-in-Migration-and-Development-Report.pdf

Khishtovani, G. (2020). *Reviewing migration and development: The role of local authorities in Central Asia*. CAREC Institute., Retrieved from https://www.carecinstitute.org/wp-content/uploads/2020/09/VFP-2020-migration-in-Central-Asia.pdf

Lacroix, T., & Desille, A. (2018). (Eds.), *International Migrations and Local Governance: A Global Perspective*. Palgrave MacMillan. DOI: 10.1007/978-3-319-65996-1

Lao, M. E. (2013). Are local governments ready for migration? In Tigno, J. (Ed.), *Interrogating Migration: New Questions and Emerging Trends in the Philippines* (pp. 28–41). Philippine Social Science Council.

Makse, T., & Volden, C. (2011). The role of policy attributes in the diffusion of innovations. *The Journal of Politics*, *73*(1), 108–124. DOI: 10.1017/S0022381610000903

Martin, P., Abella, M., & Midgley, E. (2004). Best practices to manage migration: The Philippines. *The International Migration Review*, *38*(4), 1544–1559. DOI: 10.1111/j.1747-7379.2004.tb00247.x

Nijenhuis, G. (2009). Embedding international migration: The response of Bolivian local governments and NGOs to international migration. *Environment and Urbanization*, *22*(1), 1–12.

Opiniano, J., & Ang, A. (2016). *Remittance Investment Climate Analysis in Rural Hometowns (RICART): Piloting a tool on rural hometown investing by overseas migrants. University of Santo Tomas - Research Center on Culture, Education and Social Issues*. UST - RCCESI.

Opiniano, J. (2021). *A reset for overseas migration? Recent developments in Filipinos' migration in the context of the COVID-19 pandemic (Migration Research Series no. 69)*. International Organization for Migration.

Opiniano, J., & Ang, A. (2024). Remittance investment climate analysis: Ascertaining the local development potential of overseas remittances in Philippine rural hometowns. *Asian and Pacific Migration Journal, 33*(3), 525–553. DOI: 10.1177/01171968241288259

Pertierra, R. (1992). *Remittances and Returnees: The Cultural Economy of Migration in Ilocos*. New Day Publishers.

Philippine Statistics Authority. (2020, January 28). 12 Percent of Filipino Households Have an OFW Member (Results from the 2018 National Migration Survey). PSA website, https://psa.gov.ph/statistics/national-migration-survey/node/1684064156

POEA. (1991). *POEA Annual Report 1990.*https://dmw.gov.ph/archives/annualreports/1990.htm

POEA. (1995). *POEA Annual Report 1995.*https://dmw.gov.ph/archives/annualreports/1995.htm

POEA. (2012). *POEA Annual Report 2011.*https://dmw.gov.ph/archives/annualreports/2011.htm

POEA. (n.d. – b) MOUs with local government units." A project document by POEA's Workers Education Division. (Unpublished)

Republic of the Philippines. (1991). Republic Act 7160. https://lawphil.net/statutes/repacts/ra1991/ra_7160_1991.html

Republic of the Philippines. (1995). Republic Act 8042. https://library.laborlaw.ph/r-a-8042-migrant-workers-and-overseas-filipinos-act-of-1995/

Republic of the Philippines. (2011). Republic Act 10022. https://lawphil.net/statutes/repacts/ra2010/ra_10022_2010.html

Republic of the Philippines. (2021). Republic Act 11641. https://lawphil.net/statutes/repacts/ra2021/ra_11641_2021.html

Riallant, C. (2017, January 10). Migration: An overlooked tool for local development. *OECD Development Matters*, https://oecd-development-matters.org/2017/01/10/migration-an-overlooked-tool-for-local-development/

Robinson, C. (2020). Measuring 'well-governed' migration: The IOM's migration governance indicators. In *The International Organization for Migration: The New 'UN Migration Agency' in Critical Perspective* (pp. 123-143). Springer.

Rogers, E. (1995). *Diffusion of Innovations* (4th ed.). New Free Press.

Rogers, E. (2004). *Diffusion of Innovations* (5th ed.). New Free Press.

Tacoli, C. (2010). Editorial: Governance, migration and local development. *Environment and Urbanization, 22*(1), 5–11. DOI: 10.1177/0956247810364111

Tana, J. (2004). Enhancing the performance of the Philippine public employment service office: Drawing lessons from Japan's public employment security office. Paper for the Japan Institute for Labor Policy and Training, https://www.jil.go.jp/profile/documents/Tana.pdf

Taylor, J. E., Arango, J., Hugo, G., Kouaouci, A., Masset, D., & Peregrino, A. (1996). International migration and community development. *Population Index, 62*(3), 397–418. DOI: 10.2307/3645924

Ulceluse, M. (2021, December). The local turn in the governance of emigration and its effects. Dossier, Nederlandse Vereniging voon der Verenigde Naties (NVVN). https://nvvn.nl/the-local-turn-in-the-governance-of-emigration-and-its-effects/

United Nations Economic Commission for Latin America and the Caribbean (UN ECLAC). (2020). The impact of COVID-19: an opportunity to reaffirm the central role of migrants' human rights in sustainable development. https://www.cepal.org/sites/default/files/publication/files/46354/S2000617_en.pdf

Walker, R., Avellaneda, C., & Berry, F. (2011). Exploring the diffusion of innovation among high and low innovative localities: A test of the Berry and Berry model. *Public Management Review, 13*(1), 95–125. DOI: 10.1080/14719037.2010.501616

Yeo, J., & Huang, X. (2020). Migration in public administration research: A systematic review and future directions. *International Journal of Public Administration, 43*(2), 176–187. DOI: 10.1080/01900692.2019.1672731

ENDNOTE

1 No reliable estimates are available locally on the amount of foreign cash remittances sent by overseas provincemates to Ilocos Norte.

Chapter 2
Policy Innovation in Local Governance Direct Elections of Rural Mayors in Kazakhstan for Decentralization

Raushan Nurbekova
https://orcid.org/0000-0002-7814-6697
Al-Farabi Kazakh National University, Almaty, Kazakhstan

Nurlan Muminov
https://orcid.org/0000-0001-7824-7044
Khoja Akhmet Yassawi International Kazakh-Turkish University, Turkistan, Kazakhstan

Gulmira Tokshalykovna Ileuova
Public Foundation Center for Social and Political Studies "Strategy", Almaty, Kazakhstan

ABSTRACT

The purpose of this study is to assess the importance of direct elections of rural mayors (akims) for local governance and community development in rural districts of Kazakhstan. The study focuses on residents' perceptions and a comparative analysis of settlements where elections have taken place and those where they have not. Ili district is taken as a case. The study is based on survey data and structured interviews. The results show that in localities where direct elections have already taken place, citizens perceive them positively and believe that they contribute to increasing

DOI: 10.4018/979-8-3373-0452-6.ch002

their participation in local governance. The study concludes that Kazakhstan is in the process of gradually democratising its local government system, as evidenced by the introduction of direct elections of akims. This study adds to the existing literature by analysing public perceptions of the reform and its impact on rural districts.

INTRODUCTION

The introduction of direct elections for rural mayors *(akims)* in Kazakhstan in 2021 constituted a significant milestone in the ongoing reform of local self-government, giving rise to novel opportunities and challenges within the local governance system. The reform's stated objectives included enhancing the accountability of local authorities to citizens, cultivating democratic institutions, and fostering heightened public participation in decision-making processes. Nevertheless, the question remains as to whether the direct election of akims has resulted in substantive changes in local governance, or whether its impact has been constrained.

The notion of electing local government heads in Kazakhstan was first mooted in the 1990s, but at the time this step was perceived as a potential threat to political stability, especially in the context of a systemic economic crisis (Yuvitsa, 2019). During this period, the nation's focus was on mobilising resources to address the crisis, consequently relegating the matter of local government reform to a secondary position. However, with the advent of the 2000s, the necessity for decentralisation and the devolution of certain administrative powers to the local level once more became a salient issue (Mishra, 2009). In 2001, indirect elections were held for the akims of rural districts. Subsequent to this, in 2013 and 2017, general indirect elections of akims of various levels were organised, during which the heads of rural districts, villages and towns of district importance were elected by deputies of *maslikhats* (the representative body of local self-government) (Primbetova & Tlesova, 2015).

Significant reforms in local self-government began to take shape in 2020 (Ibadildin & Pisareva, 2020; Sankhayeva & Arzikulov, 2021). In his address to the nation, President Kassym-Jomart Tokayev emphasised the importance of direct elections for heads of rural settlements, reflecting a public demand for more democratic election processes. As outlined in paragraph 140 of the National Action Plan, direct elections for akims of rural settlements, whose terms were due to expire in 2021, were scheduled for December 2021 (Zakon, 2020). Amendments to the relevant laws were officially endorsed by the President on 24 May 2021, and subsequently came into force on 5 June. By 25 June, the presidential adviser on political issues, Erlan Karin, had announced via his Telegram channel that elections for over 700 rural akims would take place on 25 July, thus marking the implementation of another significant presidential initiative. Karin emphasised the significance of this event, interpreting it as a pivotal moment that symbolised a new phase in Kazakhstan's political modernisation (Kazakhstan, 2021).

The chapter's objective is to evaluate the significance of direct elections for rural akims in terms of local governance and community development in rural districts of Kazakhstan. The study focuses on residents' perceptions and undertakes a comparative analysis of settlements where elections have taken place and those where they have not. The Ili district is selected as a case study. The chapter will demonstrate how local self-government plays a crucial role in the development of statehood in Kazakhstan, serving as an essential attribute of democracy and a foundation for civil society. The impact of local self-government on the daily lives of citizens is extensive, encompassing a broad spectrum of their quotidian concerns. Consequently, local self-government is regarded as a political institution that mitigates class conflicts, promotes socio-economic progress in specific regions, and ensures the sustainable development of the state as a whole. Empirical evidence from across the globe indicates that financial and administrative decentralisation is among the most effective organisational and economic strategies for empowering rural communities to independently manage communal property, enhance citizen well-being, and increase civic engagement. However, it is important to note that the establishment and development of such structures of self-government cannot be solely attributed to the state. Instead, they must be initiated and cultivated at the grassroots level by local communities and citizens. This underscores the relevance of the research topic.

THEORETICAL APPROACHES TO DECENTRALIZATION AND DEMOCRATIC PARTICIPATION

The question of whether decentralisation facilitates the transfer of power to the local level remains a subject of debate within the field of political science. On the one hand, theorists posit that decentralisation increases the accountability of local governments to citizens (Bardhan & Mookherjee, 2006; Treisman, 2007). Conversely, critics contend that the absence of robust democratic institutions precludes the election of local leaders from ensuring genuine transformation in governance (Kosec & Mogues, 2020). This section reviews the main theories of decentralisation and their applicability to the analysis of the direct elections of rural akims in Kazakhstan.

Decentralisation is traditionally seen as a process of transferring powers from central to local authorities (Treisman, 2007). Contemporary theories of decentralization typically categorize it into three primary types: political, administrative, and fiscal decentralization. The concept of political decentralization pertains to the transfer of authority to elected bodies at the local level. It is frequently accompanied by direct elections, augmented citizen participation in governance, and heightened transparency (Grindle, 2007). Conversely, administrative decentralization pertains to the redistribution of governance functions between the central government and regional entities, though it does not inherently entail the election of officials (Bardhan & Mookherjee, 2006). Fiscal decentralization, on the other hand, entails the transfer of the prerogative to autonomously allocate financial resources to local entities (Balaguer-Coll et al., 2010). As comparative experience demonstrates, a combination of these three forms of decentralization is necessary to achieve a redistribution of power and increased accountability. For instance, in the cases of Brazil and India, the implementation of reforms was successful due to concomitant changes in political, administrative, and budgetary institutions (Falleti, 2010; Manor, 1999).

The introduction of direct elections to the akims in Kazakhstan can be seen as an element of political decentralisation, but the question remains: Has this led to a real redistribution of power? One of the main arguments in favour of decentralisation is the hypothesis that local elections increase government accountability to citizens (Kosec & Mogues, 2020). However, empirical studies show contradictory results. In certain countries, such as Indonesia, the implementation of elections has been demonstrated to result in two notable phenomena. Firstly, there has been an observed increase in citizen participation. Secondly, there has been a decrease in corruption (Goldfrank, 2007). This indicates that the decentralization of power can potentially contribute to a reduction in corruption, provided that effective control and transparency mechanisms are in place. In China, the implementation of local elections in rural areas has not resulted in a substantial enhancement of the accountability of local leaders. The central government has maintained its authority over local politics, thereby circumventing the anticipated impact of elections on these levels of governance (Martinez-Bravo et al., 2022). The study's findings indicated that in Burkina Faso, the implementation of local elections, concomitant with enhanced transparency in financial administration, led to a reduction in the incidence of embezzlement by local leaders. Conversely, the absence of transparency exhibited no substantial influence on corruption levels (Lierl, 2017). In Tanzania, despite the implementation of political decentralization reforms and the introduction of local elections, the effective powers of local councils remain constrained. The central government maintains substantial control, resulting in tension between local politicians and administrators (Lameck, 2023). In post-Soviet countries, local elections are often formalised without changing the balance of power between the centre and the regions (Siegel, 2022).

Elections held at the local level are frequently regarded as a conduit for enhancing the accountability of local leaders vis-à-vis the citizenry. However, the efficacy with which this occurs is contingent upon the prevailing political and institutional milieu. Within the context of Kazakhstan, the effectiveness of power redistribution is potentially constrained by numerous factors. Primarily, institutional limitations manifest in the form of the inadequacy of local representative bodies and their reliance on central funding, potentially subverting the anticipated advantages associated with elections. Even in circumstances where local leaders are directly elected, the dearth of financial autonomy and legislative authority engenders a state of dependency on the central government, thereby diminishing their accountability to voters (Faguet, 2012).

Secondly, political barriers encompass the preeminent status of the executive branch and the potential perpetuation of informal control mechanisms. In countries with a pronounced vertical power structure, the central leadership wields administrative levers to exert control over the electoral process and curtail competition. A notable illustration of this phenomenon is the case of Russia, where the introduction of gubernatorial elections in the early 2000s was initially perceived as a step towards decentralization. However, subsequent events demonstrated that the mechanism for selecting candidates and the control over regional elites enabled the federal centre to maintain a dominant influence (Gel'man & and Lankina, 2008).

Thirdly, the presence of robust informal institutions, such as clientelism and patronage networks, may impede the genuine enhancement of accountability. In a number of countries, including several post-Soviet states, elected positions are utilized not necessarily to represent the interests of citizens but rather to fortify the positions of local elites with close ties to the central government (Levitsky & Way, 2010).

Therefore, even with the formal introduction of direct elections of akims, the key question remains the degree of their real independence. It is imperative to recognize that the efficacy of elections as a catalyst for decentralization is contingent upon the implementation of systemic modifications, particularly in the domain of resource distribution. The redistribution of powers and the erosion of informal control mechanisms are essential for ensuring the autonomy and impact of elected bodies. This prompts the following question: does the case of Kazakhstan represent genuine decentralisation, or is it merely a symbolic gesture?

One of the main objectives of local elections is to improve the quality of local governance and community development. In countries with strong democratic traditions, local government plays an important role in the provision of social services (Grindle, 2007). However, in authoritarian regimes, local elections do not always lead to positive change (Kosec & Mogues, 2020). Kazakhstan is in a unique position because, on the one hand, the state is introducing elections as part of democratisation reforms. On the other hand, the centre maintains tight control over the regions, which may limit the impact of elections. This makes Kazakhstan an interesting case for analysing the role of local elections in community development.

The analysis of legislative reforms is the focus of most studies on local government in Kazakhstan. Balabiev (2014) notes that the Kazakh model of local self-government is largely oriented towards the French system, in which the prefect, a representative of the central government, plays a key role. At the same time, Zhanuzakova (2013) notes that the introduction of direct elections of akims is an important step towards democratisation. However, scholars disagree: are elections sufficient for a real transfer of power to local communities?

One of the key issues is the independence of local government. Utibaev and Utibaeva (2022) argue that lower levels of government do not have sufficient powers to have a real impact on socio-economic processes. In his 2020 study, Tebayev (2020) examines the inaugural indirect local elections held in Kazakhstan in 2013, asserting that these elections signify a progressive advancement in the nation's local self-government system. In order to enhance the efficacy of local administrations, Tebayev proposes several key measures, including the augmentation of financial resources, the expansion of rural district budgets, the enhancement of transparency in the operations of maslikhats (representative bodies of local self-government), and the elevation of their status.

Siegel (2022) conducted an examination of decentralisation processes in post-Soviet Central Asia. The author posits that most countries within the former Soviet Union, including Kazakhstan, have encountered challenges in implementing effective decentralization reforms and fostering citizen engagement in governance. The exception to this is Kyrgyzstan, which, despite its shortcomings, has a high level of public participation in local government compared to other Central Asian states. Nevertheless, his study also demonstrates that decentralization does not necessarily lead to democratization. In the case of Kyrgyzstan, despite a significant expansion of local government powers, this did not lead to democratization at the national level. National authorities utilised decentralisation to consolidate their power and mitigate external pressure from international organisations. This finding carries significant implications for Kazakhstan, where the election of akims does not guarantee real autonomy of local governments unless accompanied by institutional reforms.

Sankhayeva and Arzikulov (2021) consider the features of local self-government in Kazakhstan and highlight certain characteristics of classical models of local self-government, to adapt the foreign experience to the realities of rural governance in Kazakhstan. The conclusion drawn by the authors of this study is that Kazakhstan is characterised by a continental model of local self-government, in which the significant influence of central authorities remains. The transition to direct elections of akims is interpreted as indicative of a desire to democratise political institutions. Onalbaiuly (2019) posits that the attainment of economic prosperity in Kazakhstan is contingent upon the institution of elections for akims. However, he emphasises the necessity of considering the unique characteristics of Kazakhstan, including its extensive territory and sparse population, when implementing reforms to its local government system. Furthermore, Onalbaiuly contends that Kazakhstan is still in the process of identifying the most appropriate local government model and structure that fits its specific context and best international practices.

Despite the significant focus on decentralisation issues in research, it has been demonstrated that Kazakhstan continues to exhibit a centralised distribution of resources, thereby constraining the authority of akims. The question remains, however, whether citizens' attitudes towards local authorities have changed since the introduction of elections. In Kazakhstan, the process is still ongoing, and it is important to understand how exactly the perception of the elections is changing among the population. While the existing literature covers many aspects of decentralisation, there remains a dearth of empirical evidence on the impact of elections on citizens' perceptions in Kazakhstan. This study fills this gap by analysing public opinion in the Ili district.

This section reviews the main theoretical approaches to the study of decentralisation and local elections. The review of existing literature shows that the impact of elections on accountability and community development is ambiguous and context dependent. Kazakhstan is a unique case, as elections take place in an environment of strong state control. By examining citizens' perspectives and perceptions of elections, this study contributes to the existing literature.

DEVELOPMENT OF LOCAL SELF-GOVERNMENT IN KAZAKHSTAN

Local self-government plays a pivotal role in ensuring sustainable development of territories and involving citizens in the decision-making process. In the context of Kazakhstan, this institution has undergone a protracted period of development, largely due to the centralization of power and the limited financial autonomy of local authorities (Thibault & Insebayeva, 2024). Despite the constitutional recognition of local self-government in the 1995 Constitution of the Republic of Kazakhstan (*Constitution of the Republic of Kazakhstan*, 1995), its practical implementation was constrained due to the appointment of akims (heads of local administrations) by the president or higher authorities, thereby limiting the autonomy of local governance. Nevertheless, in recent decades, the country has embarked upon a process of gradual decentralisation with the aim of strengthening the role of local authorities (Aubakirova & Aimagambetov, 2020).

The influence of the centralized model of governance inherited from the Soviet Union on local government in Kazakhstan has been significant historically. Following independence in 1991, the country initiated a gradual process of decentralization, albeit with limited redistribution of powers at the local level. The establishment of a comprehensive local governance system has been identified as a key area for modernising public administration; however, this process has unfolded in a gradual and incremental manner.

The implementation of local self-government in Kazakhstan is achieved through the establishment of local executive bodies *(akimdik)* and representative bodies *(maslikhats)*. Akimdik, presided over by akims, are responsible for the execution of executive power at the local level, while maslikhats serve to represent the interests of the population and exercise oversight over the activities of akimats (Beisembayeva et al., 2014). This system facilitates a harmonious integration of centralised management with the consideration of regional particularities, thereby ensuring a balanced and effective governance framework. The development of local self-government plays a pivotal role in the consolidation of democratic institutions and the enhancement of governance efficiency (Norton, 1994). Nevertheless, despite these advantages, the powers of local government in Kazakhstan have historically been limited due to the centralisation of power and the regions' insufficient financial independence.

The first attempts to introduce elected akims at the local level began in 2001, when experimental elections of rural akims were held in 28 rural districts based on the indirect voting mechanism (Zakon, 2001). Nevertheless, a study undertaken in 2002 by the Kazakhstan Institute for Strategic Studies (KISS) revealed that 56% of respondents in the experimental districts expressed dissatisfaction with this mechanism, asserting that the population was prepared for direct elections (Ileuova et al., 2002). This mechanism did not yield the anticipated outcomes, as the voting process was conducted through the intermediary of maslikhat deputies, rather than directly by the residents themselves.

Significant changes to the local government system commenced in 2012 with the ratification of the Concept of Local Government Development in the Republic of Kazakhstan. This document established the foundations for subsequent decentralisation and the augmentation of the powers of local authorities (Adilet, 2012). The primary steps encompassed the consolidation of a dual-tier system of local self-government, wherein at the regional and district tiers, the executive authority remained under state jurisdiction. In contrast, at the local level (rural districts, settlements, and cities of district significance), there was an envisaged augmentation of the powers of local authorities. Furthermore, the reform encompassed the establishment of budgetary autonomy for local authorities and the institution of the election of akims of rural districts as a conduit for augmenting the accountability of the authorities to the population (Adilet, 2012).

In 2013, Kazakhstan held its inaugural large-scale indirect elections of akims in 2,457 rural districts (Kosenov, 2013). However, the exclusive nomination of candidates by district akims served to limit the level of competition. Prior to 2016, the procedure for nominating candidates for the post of akim of rural districts involved the district akim conducting consultations with the local community. However, since 2016, this practice has undergone significant modification. Rather than consulting with a wide range of residents, the district akim began to hold consultations with delegates from the local community, the number of which varied from 10 to 40 people depending on the size of the district. This modification, although it facilitated the nomination process, was met with criticism from experts and the public, as it restricted the involvement of the broader population in the process of establishing local governance (ECHO, 2018, p. 8).

The term of office of the akims concluded in 2017, after which the subsequent elections of akims were conducted. Some amendments to regulatory legal acts were adopted. It was anticipated that over these four years, the mechanisms of local self-government would be refined and yield specific outcomes. On 10 March 2017, amendments were made to the Constitution of the Republic of Kazakhstan (Adilet, 2017), according to which the procedure for appointing or electing akims of cities of district subordination, rural districts, villages and settlements began to be determined by law. Consequently, the relevant amendments to the Law "On Local Public Administration and Self-Government in the Republic of Kazakhstan" were adopted on July 11 (Zakon, 2017), and subsequently came into force on July 14, coinciding with the electoral process. The amendments permitted the submission of nominations by political parties, while retaining the prohibition on self-nomination. However, the previous procedure established by presidential decree No. 555 of April 24, 2013, remained in force until October 11, 2017 (Adilet, 2013).

The most significant phase of local government reform in Kazakhstan was the introduction of direct elections of akims of rural districts in 2021. This reform, as part of the political modernisation programme, was aimed at increasing the accountability and transparency of local authorities, as well as the active involvement of citizens in the decision-making process.

An important stage in the reform of local self-government in Kazakhstan was the adoption of Constitutional Law "On Amendments and Additions to the Constitutional Law of the Republic of Kazakhstan "On Elections in the Republic of Kazakhstan" on 24 May 2021 (Adilet, 2021a). This legislative act resulted in the expansion of the electoral legislation provisions, encompassing regulations that govern the election of akims of cities of district significance, villages, towns and rural districts. Of particular note were the amendments to Articles 1, 3, 4 and 5, which saw the words "maslikhats" followed by "akims of cities of district significance, villages, towns, rural districts" added. This change was pivotal in securing the legal framework for direct elections of local akims (Adilet, 2021a).

On July 25, 2021, Kazakhstan held its first direct elections for akims of cities of district significance, villages, townships, and rural districts. A total of 1,419 self-nominated candidates and 878 candidates from six political parties vied for 730 seats (Kussainova & Ekberova, 2021). In the Almaty region, elections were scheduled for 71 akims of rural districts, with 60 positions due to the expiration of the term of office and 11 due to early resignation (Mauletbai, 2021).

In the aftermath of the elections of 18 August 2021, Decree of the President of the Republic of Kazakhstan No. 639 was promulgated, thereby approving the "Concept for the Development of Local Self-Government in the Republic of Kazakhstan until 2025" (Adilet, 2021b). The document delineated the primary directions of prospective reforms, with the objective of enhancing the efficiency of local self-government. Subsequent years have seen the implementation of amendments and supplements to the decree, with the objective of elucidating the fundamental provisions of the reform.

Direct elections of akims have become a significant instrument for enhancing accountability and transparency in governance. The new system empowers citizens to exercise oversight of the activities of local leaders, while the akims themselves are obligated to submit annual public reports on their work. In order to consolidate public control, mechanisms for expanding citizen participation in decision-making have also been introduced, including active interaction with local communities and their involvement in the discussion of key issues of territorial development (Adilet, 2021b).

A significant area of reform was the strengthening of the financial independence of local authorities. The implementation of a four-tier budget system enabled rural districts to obtain additional resources, thereby contributing to the augmentation of the revenue base of local budgets. A notable innovation was the introduction of independent local taxes and fees, in addition to the establishment of mechanisms for the redistribution of budget funds between different levels of government (Adilet, 2021b). These measures contributed to enhancing the financial stability of rural administrations.

Accordingly, during the course of the local government reforms, significant attention was allocated not only to the expansion of the powers of local authorities, but also to the augmentation of the level of civic participation. The establishment of local public councils and the concomitant expansion of their powers, in conjunction with the involvement of citizens in the elections of akims and the formation of local budgets, constituted pivotal steps in the strengthening of democratic institutions. This phenomenon resulted in a more efficient utilization of budget funds and an increase in the level of trust in local authorities (Adilet, 2021b).

A more thorough examination of these processes necessitates the consideration of a specific example: the Ili district, a pivotal region within the context of socio-economic and political interaction in Kazakhstan. This particular case study will elucidate the implementation of the overarching principles of decentralization and democratic participation at the level of a specific district.

ILI DISTRICT AS A CASE STUDY

The Ili district, located in the central part of the Almaty region, is one of the key regions not only of the region, but of the whole of southern Kazakhstan. The district is bordered by the districts of Balkhash, Karasay, Zhambyl and Talgar, as well as the city of Almaty, a factor which renders it of significant strategic importance in terms of economic and social interaction. The topography of the district is predominantly characterised by desert and steppe zones, which occupy approximately 80% of the total area. Notable geographical features include the Sartaukum sands and the Karaoi plateau. These landscape features exert a substantial influence on the economic well-being and cultural practices of the local population.

According to the 2021 census, the population of Ili district is 254,827 (Bureau of National statistics of the Republic of Kazakhstan, 2021, p. 92). The district is characterised by a multi-ethnic composition, with Kazakhs, Russians, Uyghurs, Tatars and other ethnic groups residing within its boundaries. This diversity of cultures and traditions is a distinctive feature of the district, contributing to its unique social dynamics and interactions between different groups.

The Ili district is notable for its combination of both rural and urbanised settlements, which renders it a suitable subject for analysis of local government reforms. The district is characterised by the presence of numerous rural districts and several large settlements, including the villages of Boraldai and Chapaevo, which have been selected for detailed study.

The village of Chapaevo is a typical rural settlement in the Ili district, with a population of 10,550 people as of 2021 (Bureau of National statistics of the Republic of Kazakhstan, 2021, p. 92). Its remote location, a considerable distance from any significant urban areas, engenders a reliance on local authorities for the provision of essential social services, the development of infrastructure, and the resolution of local issues. In 2021, the first direct elections of the akim of the rural district were held in Chapaevo, marking a significant stage in the reform of local self-government. This event provided an opportunity to analyse how changes in the electoral system affect the perception of power by the local population and how much the accountability of akims to citizens increases.

The largest settlement in the Ili district is the village of Boraldai, which has a population of 35,863 as of 2021 (Bureau of National statistics of the Republic of Kazakhstan, 2021, p. 91). It is one of the most developed settlements in the region, with an industrial base, developed transport infrastructure and strategic importance for the district's economy. Boraldai's strategic location in close proximity to Almaty signifies its importance as a pivotal link in the urban agglomeration. In 2014, a portion of the village's territory was incorporated into Almaty, underscoring its pivotal role in regional development.

In contrast to Chapaevo, direct elections of the akim had not yet been conducted in Boraldai at the time of the study, as the term of the incumbent akim had not yet expired. Consequently, Boraldai was utilised as a comparative case to analyse citizens' expectations before implementing the novel electoral system.

RESEARCH METHOD

The present study adopts a descriptive analysis approach, grounded in an examination of respondents' opinions. The aim of the study is to analyse public perceptions of the direct election of akims as a decentralisation tool and its impact on citizen trust, participation in governance and development of rural communities. In particular, it answers the following questions:

How does the population perceive the introduction of direct elections of akims?

What changes in expectations and trust in local authorities are observed after the elections?

What qualities do voters consider most important for a rural akim?

Do direct elections contribute to increasing citizen participation in local government?

What is the difference in the perception of the reform between residents of settlements where elections have been held and those where they have not?

To achieve these questions, the following methods were employed: surveys, structured interviews and field observations. The collection of data was conducted through the utilisation of surveys and interviews, which took place between the months of August and September 2021. This approach was adopted to ensure the relevance of the information obtained within the context of the impending and subsequent akim elections. Specifically, these methods were employed to formulate a comprehensive conceptualisation of the desired attributes of the head of a rural settlement, in addition to conducting a thorough evaluation of the prevailing infrastructure and the local governance system. The series of structured interviews and surveys conducted in the villages of Boraldai and Chapaevo in the Ili district. Four experts and opinion leaders with knowledge and experience in local elections were interviewed. Participants were selected based on their public activity and expert competencies identified during the analysis of the pre-election information field. The interviewees included public figures, entrepreneurs, directors of educational institutions and elders (*aksakals*). Prior to the interview, respondents were furnished with information materials and a consent form to ensure the anonymity and confidentiality of participation. The interviews were conducted in person, and the option of audio recording was made available to the participants. The interviews lasted between 40 and 60 minutes.

The survey method was employed to gather data from residents. During the surveys, particular emphasis was placed on two factors that determined the selection of settlements for the study. Firstly, the historical context of the development of local self-government in Kazakhstan was considered, taking into account the influence of various administrative systems that have formed this development. On this basis, the Ili district of the Almaty region was selected as an example of a territory with a developed local government system. Secondly, the experience of holding direct elections of akims was analysed, which became a key criterion in the selection of rural settlements. The study identified two distinct types of settlements. The first type is a settlement where the elections of akims took place on July 25, 2021. The second type of settlement is one in which the elections were scheduled for a later date. In the selection of settlements, factors such as distance from the district or regional centre, population size and ethnic composition were not considered. However, these parameters were subsequently analysed to interpret the results.

To ensure the representativeness of the study, the minimum required sample size was calculated. The sample size was determined with consideration for the representativeness of each locality. The sample size was calculated using the classical formula for a finite population:

$$n = \frac{N \cdot Z^2 \cdot p(1-p)}{(N-1) \cdot e^2 + Z \cdot p(1-p)}$$

where:

n is the required sample size,

N is the population size,

Z is the value for the confidence level (at 95% confidence level $Z \approx 1.96$),

p is the estimated response rate (0.5 if the exact distribution is unknown),

e is the margin of error (usually 5% = 0.05).

During the study, 770 individuals over the age of 18 were surveyed, 370 of whom resided in Chapaevo and 400 in Boraldai. Table 1 presents the demographic characteristics of survey respondents from the villages of Chapaevo and Boraldai. The age distribution in both localities is fairly balanced, although a slightly higher proportion of younger respondents aged 18–24 is observed in Boraldai, while Chapaevo has more respondents in the 65+ age group. With regard to gender distribution, the data reveal a near-equality in both villages, with a marginal predominance of female respondents.

Table 1. Demographic characteristics of respondents in Chapaevo and Boraldai villages

	Characteristics	Chapaevo	Boraldai
Age group	18-24	12,0%	16,8%
	25-34	26,4%	26,4%
	35-44	22,4%	24,8%
	45-54	17,6%	14,4%
	55-64	9,6%	12,4%
	65+	12,0%	5,2%
Gender	Male	42,8%	42,0%
	Female	57,2%	58,0%
Education level	Secondary education	22,8%	21,6%
	Secondary special education	56,0%	35,2%
	Incomplete higher education	4,8%	8,0%
	Higher education	16,4%	34,4%
Social status	Employed	74,4%	77,2%
	Unemployed	25,6%	22,8

A more pronounced divergence emerges with respect to educational attainment: while the majority of respondents in Chapaevo have received secondary special education, a substantially higher proportion of respondents in Boraldai have attained higher education. With regard to social status, the employment rate is high in both villages, with more than 74% of respondents indicating that they are employed. This suggests a relatively stable economic base, although a notable minority in both villages remains unemployed. These demographic disparities may influence perceptions of local governance and attitudes towards direct elections, a topic that will be further explored in the subsequent sections.

RESULTS

The analysis of the conditions for the organisation of direct elections of heads of local government bodies in the Ili district was conducted in the village of Chapaevo, where the elections took place, in contrast to other settlements of the municipality, where the current akims' powers have not yet expired. The post-election study was designed to make a comparison between the conditions for holding elections in Chapaevo and the situation in Boraldai, where the elections of the akim were scheduled for a later date. A survey of local residents was conducted in both settlements to assess their expectations from direct elections and the requirements for candidates for the post of akim.

As shown in Figure 1 a substantial discrepancy in the public awareness of the direct election process for akims in Kazakhstan, contingent on the geographical location of the settlement. In the village of the first type (Chapaevo), where elections have already taken place, approximately 75% of respondents are aware that akims of rural districts are elected by direct vote. Conversely, in the second village (Boraldai), where elections are yet to be conducted, the proportion of respondents aware of this procedure is considerably lower, at approximately 40%.

Figure 1. Awareness of Direct Elections of Akims in Rural Kazakhstan

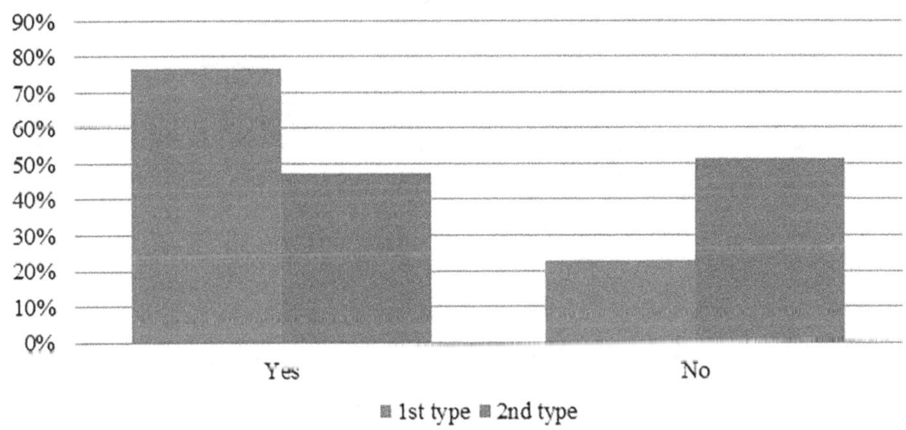

The present data underscores the impact of the actual conduct of elections on the level of awareness among citizens. The enhanced level of awareness observed in Chapaevo can be attributed to the information support provided during the electoral process, encompassing electoral campaigns, public discussions and coverage in the local media. Conversely, in Boraldai, where no elections had yet been conducted, the population may have received less information regarding the reform, which could have contributed to the observed low level of awareness.

These results suggest that the very fact of holding elections acts as a catalyst for informing citizens about the local government process. At the same time, the disparity in awareness found highlights the need for a more active information policy on the part of government bodies aimed at increasing public knowledge of the reforms, regardless of whether elections have been held in a particular rural district.

The Figure 2 shows that residents of settlements where direct elections of akims have already taken place (type one) are much more likely to express confidence in their ability to influence local governance and the decisions of the akim. In Chapaevo (type one village), most respondents believe that the new electoral system provides them with real mechanisms to influence local governance. Conversely, in Boraldai (type two village), where elections have not yet been held, the level of confidence is about 1,5 times lower.

Figure 2. Perceived Influence of Direct Elections on Local Decision-Making

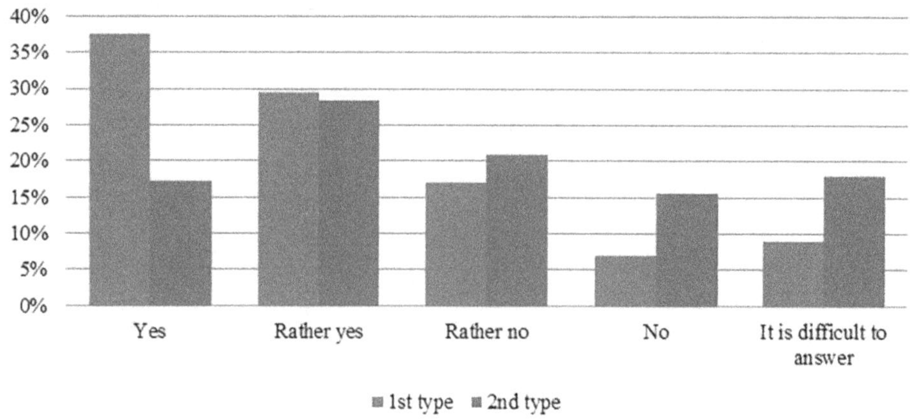

These variations may be attributable to two factors. Firstly, the residents of Chapaevo participated directly in the elections and were able to observe the process from within, thereby increasing their confidence in the new system. Secondly, the lower level of trust in Boraldai may be attributed to a paucity of information regarding the reform, as well as a lack of practical experience of participating in the akim elections.

The data substantiates the hypothesis that electoral participation fosters a sense of involvement in local governance among citizens. Nevertheless, the discrepancy in the perception of the reform between the two categories of localities underscores the necessity to augment information and education initiatives among residents of areas where elections have not yet been conducted.

The Figure 3 indicate that the majority of respondents, irrespective of the type of settlement, are of the opinion that the introduction of direct elections of akims will be advantageous for the development of their village. However, in the villages of the second type (where elections have not yet been held), the proportion of undecided respondents and sceptical citizens is significantly higher compared to the villages of the first type.

Figure 3. Expected Benefits or Risks of Akim Elections for Village Development

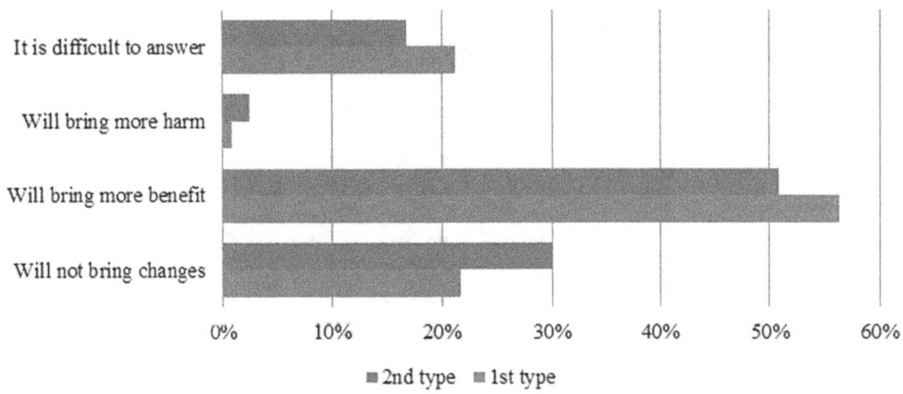

This discrepancy in perception can be attributed to a number of factors. Firstly, residents of settlements where elections have already taken place have been able to see the initial results of the reform, which has strengthened their confidence in the effectiveness of the electoral mechanism. Secondly, in the villages of the second type, there is a paucity of information and practical experience of participating in elections, which engenders greater caution in assessments.

The data demonstrate that the implementation of direct elections is predominantly perceived in a favourable manner. However, the level of confidence exhibited is contingent upon the experience of its implementation within a specific locality. These findings underscore the significance of formulating information policies and citizen feedback mechanisms to mitigate uncertainty and enhance confidence in the reform among residents of villages where elections have not yet been conducted.

An analysis of respondents' responses on the preferred qualities of a candidate for the post of village akim revealed several key trends (see Figure 4). Firstly, in villages of the second type (where elections have not yet been held), residents were found to be more likely to accept a candidate without experience in public service – approximately 50% of respondents considered this acceptable, while in villages of the first type this figure was approximately 45%. This observation may be indicative of a higher degree of flexibility in expectations among individuals residing in communities that have not yet experienced direct electoral processes.

Secondly, respondents from villages of the second type also demonstrate a greater degree of openness to non-party candidates (50%) and candidates living with disabilities (approximately 40%) in comparison to respondents from villages of the first type, where these figures are marginally lower. This finding suggests a potential inclination towards exploring novel leadership figures in contexts where electoral practices have not yet clearly delineated preferences.

Figure 4. Acceptability of Candidate Profiles by Village Type

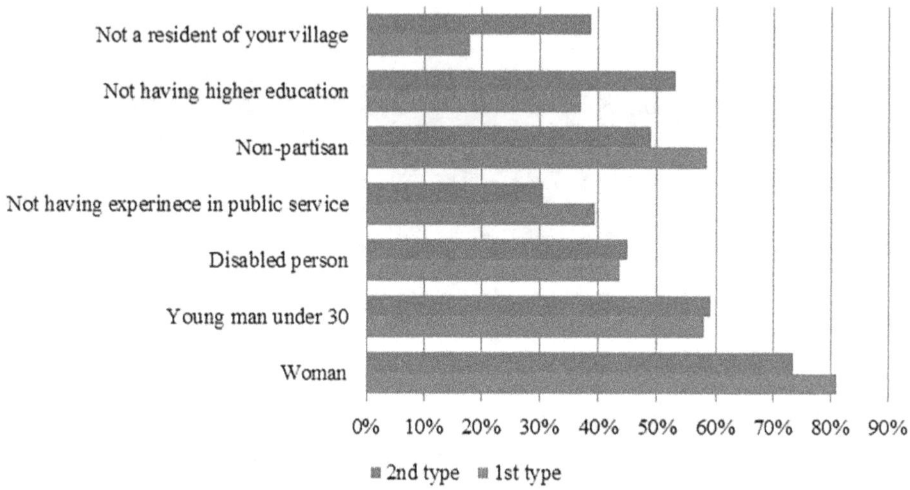

Thirdly, irrespective of the nature of the settlement, the majority of respondents (approximately 40%) consider a candidate with disabilities to be a suitable candidate for the position of akim, indicating a relatively high level of inclusiveness of views.

Fourthly, the propensity to cast a vote for a candidate under the age of 30 remains at an equally high level (approximately 60%) in both types of villages, which reflects the positive attitude of the population towards new, dynamic managers, irrespective of their experience.

Finally, the female candidate is generally perceived positively, but the approval rate is marginally higher in villages of the first type (75%) compared to villages of the second type (70%). This finding suggests that the electoral process may foster a greater acceptance of female leadership.

It is evident that the divergent preferences exhibited by residents of these two distinct settlement types are indicative of the impact of electoral experience on their perception of the electoral process and the characteristics they deem acceptable in candidates. In the villages of the second type, greater flexibility and openness to different categories of candidates is maintained, while in the villages of the first type, more specific expectations from local government leaders are already beginning to form.

The survey results (see Figure 5) demonstrate variations in respondents' perceptions of acceptable and unacceptable characteristics of candidates for the post of village akim, contingent on the type of settlement. In villages of the first type (where elections have already taken place), the majority of respondents consider it unacceptable if the candidate is not a resident of the village or does not possess a higher education qualification. In villages of the second type, a similar trend is observed, but the requirements for education and place of residence are less stringent.

Figure 5. Unacceptable Candidate Profiles by Village Type

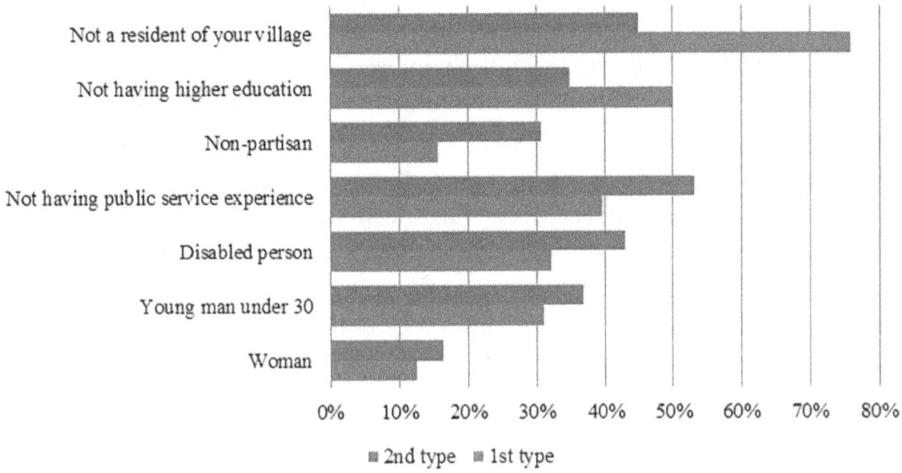

Further characteristics of candidates, including non-partisanship, a lack of experience in public service and disability, give rise to concerns. However, the differences between the two types of settlements are less pronounced. This may be indicative of the fact that for residents of the first type of villages (where elections have already taken place), expectations for candidates have become more specific, while in the second type of villages there remains greater flexibility in the perception of selection criteria.

An analysis of the preferred characteristics of the akim among respondents in both types of villages reveals that personal qualities, rather than professional competencies, play a pivotal role. In both cases, voters express a preference for qualities such as honesty, integrity, responsibility, and effective communication skills.

In the first village (Chapaevo), residents identified the following key qualities: honesty, integrity, education, responsibility, exactingness and the ability to keep promises. In addition, literacy, experience, understanding of people's problems, knowledge of the specifics of the village and professional competence were also identified as being of great importance.

In the second type of village (Boraldai), the emphasis is on qualities such as industry, attentiveness, humanity, organisation, and the ability to work with the population. Conversely, attributes such as knowledge of the village's issues, wisdom, physical strength, and erudition were deemed less significant.

The analysis of these data allows us to draw several important conclusions. Primarily, residents of the first type of villages presumably form their expectations based on past elections, which engenders a more distinct conception of what an akim should be like. Secondly, in the second type of villages, the requirements for akims are more abstract, which may reflect a lack of practical experience in participating in elections and a more general image of the "ideal leader". Finally, personal integrity and the capacity to engage with the populace emerged as paramount criteria for electors, while administrative and professional experience was found to be of secondary importance.

The data demonstrate that the perception of the ideal candidate is predominantly influenced by the experience of holding elections. In electoral districts where the process of voting has already been completed, expectations are characterised by increased structuration, whilst in those where the electoral process is yet to be conducted, there is greater flexibility in the perception of the criteria for selecting candidates.

The findings of interviews with public opinion leaders reveal an ambivalent attitude towards the level of support for the authorities and the evaluation of the activities of akims. On the one hand, respondents articulate a restrained positive opinion, and on the other hand, a neutral-negative perception, noting that the election of akims does not yet have a significant impact on the level of trust in local authorities.

In the first type of settlement (Chapaevo), respondents did not perceive any substantial changes following the elections. However, a notable proportion of respondents expressed approval of the fact that a local resident had won the elections, contrasting with the previous practice of the position of akim being occupied by appointees who were not residents of the area prior to their assuming office. This is regarded as a progression towards the consolidation of local self-government, given that local residents anticipate that an individual from their own community will possess a more profound comprehension of the local problems and requirements.

Concurrently, the interview participants unanimously emphasised that genuine positive changes in the development of local government are only possible in the long term. As one of the former akims of Chapaevo observes:

"Errors will undoubtedly be committed during the initial decades; however, these are indispensable for the success of the endeavour. At present, any individual has the potential to emerge victorious in the electoral process. I hail from the district, and it is evident that the district is a focal point of attention. The central government exerts significant influence through various means to ensure the placement of their own individuals in key positions. To illustrate this point, the regional akim possesses the authority to appoint the district akim, who in turn has the authority to appoint the village akim. It is notable that the members of the election commission are predominantly drawn from the teaching profession and hold positions of leadership. The composition of the election commission, as well as that of the public sector in general, is characterised by a preponderance of individuals with a background in education and administration. However, it is anticipated that this dynamic will undergo a shift over time" (Interviewee 1, personal communication, August 5, 2021).

This remark is indicative of a degree of scepticism surrounding the autonomy of the electoral process and the extent to which higher authorities continue to exert influence over the elections of akims. Despite the formal democratisation of the procedure, many respondents believe that the central government still wields significant influence, including control over election commissions and budget organisations.

In contrast, respondents from the second type of village (Boraldai) generally expressed a positive view on the introduction of direct elections of akims, whilst simultaneously emphasising the necessity for enhancing the political literacy of the population. It is their belief that the election of the akim will empower residents to engage more actively in the governance of their settlement, thereby fostering a greater sense of proximity between the akim and the populace. As one of the public figures of Boraldai noted:

"This is very good. It is acknowledged that there may be sceptics who predict that the electoral process will be unsuccessful due to concerns that voters may continue to elect their own candidates. However, it is contended that this is indicative of a progression towards enhanced democratic engagement" (Interviewee 2, personal communication, August 6, 2021).

This statement is indicative of a combination of optimism and lingering concerns regarding the transparency of the electoral process. Despite a general endorsement of the fundamental principle of elections, it is asserted by some respondents that the true electoral competitiveness may be constrained by administrative resources. However, the prevailing sentiment among respondents is one of support for the democratisation of the electoral system, with many considering it to be a positive development.

The question of whether elections will lead to a real improvement in governance remains unresolved. A consensus among respondents from both types of villages (Chapaevo and Boraldai) has been reached regarding the pivotal role of personal qualities, as opposed to the election mechanism itself, in determining the effectiveness of the akim. Irrespective of whether the akim is elected or appointed, the development of the settlement is influenced by his economic efficiency, responsibility and persistence.

During the study, respondents identified the general economic situation in the country as a significant factor influencing the development of rural areas. The former akim of Chapaevo emphasised the correlation between macroeconomic processes and living conditions in rural areas:

"In the 2000s, the situation was different not only in the village, but throughout Kazakhstan - there was money. This financial buoyancy led to an increase in loan activity, which subsequently stabilised. It is also noteworthy that recent salary increments have been implemented for teachers and medical professionals. Consequently, such professions are progressively being regarded as competitive in rural areas" (Interviewee 3, personal communication, August 5, 2021).

This commentary underscores the notion that the standard of living in rural areas of Kazakhstan is contingent not solely on the efficacy of local governance, but also on prevailing national socio-economic trends. It is asserted that increased public investment, higher wages, and improved social policy have a direct effect on the competitiveness of the rural economy and, consequently, the level of citizen engagement in local governance.

A salient finding from the interviews is the limited engagement of citizens in local governance processes and the absence of overt political action. Opinion leaders observe that, despite the provision of direct electoral opportunities for akims in rural settlements, residents demonstrate a passive stance in matters of governance and the development of their communities.

As one of the respondents, a manager of a transnational company from the village of Chapayevo, noted:

"In general, as a nation, we are a little far from politics. Conversely, the Kazakh nation has historically exhibited remarkable patience, yet when reserves of patience are depleted, subsequent events often unfold in a less-than-optimal manner. A pertinent example of this phenomenon is provided by the events that recently transpired in Korday. The absence of a systematic approach has been identified as a significant impediment to the formation of a cohesive political entity. The contemporary villager's political worldview is shaped by a plethora of current programs disseminated through various messengers. However, the sheer volume of information that individuals are exposed to can be overwhelming, leading to a sense of disorientation and a lack of direction. Consequently,

the populace, particularly the rural demographic, exhibits a certain degree of political passivity." (Interviewee 1, personal communication, August 6, 2021).

This commentary underscores several salient issues. Primarily, the absence of a systemic approach to political education hinders citizens from cultivating a comprehensive understanding of their rights and opportunities within the context of local governance. Consequently, the populace is either indifferent to politics or is guided by superficial sources of information. Secondly, the digital environment and the abundance of information disseminated via messengers and social networks serve to complicate the process of conscious political choice. The large flow of news and opinions often results in residents feeling disoriented, as they are unable to ascertain which actions can truly influence the development of their community. Thirdly, the historical context exerts a significant influence on the perception of political activity. The respondent observes that Kazakh society has historically exhibited a high degree of tolerance for socio-economic challenges, yet periods of crisis can give rise to pronounced public protests. This observation underscores the notion that current low levels of political activity do not necessarily imply an absence of demand for change; rather, they are indicative of the absence of adequate mechanisms for citizen involvement in the local governance process.

Notwithstanding the prevailing passivity in the political sphere, respondents have observed a gradual increase in citizens' interest in governance issues, which is primarily attributable to the development of the Internet and social networks. These platforms facilitate access to information, stimulate discussion, and can contribute to increasing the level of political literacy and public involvement in local government processes.

Concurrently, respondents lacked a comprehensive understanding of which governance format – elected or appointed – is more effective. At the time of the study, residents were unable to determine with any clarity whether the election of the akim would ensure better governance. Nevertheless, opinion leaders emphasised that the head of the settlement should be a person known to residents and who is deeply familiar with the problems of the community.

Concomitantly, respondents provided exemplification of the accomplishments of appointed akims, demonstrating notable achievements in the developmental progression of their respective rural districts. This finding indicates that the effectiveness of local government is contingent not only on the electoral process, but also on the personal qualities of the leader, his competence, and his ability to interact with the population.

The results obtained underline the intricacies inherent in the public's perception of the reform to elect the akims of rural districts. Despite an awareness of the significance of democratising local governance, citizens lack a comprehensive understanding of its efficacy. Opinion leaders acknowledge the advantages of electing the akims and recognise the ongoing impact of administrative resources.

The residents of these two types of villages acknowledge several significant benefits of direct elections, which they believe improve local governance. A recurrent benefit that has been cited with high frequency is the enhancement of local government accountability. The direct election of candidates, they posit, engenders a heightened sense of civic engagement, as residents are empowered to exercise a direct influence on the selection process. Furthermore, local residents have noted that the direct election of akims has been demonstrated to enhance the quality of decisions, as elected representatives are more responsive to the needs of their community. Furthermore, the electoral process is often characterized by heightened transparency, thereby fostering public confidence in the local governance apparatus. Surveys further reveal that respondents perceive an enhancement in their influence over the decision-making process and observe improvements in the allocation of budgetary funds at the local level. The aforementioned benefits underscore the significance of direct elections in fostering democracy and fostering citizen engagement in local governance processes. The findings lend support to the hypothesis that electoral participation fosters a sense of civic engagement and responsibility among citizens in regard to local decision-making processes.

DISCUSSION

This study explores the perceptions and readiness of local communities in Kazakhstan for the direct elections of akims of rural areas, using the Ili district as a case study. We found that residents in both first and second-type villages recognize the benefits of direct elections, with a significant awareness of the new electoral processes in areas where elections have already occurred. Additionally, the findings suggest that community members are open to diverse candidates, including those without prior public service experience, non-partisan individuals, and candidates with disabilities. The willingness to support young and female candidates indicates a progressive shift in voter attitudes towards inclusivity and diversity in local governance. These insights highlight the potential for direct elections to enhance democratic engagement and representation in rural Kazakhstan.

The findings of this study corroborate extant theoretical postulations concerning the impact of decentralisation and direct elections on local governance. As survey data demonstrated, citizens' awareness of the novel mayor election system varies considerably depending on the electoral cycle in a specific locality. This finding aligns with Siegel's (2022) assertion that the efficacy of decentralization is contingent on the degree of public engagement and awareness.

A study of rural residents' perceptions of elections reveals that these perceptions vary depending on the experience of direct voting. In the village of Chapaevo, where elections have already been conducted, the majority of respondents expressed confidence that the election of the akim provides them with a genuine mechanism through which to influence local governance. This finding aligns with the conclusions of Sankhayeva and Arzikulov (2021), who assert that the implementation of direct elections signifies a progression towards the democratisation of political institutions. Conversely, in Boraldai, where elections are yet to be conducted, a considerable segment of the population expressed scepticism, a finding that aligns with the research of Onalbaiuly (2019), who underscores that perceptions of reforms evolve as they are implemented.

The variation in public awareness regarding the direct election of akims across electoral cycles can be attributed to a multitude of factors. First, the level of education plays a significant role. Research indicates that citizens with a higher level of education are more interested in political processes and are better informed about elections (Arceneaux & Vander Wielen, 2023; Larreguy & Liu, 2024). Secondly, access to information emerges as a pivotal factor. In regions characterized by limited digital infrastructure and deficient independent media distribution, the level of awareness is typically lower, a finding that is corroborated by extant research on the impact of digital inequality (Chirwa et al., 2023). Thirdly, the media's coverage of the reform influences public interest in the elections. Active information campaigns have been shown to contribute to public engagement, while their absence may lead to a reduction in the perceived importance of elections among citizens (Şen, 2022; Smajlović & Čolakhodžić, 2023). Finally, the activity of local authorities plays an instrumental role (Dipoppa & Grossman, 2020). If akims and local governments organize explanatory work, the population shows greater interest in the electoral process. Consequently, variations in awareness levels across different geographical areas can be attributed to a multifaceted interplay of educational, informational, and institutional factors that collectively influence the extent of citizen participation in local electoral processes.

A further aspect that merits discussion is the level of trust in local authorities. As Tebayev (2020) observes, the expansion of financial autonomy for rural districts can serve as a significant catalyst for enhancing trust in local governance. The present study corroborates the finding that, in a settlement where elections have already taken place, the level of trust in the akim is higher. Nevertheless, the issue of the genuine autonomy of local authorities remains unresolved. As Siegel (2022) notes, decentralization does not necessarily lead to democratization; however, it has the capacity to enable central authorities to strengthen their control at the local level.

This study makes a significant contribution to the existing body of knowledge on decentralisation in Kazakhstan by demonstrating that the success of reforms is contingent not only on alterations to the electoral format, but also on the awareness of citizens, the level of their involvement in governance, and the real financial and administrative autonomy of local authorities. The findings of this study are likely to be of use in further research in the field of local governance and democratic transformations in post-Soviet countries.

CONCLUSION

The present study found that the introduction of direct elections of akims in Kazakhstan is perceived positively by residents of rural districts, especially in those settlements where elections have already taken place. Nevertheless, survey and interview data suggest that citizens' awareness of this reform remains limited and their participation in local governance is restricted. For instance, in Chapaevo, where elections were held in 2021, most respondents are aware of the new electoral system and believe that it can affect the level of accountability of local authorities. Conversely, in Boraldai, where elections have not yet been conducted, awareness levels are comparatively lower and citizens' attitudes towards the reform remain undecided.

The findings of this study demonstrate that the implementation of direct elections for akims in Kazakhstan has resulted in substantial shifts in the perception of local self-government among the rural population. In villages where elections have already taken place, citizens' awareness of the local governance process was higher, and their expectations of the government's effectiveness were more optimistic. However, the study also identified limitations to the reform, including the fact that although elections have contributed to greater citizen engagement, their impact on actual decision-making mechanisms remains limited.

This study makes a significant contribution to the extant scholarly debate on decentralisation by providing empirical evidence on the perceptions of the reform among citizens in Kazakhstan. Distinct from the majority of extant studies, which analyse the normative and institutional dimensions of local self-government, this paper focuses on public opinion, thus facilitating a more comprehensive understanding of the social impact of reforms. The findings of this study serve to complement extant theoretical conceptualisations of decentralisation (Bardhan & Mookherjee, 2006; Treisman, 2007) by demonstrating that the devolution of powers to local governments does not invariably result in an increase in the trust placed in them, without concomitant changes in resource allocation and accountability mechanisms. The findings of this study lend support to Grindle's (2007) conclusion that successful decentralisation requires not only institutional change but also the long-term development of democratic norms and procedures. He posits that the implementation of effective local government reforms necessitates not only the election of local leaders but also a substantial redistribution of resources. In the context of Kazakhstan, the elected akims currently possess inadequate budgetary powers, which curtails their capacity to implement development programmes without the requisite approval from higher authorities.

The analysis of the presented results also relates to the overarching theme of the collection, which is devoted to innovative approaches in local self-government. The study of direct elections of akims in Kazakhstan makes an important empirical contribution to the study of decentralization in post-Soviet countries, demonstrating both the achievements and the challenges of reforms in a centralized system of governance. The Kazakh experience can be useful for comparative studies examining the impact of local elections on community development and governance effectiveness. Moreover, situating the Kazakh experience within a broader global context, as articulated by Martinez-Bravo et al. (2022), substantiates their proposition that local elections in authoritarian or hybrid regimes have the potential to fortify local governance while concurrently functioning as a means of central government control.

The study's practical significance lies in the utilisation of its findings to enhance the local government system in Kazakhstan and other countries undertaking analogous reforms. Specifically, the study's findings highlight the necessity for a comprehensive approach to decentralisation, encompassing not only the election of local leaders but also the reform of resource allocation mechanisms. As Kosec and Mogues (2020) observe, the absence of adequate financing mechanisms in the context of decentralisation can result in a diminution of the efficacy of local governance. Consequently, it is imperative to allocate particular attention to the establishment of a sustainable financial foundation for local authorities.

Notwithstanding the valuable findings, the study has certain limitations. Primarily, the investigation is constrained to a single region, the Ili district, thereby restricting the extent to which the findings can be extrapolated to the national level. Future research could expand the geographic scope to include additional regions with different levels of economic development and different models of local governance. Secondly, the analysis is descriptive and does not cover the long-term effects of the reform. While this study has identified short-term changes in public perceptions of local governance, further research is necessary to assess the long-term impact of akim elections on local governance performance.

The implementation of direct elections for akims in Kazakhstan signifies a substantial development; however, the long-term ramifications for the local political structure remain indeterminate. The potential trajectories for further evolution are contingent on numerous variables, including the extent of political competition, the degree of oversight exercised by the central government, and the dynamics of public engagement.

One possible scenario is the strengthening of democratic decentralization, in which local elections will lead to greater accountability of akims to citizens, increased political competition, and the development of local self-government. This will necessitate additional institutional reforms, including the expansion of the authority of elected akims and the reduction of administrative control from the central government.

Alternatively, a scenario may emerge where nominal decentralization is maintained, with elections being held in form, yet real power remains firmly concentrated at the central level. In this scenario, the autonomy of akims in making independent decisions will be constrained, and the electoral process will not result in substantial changes to the political system.

Finally, the possibility cannot be discounted of a scenario of short-lived reform, in which, against the backdrop of political or economic instability, centralized governance will again strengthen, and the practice of electing akims will be curtailed or limited. A thorough examination of these scenarios indicates that effective decentralization is contingent not solely on the implementation of elections, but also necessitates a comprehensive restructuring of the prevailing institutional framework, ensuring a genuine redistribution of power at the local level.

Future research may examine the impact of akim elections on real governance and decision-making mechanisms, as well as analyse changes in civic engagement at the local level. It is imperative to consider whether direct elections contribute to the formation of more accountable and transparent institutions or remain a formality without real powers. Furthermore, it would be beneficial to investigate the political socialisation of citizens in the context of local government reform and its long-term consequences for the democratic development of Kazakhstan. As Goldfrank (2007) observes, the success of local governance reforms is contingent on citizen engagement in decision-making processes, and future research could assess the extent to which akim elections contribute to the development of an active civil society.

The results of this study are of interest to two distinct audiences. Firstly, they are relevant to the academic community studying decentralization and democratization issues. Secondly, they are also relevant to practitioners, including civil servants, politicians, and experts involved in the development and implementation of local government reforms. The presented scenarios and identified institutional barriers can be used in planning the next stages of political decentralization and increasing the effectiveness of direct elections at the local level.

REFERENCES

Arceneaux, K., & Vander Wielen, R. J. (2023). Do voters prefer educated candidates? How candidate education influences vote choice in congressional elections. *Electoral Studies, 82*, 102596. https://doi.org/https://doi.org/10.1016/j.electstud.2023.102596. DOI: 10.1016/j.electstud.2023.102596

Aubakirova, Z., & Aimagambetov, E. (2020). Problems of local self-government development in Kazakhstan. *Central Asian Economic Review, 6*(135), 46-57. https://caer.narxoz.kz/jour/article/view/272/275

Balabiev, K. (2014). Questions development of local government in the Republic of Kazakhstan and the role of international experience in its improvement. *Austrian Journal of Humanities and Social Sciences, 2*(1-2), 181–189.

Balaguer-Coll, M. T., Prior, D., & Tortosa-Ausina, E. (2010). Decentralization and efficiency of local government. *The Annals of Regional Science, 45*(3), 571–601. DOI: 10.1007/s00168-009-0286-7

Bardhan, P. K., & Mookherjee, D. (Eds.). (2006). *Decentralization and Local Governance in Developing Countries: A Comparative Perspective*. The MIT Press., https://doi.org/https://doi.org/10.7551/mitpress/2297.001.0001 DOI: 10.7551/mitpress/2297.001.0001

Beisembayeva, G., Mussina, A., & Sartova, R. (2014). Development of local government in the Republic of Kazakhstan at the present stage. *Journal of Economic Research & Business Administration, 104*(4), 32–39. https://be.kaznu.kz/index.php/math/article/view/436

Chirwa, G. C., Petro, M. L., Michael, C., Anthony, G., Boniface, D., Happy, K., & Chinsinga, B. (2023). Assessing the relationship between digital divide and citizens' political participation in Africa. *Development Southern Africa, 40*(6), 1258–1276. DOI: 10.1080/0376835X.2023.2224363

Dipoppa, G., & Grossman, G. (2020). The effect of election proximity on government responsiveness and citizens' participation: Evidence from English local elections. *Comparative Political Studies, 53*(14), 2183–2212. DOI: 10.1177/0010414020912290

ECHO. (2018). *Development of local self-government in Kazakhstan*. P. U. ECHO. https://echo.kz/images/reports/msu_echo.pdf

Faguet, J.-P. (2012). *Decentralization and popular democracy: governance from below in Bolivia*. University of Michigan Press. DOI: 10.3998/mpub.175269

Falleti, T. G. (2010). *Decentralization and Subnational Politics in Latin America*. Cambridge University Press. DOI: 10.1017/CBO9780511777813

Goldfrank, B. (2007). The Politics of Deepening Local Democracy: Decentralization, Party Institutionalization, and Participation. *Comparative Politics*, *39*(2), 147–168. https://www.jstor.org/stable/20434031

Grindle, M. S. (2007). *Going Local Decentralization, Democratization, and the Promise of Good Governance*. Princeton University Press., https://www.jstor.org/stable/j.ctt4cgd2m

Ibadildin, N., & Pisareva, D. (2020). Central Asia in Transition: Social Contract Transformation in Nazarbayev and Post-Nazarbayev Kazakhstan. In Mihr, A. (Ed.), *Transformation and Development: Studies in the Organization for Security and Cooperation in Europe (OSCE) Member States* (pp. 101–116). Springer., DOI: 10.1007/978-3-030-42775-7_7

Ileuova, G., Serazhieva, S. H., & Aljani, J. K. (2002). Analiz rezul'tatov eksperimental'nykh vyborov akimov sel'skikh okrugov. *Analytical review*(1), 15-32.

Kazakhstan, S. (2021). *Elections of 700 rural akims will be held on July 25 – Karin*. Sputnik Kazakhstan. https://ru.sputnik.kz/20210625/Vybory-700-selskikh-akimov-proydut-25-iyulya---Karin-17453504.html

Kosec, K., & Mogues, T. (2020). Decentralization Without Democracy. *World Politics*, *72*(2), 165–213. DOI: 10.1017/S0043887120000027

Kosenov, A. (2013, August 28). 370 million tenge spent in Kazakhstan on rural akim elections. *Tengrinews*. https://tengrinews.kz/kazakhstan_news/370-millionov-tenge-potratili-kazahstane-vyiboryi-selskih-240627/

Kussainova, M., & Ekberova, E. (2021). Kazakhstan hosts first direct elections of akims. *Anadolu Ajansı*. https://www.aa.com.tr/ru/мир/в-казахстане-проходят-первые-прямые-выборы-акимов/2313288

Lameck, W. U. (2023). Political decentralisation and political-administrative relation in the local councils in Tanzania. *Public Administration and Policy*, *26*(3), 335–344. DOI: 10.1108/PAP-07-2022-0077

Larreguy, H., & Liu, S. X. (2024). When does education increase political participation? Evidence from Senegal. *Political Science Research and Methods*, *12*(2), 354–371. DOI: 10.1017/psrm.2023.37

Levitsky, S., & Way, L. A. (2010). *Competitive Authoritarianism: Hybrid Regimes after the Cold War*. Cambridge University Press., https://doi.org/DOI, DOI: 10.1017/CBO9780511781353

Lierl, M. M. (2017). Elections and embezzlement: experimental evidence from Burkina Faso. *World Bank Policy Research Working Paper*(8067).

Manor, J. (1999). *The political economy of democratic decentralization*. The World Bank. DOI: 10.1596/0-8213-4470-6

Martinez-Bravo, M., Padró i Miquel, G., Qian, N., & Yao, Y. (2022). The Rise and Fall of Local Elections in China. *The American Economic Review, 112*(9), 2921–2958. DOI: 10.1257/aer.20181249

Mauletbai, S. (2021). Hope, intrigue, apathy. How were the first elections of rural akims in Kazakhstan. *Informburo*. https://informburo.kz/stati/kak-prosli-vybory-selskix-akimov

Mishra, M. K. (2009). Democratisation Process in Kazakhstan: Gauging the Indicators. *India Quarterly, 65*(3), 313–327. DOI: 10.1177/097492840906500306

Norton, A. (1994). *International Handbook of Local and Regional Government. A Comparative Analysis of Advanced Democracies*. Edward Elgar Publishing. DOI: 10.4337/9781781954225

Onalbaiuly, S. (2019). *Democratisation of local government and local governance in Kazakhstan*. University of Cambridge.

Primbetova, S., & Tlesova, A. (2015). Participation of the citizens in the decision making process at the local level as the priority of the reforming and foundation of legal capacity of the local authorities. *Actual Issues of Modern Science and Society*, (4), 13–17.

Sankhayeva, Z., & Arzikulov, A. (2021). Elections in the system of local self-government: International practices and experience of Kazakhstan. *Kazakhstan Spectrum, 97*(1), 89-99. https://doi.org/https://doi.org/10.52536/KS/vol_97_issue_1_A6

Şen, A. F. (2022). Evaluating the role of media during elections: The case of local elections of 31st March 2019 in Turkey. *Advances in Applied Sociology, 12*(4), 112–126. DOI: 10.4236/aasoci.2022.124011

Siegel, D. (2022). Decentralization, legitimacy, and democracy in post-Soviet Central Asia. *Journal of Eurasian Studies, 13*(1), 66–81. DOI: 10.1177/18793665211068525

Smajlović, H., & Čolakhodžić, F. (2023). *How Does Media Coverage Affect the Outcomes of the Elections?* MAP Social Sciences. DOI: 10.53880/2744-2454.2023.4.109

Tebayev, D. (2020). Returning to academician G. Sapargaliyev's scientific publication on self-government in the Republic of Kazakhstan. *Scientific and legal journal. Bulletin of the Institute of Legislation and Legal Information of the Republic of Kazakhstan*, *4*(62), 177–179. Advance online publication. DOI: 10.52026/1994-408X_2020_62_4_177

Thibault, H., & Insebayeva, S. (2024). The Political System of Kazakhstan. In Lempp, J., & Mayer, S. (Eds.), *Central Asia in a Multipolar World: Internal Change, External Actors, Regional Cooperation* (pp. 39–55). Springer International Publishing., DOI: 10.1007/978-3-031-63727-8_3

Treisman, D. (2007). *The Architecture of Government: Rethinking Political Decentralization*. Cambridge University Press., https://doi.org/DOI, DOI: 10.1017/CBO9780511619151

Utibaev, B., & Utibaeva, G. (2022). Improvement of the local self-government system in the Republic of Kazakhstan. *Problems of AgriMarket, 1*(1), 67-74. https://doi.org/https://doi.org/10.46666/2022-1.2708-9991.07

Yuvitsa, N. (2019). Local government in Kazakhstan: An attempt to create a national model. *Management*, *7*(1), 26–34. https://doi.org/https://doi.org/10.26425/2309-3633-2019-1-26-34

Zhanuzakova, L. (2013). Elections of akims is a real step towards the formation of the system of local self-government in the Republic of Kazakhstan. *Bulletin of the Institute of Legislation of the Republic of Kazakhstan*, *31*(3), 14–18. https://cyberleninka.ru/article/n/vybory-akimov-realnyy-shag-k-formirovaniyu-sistemy-mestnogo-samoupravleniya-v-respublike-kazahstan

Chapter 3
Digitalization in Citizen Participation and Effects on Local Governments

Hasret Duman
https://orcid.org/0000-0002-7187-7729
Hatay Mustafa Kemal University, Antakya, Turkey

Cenay Babaoğlu
https://orcid.org/0000-0002-2935-0579
Niğde Ömer Halisdemir University, Niğde, Turkey

ABSTRACT

Citizen participation refers to the ability of citizens to influence political decisions that impact their lives, forming a core aspect of democracy. While some argue that citizens lack the time, information, and motivation to engage in every public sector decision, others suggest that increased participation fosters knowledge, expertise, and community engagement. The role of public administrators in this process remains debated. However, with technological and social changes, new participation mechanisms have emerged. In particular, the rise of Information and Communication Technologies in the 2000s has transformed interactions between individuals, organizations, and governments, introducing concepts such as electronic participation. This study examines electronic citizen participation in local governments by presenting a theoretical framework, explaining participation in local governance, and analyzing practical examples. Finally, the benefits and challenges of citizen participation in local governance are evaluated.

DOI: 10.4018/979-8-3373-0452-6.ch003

INTRODUCTION

Citizen participation in public administration denotes the ability of individuals to influence policy decision-making processes that directly or indirectly impact their lives. As a fundamental component of democracy, it serves as a critical bridge between citizens and governmental institutions. This pivotal role has made citizen participation a subject of extensive scholarly debate. While some argue that expecting citizens to be actively involved in every public sector decision is unrealistic—given constraints related to time, knowledge, and personal motivation—others contend that greater participation fosters the acquisition of expertise, civic awareness, and a stronger sense of community, thereby enhancing public engagement in decision-making.

The question of how and when public administrators should involve citizens in decision-making remains an ongoing topic of discussion. However, technological and societal transformations have diversified the means of political participation, leading to the development of various participatory mechanisms. In particular, the proliferation of Information and Communication Technologies (ICTs) since the early 2000s has significantly altered the ways in which individuals, organizations, and governments interact. This digital shift has introduced new dimensions to participatory governance, most notably in the form of electronic participation (e-participation). Furthermore, according to the OECD Deliberative Database, public authorities have increasingly incorporated citizens into decision-making processes over the years. Figure 1 illustrates the number of deliberative processes undertaken by OECD member states between 1979 and 2023.

Figure 1. Number of Representative Deliberative Processes Over Time 1979-2023

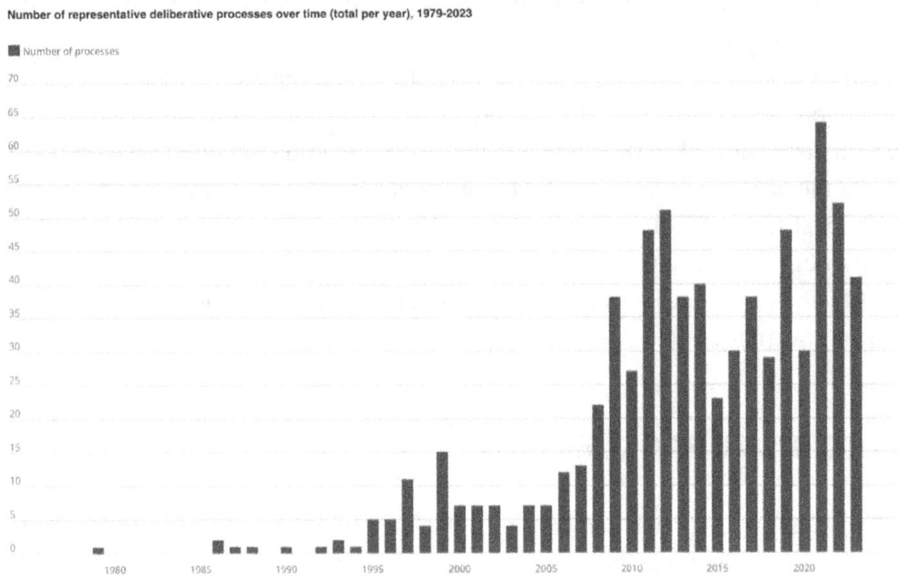

Source: OECD, 2024.

Electronic citizen participation refers to the utilization of ICTs to facilitate citizen engagement in decision-making processes. As Wirtz, Daiser, and Binkowska (2018) assert, e-participation primarily aims to: expand overall citizen involvement; enhance access to information; improve the quality of public policies; bolster public trust; reinforce shared accountability in policymaking; and increase public awareness and comprehension of policy issues.

Since the late 1990s, the widespread adoption of the internet has accelerated governmental efforts to digitize public services, resulting in the development of e-government platforms. These platforms have evolved from serving as mere repositories of information to incorporating interactive tools that enable citizen feedback. Online surveys, discussion forums, e-panels, emails, and social media platforms have gained prominence, fundamentally transforming the dynamics of citizen participation. Today, advancements in artificial intelligence and big data analytics further augment e-participation by enabling the systematic analysis of public opinion and facilitating more inclusive and data-driven policymaking processes.

Electronic citizen participation in local governance specifically pertains to the use of ICTs to foster citizen engagement in decision-making at the municipal and regional levels. This approach is integral to strengthening local democracy while enhancing transparency, accountability, and administrative efficiency. However, citizen participation is a multidimensional phenomenon, encompassing aspects such as levels of engagement, directionality, forms, timing, and technological tools. Managing these dimensions effectively to achieve the intended policy outcomes presents a complex challenge.

This study examines the digitalization of citizen participation in local governance from theoretical perspectives. First, it presents a conceptual framework that outlines the transformation of citizen engagement in public administration. Second, it addresses the nature and fundamental components of electronic citizen participation at the local level. Third, it reviews studies that explore the practical implications of e-participation initiatives in local governments. Finally, the study evaluates the benefits and challenges of the digitalization of citizen participation in the context of local governance.

THEORITICAL BACKGROUND

Although participation can be traced back to the existence of the ruler-subject relationship, its significant impact on the concept of governance is relatively recent. Following World War II, the notion of encouraging citizen involvement in public policy decision-making gained prominence. This idea was further solidified by the inclusion of the principle of ''maximum feasible participation'' in the Equal Opportunity Act enacted in the United States (UN) in 1964. These developments brought citizen participation to the forefront of public discourse (for detailed information, see Crosby, Kelly, and Schaefer, 1986: 170; Çolak, 2021: 39; Bingöl, 2022: 3). Consequently, citizen participation emerged as a pivotal topic in the literature, particularly during the 1970s. For instance, Sherry Phyllis Arnstein's seminal article *'A Ladder of Citizen Participation'* became a cornerstone in the field, influencing subsequent studies—some of which critiqued it, while others supported its framework (Sewell and Phillips, 1979; Crosby et al., 1986).

According to Arnstein, participation is a strategy for redistributing power to initiate significant social reforms. It involves decision-making processes concerning how information is shared, target policies are determined, and programs or contracts are managed (Arnstein, 1969: 216). In her *Ladder of Citizen Participation*, she identifies a spectrum ranging from non-participation, represented by disempowered citizens (such as the marginalized), to empowered groups assuming active and participatory roles. The ladder's first two rungs, *(1) Manipulation and (2) Therapy,* represent the level of non-participation. At this stage, the focus is not on enabling participation but on educating or curing participants to align with the intentions of powerholders. The next three rungs, *(3) Informing, (4) Consultation, and (5) Placation,* constitute the level of symbolic participation. Here, citizens may feel heard when they develop a genuine sense of community; however, there is no guarantee of altering the status quo. As one ascends the ladder, the power of citizens in decision-making increases. The final rungs, *(6) Partnership, (7) Delegated Power, and (8) Citizen Control,* represent the level of genuine participation. At these stages, citizens hold a significant or complete share of governance power, enabling meaningful involvement in decision-making processes.

Since the 1980s, emerging approaches in public administration have elevated citizen participation to a critical issue in public decision-making and service delivery. Efforts have been directed toward establishing accountability in public administration, strengthening participatory processes, and ensuring equity and fairness in public service provision (Çolak, 2021; Karkın, 2021; Saylam, 2021). This shift marked a transition from the passive citizen paradigm, which dominated traditional public administration, to an active citizen perspective. In the traditional approach, bureaucratic and hierarchical structures, rigid rules, and a dominant public authority constrained citizen participation. In contrast, the new public management paradigm, with its citizen-centric and flexible governance model, has fostered greater opportunities for participation (Dunleavy & Margetts, 2010; Dunleavy, et al., 2006: 467)

Figure 2. Collaboration Among Social Actors

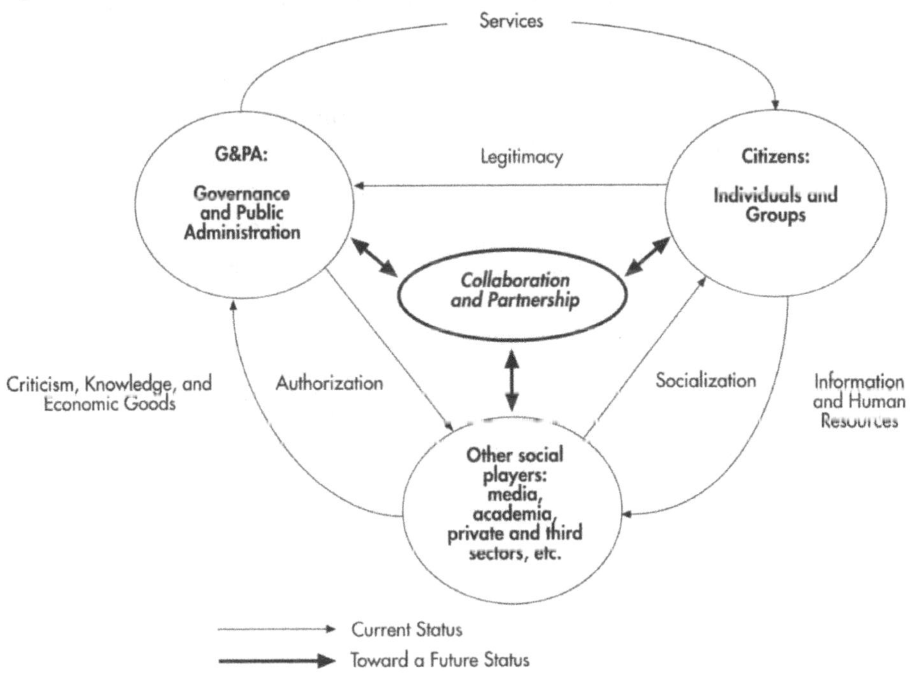

Source: Vigoda, 2002: 534.

Figure 2, developed by Vigoda (2002), conceptualizes the evolving relationships between public administration, citizens, and other social actors. In traditional relationships, citizens legitimized public administration through electoral processes and engaged socially via intermediaries authorized by public administration. In contrast, contemporary relationships involve citizens directly contributing resources such as knowledge and human capital to other social actors. These actors, in turn, participate in public service delivery by providing scientific knowledge, offering critiques of government policies, and other forms of collaboration. Consequently, the new relationships in public administration are characterized by cooperation and partnership (Vigoda, 2002; Çolak, 2021: 60).

The advent of digital technologies has not only reshaped human life but has also fundamentally transformed the governance structures of nations, institutions, and businesses. The shift from an industrial society to an information society signified the onset of the digital revolution, bringing about profound societal changes. The historical trajectory from the Industrial Revolution to the information society has been marked by successive waves of technological advancements. The First Industrial Revolution (Industry 1.0) commenced in 1776 with the invention of steam-powered machinery, revolutionizing production processes. By the late 19th century, the introduction of electrical power and mass production techniques heralded the Second Industrial Revolution (Industry 2.0), leading to unprecedented economic and industrial expansion. The 1970s witnessed the emergence of the Third Industrial Revolution (Industry 3.0), characterized by the advent of computing technologies and the rise of the information age (Knell, 2021). The term Fourth Industrial Revolution (Industry 4.0) has been adopted to describe and conceptualize new technologies such as artificial intelligence, the Internet of Things (IoT), robotics, cloud computing, and big data analytics (Fadziso, Yerram & Mallipeddi, 2022). Moreover, the social and technical innovations emerging from Industry 4.0, when considered in the context of issues like the environment, sustainability, and human rights, have paved the way for the Fifth Industrial Revolution (Industry 5.0) (Ecevit Satı, 2023: 19). These revolutions have profoundly impacted every level of society, from individuals to communities and organizations, shaping the world on a global scale (Figure 3).

Figure 3. Development of Society

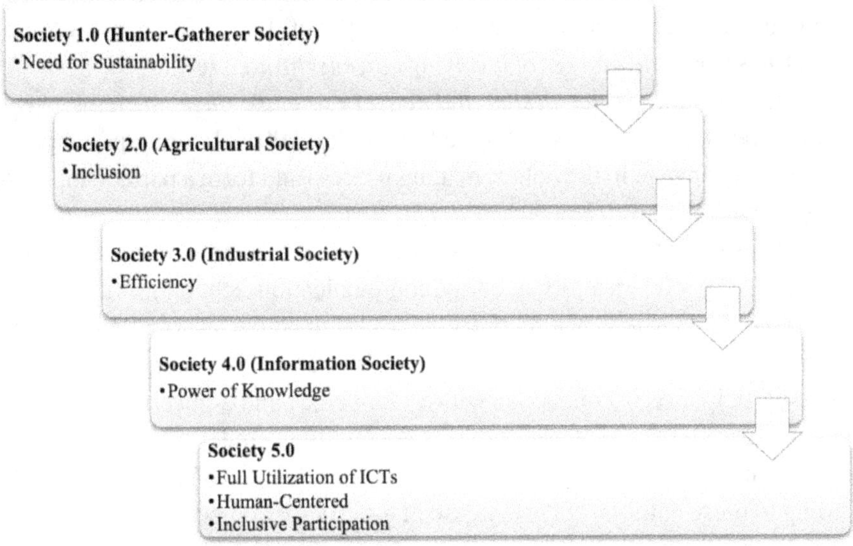

Source: Ecevit Satı, 2023: 23.

The development and widespread adoption of ICTs have increasingly linked the concept of participation to technological advancements. In contemporary society, citizens, empowered by greater access to information through ICTs, seek a more active role in shaping decisions that directly impact their lives (Babaoğlu & Leblebici, 2021: 507). Simultaneously, the knowledge and experiences of citizens and stakeholders present significant opportunities for public institutions to enhance decision-making processes (OECD, 2022). Furthermore, the degree of citizen involvement in public decision-making has been shown to strengthen public trust in government and, by extension, in public institutions (OECD, 2001). Given these dynamics, this study focuses on the electronic dimension of participation.

ELECTRONIC CITIZEN PARTICIPATION: LEVELS, DOMAINS, AND TOOLS

Electronic participation (e-participation) refers to the capacity of citizens to influence public decision-making and service delivery through the utilization of ICTs. The term derives from two key components: 'e' (electronic) and 'participation.' While the 'e' component denotes the application of digital technologies, participation signifies citizen engagement in political and administrative processes.

Consequently, e-participation represents both an expansion and a transformation of participatory mechanisms in democratic and consultative processes through digital platforms and the internet (Sæbø et al., 2008: 400-402). The United Nations (2016) defines it as "*the process of involving citizens through ICT in policy-making, decision-making, and service design and delivery to make them participatory, inclusive, and consultative*". According to the OECD (2001: 23), in e-participation, citizens actively engage in the policy-making process and form a partnership-based relationship with the government.

Wirtz, Daiser, and Binkowska (2018: 3) view e-participation as a participatory process enabled by modern information and communication technologies that involves citizens in public decision-making processes through active information exchange, thereby promoting fair and representative policy-making. Although many studies address e-participation in connection with e-democracy and e-governance, its scope is much broader and varies depending on the conditions under which citizens participate (Bannister & Connolly, 2012; Santamaría-Philco, Cerdá & Gramaje, 2019). According to these authors, not every case of e-participation pertains to political or governance-related areas.

Particularly, e-participation applications or websites enable citizens to interact with the government and participate in decision-making processes. As stated in the OECD '*Citizens as Partners*' handbook, "*strengthening government-citizen relations is a means for government to fulfil its leadership role in an open way and more effectively, credibly and successfully*" (2001: 23). For this reason, many institutions, organizations, or governments are making efforts to promote citizen participation online. According to Medaglia (2012), there was a significant increase in the number of e-participation projects in the 2000s; with the development of technological infrastructure, many new projects were created to support participation in political processes. For example, the European Union alone financed more than 35 e-participation research projects between 1998 and 2008 (Tambouris et al., 2012).

According to Phang and Kankanhalli (2008), determining the target audience of e-participation initiatives, selecting the appropriate techniques and ICT tools, and addressing the key factors for the success of the process are crucial. Therefore, it is essential for governments to plan and implement citizen participation processes effectively. The OECD, of *Guidelines for Citizen Participation Processes* outline ten steps for planning and implementing an efficient citizen participation process (Figure 4).

Figure 4. Ten-step Path of Planning and Implementing a Citizen Participation Process

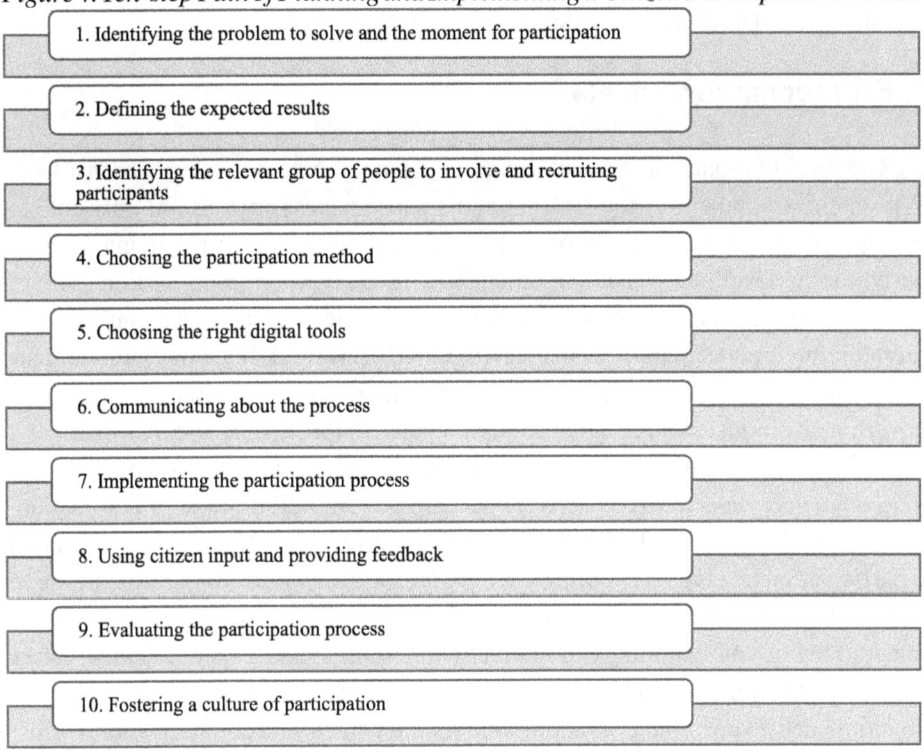

Source: OECD, 2022: 22.

According to the OECD, the initial step in designing an effective participation process is to assess whether there is a substantive issue that public involvement can meaningfully contribute to resolving, followed by a clear definition of the problem at hand. Subsequently, the expected contributions from citizens must be explicitly outlined, and the relevant individuals or groups to be involved should be identified accordingly. Once the key stakeholders have been determined, an appropriate participation management approach must be selected. Common methods include information dissemination and communication, open meetings or town hall meetings, citizen monitoring, public consultations, open innovation, citizen science, participatory budgeting, and representative negotiation processes. At this stage, it is also essential to identify and implement the most suitable digital tools to facilitate the chosen participation method. Following the selection of participation mechanisms, it is crucial to establish a continuous, transparent, and accessible communication framework to ensure effective engagement throughout the process. The implementation phase should be accompanied by regular feedback mechanisms based on the outcomes achieved, enabling a systematic evaluation of the participation process.

Finally, long-term efforts should focus on fostering and institutionalizing a culture of participation to promote sustained citizen engagement.

a. E-Participation Levels

The level of e-participation addresses the extent to which citizens are involved. With the development of the internet and smart devices, citizens are now able to engage not only by receiving information and services but also through interactions based on the level of e-participation enabled by the system (e.g., participating in online consultations or discussions, providing opinions and suggestions…). The literature on e-participation levels varies: OECD (2001) defines the political participation dimensions as follows: *Information* (a one-way relationship where the government produces and communicates information for citizens' use), *Consultation* (a two-way relationship where citizens provide feedback to the government), and *Active Participation* (citizens actively participating in defining the policy-making process and its content). Based on the OECD report, Macintosh (2004) examined e-participation levels as *e-enabling, e-engaging, and e-empowerment.* According to him, *e-enabling* refers to the use of technology to enable participation; *e-engaging* refers to the use of technology to interact with citizens; and *e-empowerment* refers to the use of technology to empower citizens. In more detail, e-enabling is when the government uses technology to address citizens' technical and communication skills; e-engaging is when the government and citizens engage in top-down consultations through various technological tools; and e-empowerment is when citizens engage in bottom-up consultations, not only as consumers but also as producers, through active electronic participation in policy-making (Macintosh, 2004: 3). Wimmer (2007: 92), on the other hand, analyzed e-participation as *e-information* (a one-way channel providing information), *e-consultation* (a limited two-way channel allowing stakeholders to contribute opinions on specific topics either privately or publicly), *e-collaboration* (a broad two-way channel where stakeholders play an active role in shaping policy proposals, although final decision-making responsibility lies with authorities), and *e-empowerment* (such as a referendum, where the final decision is left to citizens). The United Nations also examines e-participation in its E-Participation Index under three dimensions: *E-information*: Enabling participation by providing citizens with public information and access to information either proactively or upon request. *E-consultation:* Engaging citizens in contributions to and deliberation on public policies and services. *E-decision-making:* Empowering citizens through co-design of policy options and co-production of service components and delivery modalities.

b. E-Participation Application Areas

The application areas of e-participation, facilitated by the use of ICT, are diverse, with new areas emerging based on specific needs and political, social, and cultural conditions (Santamaría-Philco et al., 2019). For example, Wimmer (2007: 92) classified ICT-based e-participation application areas as follows:

- *Information Provision:* Structuring, representing, and managing information.
- *Community Building/Collaborative Environments:* Facilitating the gathering of individuals to create, advance, shape, and strengthen common agendas.
- *Consultation:* Enabling stakeholders to contribute to public or private initiatives on specific issues.
- *Campaign:* Participating in forms of collective action, such as protests, lobbying, petitions, and other actions, beyond election campaigns.
- *Election Campaign:* Supporting politicians, political parties, and lobbyists within the context of election campaigns.
- *Negotiation:* Supporting virtual group discussions, allowing for the reflection and evaluation of issues.
- *Discourse:* Supporting the analysis and representation of discourse.
- *Mediation:* Resolving conflicts or disputes in an online context.
- *Spatial Planning:* Contributing to urban planning and environmental assessments.
- *Survey:* Measuring public opinion and sentiment.

c. E-Participation Tools

A range of ICT tools facilitates interaction between citizens and the government. Online discussion forums, virtual communities, online surveys, chat systems, group support systems, email, e-panels, e-petitions, e-consultations, and e-voting are some of the ICT tools utilized for e-participation (Medaglia, 2012; Phang & Kankanhalli, 2008; Sanford & Rose, 2007; Wimmer, 2007). On the other hand, social network platforms are also an important e-participation tool, as they enable citizens to engage in the decision-making process and communicate their decisions through real-time sharing and response mechanisms (Leblebici, 2021: 52). Furthermore, according to Wimmer (2007: 92), platforms such as webcasts, podcasts, blogs, and web applications that allow users to add and edit content are also tools that, although not specifically designed for e-participation, fall into the category of widely used tools.

Due to the heterogeneous nature of e-participation initiatives, governments and practitioners decide which types of tools to use based on the level and area of application (Santamaría-Philco et al., 2019). Leblebici (2021: 55) classified e-participation tools into three categories: political discourse, policy-making, and public service delivery. Many tools, such as political party websites, social media, candidate websites, and e-voting, are used in political discourse. Tools for providing information about legislation and administrative processes, intellectual forums, gathering information about policy processes, and collecting citizens' requests are used in the policy-making process. Tools that provide e-government services and foster collaboration with citizens are used in public service delivery.

d. E-Participation Actors

In the relevant literature, e-participation actors are generally presented as citizens, politicians, government institutions, non-governmental organizations, researchers, and academics. Tambouris, Liotas, and Tarabanis (2007) classified the actors as expert administrators, elected representatives, professional stakeholders, lay stakeholders, randomly selected recruits, non-randomly selected recruits, and self-selected participants.

Citizen participation, particularly in the context of local public services, was widely and intensively practiced before the establishment of centralized state administration (Karkın, 2022: 59). Indeed, the foundation of local governments is based on the ability to observe local issues and needs firsthand and address them in collaboration with the public. When considered as the units closest to citizens, local governments make it more feasible for citizens to participate in decision-making processes.

ELECTRONIC CITIZEN PARTICIPATION IN LOCAL GOVERNMENTS

Local governments play a significant role in daily life due to their proximity to citizens and their responsibility for providing a wide range of public services. ICTs in the realm of public administration have given rise to various concepts, including e-government, m-government, e-governance, and e-participation. On the other hand, with the digital revolution of the 21st century, new technologies such as artificial intelligence, the Internet of Things, robotic technologies, cloud computing, and big data analytics have enabled the transformation of daily life and, consequently, local governments. The impact of this digital transformation on local governments has resulted in the following: real-time data collection from municipalities; improved staff efficiency and increased automation in operations; more transparent and accountable service delivery; continuous communication and information processing. Nevertheless, e-government has had a particularly significant impact on municipalities and this influence has led to the emergence of the concept of e-municipality.

Municipalities have increasingly adopted new technologies to enhance service delivery, contributing to the rapid expansion of e-participation and e-governance practices. Digital instruments, known as e-municipality services, bring numerous benefits to municipalities, steering them toward a digital future. In order to accomplish this, it is necessary to engage communities through digital channels as well as to leverage online surveys to precisely understand and meet public expectations (Pappel et al., 2018).

E-participation practices in local governments are typically used for purposes such as providing citizens with information about ongoing or planned projects, policies, budgets, and expenditures, or for collecting citizens' complaints, requests, suggestions, opinions, needs, and feedback. Various technological tools are used to serve these purposes. Local government websites, mobile applications, social media accounts, short message services, emails, online forums, negotiation or survey applications, and chatbots are some of the communication channels that facilitate e-participation services. Besides as policy-making tool for smart cities, living labs is the active participation of users and citizens, which plays a crucial role in shaping and refining urban innovation processes (Buhr et al., 2016: 28; Gascó, 2017: 1-92). Living labs could be distinguished by several fundamental components, including user and stakeholder participation, real-life environments, infrastructure, collaboration, co-creation, and innovation.

The 2030 Agenda for Sustainable Development emphasizes the importance of using ICTs to provide and manage public services at the municipal level. The United Nations E-Government Survey 2024 report highlights, in its fourth section, the need for cities to build resilient infrastructures, create green jobs, promote diversity, and foster strong social bonds within communities. It underscores the critical role of local e-government initiatives in promoting accountable, inclusive urban development strategies (UN, 2024: 135). To support and assess the development of e-government at the local level, the Division for Public Institutions and Digital Government of the United Nations Department of Economic and Social Affairs (UN DESA) and the United Nations University Operating Unit on Policy-Driven Electronic Governance (UNU-EGOV) established the Local Online Service Index (LOSI) Network. LOSI evaluates the information and services provided by local governments through their official websites. In this context, it assesses six criteria: *institutional framework, content provision, service delivery, participation and engagement, technology, and e-government literacy.* The institutional framework criterion focuses on the municipal e-government strategy, organizational structure, regulations governing access to information and privacy, and open data policies. Content provision assesses the extent to which public information and resources are available online. Service delivery focuses on the availability and provision of public services. Participation and engagement evaluate opportunities for public involvement in local government structures (Nabatchi &Amsler, 2014). The technology criterion examines the technical features of local portals. E-government literacy measures citizens' ability to make use of e-government services and e-participation opportunities. Figure 5 ranks the cities with the highest scores in the 2024 LOSI survey based on the criteria outlined above.

Figure 5. Cities in the Very High LOSI Category, 2024

City	Country	LOSI value	City	Country	LOSI value
Tallinn	Estonia	0.9271	Paris	France	0.8125
Madrid	Spain	0.9271	Reykjavik	Iceland	0.8125
Riyadh	Saudi Arabia	0.9167	Rome	Italy	0.8125
Copenhagen	Denmark	0.9063	Riga	Latvia	0.8125
Dubai	United Arab Emirates	0.9063	Zurich	Switzerland	0.8125
New York	United States of America	0.9063	Buenos Aires	Argentina	0.8021
Istanbul	Türkiye	0.8958	Zagreb	Croatia	0.8021
Berlin	Germany	0.8854	Almaty	Kazakhstan	0.8021
Seoul	Republic of Korea	0.8750	Auckland	New Zealand	0.8021
Singapore	Singapore	0.8750	Stockholm	Sweden	0.8021
London	United Kingdom of Great Britain and Northern Ireland	0.8750	Sofia	Bulgaria	0.7917
Shanghai	China	0.8646	Toronto	Canada	0.7917
Manama	Bahrain	0.8542	Doha	Qatar	0.7917
Tokyo	Japan	0.8542	Amsterdam	Netherlands (Kingdom of the)	0.7813
Kyiv	Ukraine	0.8542	Oslo	Norway	0.7813
Vienna	Austria	0.8438	Sydney	Australia	0.7708
Bogota	Colombia	0.8438	Warsaw	Poland	0.7708
Moscow	Russian Federation	0.8438	Vilnius	Lithuania	0.7604
Sao Paulo	Brazil	0.8333	Guayaquil	Ecuador	0.7500
Montevideo	Uruguay	0.8333	Tel Aviv	Israel	0.7500
Helsinki	Finland	0.8125	Luxembourg-Ville	Luxembourg	0.7500

Source: UN, 2024b: 138.

Fundamentally, both usable and well-structured technological developments in e-participation initiatives and the organizational structures and working methods of governments influence e-participation processes, activities, and outcomes (Medaglia, 2012). However, citizen participation encompasses many dimensions: government, society, culture, participation levels, direction, type, timing, and tools. Considering each of these different dimensions, managing citizen participation and achieving the desired outcomes is not always straightforward.

In their study, Tambouris et al. (2012) identified categories such as the structure of the governance regime, political culture, legal and policy environment, technological infrastructure, socio-economic environment, and cultural context as external factors, arguing that they influence e-participation processes. Similarly, Alrashedi, Persaud, and Kindra (2015) developed a user-centered e-participation model based on the intentions of users involved in e-government activities in Saudi Arabia. The study conducted an online survey with 200 Saudi citizens, and the results indicated that four variables (1- Trust in the government, 2- Attitude towards e-participation, 3- Use of social media, 4- Social influence and identity) positively affected e-participation intentions.

Schmidthuber, Hilgers, Gegenhuber, and Etzelstorfer (2017) contributed to the understanding of citizen-government interaction by analyzing survey data from users engaging with the LookatLinz (schau.auf.linz.at) platform in the city of Linz, Austria. Drawing on motivation theory and the theory of planned behavior, they explored the reasons why citizens are willing to participate in online platforms. Their findings revealed that participants who enjoyed engaging in citizen-driven activities demonstrated higher levels of activity; that experience and perceived ease of use positively influenced online participation; and that the attractiveness of open government was crucial. Additionally, they found that participants who had previously reported via traditional channels were more active in online reporting.

Yavuz (2021) examined the factors influencing electronic citizen participation in local governance, analyzing them in two dimensions: supply and demand. The supply dimension relates to the technology applications available to local governments, how frequently these tools are used, and for what purposes. Local governments differ in terms of their technological capacity and usage. The demand dimension encompasses factors such as citizens' willingness and interest in participating in local government decisions, their access to technology, and their ability to use it. The level of these dimensions influences whether citizen participation in local governance is positively or negatively affected.

Criado and Carmen Ramilo (2003) examined the local government website usage experience in the Basque Country and Madrid regions of Spain. The study addressed the citizen-oriented approach of the analyzed websites and, in this context, developed a typology for website development. Additionally, the study suggested that, in general, municipalities of different sizes possess various types of websites, with larger cities offering more advanced websites, resulting in a more dominant citizen engagement.

Karkın and Janssen (2014) evaluated municipal websites from the perspective of public value. In the study, three categories *(-content, -usability, and -quality)* were used as the evaluation metrics for websites, while six categories (*1-Accessibility, 2-Citizen Participation, 3-Transparency, 4-Responsiveness, 5-Dialogue, and 6-Balancing Interests*) were employed for measuring public value. The evaluation revealed that municipal websites performed satisfactorily in traditional indicators (content, usability, and quality), but showed weaker performance in public value criteria. According to the authors, many local government websites are built primarily around user focus and functionality rather than the creation of public value.

Babaoğlu & Akman (2022) explores the effectiveness of Facebook pages as a tool for fostering local participation. Given the growing assertion that social media strengthens citizen engagement—particularly at the local level— their study evaluates the relationship between social media and citizens by analyzing municipal Facebook pages in Türkiye. The primary focus is on the role of social media in facilitating participatory governance and enhancing citizen involvement in local decision-making processes.

Boon, Malek, Hussain, and Tahir (2020) conducted a study focusing on the participation process in e-government services and smart city programs in Petaling Jaya, Malaysia. Using thematic analysis, they carried out interviews and observations of municipal websites. In this context, the study identified the uncertainties faced by stakeholders regarding participation and provided several recommendations. Additionally, the study offered perspectives on how local governments can implement e-government in the context of public participation.

BENEFITS AND BARRIERS OF ELECTRONIC CITIZEN PARTICIPATION IN LOCAL GOVERNMENTS

Over the past two decades, governments have widely adopted e-government technologies, not only to provide online information and services but also to offer various electronic participation opportunities. To encourage citizen involvement in public affairs, governments have launched a range of e-participation channels, from simple online applications to more interactive online platforms, social media channels, and mobile apps (Choi & Song, 2020). Local governments, too, are increasingly adopting digital technologies for a variety of purposes: sharing details about their plans, goals, daily operations, and service offerings; promoting through digital platforms; promoting cities and encouraging local tourism among broader audiences; facilitating communication and consultation with a wide range of stakeholders, enabling them to engage with local governments and contribute directly or indirectly to the decision-making process; strengthening multi-stakeholder participation at the local level; reducing administrative burdens in service delivery; and ensuring more efficient communication and collaboration with citizens.

Local participation practices offer various benefits for both citizens and local governments. Particularly with the advent of Web 2.0, the cost of information and communication has decreased, and the opportunities for interaction between the government and citizens have expanded (Zheng, 2017). On the other hand, these practices are seen as a solution to the problems of representative democracy, especially the decline in political interest among the public (Oni et al., 2017). The use of ICTs to support democratic decision-making processes and strengthen representative democracy is defined as e-democracy (Macintosh, 2004). In this context, a range of tools, such as e-voting, e-panels, e-surveys, e-consultations, and e-petitions, have been implemented to encourage citizens' participation in political issues, particularly in policymaking. Through these tools, citizens can engage in the democratic process in specific areas, such as making the views of politicians known, assessing the acceptance of these views among constituents, making views or objections to political decisions known, ensuring transparency in political actions, offering the opportunity to co-formulate political decision- making in certain cases, etc. (Tambouris et al., 2007).

Transparency is one of the key elements of good governance. With the development of ICTs, transparency has become more manageable and scalable. In local governance, transparency helps prevent corruption, contributes to legitimacy, improves government performance by increasing efficiency, and promotes the principles of good governance (Grimmelikhuijsen et al., 2013). On the other hand, e-participation practices influence trust in government transparency. For instance, Kim and Lee (2012), in their study using data from an e-participation survey conducted by the Seoul Metropolitan Government, found that citizens' satisfaction with government responsiveness was positively related to their perception of influencing the government decision-making process. Additionally, they found a positive relationship between citizens' perceptions of influencing the decision-making process and their assessments of government transparency. Therefore, according to Kim and Lee (2012), there is a positive relationship between citizens' assessments of government transparency and their trust in the local government providing the e-participation program.

The involvement of citizens in local decision-making processes facilitates the adoption and implementation of these decisions (Yavuz, 2015: 274; Yavuz, 2021: 138). Moreover, local decisions made in response to citizens' complaints, requests, and demands improve the quality of municipal services. In the context of citizen participation effectiveness, Yavuz (2022) examined this issue within the scope of Nilüfer Municipality in Bursa. According to his findings, citizens place greater importance on participating in the processes of identifying service needs and problem-solving. The study revealed that citizens are most engaged in decision-making processes related to identifying solutions for local issues and needs. Another key finding from the study is that, as an aspect of participation frequency, the frequency of local participation varies according to demographic and socio-economic factors. In this regard, as age increases, participation in local decision-making processes decreases. Conversely, as education and income levels rise, participation frequency increases.

On the other hand, despite the ease of access to information due to the evolution of information, communication, and technology, participation may not reach the desired level today. E-participation studies suggest that simply establishing platforms for e-participation is not sufficient to encourage participation (Le Blanc, 2020: 17). This phenomenon can be influenced by various factors such as socio-demographic characteristics, the digital divide, the level of government digitization, staffing shortages, education, political culture, and the functionality of e-participation applications. Several studies in the literature have addressed factors such as unequal access to e-participation technologies, budget limitations, lack of information, staffing shortages, security issues, technological needs, and lack of public interest as challenges to the adoption of e-participation in cities (Schwester, 2009; Bailey & Ngwenyama, 2011; Sari et al., 2018).

One of the primary challenges in the development of e-participation is ensuring the inclusion of disadvantaged groups, such as low-income individuals, the elderly, and those with limited technological proficiency, as well as addressing deficiencies in technological infrastructure. These factors contribute to the phenomenon known as the digital divide. More specifically, the digital divide refers to disparities in both access to digital technologies and the ability to use them effectively. This divide extends beyond mere access to technological devices, encompassing the skills necessary for internet usage. Consequently, key determinants of the digital divide include economic status, educational background, age, and geographic location. Le Blanc (2020: 16) categorizes digital literacy into three key layers: (a) The ability to operate computers and navigate the internet, (b) the ability to search for and critically analyze information, and (c) the ability to utilize Web 2.0 functionalities to achieve personal objectives. Additionally, the European Digital Competence Framework expands on these competencies by identifying five core dimensions: (1) information and data literacy, (2) communication and collaboration, (3) digital content creation, (4) safety, and (5) problem-solving.

Efforts to bridge the digital divide are typically approached through infrastructure investments, digital literacy initiatives, and collaborations between the public and private sectors. However, merely establishing internet infrastructure is insufficient; the digital literacy levels of individuals play a crucial role in fostering meaningful digital engagement. Digital literacy is broadly defined as the ability to use technology effectively, safely, and ethically. For citizens to fully engage in e-participation, they must not only have access to digital platforms but also possess the ability to evaluate, produce, and disseminate information within these environments.

CONCLUSION

In the contemporary era, digitalization has emerged as a fundamental mechanism for reshaping the relationship between the state and its citizens. Particularly since the early 2000s, the rapid proliferation of Information and Communication Technologies

(ICTs) in public administration and service delivery has significantly accelerated the digitalization of governmental processes. This transformation has not only enhanced the efficiency and responsiveness of state institutions but has also fostered greater interaction between governments and citizens. As a result, digitalization has facilitated broader citizen participation in public decision-making processes, promoting civic engagement through various electronic tools and platforms.

Digitalization has become an increasingly critical topic in the fields of public administration and local governance, particularly in the context of democratic participation and transparency. The integration of digital tools —such as online surveys, e-voting, e-panels, e-forums, email correspondence, live e-chats, and social media platforms— has enabled citizens to express their opinions, share their suggestions, and engage in public discourse more effectively. These mechanisms contribute to enhancing transparency and accountability in decision-making by ensuring that governance processes are more inclusive and accessible to diverse segments of society.

In the realm of local governance, electronic participation (e-participation) refers to the active involvement of citizens in local government processes through the use of digital technologies. E-participation initiatives allow individuals to engage with governance structures without being constrained by time or geographical barriers, thereby fostering a more inclusive and participatory decision-making environment. Through these digital platforms, citizens can share their perspectives, provide feedback on public policies, and directly contribute to shaping local government decisions. This shift towards digital governance not only strengthens democratic participation but also improves the responsiveness and adaptability of local governments to the evolving needs and expectations of their communities.

As digitalization continues to advance, the role of e-participation in local governance is expected to expand further, necessitating ongoing efforts to improve digital accessibility, enhance technological infrastructure, and develop user-friendly platforms that encourage meaningful citizen engagement. By leveraging digital tools effectively, governments can create more participatory, transparent, and accountable governance models, ultimately strengthening democratic processes at both the local and national levels.

The success of the electronic participation process in local governance depends on the development of both technological and administrative capacity, the reduction of digital inequalities, and ensuring data security. Local governments must possess the technological capacity to effectively use digital tools and platforms. This is not only achievable through the establishment of platforms, but also by ensuring that digital tools are user-friendly, secure, and accessible. On the other hand, local governments need administrative capacity to manage these processes, including the systematic collection of citizen feedback, its analysis, and the integration of this data into decision-making processes. Additionally, in order for digital participation to reach a wide audience, reducing digital inequalities is crucial. Alongside policies aimed at bridging the digital divide, also ensuring data security is a critical factor. In addition, the success of electronic participation applications is linked not only to technological factors but also to citizens' socio-demographic characteristics, political values, culture, government reform, and other factors. Therefore, to enhance the effectiveness and sustainability of electronic participation in local governance, a holistic approach is required.

REFERENCES

Alrashedi, R., Persaud, A., & Kindra, G. (2015). Drivers of e-participation: Case of Saudi Arabia. *Journal of Business Inquiry, 14*(1), 1–22.

Arnstein, S. R. (1969). A ladder of citizen participation. *Journal of the American Institute of Planners, 35*(4), 216–224. DOI: 10.1080/01944366908977225

Babaoğlu, C., & Akman, E. (2022). "Participation with social media: The case of Turkish metropolitan municipalities in facebook", in *Research Anthology on Citizen Engagement and Activism for Social Change* (Edt: Mehdi Khosrow-Pour, Steve Clarke, Murray E. Jennex & Ari-Veikko Anttiroiko), Hersey: IGI, 77-95. DOI: 10.4018/978-1-6684-3706-3.ch006

Babaoğlu, C., & Leblebici, D. N. (2021). "Public participation in disability policy: The case of metropolitan Ankara", in *The Handbook of Global Challenges to Improving Public Services and Government Operations*, (Edt. C. Babaoğlu, O. Kulaç & E. Akman), Hersey: IGI, 506-524.

Bailey, A., & Ngwenyama, O. (2011). The challenge of e-participation in the digital city: Exploring generational influences among community telecentre users. *Telematics and Informatics, 28*(3), 204–214. DOI: 10.1016/j.tele.2010.09.004

Bannister, F., & Connolly, R. (2012). Defining e-governance. *e-Service Journal: A Journal of Electronic Services in the Public and Private Sectors, 8*(2), 3-25.

Bingöl, S. E. (2022). ''Kamu yönetiminde katılım üzerine geleneksel ve güncel tartışmalara ilişkin genel bir çerçeve'', in *Kamu Yönetiminde Katılım Üzerine Güncel Tartışmalar* (Edt: Ezgi Seçkiner Bingöl), Ankara: Gazi Kitapevi.

Boon, L. S., Malek, J. A., Hussain, M. Y., & Tahir, Z. (2020). Participation in e-government services and smart city programs: A case study of Malaysian local authority. *Planning Malaysia*, (18), 300 312.

Buhr, K., Federley, M., & Karlsson, A. (2016). Urban Living Labs for Sustainability in Suburbs in Need of Modernization and Social Uplift. *Technology Innovation Management Review, 6*(1), 27–34. DOI: 10.22215/timreview/958

Choi, J. C., & Song, C. (2020). Factors explaining why some citizens engage in E-participation, while others do not. *Government Information Quarterly, 37*(4), 101524. DOI: 10.1016/j.giq.2020.101524

Çolak, Ç. (2021). Kamu yönetimi, katılımcılık ve vatandaşın değişen rolü: Seçmenden ortak üretici vatandaşa. *Memleket Siyaset Yönetim, 16*(35), 37–72.

Criado, J. I., & Carmen Ramilo, M. (2003). E-government in practice: An analysis of Web site orientation to the citizens in Spanish municipalities. *International Journal of Public Sector Management*, *16*(3), 191–218. DOI: 10.1108/09513550310472320

Crosby, N., Kelly, J. M., & Schaefer, P. (1986). Citizens panels: A new approach to citizen participation. *Public Administration Review*, *46*(2), 266–278. DOI: 10.2307/976169

Dunleavy, P., Margetts, H., Bastow, S., & Tinkler, J. (2006). New public management is dead-long live digital-era governance. *Journal of Public Administration: Research and Theory*, *16*(3), 467–494. DOI: 10.1093/jopart/mui057

Dunleavy, P., & Margetts, H. Z. (2010). The second wave of digital era governance. In APSA 2010 Annual Meeting Paper, Available at *SSRN*: https://ssrn.com/abstract =1643850

Ecevit Satı, Z. (2023). *Yeni dijital teknolojiler ve dijital inovasyon yönetimi*. Der Yayınları.

Fadziso, T., Yerram, S. R., & Mallipeddi, S. R. (2022). Analyzing the progression from digital production to digital society: Industry 4.0 to industry 5.0 transition evaluation. *Journal of Fareast International University*, *5*(1), 11–22.

Grimmelikhuijsen, S., Porumbescu, G., Hong, B., & Im, T. (2013). The effect of transparency on trust in government: A cross-national comparative experiment. *Public Administration Review*, *73*(4), 575–586. DOI: 10.1111/puar.12047

Karkın, N. (2021). ''Elektronik vatandaş katılımına (E-katılım) ilişkin teorik çerçeve'', in *Kamu Yönetiminde Elektronik Vatandaş Katılımı* (Edt: Ayşegül Saylam), Ankara: Gazi Kitapevi.

Karkın, N. (2022). ''Kamu hizmetlerinde kitle kaynak kullanımı, yönetişim ve vatandaş katılımı'', in *Kamu Yönetiminde Katılım Üzerine Güncel Tartışmalar* (Edt: Ezgi Seçkiner Bingöl), Ankara: Gazi Kitapevi.

Karkın, N., & Janssen, M. (2014). Evaluating websites from a public value perspective: A review of Turkish local government websites. *International Journal of Information Management*, *34*(3), 351–363. DOI: 10.1016/j.ijinfomgt.2013.11.004

Kim, S., & Lee, J. (2012). E-participation, transparency, and trust in local government. *Public Administration Review*, *72*(6), 819–828. DOI: 10.1111/j.1540-6210.2012.02593.x

Knell, M. (2021). The digital revolution and digitalized network society. *Review of Evolutionary Political Economy*, *2*(1), 9–25. DOI: 10.1007/s43253-021-00037-4

Le Blanc, D. (2020). E-participation: a quick overview of recent qualitative trends. DESA Working Paper No. 163. https://www.un.org/sites/un2.un.org/files/2020/08/1597341830.3171.pdf

Leblebici, N. D. (2021). ''Kamu yönetiminde elektronik vatandaş katılımının sağladığı yararlar ve e-katılıma uyumun önündeki engeller'', in *Kamu Yönetiminde Elektronik Vatandaş Katılımı* (Edt: Ayşegül Saylam), Ankara: Gazi Kitapevi, 137-155.

Macintosh, A. (2004). Characterizing e-participation in policy-making. *In37th Annual Hawaii International Conference on System Sciences,* 1 -10.

Medaglia, R. (2012). E-Participation research: Moving characterization forward (2006–2011). *Government Information Quarterly*, *29*(3), 346–360. DOI: 10.1016/j.giq.2012.02.010

Nabatchi, T., & Amsler, L. B. (2014). Direct public engagement in local government. *American Review of Public Administration*, •••, 44.

OECD. (2001). Citiziens as partners: OECD handbook on information, consultation and public participation in policy-making. OECD Publishing, Paris. https://www.oecd-ilibrary.org/governance/citizens-as-partners_9789264195561-en

OECD. (2022). *OECD guidelines for citizen participation processes, OECD public governance reviews*. OECD Publishing., DOI: 10.1787/f765caf6-

Oni, A. A., Oni, S., Mbarika, V., & Ayo, C. K. (2017). Empirical study of user acceptance of online political participation: Integrating civic voluntarism model and theory of reasoned action. *Government Information Quarterly*, *34*(2), 317–328. DOI: 10.1016/j.giq.2017.02.003

Pappel, I., Tsap, V., Pappel, I., & Draheim, D. (2018). ''Exploring e-services development in local government authorities by means of electronic document management systems'', in *International Conference on Electronic Governance and Open Society: Challenges in Eurasia*, Cham: Springer International Publishing, 223-231.

Phang, C. W., & Kankanhalli, A. (2008). A framework of ICT exploitation for e-participation initiatives. *Communications of the ACM*, *51*(12), 128–132. DOI: 10.1145/1409360.1409385

Sæbø, Ø., Rose, J., & Flak, L. S. (2008). The shape of eParticipation: Characterizing an emerging research area. *Government Information Quarterly*, *25*(3), 400–428. DOI: 10.1016/j.giq.2007.04.007

Sanford, C., & Rose, J. (2007). Characterizing e-participation. *International Journal of Information Management*, *27*(6), 406–421. DOI: 10.1016/j.ijinfomgt.2007.08.002

Santamaría-Philco, A., Cerdá, J. H. C., & Gramaje, M. C. P. (2019). Advances in e-Participation: A perspective of Last Years. *IEEE Access : Practical Innovations, Open Solutions*, *7*, 155894–155916. DOI: 10.1109/ACCESS.2019.2948810

Sari, A. M., Hidayanto, A. N., Purwandari, B., Budi, N. F. A., & Kosandi, M. (2018). Challenges and issues of E-participation implementation: A case study of e-complaint Indonesia. *In2018 Third International Conference on Informatics and Computing*, 1-6. DOI: 10.1109/IAC.2018.8780467

Saylam, A. (2021). Kamu yönetiminde elektronik vatandaş katılımını etkileyen faktörler ekseninde türk kamu yönetimi için bir ortak yapım portal önerisi: Milletinkarari. gov. tr. *Kamu Yönetimi ve Teknoloji Dergisi*, *3*(1), 81–101.

Schmidthuber, L., Hilgers, D., Gegenhuber, T., & Etzelstorfer, S. (2017). The emergence of local open government: Determinants of citizen participation in online service reporting. *Government Information Quarterly*, *34*(3), 457–469. DOI: 10.1016/j.giq.2017.07.001

Schwester, R. W. (2009). Examining the barriers to e government adoption. *Electronic Journal of E-Government*, *7*(1), 113–122.

Sewell, W. D., & Phillips, S. D. (1979). Models for the evaluation of public participation programmes. *Natural Resources Journal*, *19*(2), 337–358.

Tambouris, E., Liotas, N., & Tarabanis, K. (2007). ''A framework for assessing eParticipation projects and tools'', in *2007 40th Annual Hawaii International Conference on System Sciences (HICSS'07)*, IEEE. DOI: 10.1109/HICSS.2007.13

Tambouris, E., Macintosh, A., Smith, S., Panopoulou, E., Tarabanis, K., & Millard, J. (2012). Understanding eParticipation state of play in Europe. *Information Systems Management*, *29*(4), 321–330. DOI: 10.1080/10580530.2012.716994

UN. (2020). E-government survey 2020: Digital government in the decade of action for sustainable development. https://publicadministration.un.org/egovkb/Portals/egovkb/Documents/un/2020-Survey/2020%20UN%20E-Government%20Survey%20(Full%20Report).pdf

UN. (2024a). UN E-government knowledgebase. https://publicadministration.un.org/egovkb/Data-Center

UN. (2024b). E-Government survey 2024: Accelerating digital transformation for sustainable development. https://publicadministration.un.org/egovkb/en-us/

UN - United Nations. (2016). United Nations e-government survey 2016: E-Government in support of sustainable development. Sales No. E.16.II.H.2 https://publicadministration.un.org/en/research/un-e-governmentsurveys

Vigoda, E. (2002). From responsiveness to collaboration: Governance, citizens, and the next generation of public administration. *Public Administration Review*, *62*(5), 527–540. DOI: 10.1111/1540-6210.00235

Wimmer, M. A. (2007). Ontology for an e-participation virtual resource centre. In *Proceedings of the 1st international conference on Theory and practice of electronic governance*. P: 89-98. DOI: 10.1145/1328057.1328079

Wirtz, B. W., Daiser, P., & Binkowska, B. (2018). E-participation: A strategic framework. *International Journal of Public Administration, 41*(1), 1–12. DOI: 10.1080/01900692.2016.1242620

Yavuz, N. (2015). ''Dijital çağ yönetişimi: Kamu yönetiminde ihtiyaç temelli bütünleşme çabası'', in *Kamu Yönetiminde Paradigma Arayışlar: Yeni Kamu İşletmeciliği ve Ötesi*, (Edt: Özer Köseoğlu & M. Zahid Sobacı), Dora Yayınları. 273-293.

Yavuz, N. (2021). ''Yerel yönetimlerde elektronik vatandaş katılımı'', in *Kamu Yönetiminde Elektronik Vatandaş Katılımı* (Edt: Ayşegül Saylam), Ankara: Gazi Kitapevi, 137-155.

Yavuz, N. (2022). ''Yerel yönetimlerde vatandaş katılımının etkinliği: Bursa Nilüfer Belediyesi üzerinden bir değerlendirme'', in *Kamu Yönetiminde Katılım Üzerine Güncel Tartışmalar* (Edt: Ezgi Seçkiner Bingöl), Ankara: Gazi Kitapevi.

Zheng, Y. (2017). Explaining citizens' E-participation usage: Functionality of E-participation applications. *Administration & Society*, *49*(3), 423–442. DOI: 10.1177/0095399715593313

Chapter 4
Promoting Inclusive Governance through Citizen Participation:
The Case of Switzerland's Local Decision-Making Processes

Miray Özden
https://orcid.org/0000-0001-7998-9699
Tekirdağ Namık Kemal Üniversitesi, Tekirdağ, Turkey

ABSTRACT

Citizen participation in local decision-making varies from formal mechanisms like public consultations and referenda to informal tools such as petitions and social media engagement. Switzerland stands out as a model of direct democracy, where popular initiatives allow citizens to propose legislation, and referenda enable them to approve or reject laws. Its decentralized governance grants local authorities autonomy, fostering strong public engagement. Participatory budgeting and digital democracy further enhance inclusivity, ensuring decisions reflect community needs. These mechanisms increase trust, accountability, and democratic legitimacy by directly involving citizens in shaping policies and public services. Switzerland's experience demonstrates that structured participation strengthens governance, providing valuable lessons for other countries. By institutionalizing citizen engagement and decentralizing decision-making, local governments can create more inclusive, transparent, and responsive democratic processes.

DOI: 10.4018/979-8-3373-0452-6.ch004

INTRODUCTION

Local decision-making processes are fundamental to the functioning of democratic systems, serving as the primary means through which citizens engage with their local governments and influence policies that directly affect their daily lives. These processes are central to fostering accountability, transparency, and responsiveness within local governance, ensuring that the voices of diverse communities are heard and considered in the development of policies, services, and regulations.

At the core of local decision-making is the principle of *local autonomy*, which allows municipalities and local governments to make decisions based on the specific needs and contexts of their communities. Local decision-making processes typically involve multiple stages, ranging from identifying problems or issues, consulting with stakeholders, developing policy proposals, and implementing decisions. The effectiveness of these processes often hinges on the extent to which local governments engage citizens in meaningful ways throughout each stage. Involving citizens in the decision-making process not only improves the quality of decisions but also strengthens the relationship between local authorities and the people they serve.

Effective local decision-making processes are characterized by inclusivity, where all members of the community, including marginalized groups, have an opportunity to voice their opinions and contribute to shaping local policies. This inclusivity fosters social equity and strengthens the legitimacy of local governance. Moreover, local decision-making processes that are open, transparent, and inclusive tend to result in more effective, relevant, and sustainable policy outcomes. When citizens feel empowered and included in decision-making, they are more likely to trust their local governments and participate in civic life, contributing to the overall health of the democratic system.

In addition to the structural aspects of decision-making, local governments must also consider the mechanisms through which information is shared and feedback is collected. Technology has become an increasingly powerful tool in local decision-making, particularly with the rise of e-democracy initiatives. Digital platforms and online consultations enable local governments to reach a wider audience, gather diverse perspectives, and involve citizens in real-time decision-making processes. These technologies also allow for greater transparency, as decisions and policy proposals can be easily shared and discussed within the community.

Overall, local decision-making processes are not only a reflection of the political system but also a vital part of building a democratic society where citizens are active participants in shaping their environment. The engagement of citizens in local decision-making fosters stronger communities, enhances governance, and ensures that the policies enacted at the local level are both effective and equitable. As the demands for more participatory and inclusive governance grow, local decision-making processes will continue to evolve, adapting to new challenges and opportunities for citizen engagement.

This chapter examines the importance of citizen participation in local decision-making processes and its role in fostering democratic, accountable, and responsive governance. In recent years, the need for inclusive participation in governance has become increasingly recognized as essential for maintaining the legitimacy and effectiveness of local governments. Citizen participation goes beyond just voting in elections; it involves the active inclusion of citizens in the decision-making processes that directly affect their lives, communities, and environments.

Moreover, the chapter discusses the challenges that local governments face in creating inclusive and meaningful participatory mechanisms, especially in diverse societies. These challenges include overcoming bureaucratic obstacles, ensuring equitable representation for marginalized groups, and managing the complexities of digital engagement. The role of digital technologies and e-democracy tools is also examined, illustrating how social media platforms, online consultations, and digital platforms can significantly enhance public participation and facilitate more transparent and responsive governance.

This chapter explores the critical role of citizen participation in local decision-making, with a particular focus on Switzerland's exemplary practices in this domain. Switzerland's decentralized governance model and commitment to direct democracy provide valuable insights into how participatory mechanisms can be institutionalized effectively. The Swiss system demonstrates that local governments can engage citizens in meaningful ways, ensuring that policies are not only reflective of public preferences but also rooted in the principles of accountability and transparency. Switzerland's use of local referenda, town hall meetings, and participatory budgeting, where citizens are actively involved in budgetary decisions, serves as an outstanding example of how local governments can achieve high levels of public engagement. These practices not only strengthen local democracy but also ensure that policies are more reflective of the public's preferences, fostering greater civic trust and social cohesion. Furthermore, Switzerland's strong legal framework supporting participation ensures that local governments remain accountable and transparent, continuously improving their policies based on direct input from the citizens.

The Swiss model offers valuable lessons for other countries seeking to enhance local governance through citizen participation. By institutionalizing participatory mechanisms and fostering a culture of civic engagement, Switzerland demonstrates that inclusive governance is not only achievable but also essential for building resilient and cohesive communities. The success of the Swiss system underscores the importance of decentralization, legal frameworks, and a commitment to direct democracy in creating effective local decision-making processes.

At its core, the Swiss approach highlights the transformative potential of citizen participation in governance. When citizens are empowered to engage meaningfully with their local governments, they become active participants in shaping their communities. This engagement not only improves policy outcomes but also strengthens democratic institutions, ensuring that governance remains responsive, transparent, and inclusive.

FOUNDATIONS OF LOCAL GOVARNANCE AND CITIZEN PARTICIPATION

Local governance is a fundamental pillar of democratic systems, ensuring that decision-making processes are closer to the people they affect. It encompasses municipalities, special provincial administrations, and other local entities that provide essential services such as infrastructure, public transportation, education, and social welfare. Effective local governance requires transparency, accountability, and responsiveness to community needs, fostering a system where citizens actively engage in shaping policies and services.

In today's increasingly polarized world, cities have emerged as the primary spaces where social contradictions are most intensely experienced. The demands and struggles of the working classes and other marginalized groups to access urban resources, have a say in their own lives, and express their identities within urban space often conflict with the logic of capitalist urbanization and its gains. Therefore, local development policies must address these contradictions to ensure that all urban residents can equally benefit from public services and uphold their urban rights.

Local governance being closely connected with the public gives meaning to democracy and participation. Political participation plays a crucial role in accurately identifying the needs and problems of local communities and determining effective solutions. The direct involvement of citizens in local governance not only encourages their willingness to participate but also enhances the quality of public services provided.

The realization of citizens' political participation in governance takes the form of influencing decisions, preventing the distance between the governing and the governed, and ensuring direct involvement in decision-making processes. When the public has a say in decisions, they are more likely to embrace political policies and contribute to the success of administrative practices. Moreover, a governance model that earns the trust of the communities it serves, remains responsive to public reactions, and maintains active communication with its target groups will be one that successfully fosters participation.

In addition to the methods developed to ensure participation in public institutions, the transition to the new public management approach has led to the integration of business management techniques into the public sector, resulting in a transformed governance landscape. Instead of a governing state or a solely administrating public institution, a model has emerged in which governance is based on interaction. This shift replaces the traditional approach of merely setting and enforcing rules, exercising unilateral authority, and managing from the top down with a collaborative and interactive form of governance. This evolving approach is referred to as 'governance' (Şentürk, 2008: 288).

Transformational change in governance is a global movement that has been ongoing since the 1980s. The common objectives of this movement aim to reduce the costs of governance, downsize the state, and at the same time improve the content and delivery of public services. The shift in the governance paradigm has led to a change in the scope of authority for public administrators, moving from top-down approaches to a more "pluralistic" perspective where coordination and cooperation are fundamental principles, and where network management and stakeholder involvement take center stage.

Particularly, changes in the work environments of public institutions, in terms of demands and expectations, have necessitated the redefinition of both bureaucratic and political processes in many countries. This redefinition has led to reshaping these processes in light of new tasks and methods. Administrators have observed that providing traditional services with conventional methods no longer holds meaning for citizens. Consequently, they have realized the importance of adapting new technological capabilities to governance processes. The new public management approach, which brings public administration closer to private sector principles, has contributed to the frequent expression of new principles and goals during this transformation, which has significantly impacted the way services are delivered.

The key indicators that have been effective in this transformation process include (Kettl, 2005: 5-7):

- Reducing the number of public employees while offering additional services and increasing efficiency in the public sector.
- Privatizing some services within the framework of efficiency and enhancing inter-institutional and inter-sectoral cooperation.
- Keeping pace with technological advancements, increasing the quantity and diversity of services offered through e-government approaches, improving communication between citizens and administrators, and expanding feedback mechanisms.
- Increasing authority-sharing among management levels and promoting the concept of decentralization.

- Separating service procurement from service delivery and restructuring the role of governance in public policy formation.
- Initiating performance measurement, improving the accountability of governance, and focusing more on outputs rather than processes.

Governance is derived from the concepts of administration and management. The term was first introduced by the World Bank in its 1989 report. Governance refers to a complex system encompassing public administration, the private sector, and civil society organizations, highlighting the network of relationships and mutual interactions among these entities. In this context, governance involves a broad spectrum of actors, including not only central and local government institutions but also non-governmental organizations, private entrepreneurs, and non-profit organizations, integrating them into the management system (Eryılmaz, 2013: 60).

The United Nations Development Programme (UNDP) further defines governance in terms of "*good governance*":

> *"Good governance refers to the processes by which economic, political, and administrative authority is exercised at all levels within a country. It requires that citizens and social groups have the necessary mechanisms and institutions to protect their interests and exercise their legal rights."*

The transformation of the traditional public administration concept into the New Public Management approach has also led to a shift from the classical understanding of local government to the concept of 'Local Governance.' Within this framework, local government has evolved into a multi-actor structure, incorporating various stakeholders and strengthening local networks of interaction. Gül and Kiriş (2014: 68), in their work analyzing the changing perception of governance during the transition from local government to local governance, illustrate this transformation in Table 1:

Table 1. The Transformation from Local Government to Local Governance

Traditional Local Government	Local Governance
State-centered	Public-centered
Hierarchical Relationship Between Management Levels	Peer-to-peer, stakeholder-based collaboration based on voluntary principles
Command chain	Collaborative decision-making
Order and obedience relationship	Democratic participation, team-based project work
Hierarchical and rigid organizational structures	Ad-hoc, temporary, matrix, and voluntary flexible organizations
Centralized	decentralized

continued on following page

Table 1. Continued

Traditional Local Government	Local Governance
Doing it oneself and producing directly	Enabling others (stakeholders, citizens, NGOs, companies, etc.) to do it, providing guiding support to them
Limited information sharing and privacy-oriented	Transparent, open, making information accessible
Formalistic, rule-oriented, and generally supervisory	Multi-dimensional and multi-channel local accountability and responsiveness

Reference: Quoted from Gül et al.'s (2014) book 'Local Governments and Local Politics in Turkiye.

The transition from governance to local governance has contributed to the development of innovative approaches in the delivery of traditional services, emphasizing a community-oriented understanding. Instead of the one-size-fits-all approach, innovative projects that prioritize regional development have been introduced, allowing for better identification of local needs and more effective use of resources to meet those needs.

The fundamental elements and collaboration processes brought about by governance have transformed local governments, leading them to take significant steps toward providing better services to citizens. Within the framework of new public management, steps taken to integrate concepts such as efficiency, effectiveness, performance, and quality into the operation of institutional structures have directed municipalities toward development programs that highlight local dynamics. These elements have contributed to the updating of governance through "local governance" efforts and diversified practices at the local level. Local governance represents a process that expands the scope of local governments by emphasizing multi-actor structures, dynamic systems, horizontal relationships, flexibility, and participatory mechanisms. The aim of this process is not only for local governments to provide services to citizens but also to increase their effectiveness in decision-making processes and expand inclusivity (Wilson, 2000: 51-52). Local governance refers to areas where interaction and communication within local governments are enhanced; it particularly suggests the promotion of local initiatives in the use of capital and the development of economic factors (King, Stoker, 1996: 50-56).

The relationship between local governance and citizen participation is deeply intertwined, as both concepts are central to the modernization and effectiveness of local governments. Local governance, with its emphasis on multi-actor structures, flexibility, and participatory mechanisms, is fundamentally designed to enhance the role of citizens in the decision-making processes that directly affect their lives. It shifts away from traditional top-down, hierarchical governance models and embraces a more inclusive, collaborative approach. This transition opens up new opportunities for citizens to engage with local authorities and actively shape the policies and services that impact their communities.

Citizen participation in local governance is not merely about providing feedback or voicing concerns; it is about creating a system where citizens are empowered to participate in decision-making at various levels, influencing both the direction and implementation of local policies. This participatory approach leads to more responsive governance, where local authorities can better align their services with the actual needs of the community. As noted, local governance fosters a dynamic relationship between local governments and their communities, where collaboration and communication are essential. In this context, citizen participation enhances transparency, accountability, and trust, creating a system where the government not only serves its people but works alongside them to achieve collective goals.

Furthermore, the relationship between local governance and citizen participation is particularly evident in the management of local resources and the delivery of services. Innovative projects that prioritize regional development, for instance, rely heavily on identifying local needs through citizen input. These projects enable local governments to allocate resources more effectively and tailor solutions that reflect the diverse needs of their communities. As such, the integration of citizen participation into local governance processes is not only a matter of good governance but also an essential factor in promoting sustainable, inclusive development. By fostering greater engagement, local governance models can help ensure that all citizens have a stake in shaping their community's future.

DIVERSE PATHWAYS TO ENGAGING CITIZENS

Citizen participation in local governance can take many forms, each contributing to a more inclusive, transparent, and effective decision-making process. Traditional methods, such as public meetings, referendums, and petitions, have long been used to involve citizens in governance. However, as governance structures evolve towards a more interactive and network-based model, innovative and diverse participation mechanisms have emerged. These new approaches go beyond mere consultation and enable citizens to play an active role in shaping policies, services, and development strategies.

Arblaster argues that actively involving citizens in governance processes is a crucial way to address the legitimacy crisis that democracy faces. He interprets this idea mainly through the lens of participatory democracy theory and supports his perspective with the following statement (Arblaster, 1994: 136):

"Governance should not only consult the people on what needs to be done. A healthy democracy requires that governance is not merely ready to listen to what the people (in all their diversity) have to say, but that it is obligated to do so. Leaders and governments must be acceptable to the people; given the significant gap between governance and the public in many modern societies, this likely means that rather than the people coming to governance, governance must go to the people."

Participation is a citizenship practice that emerges as the ability of individuals to influence the functioning and decisions of local government in the places where they live. The practice of participation provides citizens, as both governed and affected parties, with the opportunity to shape and influence decision-making processes. This practice carries the characteristics of a right, grounded in the principles of democratic popular sovereignty and the concept of local citizenship. Ultimately, participation aims to subject democracy and public administration to the sovereignty of the people by enabling citizens to have a voice in and shape the conditions and relationships that define their daily lives at the local level. In this sense, the practice of participation not only allows and strengthens active citizenship as a 'public subject' within a given country but also grants the right to influence collective life through democratic means (Göymen et al., 2014: 25).

The guiding principle of democracy is the existence of citizenship. The concept of citizen participation shapes the principle of citizenship as the right of individuals to take part in the political life of their country, framing it as a collective action. This principle is generally defined in terms of the different participatory models that people engage in within local governments. Since local governments are the closest administrative units to the people, they are considered a crucial platform for the implementation of participation mechanisms and democratic principles. Putnam does not define civic participation solely as political engagement; rather, he characterizes it as a connection between individuals and social life (Putnam, 2000: 17-25). In this context, citizen participation enables individuals to influence decision-making mechanisms, allowing them to perceive such influence as a means of shaping their own lives.

A strong democracy is a framework that focuses on citizens in participatory processes and highlights their commitment to engagement at this stage. Within the discourse of participatory democracy, the legitimacy of political decision-making mechanisms is shaped by the factors that either facilitate or hinder citizen participation. If citizens acknowledge these conditions, they affirm their role as a crucial pillar of a strong democracy; otherwise, they remain ineffective in improving this process. A robust democratic system is structured according to the characteristics of citizens and the conditions shaping participatory mechanisms. Implementing these conditions enhances efforts to raise awareness, educate, and empower citizens. At the same time, recognizing the challenges of citizenship allows individuals to seek ways to mitigate them (Barber, 1995: 288-295).

Citizen participation means that citizens take on leadership roles alongside administrators, actively engaging in decision-making and the development of policies that directly affect their daily lives (Walsh, 1997: 4). Therefore, resolving public policy issues in a collaborative environment and developing appropriate strategies is not an easy task. At this stage, local governments must ensure that citizens are included in the decision-making processes on matters that concern them and facilitate the organization of platforms where they can develop joint solutions. Since each policy issue is unique, it should be treated as a separate domain, requiring a tailored process for each case. Achieving the desired outcomes of participation is only possible through the implementation of realistic and effective methods.

Participatory methods that enable citizens to be involved in strategic issues and planning processes at the local level are highly diverse and extensive. Various studies in the literature emphasize these processes and methods. Establishing clear objectives in both the technical and practical aspects of participation contributes to making the process more functional while also allowing for the evaluation of different levels of participation. Therefore, in the participation process, the following key objectives should be considered:

- Ensuring that citizens can participate in identifying urban needs,
- Increasing citizen involvement in decision-making processes within local governments,
- Encouraging citizens to contribute to action plans designed to improve service delivery.

Setting these fundamental goals helps to expand local participation mechanisms (Holdar & Zakharchenko, 2002: 12–17). The successful implementation of these goals depends on identifying different levels of participation and effectively assessing their advantages and challenges. Since the participation process relies on mutual trust and interaction between administrators and citizens, the establishment and implementation of these levels depend on strengthening this relationship. These levels aim to transition citizens from a passive role to an active one, fostering a collaborative partnership between administrators and the public.

Arnstein compares citizen participation to eating spinach, stating that “in principle, no one is against it because it is beneficial for everyone.” She conceptualizes participation in three stages.

At the lowest level, decisions are made by authorities without meaningful citizen involvement, resulting in a process where participation is largely symbolic. The second stage consists of informing and consulting citizens; however, this does not guarantee that their input will influence decision-making. The highest stage represents genuine participation, where citizens actively engage in decision-making, shaping policies, and directly influencing implementation. This stage ensures meaningful and effective public participation in governance (Mapuva, 2015: 408).

The levels of participation consist of eight stages, each illustrating the degree to which citizens can influence decision-making before reaching the final stage.

The lowest rungs manipulation (1) and therapy (2) represent a lack of participation, where citizens remain passive, merely guided and informed by authorities in ways that serve institutional interests.

The next levels informing (3), consultation (4), and placation (5) are categorized by Arnstein as *"tokenism"* In these stages, citizens can voice their opinions and provide input, but there is no guarantee that decision-makers will consider their contributions. Among these, placation represents a higher level of symbolic participation, as institutions continue to retain control over decisions while offering limited engagement opportunities.

The highest rungs partnership (6), delegated power (7), and citizen control (8) mark the most meaningful forms of participation. Here, citizens engage directly in discussions with decision-makers and collaborate on policies. However, while they may share decision-making authority, they do not necessarily hold the majority of power or gain full control over governance (Arnstein, 1969: 17).

An effective participation process requires the identification of methods through which citizens will engage after designing the goals and objectives. Establishing mechanisms that enable citizens to express their views freely on matters that concern them contributes to making local governments more democratic. In this regard, incorporating citizens into local decision-making processes transforms them from mere voters into active participants in governance.

Different types and tools of participation can be utilized depending on the stage and domain of engagement. For issues affecting the entire local community, referendums may be held, or decisions can be made through prolonged deliberation and consensus-building. This approach is particularly relevant for structural changes such as urban planning, environmental regulations, or investment projects. At an individual level, digital platforms, including the internet and social media, can be used as continuous channels for communication and interaction (İzci, 2014: 34).

Various tools are used to facilitate citizens' direct participation in decision-making processes. Fung divides these participation mechanisms into at least three criteria before selecting the methods. The first criterion is who will participate in the process and how participants will be selected. Some citizen participation mechanisms, such as public sessions, are open to all stakeholders, allowing participants the opportunity to choose for themselves. In contrast, in participant applications such as focus groups or roundtable discussions, where participants are selected through specific sampling methods, the number of participants is much smaller. The second criterion concerns informing participants and their ability to influence the decision-making process. Some participation mechanisms are structured as informational meetings where citizens are not allowed to question the authorities, while in smaller participant profiles, there may be opportunities for participants to influence the authorities' opinions. The final criterion focuses on the potential impact of the outputs of the participant mechanisms on the decisions. Here, citizen participation should primarily be seen as a valuable process, regardless of whether it leads to better public policies or not (Fung, 2006: 66).

Beckley and colleagues propose an organizational framework model for participation methods. The model divides methods into direct (face-to-face) and indirect (non-face-to-face) categories, further classifying them based on the size of the group and the purpose of benefiting the participants. Among the direct methods, citizen advisory boards, focus groups, workshops, roundtable discussions, and public sessions are included. More successful tools are related to face-to-face techniques. Indirect methods include comment pages, free lines, and surveys, which, as they involve citizens submitting complaints, generally have a lower success rate compared to face-to-face methods. Additionally, new participation methods, such as electronic and web-based tools, 3D mapping, and visualization tools, are important due to their accessibility (Beckley et al., 2005: 4).

The applications designed for citizen participation can vary based on the methods used, which can be categorized into traditional and contemporary methods as a result of new developments. Additionally, they can be differentiated by the degree to which citizens can influence decision-making mechanisms, leading to classifications such as active and passive participation.

Passive participation methods are the methods in which information is shared with citizens, but the citizens are least likely to influence decisions. Passive participation methods generally emerge when institutions aim to inform a large audience. Institutions generally prefer to use passive methods for the following purposes (Figueredo, 2005: 17-20):

- To support public hearings as part of citizen participation methods.
- To inform and train citizens on issues that the institution attaches importance to
- To increase the awareness of the citizens about certain projects and initiatives
- To transform the image of the institution in the eyes of the citizens into a positive one.

Active participation methods are created in order to increase the citizens' dialogue with the authorities, to facilitate the representation of the citizens in the participation process and to improve the interaction between the citizen and the administrator. Active participation methods are among the tools that should be taken into account by institutions that attach importance to citizen participation, aim to increase the legitimacy of the decisions taken, and want to reduce distrust in political processes, because long-term opposition to the decisions to be taken can be prevented since an environment of bilateral dialogue and negotiation is created here; citizen effectiveness can be increased.

The widespread use of the Internet and the decrease in citizens' interest in traditional (offline) participation forms in this process has led to the emergence of new possibilities in terms of participation mechanisms. This situation will bring the advantages of reducing information and exchange costs, facilitating collaborative and negotiation processes, and ultimately reviewing the decision-making stages at all levels of government (Lironi, 2006:10).

E-participation is generally considered as online participation and expresses a process like traditional participation (offline) types. Here, in the decision-making stages; Conducting input research in drafting, information exchange in policy design and providing additional input complementarity, providing training and support in policy adoption and implementation, realizing information exchange in the policy evaluation process also constitute the dynamics of the e-participation process (Habermas, 1996: 17-18). Participation tools used by e-participation applications, unlike traditional participation tools, are considered as information and communication technologies. The use of these tools in the process leads up the activation of citizen participation and facilitates the citizens' access to the administrators (Al-Kodmany, 2000: 224).

The current assumption is that e-participation brings together "citizens with each other and their elected representatives" to create new possibilities for technology to improve public policy. The emergence of e-participation as a process that enables and supports democratic initiatives has brought about the inclusion of many related communication services resulting from the rapid growth and acceptance of the internet. The practice of online participation especially goes beyond traditional participation methods and is called as an attempt to break the silence of citizens in the process between elections (Wirtz, Daiser, and Binkowska, 2018: 2-3).

SWITZERLAND'S MODEL: A BENCHMARK FOR INCLUSIVE GOVERNANCE

Switzerland is widely recognized for its strong tradition of direct democracy and decentralized governance, both of which play a crucial role in shaping local decision-making processes. The Swiss political system is built on the principles of subsidiarity and federalism, which grant significant autonomy to municipalities and cantons in managing local affairs. This decentralized structure allows local governments to tailor policies and services to the specific needs of their communities, fostering a high level of responsiveness and citizen engagement.

Switzerland is a confederation composed of 26 cantons, each of which operates independently in domestic affairs with its own constitution, parliament, and government. Among these, 23 are full cantons, while three are considered half-cantons. The cantons function as federal states and exercise their autonomy within the limits established by the Federal Constitution. Legally, they hold equal status.

According to Article 3 of the Swiss Federal Constitution, *"The Cantons are sovereign except to the extent that their sovereignty is limited by the Federal Constitution. They exercise all rights that are not vested in the Confederation."* (Art:3, 1999). This grants cantons extensive autonomy in legislative, executive, and judicial matters at the cantonal level, as well as participation in governance at the federal level. Furthermore, under Article 42 of the Federal Constitution, the powers of the confederation are limited to those explicitly assigned to it, while all other matters remain under the jurisdiction of the cantons.

In practice, the implementation of federal laws is largely carried out by the cantons, allowing them significant flexibility to consider their unique regional characteristics. Additionally, when new issues arise that are not explicitly addressed in the Constitution, Article 3 ensures that these matters remain under cantonal authority, further reinforcing their broad scope of self-governance.

In Switzerland, the term *local government* primarily refers to municipalities, known as *communes*. Municipalities are considered the smallest political units (Federal Chancellery, 2013: 15). Unlike administrative subdivisions such as *regions* or *departments*, which are created by a higher-level authority and incorporated into a hierarchical administrative structure, Swiss municipalities are distinct political entities with their own legal personalities. Historically, many municipalities predate both the cantons and the Swiss Confederation itself, highlighting their deep-rooted significance in the country's governance system (Geser, 2004: 350). In addition to general-purpose municipalities, Switzerland also has specialized local government units, commonly referred to as specialized municipalities (*specialized communes*). These units are assigned responsibilities in a single specific field rather than holding broad local governance authority. Unlike municipalities in the Turkish administrative system, specialized municipalities function more like decentralized public service units. They often operate across the jurisdictions of multiple municipalities, focusing on particular areas of governance. While specialized municipalities exist across Switzerland, they are particularly prevalent in the German-speaking regions. There are over 4,000 such entities, with school administrations being the most widespread example (Fleine et al., 2005: 135).

Swiss municipalities are referred to by different names depending on the linguistic region: *Gemeinde* in German, *Communes* in French, *Communi* in Italian, and *Vischnancas* in Romansh. As the fundamental units of Swiss politics, municipalities hold significant emotional and cultural importance for many Swiss citizens (Fleiner & Misic, 2005; Steinberg, 2015). In fact, most municipalities existed before the formation of cantons and are defined by clear territorial and legal boundaries. Within their respective cantons, they exercise a form of semi-sovereignty, granting them considerable autonomy. Additionally, municipalities have the authority to confer citizenship, a power that highlights the deeply rooted, community-driven nature of Swiss political life (Fleiner & Misic, 2005).

Every municipality in Switzerland operates with at least three core bodies: the executive, the legislative, and the audit authority, with ultimate decision-making power resting with the local population. Swiss municipalities generally follow one of two structural models: bipartite or tripartite. In bipartite municipalities, governance is carried out by two main bodies—the executive branch and the electoral body. In contrast, tripartite municipalities incorporate an additional component: a municipal parliament, alongside the executive branch and the electoral body (Fleiner & Misic, 2005). The executive branch, commonly referred to as the municipial council (*Gemeinderat*), typically consists of 5 to 9 members who are directly elected by the citizens. In the canton of Bern, municipalities can choose between two governance models. Smaller municipalities often rely on a municipal assembly (*Gemeindeversammlung*) or direct voting via ballot to make decisions, whereas larger municipalities tend to delegate decision-making authority to a directly elected municipal parliament (Debela, 2020: 6).

One of the most distinctive features of Switzerland's local governance is the frequent use of direct democratic instruments such as referenda and popular initiatives. Citizens have the power to propose legislation, challenge government decisions, and vote on key policy matters at the local level. Municipalities regularly hold referenda where residents can directly approve or reject policy proposals, ensuring that governance remains participatory and transparent. This system not only empowers citizens but also holds local authorities accountable for their decisions.

Apart from referenda, Switzerland employs various participatory mechanisms to strengthen citizen engagement in governance. Town hall meetings and public consultations provide platforms for direct interaction between local officials and residents, allowing for open discussions on community issues. Participatory budgeting is another significant practice, enabling citizens to influence how local funds are allocated. This process enhances transparency and ensures that financial resources are directed toward projects that align with community priorities.

Digital tools have also become an integral part of Switzerland's participatory framework. E-democracy platforms allow citizens to access government proposals, provide feedback, and even vote on local matters online. These digital solutions expand participation opportunities, particularly for younger demographics and those who may face barriers to attending in-person meetings.

The Swiss model of local decision-making demonstrates how a well-structured system of citizen participation can enhance governance effectiveness, promote social cohesion, and increase public trust. By institutionalizing inclusive decision-making mechanisms, Switzerland serves as a compelling example for other countries seeking to strengthen democratic engagement at the local level.

Switzerland faces a decline in citizen participation across all levels of traditional democratic processes, including referenda—held regularly at national, regional, and local levels—and elections. Although citizens remain responsive to issues that directly concern them, local governments struggle to sustain consistent and institutionalized civic engagement in municipal affairs. Mobilizing residents to take an active and ongoing role in local governance presents a significant challenge for authorities.

In Switzerland, citizen participation is closely linked to trust and confidence in democratic institutions and processes. For engagement to be effective, citizens must first believe in the legitimacy and reliability of the systems they are asked to take part in. At the same time, active participation helps to strengthen the relationship between citizens and authorities, making governance more transparent, responsive, and efficient. However, fostering and maintaining this trust remains a common challenge for all democracies and cannot be achieved solely through digital or indirect means. Additionally, ensuring the inclusion and empowerment of foreign residents, marginalized communities, and vulnerable groups in political processes continues to be a significant difficulty, often falling short of democracy's fundamental promise to give every individual a voice.

Switzerland has significant practices in enhancing citizen engagement in decision-making through the use of direct democracy models. The effective implementation of these direct decision-making mechanisms ensures greater citizen involvement in governance processes. Moreover, integrating these models successfully into the system helps build and strengthen trust between citizens and authorities. To summarize these methods, direct approaches can be listed as follows (Council of Europe, 1999):

- Municipial Referendums: Municipal council decisions are presented to the municipality's voters for approval when a specified percentage of voters—

determined by the electorate's size—submit a formal request within 21 to 40 days following public announcement. Referendums can be held only on new budget categories or modifications to existing ones from the prior fiscal year, not on the entire municipal budget. Once the necessary number of signatures is collected, the state council schedules a vote for the municipality's residents to decide on the proposed measure.

- Other forms of direct participation: initiative and petition: In a municipality, all eligible voters possess the legal right to initiate discussions on specific topics by submitting a formal request, known as an initiative, to the municipal council. The number of signatures needed to validate such an initiative is defined by the referendum regulations. Additionally, the municipal electorate has the right to petition, allowing individuals to present complaints, requests, or suggestions directly to the council. Any petition that includes the petitioner's name and residence must be included in the agenda of the council's next meeting.

Source: EDA, 2022. https://www.eda.admin.ch/aboutswitzerland/en/home/politik-geschichte/politischessystem/direktedemokratie.html#:~:text=In%20Switzerland%20the%20people%20play,average%20of%20fifteen%20such%20issues.

Switzerland's citizens' initiative is a cornerstone of modern direct democracy, allowing citizens to influence political agendas by engaging directly with political institutions. This mechanism enables a minority to bring an issue before the entire electorate, ensuring their concerns receive a formal response. At the national level, the process typically involves collecting at least 100,000 valid signatures within 18 months to propose a constitutional amendment. Once this threshold is met, the initiative is put to a nationwide vote, requiring a double majority—both a majority of the popular vote and a majority of the cantons—to be adopted (EDA, 2022).

The increase in citizens' initiatives has led to a broader range of objectives (FDPA, 2018: 18):

- *Accelerator Function:* Traditionally, citizens' initiatives have served as a means to introduce new ideas. Notable successes include the Alpine Initiative (1994), advocating for environmental protection in the Alps; Switzerland's accession to the United Nations (2002); and the "Fat Cat Initiative" (2013), which aimed to limit executive bonuses in stock market-listed companies.
- *Brake Function:* Another conventional use is to halt or limit certain developments. Examples are the initiative to ban the construction of minarets (2009), the move to restrict the free movement of EU citizens (2014), and the proposal to continue the use of nuclear energy (2016).

- *Bargaining Chip:* More commonly, initiatives are employed as leverage to prompt responses from Parliament and the government, potentially leading to direct or indirect counter-proposals. Such initiatives often bring issues to the political forefront without necessarily securing majority support. Recent instances include the left-wing 1:12 initiative (2015) concerning salary ratios and the right-wing "self-determination" proposal (anticipated by 2019) addressing the balance between national and international law.

Switzerland's extensive experience with direct democracy offers several key insights (FDPA, 2018: 22):

- Maintain Low Signature Requirements: Setting high thresholds, such as requiring signatures from more than 5% of the electorate, can hinder smaller groups and diminish the effectiveness of direct democracy. In Switzerland, the requirements are approximately 1% for a referendum and 2% for an initiative.
- Allow Sufficient Time for Signature Collection: Providing reasonable timeframes ensures thorough public debate and increases the likelihood of gathering the necessary signatures. Overly short periods can limit discussion and disadvantage less influential groups. In Switzerland, there are 18 months to collect signatures for a constitutional initiative and 100 days for a referendum.
- Ensure Freedom in Signature Collection: Allowing signatures to be collected freely, without the need for official supervision, promotes direct interaction between initiative proponents and the public.
- Avoid Voter Turnout Quorums: Switzerland does not impose minimum turnout requirements for a vote to be valid, as such thresholds can undermine the democratic process by effectively counting non-voters as 'no' votes and encouraging vote boycotts.
- Limit Restrictions on Subject Matter: In Switzerland, there are few limitations on the topics that can be addressed through initiatives; only certain issues in international law are excluded. This approach ensures that citizens have decision-making rights comparable to those of their elected representatives.
- Ensure Decisions Are Binding: Direct democracy in Switzerland focuses on agenda-setting and decision-making, rather than merely consulting the public through top-down processes. This distinction ensures that public votes lead to actionable outcomes.

These principles have been integral to Switzerland's direct democracy, allowing for active citizen participation in the legislative process.

Switzerland's experience with direct democracy has served as a model for many countries; however, implementing this model elsewhere in its entirety presents significant challenges. While the constitutions of many nations allow for referendums, fully adopting comprehensive direct democracy mechanisms on the scale seen in Switzerland remains a difficult task. In Switzerland, the culture of direct democracy has developed gradually over centuries in alignment with the country's political needs. Attempting to introduce similar mechanisms through a top-down or rapid transition in other countries may result in failure due to a lack of institutional infrastructure and incompatibility with existing political cultures (Bulmer, 2014: 13-15). Below, we outline the key challenges associated with direct democracy, drawing both from Switzerland's own experience and from the difficulties encountered in other countries, along with Switzerland's responses to these challenges (demokratiezentrum.org):

- Resistance from the Political Establishment: The expansion of direct democracy entails a shift of decision-making power from elected representatives to the general public. This transition may face resistance from politically influential actors. According to political scientist David Altman, "*those who hold significant decision-making authority in a political system often oppose the redistribution of power brought about by mechanisms such as citizen initiatives and referendums.*" (Altman, 2011: 20). Historically, Switzerland has not been exempt from this phenomenon. When referendums and popular initiatives were first introduced in the 19th century, the liberal government in power frequently faced opposition from conservative factions, who repeatedly challenged government decisions through referendums, effectively blocking legislation. Following the introduction of the optional referendum in 1874 and the recognition of the popular initiative in 1891, more than half of the laws passed by parliament were subsequently rejected by the electorate, leading to legislative gridlock. This early example illustrates how direct democracy, in its initial stages, can potentially paralyze governmental processes.
- The Need for Consensus and Slower Decision-Making: Allowing public participation in every major decision can shift governance dynamics away from efficiency and speed toward consensus-building and a more deliberate pace. Switzerland's experience demonstrates that the mere possibility of a referendum forces the government and parliament to act with greater caution at every step. Opposition groups, particularly on contentious issues, can leverage the threat of a referendum to delay legislative processes (sgi-network.org). For instance, in recent years, a comprehensive CO_2 law aimed at addressing climate change was rejected in a referendum due to opposition from various interest groups, including homeowners' associations, automobile clubs, and rural representatives. Such cases illustrate how direct democracy can foster

resistance to reforms. The frequent use of referendums can also make governments more hesitant about implementing change, fearing public backlash. In Switzerland, this phenomenon is sometimes referred to as the "no reflex," whereby voters tend to reject changes they do not fully understand or perceive as complex. As a result, enacting large-scale reforms can become more difficult (sgi-network.org).

- Minority Rights and the Risk of Populism: Since direct democracy reflects the will of the majority, it can, in the absence of appropriate checks and balances, lead to decisions that undermine minority rights. The outcomes of referendums have occasionally clashed with fundamental rights and freedoms. For example, the 2009 referendum banning the construction of minarets in Switzerland faced criticism for violating religious freedoms. Similarly, extreme proposals, such as reinstating the death penalty, could theoretically be introduced through citizen initiatives. Some scholars argue that the results of popular initiatives do not always align with individual human rights principles and can jeopardize fiscal sustainability (scirp.org). In particular, populist financial initiatives may impose excessive spending obligations on the government or introduce tax reductions that threaten long-term budgetary stability. In some countries, such as the U.S. state of California, tax limitations imposed through referendums have disrupted public finances. Another risk is that economic reforms necessary for long-term stability may be blocked through referendums, as voters tend to prioritize short-term concerns over long-term economic strategies. These challenges highlight the need for safeguards to prevent direct democracy from devolving into "the tyranny of the majority."
- Ensuring Public Awareness and Preventing Manipulation: In a system where referendums are held frequently, it is crucial that voters have access to accurate and sufficient information to make informed decisions on complex issues. One challenge observed in other countries is that intense propaganda and misinformation can distort referendum outcomes (Kübler, 2024: 187-190). The influence of wealthy interest groups, which can finance large-scale advertising campaigns, raises concerns about equity in direct democracy. Switzerland has implemented unique measures to counteract this issue. Political advertisements on television and radio are prohibited, and media organizations are legally required to provide neutral and balanced coverage of elections and referendums. Additionally, before each referendum, the federal government distributes an official booklet to all voters, detailing both supporting and opposing arguments for each proposal. This approach helps limit voters' exposure to one-sided campaign materials and fosters a well-informed public debate.

A similar commitment to transparency and public participation is evident in Switzerland's legislative process. Before a significant law reaches parliament for voting, draft proposals are opened to public consultation, allowing all relevant stakeholders to provide input—a process known as "pre-consultation." This mechanism ensures that potential objections are addressed early, reducing the likelihood of a referendum crisis. Consequently, only about 5% of laws passed by the Swiss Parliament are subjected to referendums, and the majority of those that are put to a vote receive public approval. This statistic underscores how Switzerland's consensus-driven policymaking process has mitigated the risk of direct democracy leading to political deadlock.

Switzerland's structure, which serves as a model for direct democracy, has been implemented in many countries; however, it has also led to various challenges over time. In contrast, the practices encouraging direct citizen participation within the Swedish model have been successfully maintained. Undoubtedly, this success is attributed to various factors. These elements can be considered advantages stemming from both the country's historical and institutional structure as well as its societal culture:

- Historical Roots and Gradual Development: Switzerland has a long-standing tradition of direct public participation in governance, dating back centuries. Practices such as the *Landsgemeinde* (a cantonal assembly where all citizens vote in open-air meetings), which has been implemented in some cantons since the Middle Ages, highlight the deep historical roots of direct democracy. In its modern form, direct democracy was institutionalized at the federal level in the 19th century as a result of grassroots demands. Particularly, the rural uprisings and conflicts between liberals and conservatives in the mid-19th century played a crucial role in integrating referendum and initiative rights into the constitutional system (nationalmuseum.ch). This "bottom-up" development model facilitated the internalization of direct democracy by society. Rather than being introduced abruptly, these mechanisms were gradually implemented through a logical political process. Consequently, the system matured over time without radical disruptions and evolved in response to Switzerland's needs.
- Education Level and Political Awareness: The success of Switzerland's political culture is fundamentally rooted in its citizens' high level of education and the development of civic responsibility from an early age. Historians emphasize that the roots of direct democracy in Switzerland can be traced back to the country's relatively advanced education system in the 19th century. The widespread literacy and expansion of basic education enhanced the public's ability to understand and discuss civic issues. Even today, Swiss cit-

izens, who frequently encounter complex referendum topics, are experienced in acquiring information and forming opinions on these matters (democracy. community). Official brochures distributed before each vote and public media discussions significantly increase voters' ability to make informed decisions. As a result, Swiss citizens are recognized as a population with extensive experience in using direct democracy tools in a rational and mature manner. This level of maturity contributes to the stable functioning of direct democracy without excessive polarization.

- Federalism and Decentralized Governance: The federalist principle within Switzerland's political system is another factor reinforcing the success of direct democracy. The country operates as a loosely structured federation of 26 cantons, each with its own local direct democracy mechanisms. Governance follows a multi-level structure, extending from municipalities to cantons and then to the federal level. This system enables citizens to practice political participation at the local level before engaging in national decision-making (democracy.community). Since many decisions are made through local referendums, individuals gain firsthand experience in influencing issues that directly impact their daily lives. The referendum and initiative processes at the federal level are built upon this deeply ingrained participatory culture. Additionally, the federal system promotes inclusivity by representing diversity, making it easier for citizens from different linguistic, religious, and regional backgrounds to trust the decision-making process. In Switzerland—a multilingual and ethnically diverse society—direct democracy and federalism function together to institutionalize power-sharing, demonstrating that political stability can be achieved even in a highly heterogeneous population.
- Consensus-Oriented Political Culture (Consensus Democracy): Swiss politics is structured to emphasize consensus rather than conflict. Since 1959, the "magic formula" has ensured that the four major political parties share power in the Federal Council (the government). Instead of a rigid division between government and opposition, all major parties take part in governance. This consociational system works in harmony with direct democracy, preventing excessive polarization (Kübler, 2024: 190). Even groups that oppose government policies are represented within the administration, meaning that broad-based proposals rather than marginal demands tend to be presented for public voting. Additionally, to increase the chances of success in referendums, the government designs legislative proposals that can garner support from a wide segment of society. As previously mentioned, potential objections are considered early in the legislative process through a pre-consultation mechanism. Consequently, most issues put to a vote in Switzerland are well-discussed, refined, and based on common ground. This consensus-driven approach is

a key factor in the sustainability of direct democracy; without it, frequent referendums could destabilize society through constant division and polarization. Instead, Switzerland has managed to turn direct democracy into an instrument that reinforces social cohesion.

- Regulatory Framework and Safeguards: The success of Swiss direct democracy is significantly attributed to its checks and balances within the system. One of the most important of these is the double majority rule, as mentioned earlier. For constitutional amendments and major national decisions, a simple majority at the national level is insufficient; there must also be a majority approval among the cantons. This ensures that populous regions do not dominate smaller ones, maintaining a geographical balance and enhancing the legitimacy of decisions (demokratiezentrum.org). Secondly, restrictions exist to prevent the misuse of direct democracy tools. For example, initiatives that violate fundamental human rights protected under international law are not considered valid (although a broad range of topics can still be voted on under free speech provisions). A third crucial safeguard relates to campaign financing and propaganda regulations. Transparency in campaign funding is relatively high in Switzerland, and, as previously noted, media access follows principles of fairness. These regulatory measures ensure that direct democracy functions fairly and sustainably (Kübler, 2024: 190).

Switzerland's direct democracy model is the result of a combination of interdependent factors that contribute to its successful operation. A well-educated and engaged society, a strong tradition of local governance, political institutions that encourage consensus, and carefully designed regulatory frameworks all ensure the sustainability of this system. As a result, Switzerland is widely regarded as the "gold standard" for direct public participation in governance. Of course, every country has its own unique political and social conditions, making it unlikely that the Swiss model could be replicated exactly. However, the fundamental success factors of Swiss direct democracy provide valuable insights for other societies seeking to enhance citizen participation in decision-making.

CONCLUSION

Switzerland's local decision-making processes exemplify a highly developed model of inclusive governance, rooted in direct democracy, decentralized administration, and strong civic engagement. This model has demonstrated its ability to enhance political legitimacy, strengthen social cohesion, and ensure that diverse voices are represented in governance. However, while the Swiss experience provides a valuable reference point for other democracies, its success is contingent on a combination of institutional, cultural, and historical factors. This conclusion critically assesses the implications, advantages, challenges, and lessons that can be drawn from Switzerland's approach to citizen participation in local decision-making.

Switzerland's governance system fosters deep democratic engagement at multiple levels. The frequent use of referendums, participatory budgeting, and local consultation mechanisms enables citizens to have a direct and continuous impact on public policy rather than relying solely on electoral cycles. This results in:

1. *Greater Political Legitimacy:* Direct citizen participation in decision-making enhances the legitimacy of local government actions, as policies reflect collective preferences rather than elite-driven agendas. The Swiss system ensures that municipal and cantonal policies align with the will of the people, reinforcing trust in institutions.
2. *Enhanced Social Cohesion:* By giving diverse groups a voice in decision-making, Switzerland minimizes societal polarization. The principle of consensus democracy, embedded in Swiss politics, facilitates compromise and encourages inclusive policy outcomes.
3. *Decentralization as a Mechanism for Empowerment:* The autonomy granted to municipalities and cantons enables localized governance that is tailored to community needs. Rather than a one-size-fits-all approach, decentralized decision-making allows policies to be crafted in response to local social, economic, and cultural dynamics.
4. *Resilience Against Political Extremism:* The continuous engagement of citizens in governance discourages radical shifts in policy that could destabilize the political system. By ensuring that citizens have regular opportunities to shape laws and regulations, direct democracy acts as a buffer against populist or authoritarian tendencies.

These implications suggest that inclusive governance through citizen participation can contribute to democratic resilience, social stability, and effective public administration. However, despite these advantages, Switzerland's model also presents certain challenges and limitations.

Switzerland's experience provides important insights for countries seeking to enhance inclusive governance through citizen participation. The following key lessons can be drawn from its model:

1. *Balance Direct and Representative Democracy:* Switzerland has successfully integrated direct democracy into a representative system. Other countries could explore hybrid models where citizen input is institutionalized without completely bypassing parliamentary deliberation.
2. *Strengthen Civic Education:* A critical factor in the success of Switzerland's model is an informed electorate. Ensuring that citizens understand policy issues, governance processes, and economic trade-offs can prevent uninformed decision-making in referendums.
3. *Ensure Equitable Participation:* Policymakers must address participation gaps by removing barriers to engagement, particularly for marginalized communities. Targeted civic engagement programs can help increase representation across all social groups.
4. *Implement Safeguards Against Populism and Misinformation:* While direct democracy fosters legitimacy, it must be protected from manipulation. Implementing transparent campaign financing laws, independent oversight bodies, and fact-based public information campaigns can reduce misinformation and maintain public trust.
5. *Encourage Localized Decision-Making*: Switzerland's federal structure and decentralized governance model ensure that decision-making occurs closer to the people. This approach can be adapted in other contexts to enhance local government autonomy while maintaining national unity.

Switzerland's model illustrates that inclusive governance is not merely about granting people the right to vote but about ensuring meaningful and sustained engagement in decision-making. The country's multi-tiered, participatory framework offers an example of how citizens, municipalities, and national institutions can collaborate to shape policies that reflect the needs of society. However, as political landscapes evolve, Switzerland—and any country aiming to enhance citizen participation—must continue adapting its governance structures to address new challenges such as digital engagement, misinformation, and global governance pressures. The Swiss case demonstrates that while direct democracy fosters legitimacy and accountability, it must be carefully managed to ensure efficiency, fairness, and long-term democratic stability. Ultimately, the Swiss experience underscores a fundamental truth about democracy: participation is both a right and a responsibility. Ensuring that all citizens have equal access, informed choice, and real influence in governance remains a critical goal for inclusive democratic systems worldwide.

REFERENCES

Al-Kodmany, K. (2000). Public Participation: Technology and Democracy. *Urban Studies (Edinburgh, Scotland)*, *37*(2), 224.

Altman, D. (2011). *Direct Democracy Worldwide*. Cambridge University Press.

Arblaster, A. (1994). Democracy. Open University Press, 136.

Arnstein, S. (1969). A Ladder of Citizen Participation. *Journal of the American Institute of Planners*, *35*(4), 17. DOI: 10.1080/01944366908977225

Barber, B. R. (1995). Strong Democracy: Participatory Politics for a New Age. University of California Press, 288-295.

Beckley, T. M., Parkins, J. R., & Stedman, R. C. (2005). *Public Participation in Sustainable Forest Management: A Reference Guide*. Sustainable Forest Management Network.

Debela, K. W. (2020). Local governance in Switzerland: Adequate municipal autonomy cumintergovernmental cooperation? *Cogent Social Sciences*, *6*(1), 1763889. Advance online publication. DOI: 10.1080/23311886.2020.1763889

EDA. (2022). https://www.eda.admin.ch/aboutswitzerland/en/home/politik-geschichte/politischessystem/direktedemokratie.html#:~:text=In%20Switzerland%20the%20people%20play,average%20of%20fifteen%20such%20issues

Eryılmaz, B. (2013). Kamu Yönetimi: Düşünceler Yapılar Fonksiyonlar ve Politikalar.

Federal Chancellery. (2013). *The Swiss Confederation: A Brief Guide*. SFBL.

Figueredo, J. C. (2005). Publıc partıcıpatıon ın transportatıon: an emperıcal test for authentıc partıcıpatıon. In: TheDepartment of Public Afairs in the College of Health and Public Afairs at the University of Central Florida Orlando, Florida, pp. 17–20

Fleiner, T., & Misic, A. (2005). Swiss constitutional law.

Fung, A. (2006). Varieties of Participation in Complex Governance, Public Administration Review, vol. 66, Special Issue: Collaborative. *Public Management*, •••, 66–75.

Geser, H. (2004). The communes in Switzerland. Klöti, U. et al., Handbook of Swiss Politics, Neue Zürcher Zeitung Publishing, 349-391.

Gül, H., Kiriş, H., Negiz, N., & Gökdayı, İ. (2014). *Türkiye'de Yerel Yönetimler ve Yerel Siyaset*. DetayYayıncılık.

Habermas, J. (1996). Between Facts and Norms: Contributions to a Discourse Theory of Law and Democracy. MIT Press, 17-18.

Holdar, G. G., & Zakharchenko, O. (2002). Citizen Participation Handbook: People's Voice Project. International Centre for Policy Studies, 12-17.

İzci, F. (2014). Katılımcı Yerel Yönetime Genel Bakış. Göymen ve diğerleri (Ed.). Katılımcı Yerel Yönetim içinde. Kalkedon Yayınları: İstanbul, s.19-39.

Kettl, D. F. (2005). The Global Public Management Revolution. Brookings Institution Press, 5-7.

King, D. & Stoker, G. (1996). Rethinking Local Democracy. Palgrave Macmillan, 50-56.

Kübler, D. (2024). Citizen participation through direct legislation: A road to success? A perspective from Switzerland. *Global Public Policy and Governance*, *4*(2), 184–196.

Lironi, E. (2006). Lironi, E.: Potentıal and challenges of E-participation. In: The European Unıon, European Parliament's Policy Department for Citizens' Rights and Constitutional Afairs European Parliament B-1047 Brussels

Mapuva, J. (2015). Enhancing Citizen Participation in Local Governance through Participation Mechanisms. *Journal of Public Administration*, *50*(3), 408.

Putnam, R. D. (2000). *Bowling Alone: The Collapse and Revival of American Community*. Simon & Schuster.

Şentürk, H. (2008). Demokratik Katılım ve Sivil Toplum Kuruluşları. İstanbul Üniversitesi Yayınları, 288.

Walsh, K. (1997). Citizenship and Welfare: Rediscovering a Lost Dimension. *Journal of Social Policy*, *26*(4), 4.

Wilson, J. (2000). Exploring the limits of public participation in local government, Oxford university press, s 247-259.

Wirtz, B. W., Daiser, P., & Binkowska, B. (2018). E-Participation: The Role of Social Media in Citizen Engagement. *Government Information Quarterly*, *35*(4), 2–3.

Chapter 5
Digital Transformation and e-Municipality Applications in Municipalities in the Case of Pamukkale Municipality

Serdar Selman Savran
https://orcid.org/0009-0000-1539-4936
Pamukkale University, Denizli, Turkey

ABSTRACT

Today, digitalization in public administration has become a critical transformation area in terms of increasing the quality of service delivery and ensuring citizen satisfaction. In this context, municipalities are in a restructuring process based on the effective use of digital technologies in local governments. E-municipality applications provide citizens with fast, easy and time-independent access to public services; while also contributing to the more efficient use of public resources. This transformation is not only a technological investment; it also requires a participatory, transparent and solution-oriented change in management mentality. In this study, the basic dynamics of digital transformation in municipalities, the functionality of e-municipality applications and the current challenges encountered will be examined; good practice examples and strategic suggestions will be addressed specifically for Pamukkale Municipality, and a number of suggestions will be put forward to increase the effectiveness of local municipal services.

DOI: 10.4018/979-8-3373-0452-6.ch005

INTRODUCTION

In the world, the technological transformation that started in the business world has also entered homes over time. Technology, which started to enter homes with electronic home appliances, has become a tool that makes people's lives easier. Investments in internet infrastructure and smart devices in the 1990s and later have taken technology to a very advanced point. Today, the most important devices that help citizens do their personal work, follow technological developments without leaving their homes and make life easier are computers, smart phones and electronic devices that work with an operating system. The most commonly used of these are computers and smart phones. After the first computer "ENIAC" weighing 30 tons and consisting of 18 thousand lamps, computers have become quite small over time and have become a usable form that people can carry in their bags or pockets.

Smaller technological devices have made people's lives much easier. Scientific research has shown that people have become addicted to technological devices over time. Over time, computer use has become widespread in workplaces, creating a new system integrated with the world. Today, a person using a smartphone can communicate with a friend or business partner anywhere in the world at the same time and can carry out their work quickly.

Public services are services produced directly or indirectly by state legal entities and institutions with public legal entities. The general characteristic of public services is that they include public benefit. The concept of public benefit is the existence of a superior purpose while performing public services. This superior purpose expresses the individual and collective gains of citizens who benefit from public services as a result of the effective, economical and efficient use of public resources. The rapid increase in technological developments has also caused serious differences and transformations in the application of public services. Various interactive applications such as e-government applications, digitalization studies, e-municipality services provide support for improvement by addressing the static and faulty aspects of bureaucracy undertaken by individuals.

There are burdens that people who fulfill their civic duty in a country must pay in order to benefit from public services. These are generally called taxes, duties, fees and other payments. In addition to these, there are also additional fees that citizens must pay in order to benefit from municipal services. These payments, called the municipalities' own revenues, can be diversified as incomes such as goodwill and participation shares, fee schedules, movable and immovable sales, rental incomes, etc.

Today, with the widespread use of technology and digital municipality, the services provided by municipalities to the public have undergone a digital transformation and have been grouped under the name of e-services. Municipal services grouped under the umbrella of e-government and e-municipality are one of the important steps towards savings in the public sector. This digital transformation also makes the lives of citizens easier. A citizen who wanted to pay the building tax used to leave his home, go to the municipality, wait in line at the cash desk and make his payment, but now, while sitting in his comfortable bed or armchair at home, he can make this payment through the municipality's website applications using a phone, computer or a smart technological device.

Another beneficial aspect of digitalization is the ability to instantly access effective and accurate information. A large portion of the services planned to be provided by municipalities are announced to citizens via corporate websites. The tariffs and payment methods of the payments collected by municipalities are published in advance on corporate websites. Activities to be carried out within the framework of social municipality are also announced to citizens via corporate websites, operator messages and applications.

Municipalities are local actors of direct and participatory democracy. They are institutions that provide direct services to people with their large budgets, extensive service networks and extremely broad authority. Municipal administrators come to power through local elections and provide services within the boundaries of the province, district or town where they are elected. As explained in economics, human needs are unlimited and must be met with limited resources. At this point, digital municipality applications are very meaningful for municipal services to be provided fully and on time and for resources to be used effectively and efficiently. Digital municipality applications allow services to be provided at lower costs and faster. In this way, the resources saved from digital transformation can be transferred to other services for the benefit of society.

In this study, e-service applications offered in municipalities were discussed, the current situation was evaluated and a number of policy recommendations were developed to increase the effectiveness of these services.

1. TRADITIONAL MUNICIPAL SERVICES AND DIFFICULTIES IN SERVICE DELIVERY

Before explaining traditional municipal services, it is necessary to define service. Service is an abstract concept; it cannot be touched, seen, measured, and is exhausted after being provided (Sayım and Aydın, 2015: 246). Although services are abstract concepts, they usually have concrete results. For example, infrastructure and sewage services provided by municipalities are services that citizens benefit from for many years due to their nature and the results they produce. The definition and scope of services change depending on who produces them. Services provided by public institutions are called public services. Public services are services carried out under the supervision of political bodies, public institutions and organizations, and a public institution, and that observe the public interest (Yılmaz, 2008: 1224). Local public services are services produced by local government institutions within the framework of the Decentralization approach. The units with the widest authority and field of activity of local government institutions are municipalities. In this section of our study, traditional municipal services and difficulties encountered in service delivery are discussed.

1.1. Traditional Municipal Service Concept and Practices

It can be said that the concept of municipal services first emerged in Türkiye during the Ottoman Empire. In the Ottoman Empire, there was no such structure as a municipality before the Tanzimat period. The infrastructure services provided by municipalities today were carried out by the efforts of judges, foundations and guilds. Water administrations were carried out by foundations. Services such as environmental order, cleaning and sewage were shared among the citizens by the authorities (Deniz et al., 2017: 315). As can be understood from the mentioned practices, it can be said that the emergence of traditional municipal services in the Ottoman Empire was infrastructure, sewage, environmental order and cleaning and water works.

During the Ottoman period, the first municipal organization as an institution was established on June 16, 1854 under the name of Istanbul Municipality (Es, 2008: 33). At the head of this institution was a Municipality appointed by the Sultan and proposed by the government. Unlike today's municipality revenues, the Municipality did not have its own revenues; it was established to collect state taxes, duties and fees and to provide traditional public services (Karabulak, 2013: 41).

The basic duties of the municipality are to determine and supervise prices in public markets, to provide road and pavement services, to carry out cleaning works and to collect some revenues belonging to the state (Ergin, 1995: 1272). The municipality institution, which did not have its own revenues, was understandably unable to maintain its economic sustainability and was dissolved. After this dissolution, the Sixth Department of Municipality was established in 1858 in order to ensure that municipal services could continue completely and without any problems (Es, 2008: 34). After the Sixth Department was established, it provided many services in Istanbul. Among the services it provided were environmental and landscaping arrangements within the scope of urbanization activities in various districts, the construction of a hospital due to the increasing population, the lighting of Istiklal Avenue, as well as infrastructure services and cleaning works that have been ongoing since the pre-Tanzimat period (Önver, 2019: 51).

The Sixth Municipality Department, which collected the state's taxes, met its expenses from the funds allocated to it by the central organization. In addition, some taxes collected from tradesmen and citizens were used to meet the expenses of the Sixth Department (Ulusoy and Tekin, 2010: 154). As can be seen, today's contemporary municipal services in Türkiye emerged as a result of the applications tested in Istanbul, Türkiye's largest metropolis.

With the Republican era, the modern understanding of municipality expanded and spread first to other provinces outside of Istanbul and then to districts and towns. Traditional municipal services that have matured since the Ottoman period were reinforced with the Municipality Law No. 1580 and the Law on the Establishment of Metropolitan Municipalities No. 3030. The Metropolitan Municipality Law No. 5216 enacted in the 2000s (Law No. 5216 Date of Acceptance: 10.7.2004 - Chapter Three - Duties, Authorities and Responsibilities of the Metropolitan Municipality) and the Municipality Law No. 5393, (Law Number: 5393, Date of Acceptance: 3.7.2005 - Chapter Three - Duties and Responsibilities of the Municipality - Article: 14) are the current municipality laws that are still in force.

In both laws, municipalities are given important duties in addition to traditional municipal services. They perform many duties such as police, fire department, emergency aid, rescue and ambulance, city traffic, burial and cemeteries, afforestation, tourism and promotion, parks and green areas, social services, marriage procedures, development of economy and trade, vocational and skill acquisition, and construction of shelters for women and children.

1.2. Challenges in Service Delivery

Municipalities are composed of three bodies by law. These are the mayor, the municipal council and the municipal council. The mayor and the municipal council generally carry out the executive duties of the municipalities. The municipal council is the legislative body and is responsible for carrying out the duties assigned to it by law. Although they are expressed as three separate bodies, the mayor also chairs the council and the council. The fact that mayors have so much authority also brings with it drawbacks in terms of the production and equal implementation of services. Partisan practices can cause certain groups to benefit from services primarily and prevent equal distribution of services. This attitude, which turns into political despotism after a while, makes it difficult to implement social municipal services in a fair manner.

Municipalities are institutions that produce local common services. In one of its decisions, the Constitutional Court defined local common needs as follows: "*local common needs*", "*...express common expectations that are created, intensified and updated by the active situations arising from living together in the same region, and* *that are essentially local and public service in character*" (Constitutional Court, 1988: E. 1987/18, K. 1988/23). Today, municipalities have gone beyond this definition and have begun to perform duties not assigned to them by law. Due to populist approaches, many municipalities have entered a spiral of debt. Municipalities that have fallen into economic difficulties also experience difficulties in terms of service production.

The laws have paved the way for municipalities to establish companies to provide some local common services. Although these companies are established to provide services, they can turn into political parties' backyards due to partisanship. As a natural result of this, they may end up employing much more personnel than necessary over time. However, especially after subcontracting, the transfer of personnel employed by private companies other than the municipal company as a service purchase to the municipality and their subsequent unionization have increased the personnel costs on the municipalities. In municipalities where political authority has changed as a result of local elections, the situation has become even more problematic due to the new personnel hired to please their own voters. Due to increasing costs, many municipalities across the country have become seriously indebted to the Social Security Institution. Deductions are made from the shares allocated to the provincial bank due to the municipalities' debts. For this reason, many municipalities are trying to get out of debt by selling their real estate. This resource problem causes serious difficulties in the provision of municipal services.

One of the important problems in accessing municipal services is that municipalities do not give enough importance to digitalization steps. Thanks to digitalization, service delivery time can be shortened, personnel costs and numbers can be reduced, and thus more resource waste can be prevented. In addition, digitalization and e-municipality services are of great importance for people living in rural areas to benefit from municipal services effectively and efficiently. Unfortunately, in municipalities where digitalization is not fully operational, citizens who cannot leave their homes due to various reasons such as agricultural and livestock work, disability, and illness can obtain information about municipal services and benefit from these services, which is not as desired.

One of the most important reasons for the disruption of services is the change in voter behavior. Some voters living within the municipality borders act with the understanding that "*you were elected with my vote, you will do what I want*" and therefore expect municipalities to provide services that are personal and not within the municipality's scope of duty. The changing service perception of citizens is transforming municipal administrators who are concerned about votes from being public institution managers into politicians who act with the concern of maximizing votes. These politicians who are trying to maximize their votes are using municipal resources recklessly. The frantic transfer of resources to personalized services is causing disruption of services, including traditional services.

Another reason for difficulties in service delivery is corruption. The lack of transparency in the management processes of municipalities, their departure from participatory democracy practices and the inadequacy of accountability and control mechanisms to citizens seriously increase the waste of resources. Digital transformation practices will strengthen local democracy and ensure that the public has a say in municipal administration. As can be seen, one of the problems of non-digitalized municipalities is the inability to manage resources, time and processes properly.

2. TRANSITION PROCESS TO E-MUNICIPALITY SERVICES AND THE CONCEPT OF E-MUNICIPALITY

Along with technological developments, innovations have occurred in the development and transformation of public services in the world. The investments made by the public sector in technological infrastructure have increased the speed, effectiveness and efficiency of service delivery. As a result of this change and transformation, the concept of e-service has emerged. Although e-service applications were initially implemented as central administration services, they were later reflected in the services of local governments. The digital transformation experienced in the world and in Türkiye and the e-services implemented as a result of this are explained in this section.

2.1. Digital Transformation

Digitalization is defined by Mckinsey as a new technique in which services are quickly designed in businesses and presented to managers and stakeholders through technology (Sucu, 2021: 6). As a concept, digitalization was first expressed in an article in the North American Journal in 1971. Although the concept of digitalization was first put forward for private sector applications, it has now been used by the public sector, especially after 2000 (Çeliksoy and Akça, 2024: 454).

In other words, digitalization can be defined as the use of digital technologies to improve and change business processes, as well as transform them (Baykara, 2024: 104). Digital transformation is defined as *"the holistic transformation of human, business processes and technology elements aimed at increasing economic and social welfare through the use and development of digital technologies"* according to Article 526 of the Presidential Decree No. 1.

The first digitalization movement of the Turkish public administration took place in 1998 with the establishment of the Kamu-Net Technical Board, and then the e-Transformation Türkiye Project was launched in 2003, and continued with the Information Society Strategy covering the years 2006-2010 published in 2005 (Ölmez, 2021: 4). In addition to such digitalization efforts, some public institutions and organizations have started to offer various e-application services in order to deliver the public services they produce to citizens more quickly and comfortably. The Central Population Administration System (MERNIS), the Customs Systems Automation Project (GİMOP), the Tax Offices Automation Project (VEDOP), the National Judiciary Network Project (UYAP), and the Police Information System (POLNET) can be given as examples of these applications (Çeliksoy and Akça, 2024: 460).

As an important step within the scope of digitalization infrastructure studies, the program called "*National Technology Move*" initiated by the Ministry of Industry and Technology, which aims for local and national development in the field of technology. Türkiye, which is dependent on foreign sources in many technological fields, especially in the defense industry, has made significant investments in technology in the last 15 years thanks to the determined attitude of the current government. The process called the National Technology Move has 5 basic elements. These are; "*High Technology and Innovation*", "*Digital Transformation and Industrial Move*", "*Entrepreneurship*", "*Human Capital*" and "*Infrastructure*" (Bulut et al., 2024: 122). TEKNOFEST competitions are organized every year within the scope of the national technology move. Here, young entrepreneurs have the opportunity to introduce their ideas and projects in technological terms.

Within the scope of public sector digitalization studies, the Ministry of Transport and Infrastructure created the e-Government Strategy Document in 2016. The National e-Government Strategy and Action Plan document covering the years 2016-2019 primarily targeted issues such as making digitalization and the e-government ecosystem effective and sustainable, increasing participation and transparency, increasing digital transformation in public administrations, and strengthening the technological infrastructure (Çeliksoy and Akça, 2024: 463).

In order to ensure institutional transformation in Türkiye, the Presidency Digital Transformation Office was established in 2018. The aim of this office is to coordinate the digitalization steps of institutions, ensure data security and accelerate integration with new technologies such as artificial intelligence. The Digital Transformation Office has undertaken tasks to ensure that Türkiye can take its place in the field of technology with the support and digitalization efforts it provides to institutions in terms of the transformation of e-government, e-municipality and other e-applications. (Çeliksoy and Akça, 2024: 463). The Digital Transformation Office, which continued its activities for five years, was closed by decree numbered 183.

The indispensable part of digital transformation is the developments in internet providers. Studies on computer networks in Türkiye first started in the 1980s. The leading institutions working in this context were Ege University, Middle East Technical University, Boğaziçi University and TÜBİTAK. The internet first came to Türkiye in 1987 with the Turkish University and Research Institutions Network (TÜVEKA) established under the leadership of Ege University. In order to expand this network covering only universities, a network called TR-NET was established by Middle East Technical University and TÜBİTAK, and the internet was connected for the first time in 1993 via NSFNET, a leased line with a speed of 64 Kbps (TÜBİTAK, January 5, 2025).

The use of the internet in workplaces and its entry into homes first occurred in 1996. Thanks to the TURNET project implemented by Türk Telekom, Superonline and ULAKNET created by TÜBİTAK, the internet began to spread rapidly and become a part of our lives (Saka, 2019: 9). Towards the end of the 1990s, the increase in computer use in homes also increased the number of dial-up connections. Internet cafes began to provide services for citizens who did not have computers at home.

The early 2000s are considered to be the years when technological developments gained a different phase. In this period, called the millennium age, digitalization steps accelerated as a result of advanced computers, the first versions of smart phones, and ADSL internet services. The economic policies implemented between 2002 and 2010 increased the welfare of the people and facilitated access to the internet. Increases in purchasing power accelerated the access of households and workplaces to computer technologies. As of 2005, the number of ADSL users in Türkiye exceeded two million (www.ccell.com.tr).

The increase in internet providers has increased competition and led to more investment in internet infrastructure. In Türkiye, fiber internet infrastructure work was first started by Turkcell Superonline in 2008. Thanks to the increase in fiber internet providers such as Uydunet, Türk Telekom and Vodafone and their competitive advantage, the number of fiber internet users, excluding mobile lines, has reached 19.8 million today. Rapid transformations in smartphones, 3G services that started in 2009 and 4G and 4.5G mobile broadband services that were developed later have caused a significant increase in the number of mobile broadband users. According to 2024 data, there are 74.4 million mobile broadband internet users (www.aa.com.tr).

It can be said that e-services have emerged as a natural result of digital transformation. Despite the potential benefits offered by e-government applications and e-municipality services, there are various difficulties in the implementation process, especially in developing countries. Overcoming these difficulties and establishing an effective digital infrastructure is of critical importance for municipalities to fully benefit from the benefits offered by information and communication technologies. The success of e-municipality services depends on the level of development of the information and communication technology infrastructure of the country, region or city. (Moon and Norris, 2005: 43-55). The effectiveness of e-municipality services is directly related to the general development levels of countries. For example, according to the Global Information Technology Report 2009-2010, Türkiye ranks 69th with a score of 3.68, and its position in the information technology readiness index, which was 48th in 2006, has dropped to 69th place (Yaman et al., 2013: 207-220).

It is seen that countries with successful applications with e-government services also reflect their success in e-municipality services. According to an international study, 1,797 e-government portals of 198 countries were examined and regional differences were determined according to the performance of the application. Among these regions, the North America region stood out as the most developed region. It is followed by Asia, Western Europe, Pacific Islands, Middle East, Eastern Europe, South America, Russia, Central Asia, Central America and Africa. (Varnalı, 2025: 246). As can be seen, countries that direct technological developments, invest in technology and strengthen their technological infrastructure have outperformed others in e-municipality services.

The "e-municipality information system" developed by the Ministry of Interior is one of the local legs of digital transformation in Türkiye. The e-municipality information system project is considered to be among the largest projects in Türkiye in terms of savings it will provide. It is estimated that Türkiye will rise 30 places in the World Bank's business ability index by completing the business opening and work permit processes electronically thanks to this project. The e-municipality information system, which is offered to municipalities free of charge, will provide citizens with the opportunity to receive uninterrupted service independent of time and space (MUNICIPALITY, January 3, 2025).

There are 67 modules in the E-Municipality Information System, which is offered to citizens via the e-government portal, according to the data of 2025. 45 of these are offered by the Ministry of Internal Affairs and 22 by the Ministry of Environment, Urbanization and Climate Change. Examples of these modules are; E-Municipality EBYS Document Verification, E-Municipality EBYS Document Tracking, Municipality License Application, Municipality License Application Inquiry, E- Municipality Petition Registration, Municipality Information Acquisition Applications services (MUNICIPALITY, January 3, 2025).

The "*Local Information System*", which started to be actively used by the General Directorate of Local Administrations as of 2022, is one of the steps of digital transformation in municipalities. The local information system aims to actively follow the tasks assigned to the Ministry by the Presidential Decree, identify the needs of institutions, establish service standards in the work carried out, coordinate in situations where rapid decisions are required, such as disasters, and ensure preliminary adaptation to changes in legislation (CSB, February 7, 2025).

Another stage of digital transformation that constitutes central personnel management is the "Public Personnel Information System" implemented by the Presidency Strategy and Budget Presidency. This central personnel database bank, which was created as of 2024, was opened to the use of public institutions and it was requested to keep up-to-date and detailed data regarding the status, title, qualification, seniority and number of employed personnel. The regular, effective and efficient execution of public services is possible by employing sufficient personnel in terms of quantity and quality and their balanced distribution. Controlling the personnel employed throughout Türkiye with instant data entries from a single center reveals the point reached in state personnel management.

2.2. The Concept and Importance of E-Municipality

According to the official inventory of the Ministry of Interior, there are 30 metropolitan municipalities, 51 provincial municipalities, 519 metropolitan district municipalities, 403 district municipalities and 400 town municipalities in Türkiye (INTERIOR, April 1, 2025). Increasing population numbers and Türkiye's geographical features cause some difficulties in providing municipal services. This situation also increases service costs. A large part of the municipalities, especially provincial and central district municipalities, have switched to the digital municipality approach in order to minimize their expenses and produce more effective, more transparent and more efficient services.

Technological developments, advances in telecommunication infrastructure, the spread of satellite devices and internet providers have led to the maturation of the concept of e-service. E-government applications have been implemented by public service providers in order to deliver public services to citizens in the fastest and most effective way. E-government is the name given to the provision of public services over the internet. Although it was first seen in the United States and England in the 1950s, the modernization process began in the 2000s (Mecek, 2017: 1816). Especially after the millennium, developing computer technology and internet infrastructure have expanded the scope of e-government services. In Türkiye, e-government applications were put into practice in 2008 under the name of "e-government gateway". Although there were some problems at first, these problems were resolved over time and the scope and quality of service provision were increased.

The concept of e-municipality, which has become an integral part of the concept of e-government, was first implemented in Duisburg, Germany, Tilburg, Netherlands, Forum, Denmark, Braintree, England and Phoenix, USA (Erdoğan, 2019: 557). In Türkiye, Antalya Metropolitan Municipality, Bitlis Provincial Municipality and Malatya Battalgazi Municipality were selected as pilot units within the scope of the e-municipality information system project by the Ministry of Internal Affairs. (MUNICIPALITY, January 14, 2025).

Over time, more municipalities have been integrated into e-government and e-municipality applications developed by the central administration. The implementation of e-services by municipalities has been made mandatory by the Presidency and various institutions through norms and internal operations. In this direction, municipalities provide e-municipality services through their corporate websites. Currently, 485 municipalities from 81 provinces have adapted to e-services accessed through www.turkiye.gov.tr and have started to provide services to citizens through this portal. In addition to these services, 30 local service providers affiliated with municipalities providing transportation, sewage, water, etc. services also provide services through the e-government portal, including information and application services (TÜRKİYE, April 1, 2025).

The concept of e-municipality has been defined in various ways in the literature. E-municipality services are not just about creating a municipality website, but also about providing administrative and social processes electronically to all stakeholders who are parties to public services, without any time or space constraints, in a fast, effective and efficient manner (Henden and Henden, 2005: 64). E-municipality, which is the abbreviation of the concept of electronic municipality, is expressed as municipalities providing fast, easy, transparent and high-quality services by managing city-related services through information and communication technology-based applications and institutional websites (Güven, 2022: 1623). E-services form the basis of e-municipality. The concept of e-service is the process of providing services to citizens through institutional websites with various software or programs without the direct intervention of the personnel involved in the provision of services.

According to another definition, the concept of e-municipality is a tool that enables the administrative decisions, plans and programs, controls and audits taken by the municipality to be shared with the public using internet technologies in accordance with the principles of participatory democracy; breaking the chains of the spatially confined service style of the classical management style, and providing the shortest and fastest access to the desired information 24 hours a day, 7 days a week (Çoruh, 2009).

E-municipality applications are important technological developments that not only provide citizens with direct access to services, but also have significant benefits, increase the quality, speed, efficiency and effectiveness of services, and reduce service production costs as much as possible. Thanks to e-municipality applications, paperwork costs, which are one of the basic problems of bureaucracy, are largely eliminated. Before e-municipality services, citizens used to make tax and fee payments, requests and complaints, and social service applications by going directly to the municipality by taking time off from their work and social time. Citizens who could not get permission from work or could not access these services for an important reason were deprived of many services. Again, people who delayed their tax payments due to opportunities they did not have were burdened with more debt as a result of the addition of additional receivables to these payments. E-municipality applications also contribute greatly to the implementation of the constitutional rights of equal opportunity and justice in taxation in these times when people can access the internet from their homes or work.

Another aspect of e-municipality services is their contribution to participatory democracy. Article 15 of the Municipality Law No. 5393 states that "The municipality *may conduct public opinion polls and research in order to determine the views and opinions of town residents regarding municipal services.*" It is stipulated that municipal administrators can produce services by receiving the demands and opinions of the public. People directly participate in administrative services through surveys or project proposals directed to them through e-services. The fact that citizens directly determine service priorities maximizes service benefits and strengthens local democracy.

The Covid-19 pandemic, which has caused many social consequences, has made a great contribution to the realization of how important e-municipality services are. This pandemic, which was first seen in Wuhan, China in December 2019 and spread all over the world, was declared a pandemic by the World Health Organization. This pandemic, which caught hospital systems unprepared all over the world, caused the death of many people. The pandemic period, during which people affected by the pandemic were quarantined and curfews were implemented to reduce the spread, caused a serious transformation in e-commerce and e-services. People who could not leave their homes ordered their daily needs from digital environments. Municipalities also significantly eased the burden on the central government during this period and ensured that the pandemic process was overcome in the lightest way. During the pandemic process, citizens reached public services without any disruption thanks to e-municipality services.

According to the additional article 3 of the Law No. 5393 on Municipalities, "*municipalities use the e-municipality information system, which carries out all kinds of administrative work and transactions, in order to carry out the duties and services assigned to them by legislation and to finalize the applications made by* citizens. The Ministry of Interior is authorized to establish and operate the e-municipality information system, to determine the policies regarding data storage, data transmission and data sharing, to determine the working procedures and principles and to establish a central service standardization regarding this system.", it has been made mandatory for municipalities to use the e-municipality information system. Due to this revolutionary application, it is aimed to save 3 billion liras annually since all works and transactions can be carried out electronically in a common infrastructure from a single database.

3. PAMUKKALE MUNICIPALITY DIGITALIZATION AND E-MUNICIPALITY SERVICES APPLICATION AREAS

It has been stated above that Antalya Metropolitan Municipality, Bitlis Provincial Municipality and Malatya Battalgazi Municipality were selected as pilot units by the Ministry of Internal Affairs within the scope of digitalization studies. In this section, digital transformation and e-municipality services are explained in detail in the context of Denizli Province Central District Pamukkale Municipality.

3.1. E-Municipality Services

Pamukkale District was established as the central district in 2014 when Denizli province became a metropolitan municipality. The district population was announced as 345,850 according to 2024 TÜİK data (TÜİK, April 5, 2025). Again, according to TÜİK data, the district, which has a population greater than 27 provinces, has an area of approximately 823 km2. It is one of the districts that is difficult to manage with its wide geography and population density. Pamukkale Municipality started its services with the local elections in March 2014. Pamukkale Municipality continued its services in the Denizli Metropolitan Municipality service building due to the lack of a service building in the first months of its operation. The municipality, which continued its services here for a few months, later moved to the main campus allocated to it by Denizli Metropolitan Municipality, where it currently serves. The new establishment of the municipality and the physical inadequacies related to this negatively affected the managers and employees of the period. Reasons such as lack of machinery and equipment, insufficient personnel, inadequate physical environments and inadequate tools and equipment used by employees have caused disruptions in services.

Pamukkale Municipality has resolved the problems experienced in the services with new personnel recruitment and institutional adaptation processes. It has integrated into e-government and e-municipality services by creating its technological infrastructure in a short time. Links for practical access to e-municipality and e-government services have been placed on the corporate website of Pamukkale Municipality. The sub-access links under the "*E-municipality*" box, which is one of these links, are given below.

Figure 1. Pamukkale Municipality Website Interface (e-Municipality)

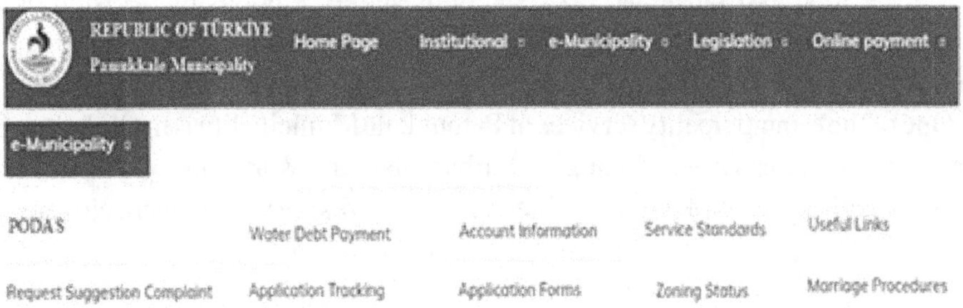

Source: *PB, https://www.pamukkale.bel.tr/*

The transition to digital archive application, thanks to the Project Approval and Digital Archive System (PODAS) used by Pamukkale Municipality, is a revolutionary development in project approval and license processes. This project, which allows projects and related documents to be stored, managed and archived securely in a completely digital environment, has saved the municipality and its employees time, cost and resources while getting rid of the burden of physical documents (PODAS, February 5, 2025).

Pamukkale Municipality does not collect water because it is a district municipality. However, as an e-municipality service, a water debt payment link is provided on the website. With this link, citizens are directed to the Denizli Sewerage and Water Administration's internet address and are able to pay their water debts securely.

In the account information section, there are tax office information, bank account information, postal check numbers and cash register addresses for those who will make the payment. Service standards and useful links are also presented to the citizens. Municipalities mostly establish request, suggestion and complaint units called white desk to increase service quality and standards. Pamukkale Municipality has also established a unit called "*Pamuk Desk*" under the Press, Broadcasting and Public Relations Directorate. Thanks to this unit, which was later named "*White Desk*", direct democracy practices, one of the most important functions of local governments, come to life. Within e-municipality applications, receiving Pamuk Masa applications online contributes to democratic participation processes. At the same time, it provides the opportunity to intervene in complaints in the fastest way.

Among the services provided online by municipalities via e-municipality servers are social municipality services. The demographic structure of Pamukkale Municipality, the abundance of rural settlements and the high number of neighborhoods called slums where people working in the lower income group live densely, bring social municipality services to the forefront. Citizens whose household income is below the specified limit are provided with social assistance such as education assistance, food assistance and tax reductions and exemptions by decision of the municipal council. Citizens who want to benefit from social assistance can apply via the website and e-municipality services.

One of the e-municipality services of Pamukkale Municipality is the link showing zoning status information. Zoning and urban planning works are one of the most intensive activity areas of municipalities. Zoning works are works where citizens can get results in a long time due to the large size of the documents related to zoning, the inconvenience of physical storage conditions and the slowing down of bureaucratic processes by archive services. When the negative attitudes and behaviors of the employees are added to this, these processes become unbearable for many people. Therefore, being able to view zoning status documents online and get their printouts is a revolutionary application. Citizens can see the zoning status of their plots and lands or houses with a single click via e-municipality services.

The last of the services under the e-municipality link is marriage services. Citizens who want to get married can see the documents required for marriage, legal regulations that will prevent marriage, the addresses and phone numbers of Pamukkale Municipality marriage offices and finally the rental fee tariffs of marriage halls through this link. Pre-marriage processes are the most tiring processes for couples and families. In these processes that require as much time as possible, Pamukkale Municipality's providing these services online is a great convenience for couples.

3.2. Online Transactions

The revenues of municipalities are divided into four groups: own revenues, shares received from the central budget, transfer revenues and borrowing revenues. The most important of these revenues are the shares received from the central budget. The payment of these shares is transferred to the Bank of Provinces by the Ministry of Treasury and Finance to be made no later than the tenth day of each month. Municipalities carry out their important investments and expenditures through these shares. Another important revenue for municipalities is own revenues. Own revenues are; taxes, duties, fees, participation shares, honoraria, sales revenues of movable or immovable properties, rental revenues, revenues obtained from fee schedules, parking revenues, donations, interest and penalty revenues and other revenues. In order for this revenue to be collected quickly without causing a decrease in public resources, online payment services are offered to citizens by municipalities as a convenience.

On the Pamukkale Municipality website, under the online transactions link, there are e-government payment, e-government login, individual payment, corporate payment, non-membership SMS payment, account information and cashier addresses. Citizens who will make payments using online payment channels can log in via e-government and make their payments by saving time and space and minimizing payment costs with the guidance they will receive. In addition, payments can be made with direct payment options other than the e-government channel (www .pamukkale.bel.tr).

Online payments are a great convenience for citizens. Today, almost every citizen benefits from e-municipality services by connecting to online services from internet providers via smart phones, tablets or computer technologies. The ease of payment provided to citizens by Pamukkale Municipality, which operates in a large area of 823 km2, increases citizen satisfaction and service quality. The online payment interface of Pamukkale Municipality is presented in Figure 2.

Figure 2. Pamukkale Municipality Website Interface (Online Payments)

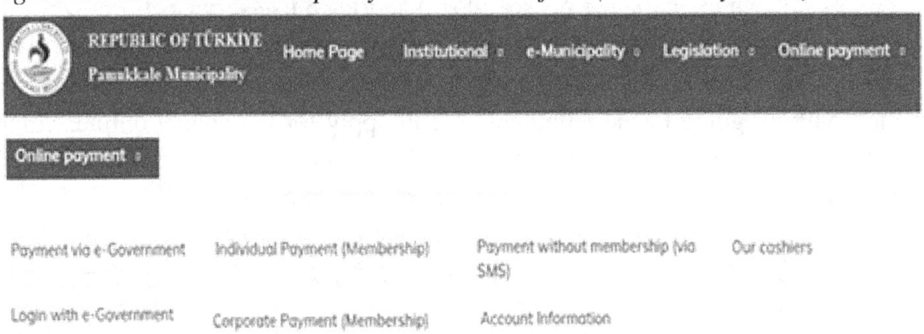

Source: PB, https://www.pamukkale.bel.tr/

3.3. Shortcut Links

One of the digitization steps of Pamukkale Municipality is the shortcuts that it offers to citizens on the homepage of its website. The shortcut links, which provide great convenience especially for elderly individuals who do not have sufficient skills in using technological devices and want to access municipal services, carry e-municipality services to a different point. Some of these links, which also include applications that contribute to local democracy and social municipal activities, are given below.

The most important organ of the municipalities is the municipal council. Municipal councils carry out the duties assigned to them by law and subordinate norms. The municipal council is elected. It meets in the first week of each month under the chairmanship of the mayor. The municipal council, whose agenda is determined in advance, undertakes important duties in terms of the implementation of local common services. In modern local institutions, public participation in the administration and transparency in administration are important topics. Pamukkale Municipality has taken an important step in terms of transparent municipalism with the options of the council agenda, council decision summaries and committee reports in the shortcuts section. Thanks to these open sources, citizens are provided with direct access to information, and a citizen control mechanism has been put into practice. The fact that the decisions taken by the municipality's decision-making bodies and affecting all citizens within the municipal borders are open to the public also increases trust in the administration.

the shortcuts section is the on-call pharmacies application. This data, which is generally shared by municipalities that provide digital municipal services, makes people's lives easier and allows citizens to quickly access pharmacy address and phone information in cases where access to the on-call pharmacy is urgent.

Pamukkale Municipality offers social and sports course services for citizens in some service buildings, primarily Aktepe Social Facilities. With the course application link in the shortcuts section, people can get information about the courses opened without going to the municipality and apply for the course online. Some examples of courses opened in Pamukkale Municipality include fitness, guitar, football, athletics, needlework, marbling, handicrafts, English, etc.

As presented in Figure 1 below, other applications in the shortcuts section have been put in place to increase service quality and respond to the changing expectations of citizens.

Figure 3. Pamukkale Municipality Short Cut Service

Source: PB, https://www.pamukkale.bel.tr/

3.4. Mobile Application

Mobile broadband services in Türkiye have reached an average of 74.4 million people. The most widely used mobile service device is the smart phone. Thanks to technological developments, phones have evolved and today they play an active role in performing digital services as well as making calls. Along with phones, smart devices such as tablets also make people's lives easier. Smart devices, which reach a wide range of users, regardless of age, provide citizens with easy and fast access to e-services.

Pamukkale Municipality has kept up with the rapid changes in smartphones and devices, as well as its website content. Citizens can access up-to-date news about the municipality through mobile applications whose software is provided by the municipality and rented or purchased from another company, and they can benefit from many applications such as pharmacies on duty and directions, road conditions, pick and send and zoning status.

Citizens can also quickly forward their requests, suggestions and complaints to municipal employees through mobile applications.

Pamukkale Municipality has established Wi-Fi stations at 21 different points within the district borders in order to facilitate citizens' access to the internet and to popularize the use of digital municipal services. Citizens have free internet access thanks to this service and can charge all their mobile devices at these points (Pamukkale Municipality, 2024: 38).

3.5. Digital Governance and Participatory Democracy Practices

The concept of management is one of the oldest concepts that determines the hierarchy and distribution of tasks among people since the existence of humanity. Although the definition of the concept of management could not be made in the periods when the first people lived, it can be said that there was a form of management in agricultural and hunting activities and tribal life. The literal meaning of the concept of management is the organization or the entire activities of directing and organizing an organization in a coordinated and cooperative manner towards a specific purpose. The concept of management is a concept that we encounter in every area of life. Whether it is family life, the activities of a large company or the goods and services produced by the public sector, they all have a management process. Over time, the management function has changed and has become unable to meet the expectations of employees, entrepreneurs and citizens. The concept of governance, which has entered our lives especially in the period after 1990, has begun to be used as a remedy for the deficiencies of the management function.

The concept of governance was first mentioned by the World Bank in 1989, when it prepared a report on the development of Africa. The concept referred to as the "governance crisis" in this report tried to explain the problems of the political power in the management processes. According to the World Bank report, the term "governance" is synonymous with "healthy development management". In other words, the concept of governance means healthy development management (Güler, 2003: 102).

When defining the concept of governance, a distinction should be made between private sector and public institutions. For a large-scale company in the private sector, the concept of governance means the participation of not only top-level managers and capital owners but also all stakeholders in the planning and implementation stages of business activities such as human resources, production, and marketing. The concept of governance is a bit different in public institutions. In terms of public institutions, governance covers the participation of non-governmental organizations, professional organizations and chambers, private sector companies, service-based management organizations, especially citizens and public personnel who receive service in the management and decision-making processes (Özgökçeler, 2014: 71).

The concept of digital governance in municipalities is the process of direct participation of the public in management and decision-making processes through e-municipality services with websites and smart applications offered through digital infrastructure and broadband services.

The statement in the 2025-2029 5-year strategic plan of Pamukkale Municipality, " *Since Pamukkale Municipality has adopted the participatory governance model in all its services in its new term, it will continue on its path by utilizing traditional and innovative tools in order to increase participation in its work and decision-making mechanisms. It should be particularly emphasized that our municipality believes that the people living in Pamukkale district have a say in the area they live in and therefore encourages their active participation in decision-making processes at every step. In this context, the same understanding and belief has been maintained in the "Pamukkale Municipality 2025-2029 Strategic Plan" studies prepared with a participatory approach. Our municipality has carried out a two-dimensional study, one citizen-based and the other institution-based, in order to ensure external stakeholder participation in strategic plan studies.*" clearly reveals the importance the municipality attaches to governance and participatory democracy.

With this visionary perspective, Pamukkale Municipality conducted a comprehensive survey in 2024 to obtain suggestions and opinions from citizens. External stakeholders expressed the services that the municipality should maintain within the scope of the survey, as shown in Figure 5.

Figure 4. Municipal Services

- Municipal Services
- Green Area
- Park and Garden Cleaning
- Cleaning and Solid Waste Collection
- Road, Pavement and Asphalt Works
- Pest Control Services
- Development, License and Building Inspection
- Urban Transformation and Regulations
- Protection of Historical and Cultural Texture

Source: *Created by the author.*

Apart from these, services for women, elderly and children, services and social aid for the disabled, vocational courses, activities for young people, foreign language, sports, education courses, neighborhood markets, cultural tours, play groups in parks and maintenance and repair of existing ones, ensuring the security of parks, announcement and security camera systems, nursery and day care center, elderly care center, public bread and public milk are the services expected from the municipality by external stakeholders (Pamukkale Municipality, 2024: 30).

One of the best tools for implementing participatory democracy is surveys. Surveys conducted in the past were not preferred much by municipalities and institutions in terms of both time and cost. However, with the development of technology today, a significant portion of surveys are conducted in digital environments or via telephones rather than face-to-face on the streets. This application has begun to be used frequently by municipalities because it shortens the time spent on surveys and reduces survey costs. It is one of the basic teachings of political science that political authorities who come to power through elections measure citizens' expectations at certain intervals. Pamukkale Municipality also measures citizens' expectations at certain intervals by organizing digital surveys, as it does for the 2025-2029 strategic plan.

Another good work done by the municipality in terms of participatory democracy and digital governance practices is the live broadcasting of council meetings to the public. Thanks to these meetings, the public can directly access the decisions made by the municipality for them. Again, the fact that citizens can convey their demands, suggestions and complaints to the relevant units of the municipality in the fastest way possible through digital channels is one of the best examples of direct democracy.

3.6. Digitalization Studies for Personnel

Digitalization has serious benefits for internal stakeholders, employees and administrative processes, as well as external stakeholders. Equipping the working environments of the personnel with technological tools has caused cumbersome bureaucratic processes to become functional. Before the digital transformation, physical documents were used. Especially after the integration of the EBYS system into the municipalities, correspondence began to be made through the system. While the correspondence made through the system increased the speed of the completion of the transactions, it also resulted in more service output with less personnel. According to the strategic plan data, Pamukkale Municipality provides services with 376 Desktop computers, 57 Notebooks, 119 Printers, 8 Physical and 40 Virtual Servers, and 2 Firewalls as a result of the digital transformation of the physical environments of the personnel (Pamukkale Municipality, 2024: 38).

SAYSIS, which was one of the digitalization steps used before switching to the EBYS system in Pamukkale Municipality, is still actively used. In particular, personnel salaries and other payments are made through this system. In addition, system users can digitally communicate their requests and complaints to the relevant unit managers through the system. With systems such as EBYS and SAYSIS, data entry through the system instead of preparing some documents in a physical environment saves on document costs. It also increases the number of daily transactions of the personnel. In addition to the cost advantage, reduced paper consumption also makes a significant contribution to sustainable environmental practices.

Pamukkale Municipality uses some software so that its personnel can perform the tasks in their job descriptions in the most efficient and effective way. Examples of these are NETCAD, LUMİON, STA4CAD, İDECAD, SKETCHUP, MS OFFICE, COREL DRAW and EDİUS, LOG and SIEM, Estimated Cost and e-Profit software, Legislation Jurisprudence Program and Execution Follow-up Program software, Occupational Health and Safety software (Pamukkale Municipality, 2024: 38). These software shorten the work completion time of those who receive service and enable those who receive service to benefit from the services in a shorter time.

Pamukkale Municipality organizes digital surveys for its employees every year. When these surveys are analyzed, a satisfaction rate of approximately 80% was found in the subjects of "*adoption of the principles and values of the municipality, senior management knowing and caring about employees, easy access to senior management and communicating problems, easy access to needed information, provision of necessary resources for work environment improvement activities, sufficient technological infrastructure, satisfaction with communication with colleagues, and the belief that there is a system where problems are communicated to decision makers"*. The future expectations of the staff in the survey were nursery services, guesthouses, social facilities and cultural tours (Pamukkale Municipality, 2024: 31).

Digital surveys targeting employees are widely used due to the speed at which they are conducted and the ability to quickly analyze data through systems. Employees are often unable to openly express their requests, suggestions, and complaints because they fear political pressure. Surveys provide them with freedom in this regard. In this way, data is obtained accurately. By analyzing the data obtained, quick solutions are produced for employees' requests and complaints. The 80% satisfaction rate found in the surveys is also important in this context.

One of the digitalization efforts of Pamukkale Municipality personnel is online training. In-service trainings increase the quality and competence of the personnel. The personnel participate in the trainings provided by the Human Resources and Education Directorate, especially through the Presidency distance education portal, at certain intervals. Various trainings are also provided online by the Union of Municipalities of Türkiye throughout the year. The biggest benefit of online trainings is to save time without interrupting the work. In addition, the trainings contribute to both the personal and professional development of the employees, and also contribute positively to the municipal budget within the scope of the savings measures circular.

4. DISCUSSION AND POLICY RECOMMENDATIONS

Today, with the rapid development of technology, digitalization has radically changed the lifestyles of individuals, institutions and societies. This process has a wide range of effects, from the transformation of economic structures to the evolution of education systems and the reshaping of social relations. Digitalization not only increases the use of technology, but also encourages efficiency, competition and innovation.

Various steps have been taken in Türkiye since the 1980s for digitalization. Public investments in internet infrastructure and e-services in particular have accelerated digital transformation. The digital infrastructure services developed by the central administration and the free use of these services by local governments have cured the faulty aspects of bureaucracy and improved data processing times. It has also enabled local governments to save space, time and cost.

Although Pamukkale Municipality was established in 2014, it has adapted quickly to digital transformation. It is thought that the plain and simple nature of the Pamukkale Municipality website, which is easily usable by citizens of all ages, increases the usability of e-services. Especially in the "Shortcuts" section, the fact that the services that citizens expect most from the municipality are visible on the main screen is an important success in web page usage. E-municipality and online payment channels also enable people who benefit from municipal services to benefit from the services effectively and efficiently, while also creating a digital habit in the citizen.

Pamukkale Municipality has equipped the physical working environments of the personnel with technological devices. When the 2025-2029 strategic plan data is examined, it is seen that there are a sufficient number of smart devices such as computers, printers, and notebooks in the service units. In addition to these smart devices, it can be said that the broadband infrastructure has been established by the municipality in a healthy way. In addition, it is seen that many applications and software that help the personnel to receive public service are offered to the use of the personnel. The digital transformation of the working environments and tools for the personnel is an important step for the municipality.

At the institutional level, it is stated that digitalization is not limited to making technology investments; it also includes areas such as corporate culture, leadership approach and employee competencies. The digital transformation in Pamukkale Municipality's service approach is a natural result of the participatory leadership mission. The fact that local elements also have a say in the administration thanks to digital applications is a good example of participatory democracy and governance principles. Making municipal council decisions open to the public online, announcing council and commission decisions to the public via the website, online surveys conducted at regular intervals to measure citizens' demands and expectations, and requests, suggestions and complaints received through the white table show that citizens are effective in decision-making processes.

In the world, especially after the industrial revolution, personnel management has gradually transformed into the concept of human resources management. The establishment of unions and the legal rights gained by employees accordingly have led to the physical transformation of work environments and the regulation of working hours. In addition, many studies have been conducted on how to get the most efficiency from personnel with developing personnel approaches. At this point, instead of the concept of personnel management that focuses only on the output produced by the personnel, human resources management that focuses on people has begun to be implemented. The human resources management concept, which has also been implemented in the public sector in recent years, expresses an integrated approach. This method regulates the working standards of employees according to modern rules and laws. When Pamukkale Municipality practices are examined, it is seen that human resources management operates successfully. Especially thanks to digital transformation, a correct bridge has been established between managers and personnel. Personnel satisfaction surveys conducted every year, online trainings that increase the personal development and skills of the personnel, modern working environments and a holistic management approach show that Pamukkale Municipality has successfully digitalized in human resources management. For the sustainability of a successful digital transformation, the institution must have a structure open to change and adopt a continuous learning approach.

Digitalization has made access to information easier, while also bringing issues such as privacy and security to the agenda. The most important problem of digitalization for institutions is keeping personal data secure. Pamukkale Municipality servers contain personal data of citizens and personnel. The fact that this data falls into the hands of malicious people will create a serious security problem. The municipality, which is rapidly implementing digitalization steps, should place more emphasis on security services and increase its measures against attacks in the digital environment. Considering the information provided for the security of servers in the municipality's 2025-2029 strategic plan, it is thought that more investment should be made in data security.

Digital services allow citizens to carry out municipal transactions faster and easier. However, this rapid development of digitalization has also brought about new social problems such as digital inequality. Factors such as age, education level and economic status in particular affect access to digital opportunities and create a new social separation. Within the scope of digitalization studies, Pamukkale Municipality should act according to the principle of "*equal citizenship*", which is the basic rule of democracy, by correctly planning the disadvantages of its large surface area and the large number of rural neighborhoods. In order not to create a new "*Elite digital class*", as much investment as possible should be made in the steps of digitalization of citizens.

As a result, digitalization and e-municipality studies have made the lives of the majority of people living in the country significantly easier. Türkiye has made significant investments in terms of adaptation to technological developments. Investments made in the defense industry in particular have been a pioneer in the development of technology. Technological developments have also directly affected digitalization. The support of the private sector to the increasing digitalization studies in the public sector has created a new digital vision in Türkiye. Local services are at the forefront of the application areas of this digital vision. Local governments are the public institutions that provide the closest and most direct service to the public. Pamukkale Municipality's studies in the field of digitalization and e-municipality are considered to be a useful and successful example of the steps that local governments should take in the digital transformation process.

REFERENCES

Bulut, MA, Birgili, B., Koçoğlu, M., & Gülünay, O., Et. (2024). Contributions of Technology and Science Centers to the National Technology Move and the Example of T3 Foundation. *Babur Research, 3*(2), 117–132.

Çeliksoy, E., & Akça, A. (2024). Digital Transformation Process in Public Administration in Türkiye. Çankırı Karatekin University Journal of Social Sciences Institute, 15(2), 445-486. Https://Doi.Org/10.54558/Jiss.1426480

CSB. (2025, February 7). Republic of Türkiye Ministry of Environment, Urbanization and Climate Change, General Directorate of Local Administrations. Ministry Circular on the Use of Local Information System Published, https://Yerelyonetimler .Csb.Gov.Tr/Yerelbilgi-Sisteminin- Kullanilmasina-İliskin-Bakanlik-Genelgesi-Yayimlanmistir-Haber-266965

Deniz, A., Akarçay, P., & Karakaş, A. (2017). Development of Municipality in the Ottoman Empire and Modernization Efforts. *Academic Perspective International Refereed Journal of Social Sciences*, (64), 314–325.

Erdoğan, O. (2019). E-Municipality Applications in Local Governments: Ministry of Internal Affairs E-Municipality Information System. *Süleyman Demirel University Journal of Faculty of Economics and Administrative Sciences, 24*(3), 551–566.

Ergin, O. N. (1995). Mecelle-I Umur-I Municipality. Istanbul Metropolitan Municipality Culture Inc. *Publications, 2*(2).

Es, M. (2008). Local Administrations in the Ottoman Empire. *Local Politics Journal*, (27), 29–38.

Güler, B. A. (2003). Governance: All Power to Capital. *Praxis (Bern), 9*, 93–116.

Güven, A., (2022). "Provincial Administrations in Türkiye Within the Context of E-Municipality Applications

Henden, H. B., & Henden, R. (2005). Changes in Service Provision of Local Governments and E-Municipality. *Electronic Journal of Social Sciences, 4*(14), 48–66.

Karabulak, S. (2013), "Municipal History in Turkish Public Administration" Istanbul Aydın University, Institute of Social Sciences, Department of Political Science and International Relations, Master's Thesis, Istanbul.

Mecek, M. (2017). E-Government and E-Municipality: Conceptual Framework and Review of Studies on Municipality Websites in Türkiye. Süleyman Demirel University Journal of Faculty of Economics and Administrative Sciences, 22 (Kayfor 15 Special Issue), 1815-1851.

Moon, J., & Norris, D. (2005). Does Managerial Orientation Matter? The Adoption Of Reinventing Government And E-Government At The Municipal Level January. *Information Systems Journal, 15*(1), 43–60. Https://Doi.Org/10.1111/J.1365-2575 .2005.00185.X. DOI: 10.1111/j.1365-2575.2005.00185.x

Ölmez, M. (2021). Digital Transformation and E-Commerce in Public Policies in Türkiye: A Model Proposal. *Journal of Public Administration and Technology, 3*(1), 9–33.

Önver, Ş. B. (2019). Sixth Department-I Municipality and Comparison with Today's Municipal Services. *Takvim-I Vekayi, 7*(1), 37–72.

Özgökçeler, S. (2014). An Effective Concept in Local Development: "Local Governance" [Bursa City Council Example]. İş, Güç. *Journal of Industrial Relations and Human Resources, 16*(1), 67–82.

Saka, E. (Ed.). (2019). *Internet History of Türkiye (New Media Studies V)*. Alternative Informatics Association., https://ekitap.alternatifbilisim.org/ymc5_turkiye _internet_tarihi.html

Sayım, F., & Aydın, V. (2015). A Theoretical Study on the Interaction of Service Sector Characteristics and Unsystematic Risks with Sector Securities. *Dumlupınar University Journal of Social Sciences*, (29), 245–262.

Ulusoy, A., & Akdemir, T. (2010). *Local Administrations Theory - Application - Finance*. Seçkin Bookstore.

Varnalı, T. (2025). E-Municipality in Türkiye: Digitalization Path of Local Governments and Application Analysis. *International Anatolia Academic Online Journal Social Sciences Journal, 11*(1), 237–259.

Yaman, K., Aşgın, S., Yetişken, Y., & Aksoy, E. (2013). Comparative Analysis Of The E-Municipality Applications In Türkiye: The Case Of Western Black Sea Region. *Celal Bayar University Journal of Management and Economics., 20*(1), 207–220.

Yilmaz, D. (2008). The Concept and Criteria of Public Service in Turkish Law. Gazi University Faculty of Law Journal, XII(1-2).

Chapter 6
Migration Policies of Local Governments in France

Oğuzhan Erdoğan
https://orcid.org/0000-0003-3809-6688
Burdur Mehmet Akif Ersoy University, Burdur, Turkey

Çiğdem Pank Yildirim
https://orcid.org/0000-0002-7084-313X
Muğla Sıtkı Koçman University, Muğla, Turkey

ABSTRACT

Local governments in France are structured in a tripartite system consisting of "municipal", "departmental", and "regional" administrations. Since French local governments are founded on the principle of centralization, they operate under strict supervision from the central government. The aim of this study is to reveal the transformation caused by migration in France and to evaluate the effects of local migration governance on migrants. In line with this aim, the study examines the migration policies of local government units in France and reveals the current state of migrant welfare at the local level. First, the concept of migration governance and policy is addressed. Second, it discusses what has been done regarding migration management in France. Lastly, it explains the migration policy of local governments in France, evaluates the condition of migrants, and discusses these issues. The study employs the method of document analysis.

DOI: 10.4018/979-8-3373-0452-6.ch006

1. INTRODUCTION

Migration is a complex and multifaceted social phenomenon that arises from human mobility and unlimited needs and demands. With migration, significant changes can occur in the political, economic, and social structures of countries. These changes can affect both the countries of origin and the destination countries. Therefore, migration has become a crucial element that states incorporate into their strategies and policies. To avoid being negatively affected by the transformations caused by migration, states attempt to frame migration governance within a structured context and develop relevant policies and strategies. Migration policy, in general, is a roadmap specifically created for a country to manage internal and external migration. Local governments play as significant a role as central administrations in a country's migration policy. Local administrations also develop policies and strategies to manage the transformations caused by migration at the local level. This situation extends their role beyond simply meeting the communal needs of local populations and assigns them new responsibilities. Migration, as a complex and comprehensive issue, is widely discussed in many countries around the world and has become central to the lives of societies. European countries also see migration as a major issue and develop and implement policies to manage it. France stands out as one of the most experienced countries in developing migration policies. France has a long migration history due to heavy immigration from its former colonies. Since the 19th century, it has been one of the countries in Europe receiving the highest number of migrants. France developed its immigrant integration model based on the republican values brought by the 1789 French Revolution. Terrorist attacks that occurred in France during 2015-2016 led to a division between Muslim and non-Muslim migrants in French society. President Macron, elected in 2017, has taken a negative stance regarding migrant policies.

Macron's approach to migrants has also influenced the strategic decisions of local governments regarding migration management. France, a unitary state governed by a semi-presidential system, has a tripartite structure of local administrations: "municipal", "departmental", and "regional" units. These local governments, established on centralist principles, are under strict supervision by the central authority. The purpose of this study is to highlight the changes migration has brought about in France and assess how local migration governance affects migrants. For this purpose, the migration policies of local government units in France are examined, and the well-being of migrants at the local level is revealed. The study begins by addressing the topics of migration governance and migration policy. Then it discusses actions taken in France concerning migration management. Finally, it explains how local governments in France manage migration and evaluates and discusses the situation of migrants. Document analysis is used as the research method in this study.

2. THE CONCEPT OF MIGRATION

Migration is a phenomenon as old as human history. According to the International Organization for Migration (IOM, 2023), migration is defined as the process by which individuals or communities move permanently or temporarily from one place to another due to economic, social, political, or environmental reasons. Throughout history, migration has played a vital role in shaping civilizations, fostering cultural interactions, and evolving social structures. Today, migration continues to be a global phenomenon that impacts individuals and societies in various ways. The underlying causes of migration are generally examined under two categories: "push factors" and "pull factors." Push factors are adverse conditions that compel people to leave their place of residence. These include war, poverty, natural disasters, unemployment, political oppression, conflict, and environmental degradation. Pull factors, on the other hand, are attractive elements in destination areas such as better living conditions, job opportunities, educational prospects, political freedom, and security. When these factors combine, people decide to migrate in hopes of a better life for themselves and their families (Lee, 1966).

Climate change, wars, economic crises, political pressures, and social reasons all contribute to migration movements. Today, both developed and developing countries face the economic, demographic, political, and cultural consequences of migration (Castles, de Haas & Miller, 2014). The multidimensional nature of migration necessitates that research in this field be approached from an interdisciplinary perspective. Migration, which affects societies in many ways, consists of four elements: spatial, temporal, causal, and status-based. Spatial element refers to the movement from rural to urban areas or from one country to another. Temporal element defines whether migration is permanent, temporary, or seasonal. Causal element encompasses the economic, political, environmental, familial, or personal reasons behind migration. Status-based element distinguishes between voluntary, forced, documented, and undocumented forms of migration.

Migration is classified according to different criteria: time, direction, and reason (UNHCR, 2022):

- Time-based migration types are divided into "temporary migration" and "permanent migration." Temporary migration includes seasonal workers, student exchange programs, and other time-limited movements. Permanent migration refers to migration carried out with the intention of permanent settlement.
- According to direction, migration types are divided into two categories: "internal migration" and "international migration." Internal migration refers to the movement of individuals within the borders of a country, typically

from rural areas to urban centers. In Turkey, significant internal migration movements have occurred since the 1950s with the onset of industrialization. International migration involves moving from one country to another. These migrations have social and economic impacts on both the sending and receiving countries. In short, international migration crosses national borders.

- According to the cause, migration is classified into two types: "forced migration" and "voluntary migration." Forced migration refers to the displacement of individuals against their will due to reasons such as war, natural disasters, or political oppression. Refugees are included in this category. Voluntary migration occurs when individuals choose to relocate of their own accord, typically in pursuit of better living conditions or career opportunities.

Migration has economic, social, cultural, and political impacts on both sending and receiving societies. The economic impact of migration includes imbalances in the labor market, brain drain, or the devaluation of labor. The social impact involves multiculturalism, social cohesion, or exclusion. The demographic impact refers to changes in population structure, such as aging or rejuvenation (Faist, 2000). For migrants themselves, migration can provide advantages such as access to better job opportunities, education, and healthcare services; however, it may also lead to difficulties such as cultural adaptation problems, discrimination, and alienation. In receiving countries, while migration contributes to labor force growth and cultural diversity, it may also cause infrastructure problems, housing shortages, and social tensions due to rapid population increases. Labor market diversification, cultural enrichment, and issues of social cohesion and integration may arise. Additionally, xenophobia and anti-immigration policies may become prevalent. In sending countries, migration may lead to population decline, economic stagnation, and an aging population. Brain drain and labor force loss are common consequences. At the same time, remittance flows emerge, and changes occur within the social structure (Faist, 2000). In migration studies, there are four main theories developed by various academic disciplines. These are: the "Classical Economic Theory," the "New Economics of Migration," the "World Systems Theory," and the "Network Theory and Social Capital." These theories can be briefly explained as follows:

- *Classical Economic Theory*: Migration occurs based on individuals' expectations of economic gain and serves to balance labor market disparities. This theory explains migration as the rational behavior of individuals (Harris & Todaro, 1970). According to this theory, migration is driven by individuals' desire to maximize their income. Migrants tend to move from low-wage regions to high-wage regions (Todaro, 1969).

- *New Economics of Migration*: The decision to migrate is not made at the individual level but rather at the household level. Families encourage migration as a strategy to diversify income and minimize risk (Stark & Bloom, 1985).
- *World Systems Theory*: The core-periphery relations of the capitalist system make migration inevitable. Economic dependency and colonialism explain the flow of migration from peripheral countries to the core (Wallerstein, 1974). According to this theory, migration is seen as a result of capitalist modes of production (Portes and Walton, 1981).
- *Network Theory and Social Capital*: According to this theory, migrant communities facilitate the migration process by supporting subsequent migrants. In addition, social networks reduce the cost of migration and make it more sustainable over time (Massey et al., 1993).

The rise of anti-immigration rhetoric is increasing political polarization (Betts & Collier, 2017). Refugee crises continue to occur, with conflict zones such as Syria, Afghanistan, and Ukraine generating new waves of migration (UNHCR, 2022). Current migration trends are largely characterized by "climate migration" and "irregular migration," both of which bring additional challenges. In the context of climate migration, movements driven by droughts, floods, and natural disasters are on the rise. In the context of irregular migration, the living conditions of undocumented migrants and border control policies have become central issues of debate (IOM, 2023).

3. MIGRATION MANAGEMENT

Today, migration is a multidimensional phenomenon that is not limited to individual decisions but constantly occupies the agenda of states and international organizations. While migration movements are gaining momentum due to increasing wars, climate crisis, economic inequalities and globalization, the management of this process has also become of great importance. Migration management is the whole of policies that protect the rights of individuals, ensure social harmony and support sustainable development. Increasing forced and voluntary migration movements on a global scale have made it necessary for states and international actors to restructure their migration management methods. In the context of international examples and multi-level governance, the counterparts of migration management at both national policies and local practices are discussed.

Migration management is the whole of policies, strategies and practices developed by states, international organizations and civil society actors to regulate the mobility of individuals and communities. Migration management covers not only border controls but also dynamics such as the integration of migrants, the protection of their rights, the prevention of illegal migration and brain drain. Migration management also covers planning, regulation and implementation activities related to the causes, processes and consequences of migration. This management process directly affects the domestic and foreign policies, security strategies, social service provision and economic planning of states. An effective migration management should not only protect migrants but also consider the stability and well-being of the receiving societies. Therefore, migration management requires balancing both human values and strategic interests. Migration in the 21st century is not only the spatial movement of people, but also a multi-layered phenomenon with socioeconomic, cultural and political effects. The International Organization for Migration (IOM) defines migration management as follows (IOM, 2004): "Migration management includes legal, administrative and practical frameworks for planning, implementing and evaluating migration. According to the International Organization for Migration (IOM, 2023), there are 281 million international migrants worldwide. This increasing mobility has necessitated that migration be addressed not only as a border security issue but also from the perspectives of development, human rights, social cohesion and security.

In this context, "migration management" refers to the entirety of multi-actor and multi-level policies that regulate the arrival, stay, settlement and return processes of migrants (Betts, 2011). Migration management refers to a governance area that is not only subject to the singular authority of the state, but also includes international organizations, local governments, civil society and the private sector. The concept of migration management aims to establish a balance between the control and direction of migration flows and the protection of migrants' rights. Migration management has two dimensions: "horizontal dimension" and "vertical dimension". The horizontal dimension; refers to actors such as the state, NGOs, international organizations, and the private sector involved in the migration process. The vertical dimension refers to decisions and practices taken at international, national, regional, and local levels (Papademetriou, 2005).

Migration management has historically been addressed in three main stages. These are; "Nationalist Model (1945-1970)", "Multi-Actor Governance (1980-2000)", "Global Governance and Solidarity (after 2000)". In the nationalist model, migration policies were determined only according to national security and labor needs. In multi-actor governance, the role of international organizations (UNHCR, IOM, EU) in migration policies has increased. Global governance and solidarity are evaluated with the principles of migration, sustainable development, human rights, and global coordination (Castles et al., 2014). Types of migration management; It is divided into three as "forced migration management", "voluntary migration management" and "irregular migration management". Refugees, asylum seekers and climate migrants are included in forced migration management. Voluntary migration management refers to migrations made for reasons such as work, education and family reunification. Irregular migration management is used to describe illegal migration and undocumented migrants (Papademetriou, 2005). The main objectives of migration management are; supporting regular migration, combating irregular migration, protecting migrant rights, socio-economic integration, ensuring national security and combating human trafficking (Castles et al., 2014). A number of elements should be taken into consideration in order to manage migration in a healthy way. The basic elements of migration management are; "Policy and Legal Framework", "Inter-Institutional Coordination", "International Cooperation", "Integration Policies", "Data Collection and Information Management" are divided into five:

In the political and legal framework, states create laws and national migration policies to regulate migration movements. Laws determining the status of migrants, international agreements, border security and asylum systems form the basis of migration management. An effective legal framework protects the rights of migrants while also making it possible to combat irregular migration. In this framework, tools such as visa regimes, work permits, asylum systems, and citizenship laws are used. At this point, importance is also given to national security, and the national security process covers the prevention of illegal crossings and identity verification processes. Border agencies such as Frontex (EU) and ICE (USA) operate in this area. The critical debate at this point focuses on whether security or human rights are more important (Guild, 2009). Migration management is not only the responsibility of the state. In inter-institutional coordination, migration management constitutes a multi-actor process. These actors; government institutions such as the ministries of interior, foreign affairs, labor and social services, municipalities and local governments, non-governmental organizations, international organizations (IOM, UNHCR, EU) (Guild, 2009).

- International cooperation is also one of the most fundamental elements of migration. Since migration is often a cross-border process, it necessitates international cooperation. This situation becomes especially important in the fight against irregular migration and in refugee crises. International initiatives such as the United Nations' "Global Migration Compact" aim to manage migration in a safe, orderly and dignified manner. Similarly, regional structures such as the European Union are also trying to develop common migration policies (Betts, 2011).
- Integration policies are also one of the important elements of migration. In the context of these policies; language courses, educational opportunities, access to the labor market and social participation should be supported to facilitate the economic, social and cultural adaptation of migrants (Betts, 2011).

- In data collection and information management, data-based decision making is important for effective migration policies. Accurate analysis of migration movements is possible by providing decision makers with a solid data infrastructure. Population statistics, employment data and social service needs play a critical role in this process. Population movements, migrant profiles, needs and risk analyses need to be continuously monitored (Betts, 2011).

Migration management models and approaches are divided into three. These are; "Restrictive Model", "Human Rights Based Model" and "Economic Benefit Based Model". The restrictive model is generally security-focused. In this model; preventing irregular migration, border controls, and return practices are at the forefront. The external border policies of the European Union are examples of this model. In the human rights-based model; the welfare, integration and protection of human rights of migrants are essential. In this model, international legal norms (e.g. 1951 Geneva Convention) are taken as basis. In the economic benefit-based model, migration is evaluated in terms of contribution to the labor market and development potential. The point system migration policies of Canada and Australia are examples of this model (Ruhs, 2013). Global and regional actors play an important role in migration management. Global actors; "The UN Refugee Agency (UNHCR)", which deals with the definition and protection of refugee status, "International Organization for Migration (IOM)", which deals with the management of migration in a manner worthy of human dignity, "Global Compact for Migration", which aims for safe, regular and humane migration. Regional actors; European Union's "Common European Asylum System (CEAS)" and "Dublin System", African Union's "MERCOSUR", which represents intercontinental migration agreements and cross-border cooperation (Zapata-Barrero et al., 2017).

Local governments also play an important role in migration management. Local level migration management emerges on the basis of some practices. These are; shelter and housing policies, language education and social services, participatory and inclusive democracy mechanisms, immigrant-friendly cities (such as Sanctuary Cities, Intercultural Cities) are examples that expand immigrant rights at the local level (Zapata-Barrero et al., 2017). Migration management faces many challenges remains. In the face of intense migration flows, especially from war and crisis regions, the capacity of countries may be insufficient, and problems such as irregular migration and human trafficking come to the fore. In addition, the increase in anti-immigration sentiment with populist discourses can fuel social polarization. Today, there can be problems and critical discussions regarding migration management such as irregular migration and border security, sharing the burden of refugees, integration of immigrants and discrimination, brain drain and losses of source countries, migration due to climate change (environmental migration). Irregular migration and human trafficking require combating fundamental causes beyond border security. Climate change and migration are giving rise to a new wave of forced migration. Political polarization can emerge, and the rise of anti-immigration policies complicates management. The role of civil society is also important in migration management. In this context, aid organizations, NGOs and activist groups often fill the gaps left by the system (Baldwin-Edwards and Kraler, 2009).

4. LOCAL GOVERNMENTS AND MIGRATION

The increasing migration movement on a global scale has expanded the area of responsibility of local governments as well as national governments. Since cities are the first points of contact and living spaces of migrants, the role of local actors in migration management is becoming more and more important every day. The problems faced by migrants are often concentrated in local service areas such as health, housing, education, and employment. For this reason, local governments are in a critical position in terms of migrants' social cohesion and integration into urban life. Although migration is inherently addressed in national and international policy areas, the most concrete effects of migration are felt at the local level. Because processes such as migrants' settlement, access to public services, and social cohesion fall directly under the responsibility of local governments. For this reason, the relationship between local governments and migration has become an indispensable part of migration management today. Municipalities and local governments are actors who directly observe the structural and social inequalities faced by migrants and have the capacity to produce solutions in this area (Scholten & Penninx, 2016). Migration policies are no longer determined solely by national governments; It is shaped by the interaction of local, regional, national and transnational actors in the context of multi-level governance (Hooghe & Marks, 2003). In this context, "localization" refers to the process in which migration policies are implemented by local governments and are often reshaped according to local needs. "Locality of integration" is directly related to the quality of local services in areas such as social adaptation of migrants, housing, education and employment (Penninx, 2009).

Local governments include public institutions that provide services at the city level, primarily municipalities. Since a large portion of immigrants head towards urban areas, local governments must plan and diversify their services by taking this new population into account. Most of the basic services that immigrants need, such as housing, water and sewage, education, social assistance, and language courses, are provided directly through local governments. The role of local governments in migration varies from country to country, but is most commonly seen in the areas of service provision, social cohesion and integration, participation, and representation. Within the scope of service provision, local governments are the first public authorities to provide direct services in areas such as housing, education, health, social services, cultural and social participation, and employment services in cities where immigrants live (OECD, 2018; Zapata-Barrero et al., 2017). In the context of social cohesion and integration, municipalities develop projects on issues such as the integration of immigrants into local society, the promotion of cultural interactions, and the fight against discrimination. Integration efforts are usually carried out in cooperation with NGOs, universities, and immigrant associations. In the context of participation and representation; some local governments create structures such as advisory boards and immigrant councils for the participation of immigrants in the administration. These mechanisms are important in terms of equality of representation and inclusiveness (Penninx, 2009).

The housing shortage and pressure on infrastructure experienced by newly arrived immigrants constitute one of the first issues that local governments must solve. Access to education for immigrant children and the language proficiency of individuals who will receive education in a language other than their mother tongue are among the important issues. Social assistance such as psychosocial support, counseling services, and guidance can facilitate the social adaptation of immigrants. Cultural activities, efforts to increase mutual understanding, and collaborations with civil society are important tools in this process. The factors that are effective in shaping the migration policies of local governments are; "National Policy and Legal Framework", "Migration Profile of the City", "Political Local Government Approach". The area of action of local governments largely depends on the legal framework drawn by the central government. However, in some countries such as Germany and Sweden, it is seen that the local level participates more actively in the policy-making process. The number, diversity and needs of immigrants directly affect the shaping of local policies. For example, in cities hosting a high number of refugees, health, housing and psychosocial support are prioritized. In the context of the political local government approach; the approach of municipalities to immigrants may vary depending on the ideological stance of the local government. While participatory, human rights-based municipalities can follow more inclusive policies, security-oriented approaches can lead to exclusionary practices (Caponio and Borkert, 2010). In particular, inclusive municipalities participate in international networks such as the network of immigrant-friendly cities (Cities of Migration, Eurocities) to both share experiences and try to influence national policies (Scholten&Pennix., 2016).

Municipalities are the closest public institutions that ensure the participation of immigrants in urban life. They do not only provide services; they also build social bridges between local people and immigrants. They have roles such as ensuring that cultural differences are tolerated, reducing discrimination and reinforcing a culture of solidarity. For example, some metropolitan municipalities establish Migrant Solidarity Centers to provide multilingual consultancy services to immigrants and inform them about their legal rights. Local governments face many difficulties such as "lack of financial resources", "lack of planning" and "polarization and prejudices in society" in the face of increasing migration. Local governments may not have sufficient budget and expertise in providing services to immigrants. This situation can cause a disruption in integration, especially in places where the central government provides limited support. As the immigrant population increases, the service burden also increases, but the lack of sufficient budget transfers from the central government can put municipalities in a difficult situation. In addition, there may be planning problems and difficulties in adapting to the rapidly changing demographic structure. In addition, polarization and prejudices in society and negative perceptions towards immigrants can disrupt local integration policies. There are uncertainties between the legal status of immigrants and their right to access services. This can lead local actors to take legal risks when providing services. In environments where anti-immigration rhetoric is on the rise, it can be politically difficult for local administrators to implement immigrant-friendly policies (Garbaye, 2005).

In Europe, cities such as Barcelona, Berlin and Amsterdam stand out with their immigrant-friendly policies, language education and social cohesion projects. In Spain, the Barcelona Municipality offers cultural participation projects and multilingual consultancy services for immigrants. In Germany, the Berlin Municipality establishes social service centers in immigrant neighborhoods and provides integration consultancy. In the Netherlands, the Amsterdam Municipality implements neighborhood-based integration policies and ensures the inclusion of immigrants in participatory budgeting processes. In France, the Lyon Municipality implements cultural events and neighborhood-level social cohesion projects for immigrants' participation in social life. In Sweden, the Malmö Municipality runs multilingual information systems and mentor programs for immigrant youth's access to education and employment (Bernt, 2019).

5. MIGRATION MANAGEMENT IN FRANCE

France, as one of the major immigrant-receiving countries in modern history, has developed different policies against migration movements in various periods. From industrialization to the post-colonial period, from economic crises to today's security-centered approaches, migration policies have been in a constant transformation. Migration policies initiated to meet the post-industrial labor force need have gradually taken on a more complex structure focused on social harmony, security, identity and integration. Anti-immigration sentiment and discussions on the cultural identities of immigrants have become determining factors in the direction of policies, especially since the 1980s. France's migration policies have been influenced by both post-colonial developments and geopolitical dynamics in Europe. France has historically been one of the countries that receive the most immigration in Europe, and the phenomenon of migration has become an important determinant in many areas, from economic development to social integration, from identity politics to security strategies.

France, one of the countries that receives the most immigration in Europe, has been living side by side with the phenomenon of immigration for many years. The migration movements that started in the 20th century to meet the need for labor have gained a socio-political dimension over time, leading to migration management becoming a central public policy. Today, migration in France has become a multi-dimensional issue discussed within the framework of security, economy, social harmony and human rights. France is one of the countries with the most deep-rooted immigrant communities in Europe. For this reason, immigration management has been a policy area that is constantly changing in both its historical and current dimensions. The subject of "Migration Management in France" is quite multi-layered in terms of historical development, legal framework, institutional structures, implemented policies and current discussions. France's immigration management has been shaped by significant legal changes and political discussions in recent years. This process is carried out with the effort to establish a balance between economic needs, integration policies and security concerns. France's immigration experience began with industrialization in the late 19th century. After World Wars I and II, large-scale immigration flows occurred primarily from Italy, Poland and Spain, and later from former French colonies (Algeria, Morocco, Tunisia, Senegal etc.) to fill the labor gap. With the oil crisis in the 1970s, immigration policies changed; temporary and controlled immigration practices came to the fore instead of permanent settlement. However, these policies could not prevent permanent settlement through the reunification of immigrant families.

With industrialization, the increasing need for labor in France led the country to attract immigrants, especially from neighboring countries. During this period, immigration was largely free and state intervention was limited. There was an influx of immigration from Belgium, Italy and Spain. The French Citizenship Law of 1889 allowed the integration of immigrants based on the principle of citizenship based on place of birth (jus soli). Immigration policy was based mainly on the principle of freedom (Noiriel, 1991). The post-war reconstruction process made France dependent on labor once again. During this period, immigration from the colonies became very important. Immigrants, especially from North African countries such as Algeria, Morocco and Tunisia, radically changed the ethnic structure of French society. After Algerian Independence in 1962, many Algerians immigrated to France. During this period, most of the immigrants were employed as industrial workers. Permanent migration waves began with family reunification. However, no serious structural measures were taken for the social integration of immigrants during this period, and isolated communities formed in the suburbs (Temime, 1999). The historical phase of immigration in France is expressed as follows (Weil, 2005; Brubaker, 2020):

- *1945 Ordonnance*: It is the first comprehensive regulation that brought the hiring of immigrants under state control. In the 1945-1974 period, economic immigration policies were developed and immigration was encouraged due to the need for labor. In the post-1974 period, immigration restrictions began with the economic crisis and "family reunification" came to the fore (Weil, 2005; Brubaker, 2020). In the post-World War II period, France experienced a serious labor shortage while restructuring its industry under the influence of the Marshall Plan. Immigration was one of the main tools in meeting this need. The 1945 Ordonnance sur l'entrée et le séjour des étrangers laid the foundations of modern immigration policy. The immigration policy was guided by a dual contract system and both the employer and the state accepted immigrants. Mass migration waves began from former colonies such as Algeria, Morocco and Tunisia (Temime, 1999).
- *The 1973 Oil Crisis* was a turning point in immigration policies. Labor migration was stopped with the economic recession, but most immigrants in France became permanent. Labor migration was officially stopped in 1974. However, family reunification practices changed the demographic structure of immigration. This period was a transition period in which immigrants began to become permanent citizens rather than "guest workers." The economic contraction following the 1973 Oil Crisis caused a sharp transformation in immigration policies. In 1974, the government decided to stop economic immigration. New immigration restrictions were introduced. Permanent immigration was tried to be prevented. Instead of integrating immigrants into the country, "return" was encouraged. However, these policies were not successful; the immigrant population continued to increase through the reunification of immigrant families and birth rates (Schnapper, 1991).
- *1980s-1990s*: This is a period of intense debates on integration, security-focused approaches, secularism and citizenship. During this period, deportation practices increased with the Pasqua laws (Weil, 2005; Brubaker, 2020). During the 1980s and 1990s, the integration of immigrants into French society began to be discussed. At the same time, immigration became a political issue in the context of social harmony, cultural conflict and security. In 1981, the Socialist government provided collective residence permits to illegal immigrants. In 1993, the Pasqua Laws made it difficult for immigrants to be-

come citizens and expanded deportation powers. Immigration increasingly began to be framed as a "public threat". Within the framework of the principle of "laïcit"", the headscarf ban came into effect in 2004. Immigration was increasingly defined as a problem of cultural harmony and associated with security concerns (Kepel, 2012).

- *1990s-2000s*: In the 1990s, immigration debates began to focus on security, identity and integration. Increasing refugee applications, illegal immigration and European Union border policies led to a new direction in France's immigration policies. The 1993 Pasqua Law made it more difficult to obtain a residence permit. The 2003 Sarkozy Law further increased security-oriented policies. Problems such as discrimination and ghettoization led to social debates. In France, discussions of "secularism" frequently overlapped with the cultural identity of immigrants (Brubaker, 2020).
- *After 2010s*: In recent years, migrations due to the Syrian Civil War, conflicts in Africa and climate change have brought new crises throughout Europe. During this period, France has made its migration policies more controlled and selective. The 2018 Migration Law has shortened the asylum period and accelerated deportation processes. The motto "Controlled for migration, effective for asylum, successful for integration" has been adopted. France is open to qualified labor but has a stricter stance against irregular migration. While opposition to migration is rising at the social level, criticisms of inadequacy in integration policies continue. The Macron government supports a selective migration model based on the need for labor by adopting a "qualified migration" approach. Social cohesion policies are shaped around "republican values" and an attitude distant from cultural pluralism is maintained (Brubaker, 2020).

In France, immigration has long been at the center of public policy with its economic, social and political dimensions. Since the mid-20th century, immigration management has shifted from being a solely labor-based policy area to a broader spectrum such as border control, management of integration processes and cultural adaptation. In this context, immigration management has become a multi-actor and multi-layered governance process (Geddes & Scholten, 2016). Immigration policies in France are based on the Constitution, European Union directives and international agreements. France is a party to the European Convention on Human Rights and the 1951 Geneva Convention Relating to the Status of Refugees. The French Constitution is based on the equality and human rights of all individuals (especially the 1789 Declaration of the Rights of Man and of the Citizen) (Fassin, 2011).

The basic legal documents regarding immigration in France are:

- CESEDA (Code de l'entrée et du séjour des étrangers et du droit d'asile): It regulates the rights of foreigners to enter, reside and seek asylum in France (Fassin, 2011).
- LOPPSI II (2011): It is the law that brings together security and immigration policies (Fassin, 2011).
- Collomb Law (2018): It has brought important changes regarding asylum and immigration, such as shortening the periods, accelerating deportation procedures and combating irregular immigration (Fassin, 2011).
- A New Comprehensive Immigration Law (2024): The new immigration law, which entered into force in January 2024, aims to combat irregular immigration while promoting integration. In terms of integration and residence; French proficiency has been introduced for those who want to obtain a multi-year residence permit. A special residence permit has been granted for irregular immigrants working in the health sector. There are limits on the number of renewals of some temporary residence permits (Fragomen, 2024). Foreign children born in France must apply for citizenship between the ages of 16 and 18; automatic citizenship has been abolished. Citizenship applications of foreigners who commit crimes may be rejected. Deportation of people convicted of minor crimes has been made easier (Le Monde, 2023). The new law has been criticized by human rights advocates and opposition parties. In particular, issues such as the deportation of people who came to France as children and the disruption of family unity have been controversial. In addition, the concept of "threat to public order" has been expanded, making deportation of people convicted of minor crimes easier (Reuters, 2025).

France's migration policies are being brought into line with the European Union's new Pact on Migration and Asylum. In this context, strengthening border controls and combating irregular migration are at the forefront. It is also stated that France is preparing a new migration law for 2025, which aims to extend detention periods and tighten residence permit criteria. In France, the "Ministère de l'Intérieuré is the main agency responsible for immigration and asylum management. The "OFII (Office Français de l'Immigration et de l'Intégration)" works on the integration of immigrants, social support and housing. It is the French immigration and integration office. The "OFPRA (Office Français de Protection des Réfugiés et Apatrides)" evaluates asylum applications. It is the "French Office for the Protection of Refugees and Stateless Persons". The "CNDA (Cour nationale du droit d'asile)" examines appeals against OFPRA decisions (Ministère de l'Intérieur, 2023; OFII, 2022). Since France is a member of the Schengen area of the European Union, its border policies are shaped within the framework of the EU. However, after the 2015 refugee crisis, controls at the national level have been tightened. France has adopted policies aimed at stopping immigrants, especially those coming from Italy and Spain, at its borders (Fassin, 2011). France aims to integrate immigrants into French values with the understanding of "republican assimilation." In this context, the French integration model is based on the principle of republican universalism. In this model, immigrants are expected to adapt to society as individuals. Language education, secular education and citizenship courses are made mandatory. In short, learning French is encouraged. Integration agreements (CAI, contract d'accueil et d'intégration) are implemented. Newly arrived immigrants are provided with language courses, civics education and labor market integration. Adherence to French values is emphasized in citizenship applications. Social integration courses are organized and immigrants are given seminars on topics such as French history, secularism and equality (Schnapper, 1991; Brubaker, 2001). Local governments and civil society play an important role in France's migration management. Local governments are the practical implementers of integration. They play a key role in providing services such as housing, education, social services and language courses. Municipalities are important actors in providing immigrants with access to shelter, health, education and social services. Large cities such as Paris, Marseille and Lyon carry out various integration projects. These municipalities provide support to immigrants with "guest houses" (centre d'accueil), counselling centres and multicultural activities. Civil society organisations also provide legal support, psychosocial assistance and accommodation services to refugees. For example, "France Terre d'Asile" advocates for the right to asylum. "La Cimade" plays an active role in protecting and supporting immigrant rights. However, the equality of these services varies according to local resources and political will (Joly, 2005).

Immigration in France is a subject of intense political debate, especially during election periods. Anti-immigration rhetoric is promoted by far-right parties; this situation increases polarization in society. The main problems encountered at this point are; overloading of the asylum system, social exclusion and unemployment in the suburbs, Islamophobia and xenophobia in society, problems in the integration of immigrant youth into education and the workforce. Social disharmony and separation occur, and the exclusion of the immigrant youth in the suburbs causes integration policies to be questioned. There is a dilemma regarding security and human rights, and the fact that immigrants are seen as security risks increases social polarization. In addition, there is frequent tension between EU policies and national interests (Kepel, 2012). New factors such as the Ukrainian War and climate change have made it necessary for France to re-evaluate its immigration capacity. The types and policies of immigration in France can be summarized as follows (Weil, 2005a):

- *Legal Immigration*: It is aimed at immigrants who come for reasons such as work, education, family reunification. French language education and citizenship information programs are offered with the Integration Agreement (CIR).
- *Asylum:* France is a party to the EU's Dublin III regulation. Applications are evaluated by OFPRA. As of 2023, there has been an increase in asylum applications.
- *Irregular Immigration*: Strict controls are applied against illegal entry and stay, and deportation procedures are accelerated. It is carried out with applications such as police checks, detention centers (CRA), and "deportability".

5.1. MIGRATION POLICIES OF LOCAL GOVERNMENTS

France, as one of the countries that receives the most immigration in Europe, has been developing policies at different scales for many years to ensure the integration of immigrants into social life. Although the national government is mostly at the center of these policies, the actors that most directly affect the daily lives of immigrants are local governments. Municipalities, city councils and regional administrations are responsible for meeting the needs of immigrants in many areas, from housing to education, from social integration to employment. Despite the determination of national immigration policies, municipalities play critical roles in the participation of immigrants in social life. The strategies implemented by local governments, especially in the areas of housing, education, social services and cultural integration, are of great importance for the sustainability of France's multicultural structure. The phenomenon of migration is a process that shapes not only national borders but also the social fabric of cities. In countries that have been receiving immigrants for a long time, such as France, the role of local governments in this transformation process is becoming increasingly important. The areas where immigrants live most densely are cities and suburbs; therefore, the services that immigrants encounter in their daily lives are generally provided at the local level (Barou, 2009).

The institutional structure of immigration policies in France is also important for local governments. In France, the central government (especially the Ministry of the Interior) is the main actor in the formation of immigration policies. However, with the "Decentralization Law" of 1982, local governments were given broader powers; the responsibilities of municipalities were increased, especially in the areas of social services, housing and education. In the implementation of immigration and integration policies, municipalities operate at the région (region), département (province) and commune (municipality) levels. Each level manages programs for immigrants in a different service area (Le Galès, 2002). In France, there are three levels of government: the central government, regional governments (régions, départements) and local governments (communes, municipalities). Although local governments have limited direct authority over immigration, in practice they are among the most important providers of social services. The main areas of authority of local governments in France are housing and housing policies, education and school services, public transport and urban infrastructure, social assistance services, cultural activities and social integration programs. These tasks are directly related to the basic needs that immigrants face in their environment. For this reason, the practical influence of local governments is gaining a dimension that goes beyond the limits of legal authority (Le Galès, 2002). In recent years, French municipalities and local authorities have been trying to develop participatory and inclusive policies towards immigrants. These policies can be grouped mostly under the following headings:

- *Housing Services*: Local governments are developing temporary accommodation centers (CADA) and social housing projects for asylum seekers and registered refugees. While housing shortages are a significant problem, some municipalities are running special housing programs to increase social solidarity. Housing is one of the most basic needs of migrants. Local governments are trying to respond to this need through social housing production (HLM - Habitation à Loyer Modéré) and temporary housing solutions (Groupe URD, 2020). For example, the Maison des Réfugiés, managed by the Municipality of Paris, provides both housing and consultancy services for refugees (Ville de Paris, 2022).
- *Language and Citizenship Education*: Language education, which is seen as the fundamental step in the integration of immigrants into French society, is often provided at the local level. Municipalities organize French courses, citizenship workshops and vocational training in cooperation with voluntary organizations. Municipalities undertake important duties, especially in the integration of newly arrived immigrant children into the school system and in the learning of French by adult immigrants. Family support centers and neighborhood reading houses play an active role in this process (Ichou, 2013).
- *Social Services and Integration Programs*: Local social service units create various support mechanisms for immigrants to find work, access social assistance and benefit from health services. In this process, structures such as the Centre Communal d'Action Sociale (CCAS) play an important role (Wray, 2021).
- *Social Cohesion and Cultural Participation*: City governments are developing projects that encourage communities from different origins to live together peacefully. Within the framework of the "living together" (vivre ensemble) principle; organizations such as cultural festivals, neighborhood meetings, community centers are supported. Municipalities support cultural

events that bring different ethnic groups together within the framework of the "living together" (vivre ensemble) approach. The Municipality of Strasbourg is shown as an exemplary implementer in this regard (Strasbourg Ville et Eurométropole, 2023). The Municipality of Lyon is also shown as an example. Lyon has taken various initiatives to make integration policies sustainable at the local level, especially since the 1990s. Within the scope of the "Lyon Ville Refuge" (City of Refuge Lyon) project; accommodation is provided to people seeking international protection, vocational training and psychosocial support are provided in cooperation with civil society (Ville de Lyon, 2021). This model ensures that refugees are not seen as passive recipients but as active participants in city life.

- *Consultancy and Legal Support for Immigrants*: Especially in big cities, "immigrant consultancy centers" have been opened where immigrants can receive support on administrative procedures. These centers provide guidance on issues such as preparation of documents, residence permit applications and access to social assistance.

Examples of successful local practices in France can be given (Wray, 2021):

- *Municipality of Paris*: Paris is the city with the largest immigrant population in France. The Municipality of Paris provides social support to immigrants and refugees through centers such as the "Maison des réfugiés" (Refugees House), organizes preschool French preparatory courses for children, and develops integration projects with civil society organizations.
- *Municipality of Lyon*: In Lyon, the municipality carries out social housing projects for refugees and asylum seekers, special support programs for female immigrants, and cultural mediation work.
- *Municipality of Strasbourg*: Strasbourg is an active municipality in immigration and human rights issues due to being the headquarters of the Council of Europe. The Municipality of Strasbourg stands out with its multicultural education programs and equality-based social services.

In France, the issue of cooperation between local governments and civil society organizations is also important. In France, local governments work in cooperation with civil society organizations to both expand their service area and increase social acceptance. Organizations such as Emmaüs, Secours Catholique, and La Cimade are important actors working directly with immigrants. Capacity building is provided in the areas of social integration, education, and legal support through joint projects (Wray, 2021).

Local governments in France face several obstacles when providing services to immigrants:

- *Insufficient resources*: The lack of sufficient funds from the central budget makes it difficult to sustain services. Appropriations from the central government remain limited and the capacity of municipalities to generate resources is weakened (Bozec & Simoulin, 2018).
- *Limitations of authority*: Many decisions on immigration status are made at the national level, and local governments are the implementers of these decisions. In particular, decisions on immigration status and deportation are the monopoly of the central authority.
- *Social pressures and political polarization*: Municipalities that support immigrants may be criticized by some political groups. In some cities, anti-immigrant and discrimination make it difficult to sustain local practices.

A multi-actor and participatory governance approach is essential for the success of immigration policies. It is recommended that local governments cooperate more with civil society, include immigrant representatives in decision-making processes, and use European Union funds more effectively (Penninx, 2009).

6. CONCLUSION

Migration is a phenomenon as old as human history, but more complex and multidimensional today. It is one of the important issues that occupy the world agenda today. Understanding the reasons for migration and managing this process in a humane and sustainable way is of great importance both in terms of protecting the rights of individuals and ensuring the balanced development of societies. The fundamental problems of the modern age, such as globalization, war, climate change and inequality, are reshaping the causes and consequences of migration. Therefore, migration must be addressed not only with security or economic issues, but also with human rights, development and global justice issues. When managed correctly, migration can turn into opportunities for both migrants and migrant-receiving societies. For this purpose, a balanced, human rights-based, inclusive and data-based migration management approach should be developed. With long-term planning, international cooperation and policies that prioritize social harmony, migration can become a part of sustainable development. Migration management should be addressed not only in the context of protecting borders but also in the context of providing decent living conditions, supporting social harmony and building global justice.

Recommendations for effective migration management:

- Multi-level governance principles should be adopted.
- The participation and representation of migrants should be strengthened.
- Rights-based and human-centered policies should be expanded.
- International solidarity should be redefined with the understanding of responsibility sharing, not just burden sharing.

Although migration is a process that develops on a global scale, its effects are felt at the local level. Therefore, it is vital that local governments develop conscious, inclusive and sustainable policies on migration. Ensuring peaceful coexistence between local people and migrants is only possible with strong local migration management. In this process, local governments need to be supported, educated and empowered. The role of local governments in migration management is not limited to providing services only; it is also critical in terms of building social cohesion, promoting participation and implementing rights-based policies. Therefore:

- Local governments should be given more financial resources and legal authority.
- Migrant communities should be included in participatory policy-making processes.
- Coordination between central and local actors should be strengthened.
- In order to increase the effectiveness of migration policies, local governments should be integrated into the process not only as implementers but also as policy makers.

In France, immigration policies have historically been shaped by economic needs, political preferences and social dynamics. This process, from industrialization to the post-colonial period, from security-oriented approaches to integration problems, has caused the state to perceive immigration sometimes as a resource and sometimes as a threat. The greatest responsibility facing France today is to develop participatory and inclusive policies that respect the rights of both locals and immigrants, making migration manageable, fair and sustainable. France's immigration policies have historically been shaped by economic needs and political concerns; over time, they have gained dimensions based on human rights, security, national identity and integration. The immigration-friendly structure of the 19th century has been replaced by a more selective, controlled and security-focused immigration regime today. This historical transformation is a reflection not only of France's domestic policies but also of the immigration policies developed at the European Union level. In the coming period, the need for more inclusive and fair immigration policies to ensure social cohesion and the sustainability of the multicultural structure is increasing.

France's immigration policies have historically emerged from economic necessities and have evolved over time into political, cultural and security-based approaches. In this process, from the free immigration period of the 19th century to the selective and security-focused policies of the 21st century, the status of immigrants has become increasingly regulated and their rights have become more debatable. This transformation is not only in the legal framework, but is also directly linked to France's understanding of national identity, secular practices and citizenship regime. It is vital for social cohesion that future migration policies are more inclusive, egalitarian and based on human rights. France is one of the countries that experiences migration as both a challenge and an opportunity. Developing a participatory and inclusive migration management approach that considers the balance between security and human rights is essential to ensure social cohesion in the long term. As one of the central countries of Europe, France has the potential to shape not only its own future but also the general direction of the continent with the steps it will take on migration. In France, immigration management is a public policy that historically emerged from economic needs, but has now spread to complex areas such as integration, security, citizenship and multiculturalism. The state's governance of immigrants is shaped not only by legal regulations, but also by local practices, social reactions and international obligations.In order for France to be successful in migration management in the future, it needs to adopt more participatory, inclusive and rights-based approaches.

In France, migration management is shaped not only by national policies but also by local practices and initiatives. Local governments are one of the most effective actors in finding solutions to the problems that migrants face in their daily lives. The inclusive, human rights-based and social cohesion-oriented policies of municipalities and regional authorities contribute to managing migration as a social asset rather than a crisis. In the future, empowering and resource-supporting local governments is a critical step to making immigration policies in France more equitable and sustainable. In France, local governments play a key role in providing services that directly affect the daily lives of immigrants. Local policies in the areas of housing, education, social services and cultural integration are decisive in terms of the integration of immigrants into society. However, developing more sustainable and inclusive policies in these areas will be possible by both increasing financial resources and strengthening administrative powers. Considering the impact of immigration on urban life, it is essential that local governments are supported more in this regard.

REFERENCES

Baldwin-Edwards, M., & Kraler, A. (2009). *REGINE: Regularisations in Europe*. ICMPD. DOI: 10.5117/9789085550082

Barou, J. (2009). Immigration et intégration en France: État des lieux. *Regards Sociologiques*, *37*, 25–45.

Bernt, M. (2019). Migration and Urban Governance in Berlin. *Urban Research & Practice*.

Betts, A. (2011). *Global Migration Governance*. Oxford University Press. DOI: 10.1093/acprof:oso/9780199600458.001.0001

Betts, A., & Collier, P. (2017). *Refuge: Transforming a Broken Refugee System*. Penguin Books.

Bozec, G., & Simoulin, V. (2018). Les politiques publiques locales de l'immigration. *Revue française d'administration publique*, 167(3), 599–616.

Brubaker, R. (2001). The return of assimilation? Changing perspectives on immigration and its sequels in France, Germany, and the United States. *Ethnic and Racial Studies*, *24*(4), 531–548. DOI: 10.1080/01419870120049770

Brubaker, R. (2020). *Laïcité, Integration and Citizenship in Contemporary France. Ethnic and Racial Studies*, *43*(3), 405–424.

Caponio, T., & Borkert, M. (2010). *The Local Dimension of Migration Policymaking*. Amsterdam University Press. DOI: 10.5117/9789089642325

Castles, S., de Haas, H., & Miller, M. J. (2014). *The Age of Migration: International Population Movements in the Modern World*. Palgrave Macmillan. DOI: 10.1007/978-0-230-36639-8

Ministère de l'Intérieur. (2023). *Rapport annuel sur l'immigration*.

Faist, T. (2000). *The Volume and Dynamics of International Migration and Transnational Social Spaces*. Oxford University Press. DOI: 10.1093/acprof:oso/9780198293910.001.0001

Fassin, D. (2011). *Humanitarian Reason: A Moral History of the Present*. University of California Press.

Fragomen (2024). France: New Comprehensive Immigration Law Introduced. https://www.fragomen.com/insights/france-new-comprehensive-immigration-law-introduced.html?utm_source=chatgpt.com, Erişim tarihi: 10.03.2025.

Garbaye, R. (2005). *Getting Into Local Power: The Politics of Ethnic Minorities in British and French Cities*. Blackwell Publishing. DOI: 10.1002/9780470761625

Geddes, A., & Scholten, P. (2016). The politics of migration and immigration in Europe. *Sage (Atlanta, Ga.)*. Advance online publication. DOI: 10.4135/9781473982703

Groupe URD. (2020). *L'accès au logement des personnes réfugiées en France.*

Guild, E. (2009). *Security and Migration in the 21st Century*. Polity Press.

Harris, J. R., & Todaro, M. P. (1970). Migration, Unemployment and Development: A Two-Sector Analysis. *The American Economic Review*, *60*(1), 126–142.

Hooghe, L., & Marks, G. (2003). Unraveling the Central State, but How? Types of Multi-level Governance. *The American Political Science Review*, *97*(2), 233–243.

Ichou, M. (2013). Différences d'origine et performances scolaires. *Revue Française de Sociologie*, *54*(3), 463–498.

International Organization for Migration IOM. (2004). *Glossary on Migration*. International Organization for Migration.

International Organization for Migration (IOM). (2023)... *World Migration Report*, •••, 2023.

Joly, D. (2005). *L'intégration des immigrés en France: Entre assimilation et multiculturalisme.Revue Européenne des Migrations Internationales*, *21*(2), 39–59.

Kepel, G. (2012). *Banlieue de la R"publique*. Gallimard.

Le Galès, P. (2002). *Gouverner par les instruments*. Presses de Sciences Po.

Lee, E. S. (1966). A Theory of Migration. *Demography*, *3*(1), 47–57. DOI: 10.2307/2060063

Massey, D. S., Arango, J., Hugo, G., Kouaouci, A., Pellegrino, A., & Taylor, J. E. (1993). Theories of International Migration: A Review and Appraisal. *Population and Development Review*, *19*(3), 431–466. DOI: 10.2307/2938462

Monde, L. (2023). *What's in France's controversial immigration law?*https://www.lemonde.fr/en/france/article/2023/12/20/what-s-in-france-s-controversial-immigration-law_6361995_7.html?utm_source=chatgpt.com#, Erişim tarihi: 10.03.2025.

Noiriel, G. (1991). *La tyrannie du national: le droit d'asile en Europe, 1793–1993*. Calmann-Lévy.

OECD. (2018). *Working Together for Local Integration of Migrants and Refugees*. OECD Publishing.

OFII (Office Français de l'Immigration et de l'Intégration). (2022). *Bilan annuel*.

Papademetriou, D. (2005). *The Global Struggle with Illegal Migration: No End in Sight*. Migration Policy Institute.

Penninx, R. (2009). Decentralising Integration Policies: Managing Migration in Cities, Regions and Localities. *International Migration (Geneva, Switzerland)*, *47*(5), 1–19.

Portes, A., & Walton, J. (1981). *Labor, Class, and the International System*. Academic Press.

Reuters. (2025). From France to Mali, a deportee's struggle far from home. https://www.reuters.com/investigates/special-report/migration-europe-africa/, Erişim Tarihi: 10.03.2025.

Ruhs, M. (2013). *The Price of Rights: Regulating International Labor Migration*. Princeton University Press.

Schnapper, D. (1991). *La France de l'intégration*. Gallimard.

Scholten, P., & Penninx, R. (2016). The Multilevel Governance of Migration and Integration. In Zapata-Barrero, R., & Triandafyllidou, A. (Eds.), *Addressing Tolerance and Diversity Discourses in Europe*. Palgrave Macmillan. DOI: 10.1007/978-3-319-21674-4_6

Stark, O., & Bloom, D. E. (1985). The New Economics of Labor Migration. *The American Economic Review*, *75*(2), 173–178.

Strasbourg Ville et Eurométropole. (2023). *Rapport d'activit"s sur l'int"gration*.

Temime, E. (1999). *Histoire de l'immigration en France*. Paris: La D"couverte.

Todaro, M. P. (1969). A Model of Labor Migration and Urban Unemployment in Less Developed Countries. *The American Economic Review*.

UNHCR. (2022). *Global Trends: Forced Displacement in 2022*.

Ville de Lyon. (2021). *Lyon Ville Refuge: un engagement de solidarit"*.

Ville de Paris. (2022). *Maison des Réfugi"s – Rapport annuel*.

Wallerstein, I. (1974). *The Modern World-System*. Academic Press.

Weil, P. (2005). *La France et ses étrangers: l'aventure d'une politique de l'immigration de 1938 à nos jours*. Gallimard.

Weil, P. (2005a). *La République et sa diversité: immigration, intégration, discrimination*. Seuil.

Wray, H. (2021). *Migration and Local Governance*. Palgrave Macmillan.

Zapata-Barrero, R., Caponio, T., & Scholten, P. (2017). Theorizing the 'Local Turn' in Immigration Policies. *International Review of Administrative Sciences, 83*(2), 241–260. DOI: 10.1177/0020852316688426

KEY TERMS AND DEFINITIONS

Migration Management: Migration Management is a multidimensional public policy area that encompasses the entire process of planning, organizing and monitoring the movement of individuals from one country to another or from one place within a country to another. This management process includes many elements such as organizing legal migration routes, combating illegal migration, border security, protecting refugee and asylum seeker rights, and developing social cohesion policies. An effective migration management aims to both protect the rights of migrants and balance the social, economic and security concerns of the host society.

Migration and Integration: Migration and Integration refers to the process of establishing and strengthening social, economic, cultural and political relations with the society to which individuals migrate from one country to another or from one region to another. While migration begins with the individual changing location, integration is a dynamic and multifaceted process that aims for the mutual adaptation of this individual with the new society. Effective integration policies strengthen social harmony and social cohesion by supporting immigrants' access to rights in areas such as education, employment, housing, health and citizenship.

Refugees: Refugees are people who seek refuge in another country due to fear of persecution due to their race, religion, nationality, membership in a particular social group or political views and who seek international protection. This definition was established in international law by the United Nations Refugee Convention of 1951. Refugees have a special protection status because they are unable to return to their country due to reasons such as war, internal conflict or human rights violations. Their access to basic rights, security and decent living conditions are guaranteed by national and international law.

Local Governments and Migration: Local Governments and Migration refer to the critical role played by municipalities and other local institutions in solving the problems faced by migrant and refugee populations. Since migrants' basic needs such as housing, health, education, social services and social cohesion are met directly at the local level, local governments are at the forefront of managing migration. At the same time, they assume important responsibilities in areas such as implementing social cohesion policies, promoting cultural interaction and developing relations between local people and migrants. Effective local migration policies support the well-being of both migrants and the host society.

Local Governments and Immigration in France: Local Governments and Immigration in France refers to the central role played by municipalities and local authorities in the provision of services and social integration processes for immigrants and refugees. Although immigration policies in France are determined at the national level, a large portion of services such as housing, education, health, language education, social assistance and integration are carried out by municipalities, regional councils and departments. In particular, metropolitan municipalities (such as Paris, Lyon, Marseille) aim to strengthen social integration by developing social policies for immigrants in cooperation with civil society organizations.

Immigration Laws: Immigration laws refer to the legal framework that regulates the entry, exit, residence and working conditions of individuals from one country to another. These laws determine the legal status of immigrants (e.g. tourist, student, worker, refugee), their admission process to the country, the duration of their stay, the methods of acquiring citizenship and the cases of deportation. Immigration laws also cover areas such as combating irregular migration, taking measures against human trafficking and evaluating international protection requests.

Immigrants: Immigrants are people who move from their home country to another country for various reasons or are temporarily in that country. Immigrants usually migrate for reasons such as economic opportunities, education, family reunification, war, internal conflicts or natural disasters. Immigrants can have legal or irregular status and can sometimes be classified with different legal definitions such as refugees or asylum seekers.

Chapter 7
Good Practice Policies Examples in America's Local Governments and their Ethical Considerations

Daniel Uriel Scott
https://orcid.org/0009-0004-9925-7435
Niagara University, Buffalo, USA & NWCU Law School, Sacramento, USA

ABSTRACT

Local government leaders can promote transformative progress to foster change in their communities through policies. Cities in the United States are affected by complex and interconnected issues related to land use, transportation, waste management, and housing that have evolved to fulfill residents' needs. The housing good practices identified include overlay zones, adaptive reuse, and form-based code. The transportation good practices discussed are complete streets and leveraging ride sharing. In the case of waste management, the good practices are mandatory recycling and compositing ordinances and youth educational programs. Each of the good practices is associated with ethical considerations. Policy changes often result in inequitable outcomes, which can cause ethical concerns. There is a need for future researchers to assess the ethical considerations associated with the identified good practice policies. In essence, good practice policies positively impact local government functions concerning land use, transportation, waste management, and housing.

DOI: 10.4018/979-8-3373-0452-6.ch007

INTRODUCTION

Local governments are uniquely positioned to address the complex problems that impact their communities by implementing system-level changes using policies. The use of land, transportation, waste management, and housing are some of the areas that require current thinking to promote sustainability in communities. A prevalent problem when it comes to policymaking in most local governments is the limited opportunity to explore the root causes or issues and gather adequate evidence to determine how the proposed changes can promote equity in communities. Instead, local governments often focus on developing single-issues solutions, instead of collaborating with the different sectors and agencies to ensure that the policy changes foster equity (Scally et al., 2023). The lack of a holistic approach at the local government level can often result in the implementation of policies that yield inequitable outcomes for communities. Achieving equitable outcomes and sustainability requires local governments to engage in effective initiatives to assess the complexities associated with land, transportation, waste management, and housing. The complexities of addressing land use, transportation, waste management, and housing increase policymakers' susceptibility to information on suitable approaches for addressing the problems.

Local governments can introduce policies that promote system change in four phases (Scally et al., 2023). The first phase involves articulating the problem, identifying the root causes, and setting goals. During this phase, the community problem associated with the root cause of the issue is recognized. Evidence supporting the scope of the problem and an explanation of why past work initiatives were not effective are identified, underpinning the development of a call to action rationalizing the need for the local government to act. Articulating the problem involves the local government communicating the challenges. Identifying the root cause requires local government teams to determine why the issue exists. Setting goals involves local governments writing impact statements on the desired outcomes or reality that will be the product of the proposed policy and systems change (Scally et al., 2023).

The second phase consists of mapping the policy ecosystem, identifying policy solutions, and assessing feasibility and impact (Scally et al., 2023). The aim of the second phase is policy transference, which involves selecting the available option, based on the most feasible policy proposal, ensuring maximization of the desired impacts. Policy transfer offers an opportunity to apply the best practices at local government levels, promoting in capitalizing on the proven success of other jurisdictions. Good or best practice policies are characterized as clear, measurable, specific, and budgeted (Scally et al., 2023).

Phase two can be achieved by assessing the relevant data from promising models of other municipalities or cities, existing policy assessments that illustrate the impact of different options, responses from internal conversations with local officials, and external meetings with major organizations. During the phase, several workshops with various stakeholders who can offer essential insights related to the ecosystem's details to assist local government officials in determining the change momentum and identify potential barriers to policy adoption and implementation are conducted. Engaging policy experts from research organizations or universities can assist local governments identify potential solutions from other geographical areas (Scally et al., 2023).

Mapping a policy ecosystem involves teams identifying promising policy options that can be used to address the identified root causes (Scally et al., 2023). An ecosystem map is made up of stakeholders who are private, public, and nonprofit sector actors who control, support, influence, or oppose policy options. When mapping a policy ecosystem, it is essential to assess the impact of the policy options on equity. Additionally, understanding the general public's opinion and perception is essential. Identifying policy solutions requires the team to engage in dialogue with public officials, and staff within the local government (Scally et al., 2023). An internet search can be used to identify recent reports or articles by national, regional, or local organizations and professional associations for examples of suitable or promising policies. The team can also collaborate with a consultant or partner with a local university or research organization to perform a more in-depth and formal assessment of the academic and policy research containing the results, outcomes, and impact related to policy (Scally et al., 2023).

The assessment of the feasibility and impact of the identified policy options helps in determining the most applicable choice (Scally et al., 2023). Feasibility is determined through different options such as the budget, staff capacity for implementation, rationale, political dynamics, the impact of the market, partner organization capacity, federal spending, and public perceptions. An assessment of the feasibility and impact helps determine whether the policy will reach the intended populations and decrease the disparities. Also, it promotes determining if the scope is big enough to reach the intended population. Assessing whether the policy will result in equitable outcomes over time and achieve system change goals is core. An assessment of the feasibility of different policy solutions enables local governments in understanding any potential trade-offs between the available options. A feasibility assessment is essential because it can assist in determining how any substantial hindrances can be addressed, evaluating whether the issues can be resolved or mitigated (Scally et al., 2023).

The third phase is made up of developing a policy proposal and creating a change roadmap (Scally et al., 2023). The roadmap provides the team with the steps to take during policy change. The written policy proposal is a holistic action plan that outlines how the local government can enact the changes. Successful policy changes need to have a compelling rational outlining the urgency of the issues and practicality. The roadmap contains any strategies or tactics for overcoming any issue that might emerge. An effectively developed road map provides a range of actions that can be adopted to support policy adoption. A policy proposal should contain an explicit statement of the change, information on the persons responsible, and a rationale for why action is needed (Scally et al., 2023).

The fourth phase involves enacting policy and implementing and measuring success (Scally et al., 2023). The enactment of the policy mandates the city team to focus on implementing, budgeting, and establishing a regular policy and program for assessing the achievement of the outcomes. It is essential to determine the measures that will be an indicator of the outcomes. Tracking the outputs and outcomes of the process is indispensable because it offers insights into the manner the process results in systems and policy changes (Scally et al., 2023).

The focus of this chapter is discussing the good practice policies examples in America's local government and their ethical consideration. Specifically, the focus of the good practice policies is related to land use, transportation, waste management, and housing. First, the author began by introducing the concepts of focus to make the reader aware of good practices and policy transfer. Second, the author provided background information on land use, transportation, waste management, and housing policies in America's local governments. Third, a discussion on good practice examples in land use, transportation, waste management, and housing policies, together with their ethical considerations are provided.

Fourth, the researcher provided recommendations that policymakers can use to promote the adoption of relevant good practice policy examples in their contexts. Fifth, in future research works, the author explained the gaps relating to exploring the ethical considerations linked to good practices that should be addressed. The conclusion contains the major takeaways from the chapter.

The first strength of this book chapter is that the information included was based on credible and reliable sources such as peer-reviewed articles and publications by research organizations, federal and local governments, and consultancy firms. The evidence supports that there is current and credible literature on the topic. The second strength is that the good practices discussed are based on real-life case studies in the United States, which supports the relevance of the information provided. The third strength is that the chapter has been structured into clear headings to provide readers with a clear overview of information, making it easier to understand the core concepts discussed.

The first weakness of the chapter is that information was retrieved from secondary sources, which could be subject to publication bias. It is possible that only the positive aspects of the good practices were published, which could limit gaining a comprehensive overview of the outcomes. The second weakness is that the content in this book is based on the United States, which limits transferability. The political structure in the United States could differ from what is practiced in other countries, which might limit the application of the discussed good practices. The third weakness is that the author of this book does not claim to have provided an exhaustive discussion on land use, especially from an agricultural perspective. The focus on land use in this book is mainly related to transportation and housing. The author does not also claim that the provided good practice policies in this chapter are the only ones available or are superior to the other that have been implemented in different parts of the United States. The good practices included were selected based on their outcomes and the availability of credible and reliable information on their feasibility and sustainability.

Best practices are essential in all areas that require planning because they are indicators of effective approaches or standards that promote evidence-based policymaking (Blake et al., 2021). The good practices discussed related to land use include compact development and affordable and diverse housing. The ethical consideration associated with compact development is that if the strategy is applied in areas with low-income residents, an increase in property value could occur, displacing the original residents. An ethical consequence of by-right development is that it limits community input, which could cause the construction of projects that are incompatible with the neighborhood's surroundings, resulting in congestion, pollution, and strain on the available infrastructure.

The housing good practices identified include overlay zones, adaptive reuse, and form-based code. Overlay zones can result in the exclusion of the near-poor segment from housing. In the case of adaptive reuse, older buildings could contain hazardous materials that require expensive and disruptive remediation approaches. Free-based code can result in the displacement of existing residents, gentrification, and inequity.

The good practices for transportation discussed are complete streets and leveraging ride sharing. Complete street development and construction can adversely impact the environment. Leveraging ridesharing is that subsidized rides and bicycles could disproportionately benefit higher-income residents who can use the on-demand services. Leveraging ridesharing might not be accessible to individuals with disabilities who need specialized transportation, which causes disproportionality. Ridesharing is limited geographically, which can hinder access for some individuals. In addition, ride-sharing could increase traffic congestion if individuals shift from walking or cycling to ride-hailing.

Waste management good practices are mandatory recycling and compositing ordinances and youth educational programs. Mandatory recycling and compositing could result in an infringement of individual freedom. Notably, youth educational programs are an oversimplified solution to waste management.

The information provided in this chapter could be beneficial to researchers, students, and practitioners because the author provides explanations of the best practices that have been used in the implementation of policies. The relevance of the chapter to researchers is that the content could add to their knowledge base on public administration and local governance, providing a foundation for future scholarship. For students, the chapter offers real-world examples of effective policy implications, which could enhance their understanding and critical thinking relating to the complexities of local government and the essence of ethical considerations.

The benefit for the practitioners is that the information provided could inform policy transfer. The author is cognizant that the transferability of best practices can be influenced by factors such as cultural, demographic, and resource differences. When providing recommendations for policy transfer, the author rationalized the need to personalize the best practices in the adopter's context.

BACKGROUND OF LAND USE, TRANSPORTATION, WASTE MANAGEMENT, AND HOUSING POLICIES

Policies at the local government influence land use, transportation, waste management, and housing, which have an impact on lifestyles and the environment (Lowe et al., 2022). For instance, policies on planning, specifically those on land use, taxation and regulations on housing and car use have an impact on economic development. As such, it is indispensable for the policies that influence land use, transportation, waste management, and housing to be founded on the best practices. Policy ideas to address issues relating to land use, transportation, waste management, and housing can emerge from a range of sources. A prevalent problem of local government leaders and staff is determining whether the identified policy ideas can address or mitigate the prevailing causes of community problems. Accordingly, there is a need to holistically address the prevailing complex community problems. In the subsequent section, a background of policies related to land use, housing, transportation, and waste management is provided. An understanding of the historical evolution of land use, housing, transportation, and waste management policies is essential because it provides the reader with a contextual understanding of how the current challenges emerged. Historical knowledge also offers leaders an understanding of the limitations of the implemented policies, offering rationale for meaningful reforms.

Shaping the Landscape: A History of Land Use Policy

In the United States, land use is influenced by local, state, and national governments. The federal government in 1924 published the Standard State Zoning Enabling Act, which offered a framework for states to define local governments' power on zoning (United States Department of Commerce, 1924). The premise of zoning was to decrease congestion in the streets, enhance health and general welfare, offer adequate light and aid, decrease overcrowding, overcome undue population concentrations, and ensure adequate provision of public services such as water, transportation, sewage, parks, and schools (United States Department of Commerce, 1924). Over time, zoning rules have been modified to accommodate requirements related to promoting resilience to natural disasters and enhancing efficiency (Martin et al., 2020).

Local governments are also responsible for funding different public services such as crime prevention, transportation, schools, and water infrastructure (Schuetz, 2023). The construction of additional housing in a city or county results in a rise in the demand for public services. Initially, local zoning was used as a tool for limiting the pace, quantity, and size of development. In essence, local zoning was applied as an approach for constraining urban growth and density (Schuetz, 2023). An essential factor considered by the local government when regulating development is whether new houses would result in adequate revenue via impact fees or property taxes to offset the expenses of the public service provided to the new residents. Zoning regulations such as issuing apartment bans are done to limit development (Schuetz, 2023).

Often, zoning regulations are not based on best practices, but pressures from voters or community members who desire to limit the development of moderately priced housing as it would change the neighborhood and decrease property value. Older, wealthy White homeowners in communities tend to dominate meetings that are held to approve proposal developments, hindering what they deem as unwanted housing projects (Einstein et al., 2019). As a result, local government can adopt restrictive zoning initiatives hindering the number of new developments and allowing only expensive new houses, decisions that are solely founded on fiscal and political perspectives (Manville et al., 2020; Schuetz, 2023).

The restrictions can hinder the development of well-functioning markets, causing limited housing projects to be developed, which consequently creates a demand, exacerbating the cost (Bernstein et al., 2021). Increased zoning restrictions can be attributed to the prevalence of the housing affordability crisis, exacerbated wealth disparities, and rising economic and racial segregation (Manville et al., 2020). Restrictive land use initiatives limit the economic opportunity for low and moderate-income households. A consequence of restrictive zoning is that organizations in such regions have challenges attracting and retaining employees because the workers require high wages to afford housing (Airgood-Obrycki et al., 2024; Schuetz, 2023). The increased cost of housing in cities such as New York, Boston, and San Francisco limits workers from relocating to the areas as most affordable housing tends to be located on the urban periphery, away from public transportation and job centers (Schuetz, 2023). The consequences are longer commutes and traffic congestion (Crump et al., 2020). Additionally, restrictive zoning policies can lead to financial instability because individuals spend most of their income on rent (Airgood-Obrycki et al., 2024; Schuetz, 2023).

Land use planning involves authorities assessing the most appropriate utilization of land, based on economic, social, and environmental factors (Hivo, 2023). The land planning process involves assessing different interests to achieve holistic and sustainable development in a geographical area. The different factors considered during land use planning include population density, natural resource availability, and existing infrastructure. The careful consideration of the factors enables authorities to make informed decisions that will impact the future of the community.

Effective land use planning is essential because it offers a framework for influencing communities, protecting natural resources, and improving the quality of life. Land use planning should be performed strategically to overcome any conflicts that could undermine efficient development. Core components in land use planning are natural resource preservation and fostering social equity through affordable housing, accessible transportation, and availability of amenities for a diverse population (Hivo, 2023). Local governments have a core role in land use planning because the authorities are responsible for making decisions related to issues such as zoning regulations, development permits, and urban growth boundaries. The decisions made by local government officials have a direct and significant impact making it essential for the authorities to balance the residents' developers, businesses, and environmental organizations effectively (Hivo, 2023; Lark et al., 2017). Based on the synthesized literature, there is adequate evidence on the history of land use policies. Researchers have conducted research on how local factors influence land use policies (Airgood-Obrycki et al., 2024; Bernstein et al., 2021; Crump et al., 2020; Hivo, 2023; Lark et al., 2017; Schuetz, 2023). The literature supports providing an informed overview of the background on land use policies.

A Historical Overview of Housing Policies

Since the 1930s, America has been experimenting with housing policies (Karki, 2023). The policies focused on housing design, construction, and demolition and were developed by architects, congressmen, presidents, activists, and real estate professionals. Conversely, despite the collaborative initiatives, it has been challenging to achieve success in public housing. For instance, in the early 20th century, it was believed that enhancing the residential environment would promote the condition of the marginalized, an assumption adopted by Britain. As a result, the Freman Zeilenbau housing style was adopted, but in the early 1960s, it was abandoned without a specific good reason. There are examples of other housing design experiments such as Pruitt-Igoe public housing projects and Robert Tailor Homes that have been unsuccessful across the United States, partly because the users' needs were not considered (Karki, 2023).

In addition to experimenters, the issue in the United States' housing market can be attributed to economy maximizers, who perceived public housing as a strategy to revolutionize the construction industry, instead of addressing the issue of shelter among the marginalized (Karki, 2023). The 1929 to 1939 Great Depression resulted in the federal government being involved in public housing by supporting private constructors and industries dealing with building materials (Office of Policy Development and Research, 2020). The legislations introduced during the period included the Federal Home Loan Bank Act (1932), Homeowner Refining Act (1933), National Industrial Recovery Act (1933), National Housing Act (1934), and United States Housing Act (1937). The aim of the Federal Home Loan Bank Act was to make homeownership more affordable by advancing funds to house mortgage lenders who historically did not have access to the Federal Reserve System (Govinfo. n.d.a). The purpose of the Homeowner Refinancing Act, which is also known as the Homeowners' Loan Act was to offer emergency relief by providing homeowners or potential ones money or refinancing their mortgages (Fraser, 1933). The goal of the National Industrial Recovery Act was to assist the United States recover from the Great Depression, which indirectly affected housing by enabling the Public Works administration to fund the development of public housing projects to decrease shortages and stimulate the economy via large-scale construction projects (National Archives, 1933).

The focus of the National Housing Act was to make homeownership more accessible by improving construction and standards, promote home mortgages affordability, and support the construction and repair of homes to stimulate the economy (United States Department of Housing and Urban Development, n.d.). The United States Housing Act was intended to improve housing conditions, mitigate discrimination, and foster homeownership (Govinfo, n.d.b). After the Great Depression, the Housing Acts were enacted in 1949 and 1954. The United States Housing Act of 1949 expanded the federal government's role in mortgage insurance and housing construction. The Act was aimed at addressing the declining urban housing, improving standards, while decreasing housing costs, offering decent homes for low-income families, and eliminating slams (American Planning Association, 2014). The 1954 Act redefined urban liberalism, which included revitalizing aging cities and suburbs, offering assistance for the rehabilitation and conservation of blighted areas, mandating mortgage insurance for lower-cost housing and urban renewal areas, and requiring communities to create a plan to eliminate slams before being provided with federal funding (Flanagan, 1997).

In the United States, fair housing has been a challenge, an issue that has been attributed to local governments' reluctance to adopt policy changes recommended by federal and state government agencies (Monkkonen et al., 2024). In particular, the Affirmatively Furthering Fair Housing (AFFH) went unenforced for more than 40 years (Monkkonen et al., 2024). The Fair Housing Act was passed by Congress in 1968, prohibiting discrimination in the sale or rental of houses. The Act required all executive agencies to administer their housing and community development programs in manners that promote fairness. The goal was to ensure that the United States Department of Housing and Urban Development increased the supply of housing, ensuring it is accessible to all devoid of discrimination based on race, family status, disability, or any other protected attributes.

The New Federalism promoted by President Nixon, undermined Gorge Romney's (the then secretary of the Department of Housing and Urban Development) initiative to deny funding to wealthy municipalities that had exclusionary practices (Steil & Kelly, 2019). In 1974, the Housing Community Development Act consolidated different federal funding streams into the Community Development Block Grant (CDBG), which was aimed at offering decent housing and sustaining living environment and promoting economic opportunities, mainly for individuals of low and moderate incomes. Conversely, there was no reference to the Fair Housing Act. In 1983, 1988, and 1995, Congress amended the CDBG, specifying that the Department of Housing and Urban Development should only issue grants if the grantees purposed to promote fair housing. Despite the initiatives, it has been challenging to eliminate fair housing (Monkkonen et al., 2024; Steil & Kelly, 2019).

In 2015, the United States Department of Housing and Urban Development developed a final AFFH rule that required grantees such as local governments to assess fair housing issues and create meaningful approaches to address the problems (Monkkonen et al., 2024; Steil & Kelly, 2019). The AFFH rule has the potential to decrease disparities in neighborhoods by reducing exclusionary zoning restrictions and lack of affordable housing. Per the AFFH rule, the American Department of Urban Development offers grant recipients data on segregation and disparities in accessing housing opportunities.

In 2017, the 2015 AFFH rule was revised to indicate that grantees are required to conduct a standardized assessment of fair housing (Steil & Kelly, 2019). Other notable changes included requiring the Department of Housing to provide municipalities data on segregation and disparities related to housing, necessitating the creation of specific measurable goals and actions, and performing planning and assessment indispensable to determine future funding. Monkkonen et al. (2024) in their assessment, evaluated fair housing programs in eight municipalities. In the assessment, 200 fair housing programs were evaluated, out of which 17% were identified as having meaningfully advanced fair housing goals. Contrastingly, 36% were considered as somewhat meaningful, and 47% identified as not meaningful. The limited meaningfulness can be associated with most cities failing to modify their land-use plans to allow affordable housing in high-end neighborhoods. A mismatch in planning was identified because the affluent, majority-White cities that had the most meaningful fair housing programs focused on the construction of affordable housing in the last prestigious neighborhoods (Monkkonen et al., 2024).

The trial-and-error approach in United States public housing experimentation is a prevalent problem, which supports the need for best practices (Karki, 2023). In 2021, there were approximately 40 million American households were burdened by housing costs because they spent more than 30% of their income on their mortgages (Joint Center for Housing Studies, 2023). Out of the 40 million, approximately half were significantly burdened because they spent over 50% of their incomes on housing. Additionally, over half a million Americans experience homelessness on any given night (Joint Center for Housing Studies, 2023). The crisis in the United States can be attributed to the fact that most housing projects looked good physically, but failed socially, particularly because they did not address the needs of the underprivileged and underserved communities. The issue emerges when the people impacted by the problem are not consulted. Accordingly, there is a need for policies to be founded on good and best practices to promote achieving a suitable outcome. The next section contains a historical overview of the transportation policies in the United States.

The Evolution of Transportation Policy

Most transportation for a millennium has been by walking, water transportation, or animal (Deakin, 2021). Conversely, the transportation industry in the United States has because of the intersection of private interest and public good (Baker & Critchlow, 2020). The national and local governments had significant roles in the development of the different transportation modes, specifically roads, highways, canals, railroads, and airways. The American transportation policy can be categorized into three; the Whig era (1820s to 1880s), the second regime; regulation (1880s to 1970s), and the third regime; deregulation (1980s to present) (Baker & Critchlow, 2020).

The Whig era involved the first transportation revolution, which occurred because of a near disaster of the United States' victory over Great Britain in the 1812 war. The lack of roads to transport troops and supplies in the interior parts of the country created the need for new infrastructure. The construction of roads and canals occurred through a collaboration between state government and private investors. At the time there was a lack of federal regulation of canals, hence the process occurred through state support. The passing of the Pacific Railway Acts in 1862 and 1864 resulted in the construction of a transcontinental railroad across the West (Baker & Critchlow, 2020).

The second regime was characterized by regulations that dominated the American transportation industry (Baker & Critchlow, 2020). For instance, the Hepburn Act was enacted in 1906 to provide just reasonable rates for the railroads. The Valuation Act of 1914 mandated the Interstate Commerce Commission (ICC) to assess the railroads worth assisting in determining the rates. The signing of the Adamson Act in 1916 introduced an eight-hour workday, improving workers' work-life who used to report for long hours at low pay and dangerous conditions. The passage of the Esch-Cummins Act or the Transportation Act of 1920 decreased the federal government's control of railroads, increasing the ICC's ability to determine the minimum rates. The enactment of the National Highway Act promoted the construction of highways throughout the United States. Increased automobile ownership because of the mass production of vehicles promoted the demand for good roads movement (Baker & Critchlow, 2020).

Federal subsidies in the 1920s were introduced to support air travel and air mail (Baker & Critchlow, 2020). The Air Mail Act of 1925 was passed to encourage commercial aviation. Safety was an issue in aviation, which resulted in the signing of the Air Commerce Act, but the problem persisted. In 1935 another Air Mail Act was introduced, allowing private airlines into the industry. The Transportation Act of 1940 provided the ICC with continued authority over transportation. When the National Defense Highway Act was passed in 1956, the government invested $50 billion in the construction of interstate highways, which were often alongside railroad routes. The increased road networks and taxes created a crisis for railroads, and while the Transportation Act of 1958 was introduced to promote deregulation, less than 20% of all travel was conducted by rail. In efforts to resolve the crisis in railway transportation, the Regional Rail Reorganization Act was passed allowing the Federal Railroad Administration to loan the Easter and Midwestern railroads, but the initiatives could not mitigate the industry from bankruptcy. The Rail Reorganization and Regulatory Reform Act was enacted in 1976, but the high inflation and decreased carloads hindered the crisis in the rail industry (Baker & Critchlow, 2020).

The third regime was focused on the deregulation of transport in the United States (Baker & Critchlow, 2020). The signing of the Airline Deregulation Act in 1978 promoted decreasing prices, with the entry of airlines into the market, fostering competition. The 1980s Motor Carrier Act deregulated the trucking industry, resulting in price control being determined by major companies, which resulted in increased shipping costs. The Surface Highway Transportation Act was introduced in

1982, standardizing the minimum weight and height of tracks ferrying goods on the interstate highway. The Staggers Rial Service Act supported the deregulation of the railway industry, resulting in mergers and privatization, helping resolve the sector's crisis, which was also supported by the introduction of new technologies (Baker & Critchlow, 2020).

The Intermodal Surface Transportation Efficiency Act of 1991 offered a multi-modal approach to transportation funding and planning and provided frameworks for decreasing congestion, improving air quality, and performance monitoring of bridges and highways (Deakin, 2021). The act also provided metropolitan planning organizations with more power and responsibilities. Notably, by 2020, from a federal perspective, transportation policies had stalled for years. Then in 2021, the Bipartisan Infrastructure Bill was signed, allowing the investment of $550 billion in roads, rails, and electric vehicles (The White House, 2021).

Transport has a significant impact on a nation. For instance, city designs are influenced by the transport modes available. Transportation affects land use, but the separation of policies related to such core aspects has an adverse impact. For instance, the spread out between jobs and homes has increased commutes via personal vehicles because transit services are not at par with Americans' needs (The Transport Politic, 2019). In the subsequent section, a discussion on the evolution of waste policies is included.

The Changing Waste Policy

The evolution of waste management policies has been supported by the need to protect public health and promote a conducive environment (Ross & Law, 2023). Minimal sanitary regulations in the United States can be traced back to the 1600s (Jay, 2010). For example, Boston officials prohibited fish and garbage from being disposed of in common areas in 1634. The lack of waste management policies in the 1800s resulted in an outbreak of diseases such as cholera and yellow fever. As the 19th century ended, the need to have organized systems for waste management became apparent. In 1965, congress passed the Solid Waste Disposal Act, making it the first federal initiative for waste management (Govinfo, 2022). The aim of the Solid Waste Disposal Act was to help state and local governments figure out the technical and financial aspects of creating and managing waste disposal programs. The act provided a framework for guiding the collection transportation, recovery, and disposal of solid waste (Govinfo, 2022).

The Resource Conservation and Recovery Act was passed in 1976 to govern the disposal of solid and hazardous waste. The goal was to promote human health and the environment, conserve energy and natural resources, decrease waste, and ensure effective management (United States Environmental Protection Agency, 2024a). In

1984, Congress amended the Resource Conservation and Recovery Act through the enactment of the Hazardous and Solid Waste Amendments to encourage waste minimization and phase out the disposal of hazardous waste on land (United States Environmental Protection Agency, 2024b). In the following sections, the focus is on good practice examples for land use, housing, transportation, and land use waste management

GOOD PRACTICE EXAMPLES IN LAND USE AND ETHICAL CONSIDERATIONS

The development of good practices is important in assisting communities in creating more opportunities for attainable and affordable housing by implementing sustainable growth and development patterns. The identified good practices are related to compact development, affordable and diverse housing, and growth management. In the subsequent sections, I have provided good practice examples related to land use and housing implemented by different local governments.

Compact Development: A Land Use Good Practice

Compact development fosters sustainable growth by applying existing utility and transportation infrastructure to concentrate development in smaller and more accessible areas. In a compact development set-up, there is usually a blend of multiple-use development in one area, serving the purposes of residential, commercial, retail, employment, and entertainment. The development strategy assists in directing growth in areas closer to services and jobs. The benefits of compact development include helping revitalize communities, improve amenities, and increase housing options. Additionally, compact development protects exurban areas such as agricultural land, wilderness, and open spaces (Bibri et al., 2020). Compact development has been supported to encourage people to drive less and walk more, which decreases transport-related greenhouse gas emissions (Jama et al., 2024). An additional advantage is that compact development promotes better connectedness because residential and commercial areas are not separated from each other, with places where individuals live, shop, and work being easily accessible (Jama et al., 2024).

Portland has focused on concentrating its population increase within a compact urban area to avoid any sprawl that could have led to a significant loss of agricultural land and greenspaces (The Housing Agency, 2024). Portland's focus is to grow up, instead of outwards, which is in alignment with compact development. The state's compact development is consistent with the Urban Growth Boundary introduced in the 1970s, which controls urban expansion onto forests and farmlands. The boundary aims to manage urban sprawl and not to stop the process. Consequently, its boundaries are adjusted when and where necessary based on the statewide planning goals (The Housing Agency, 2024).

In addition to protecting agriculture and farmland, the compact development in Portland is performed to promote economic prosperity, enhance human wellness, improve environmental health, and enhance equity (Portland.Gov, 2018; The Housing Agency, 2024). According to Portland's comprehensive plan, achieving compact urban growth to achieve economic prosperity includes investing in industrial brownfields and increasing business areas in urban environments to employ within the city to the increasing population (Portland.Gov, 2018). The success of Portland's compact development is evidenced by having 2.8% of people commuting to work via bicycle (Griggs, 2024).

Pearl District, which is in the northwest of Portland's downtown core is a perfect example of compact development (The Housing Agency, 2024). In the early 1980s, the area surrounding NW 13th Avenue next to downtown Portland was mainly an abandoned brownfield site. Conversely, after applying compact development, Pearl District has become among the most sought-after neighborhoods in Portland. Pearl District is zoned as mixed-use, containing apartment blocks, coffee shops, grocery stores, loft conversions, office buildings, and recreational spaces. The district is a case study of the role of planning and coordination in effectively achieving compact growth. The core design features of Pearl District include access to green spaces, convenient public transit, connectivity through the neighborhood, small block sizes, and areas designated as mixed-used zones (The Housing Agency, 2024).

Another example of compact development containing higher density mixed-use development is one that was implemented in Mile High Greyhound Park at Commerce City Colorado (Colorado Department of Local Affairs, 2024a). Mile High Greyhound Park, a previous 65-acre racetrack and entertainment site was transformed into a diverse mixed-use community hub, containing a variety of residential housing options. The mixture of residential uses was to accommodate the increased population densities in the area (Colorado Department of Local Affairs, 2024a).

Ethical Considerations

Compact development is a moral and responsible strategy that requires effectively planning and executing urban development projects by local authorities. The initiative ensures that development benefits all community members without resulting in any undue harm to the environment or displacing individuals through unethical practices. As such, effectively implemented compact development ensures that all residents can access the required services, amenities, and infrastructure (Portland.Gov, 2018). Contrastingly, in cases where compact development is not performed effectively, it could result in gentrification and displacement. Gentrification and displacement occur when local authorities do not prioritize equity and transparency. Accordingly, there is a need for accountability in the planning and implementation of compact development. When compact development is performed in areas that have low-income residents, it could increase property value, forcing the original residents out because of higher rents and housing costs.

An environmental impact is that compact development could increase temperature because of urban densification (Iizuka et al., 2020). For this reason, local governments need to consider the sustainability of compact development, to prevent increasing temperature. Responsible compact development needs a balance in environmental stewardship, density, and social justice to prevent the creation of new types of inequities.

Affordable and Diverse Housing

Affordable housing is essential in society because it influences economic mobility (Chakraborty & McMillan, 2022). Accordingly, implementing a best practice such as "by-right" affordable housing, where developments are approved through a staff-level administrative process, rather than a discretionary approval approach can improve housing affordability. The best practice could assist in decreasing the expenses, time, and barriers associated with house development (Barrall & Monkkonen, 2024). "By-right" development allows affordable housing the be approved in the relevant zone districts, mitigating the need for more hearings.

An example of the application of "by right" affordable housing best practice is the Greeley, Colorado 2021 development code. The practice provides more housing options for different income levels throughout the community. The "by right" development allowed different residential product types throughout the community to gain new and infill opportunities. The update in the local code assisted the city in promoting missing middle housing opportunities throughout existing and emerging neighborhoods.

A second example of a best practice for promoting affordable and diverse housing is the Southeast Colorado Economic Development District (SECED). The project in Southeast Colorado involved the SECED and local governments partnering to create a subsidiary and incentive program to underpin the development of new housing units (Colorado Department of Local Affairs, 2024b). The partnership enabled leveraging local resources, resulting in incentivized housing developments, which was achieved through grants, donations of publicly owned land, and regional coordination. The communities provided publicly owned land where the houses were developed. Subsequently, the SECD partnered with the communities to develop horizontal infrastructure using grants and available resources (Colorado Department of Local Affairs, 2024b).

Ethical Considerations

An ethical issue that could emerge is that by-right development could result in minimal community input, because of the lack of local authorities considering the concepts of collective good and democratic participation. The lack of meaningful engagement can cause the construction of projects that are incompatible with the surrounding neighborhood, which could adversely affect the residents, infringing the principle of community well-being. Unrestricted development could cause overcrowding, congestion, pollution, and strain on existing infrastructure, creating dilemmas between sustainability and resource management. Accordingly, local authorities need to practice responsible stewardship to ensure that balance between development rights and community needs are achieved. The ethical consideration that could emerge from affordable housing subsidies and initiatives is the dilemma of determining how limited resources should be allocated among the eligible applicants, an indicator of the lack of equitable resource distribution by local authorities. There exists a dilemma in determining whether priority should be given to the elderly, families with children, individuals with disabilities, or people experiencing homelessness. The dilemma emerges when there lacks transparent and just processes in local government related to social justice prioritization and minimizing the potential for discriminatory decisions, ensuring all individuals are treated with dignity.

GOOD PRACTICE EXAMPLES IN HOUSING AND ETHICAL CONSIDERATIONS

Despite the prevailing housing crisis in the United States, some local governments have adopted effective approaches that have facilitated decreasing the disparities (Joint Center for Housing Studies, 2023). The identified best practices include affordable housing overlay zones, form-based code, and adaptive reuse. A discussion of the best practices and their associated ethical considerations are discussed in the subsequent section.

Good Practice One: Overlay Zones

The first best practice is the use of overlay zones, which are often applied to protect historical buildings, waterfronts, wetlands, and steep slopes. Additionally, overlay zones can be used to support specific development projects such as affordable housing. In the case of Oakley and Salt Lake City, an overlay zone was introduced to promote affordable housing (Salt Lake City, 2020; Terner Center, 2019).

The affordable housing overlay in Oakley, California was introduced in 2005 when the city up-zoned 16 acres from commercial and light industry uses to "by-right" multifamily development (Terner Center, 2019). As a result, seven affordable housing developments, totaling 509 units in low-income families have been established. The use of overlay zones encourages the development of affordable housing by offering developers incentive packages such as fee waivers, decreased parking ratios, and enhanced density bonuses. Affordable housing overlay zones require that 25% and 100% of units in a development be affordable for households earning 50% to 80% of the area median income (Terner Center, 2019).

Oakley's is a successful affordable housing overlay program because it increased the number of multifamily units, achieving the city's regional housing needs allocation for low and very-low-income categories (Terner Center, 2019). In 2006, the Corporation for Better Housing (CBH) bought 16.3 acres and developed multi-purpose, 100% affordable houses. In 2000, Oakly had 7,946 housing units (7,363 single-family units; 164 multifamily units), which in 2008 changed to 10,748 (10,228 single-family units; 134 multifamily units). Later in 2016, all housing units increased by 14% from 2008 to 12,294 (11,412 single-family units; 506 multifamily units) (Terner Center, 2019).

A second example is Salt Lake City's Affordable Housing Overlay. According to the American Planning Association (2007), an overlay is a zoning district that is applied over one or more predetermined areas to establish additional or stricter criteria and standards on the affected properties. While the project is not yet completed, the goal is to offer affordable housing and enhance the residential district in the city. The overlay zone will contain three core elements, (a) modification of density limits, (b) change of lot requirements, and (c) accommodation of adaptive reuse. The core elements are focused on encouraging the production of affordable housing, instead of making it a requirement. The proposed modification is permitting additional height, decreasing development standards without compromising quality, allowing more housing types, and offering process waivers. The overlay aims to offer developers more choices by providing additional benefits to projects that promote the supply of affordable houses (Salt Lake City, 2020).

The suitability of overlay zones is the best practice that encourages the development of affordable houses without additional costs to developers and governments. The affordable housing overlays create value by eliminating the lengthy entitlement processes, such as the need to amend the general plan. Accordingly, affordable housing overlays can impact a city's comprehensive housing affordability strategy by targeting specific areas for better development.

Ethical Considerations

Although restricting each project to provide affordable rents or sale prices would reduce the cost of shelter, it would still exclude householders earning between 80% and 120% area's median income, resulting in ethical concerns related to equitable access and social inclusion. The exclusion of the near-poor segment of the population could reinforce existing social divisions. It is essential to consider how the 50% to 80% area median income provision can be adjusted over time to prevent the occurrence of housing insecurity. Local authorities' lack of flexible and adaptable frameworks the prioritize citizens' needs can adversely impact long-term resilience and social justice.

Good Practice Two: Adaptive Reuse

The second-best practice is the use of adaptive reuse, which involves converting existing buildings that have functional and/or economic obsolescence into viable residents. An example of adaptive reuse is a medical office building for the University of the Pacific's Arthur A. Dugoni School of Dentistry (Terner Center, 2021). The building constructed in 1967 was redeveloped into a market-rate condominium tower in 2017. The developed building contains two parts. The first part is the main building that went through adaptive reuse. The second part was a set of 10 condominium townhouses that were converted into a spaces surface parking lot. The building was converted into 230,000 square feet, containing nine levels, hosting 66 residential condo units that contain two basement levels accommodating 98 parking spaces. Adaptive reuse projects can result in expedited building approvals, especially in areas where new development is significantly regulated (Terner Center, 2021). However, in The Pacific's case, the building was considered non-historic, which allowed the design and development team to completely strip the building and replace the interiors. The case study is an example of how adaptive reuse has the potential to offer quality, infill residential units, especially in places without vacant sites for new housing developments (Terner Center, 2021).

Another example of adaptive reuse is the construction of Mill Street Square, which began in 2021 (Office of Policy Development and Research, 2024). The former Argus Mill dating back to the 1870s had been listed in the National Register of Historic Places since 1986, but the building had been vacant for years. The site also contained two historical structures (the Thompson and Ryle Houses) and a large surface parking lot that was owned by the Peterson Parking Authority. In the adaptive reuse, the mill building, parking lot, and the two houses were incorporated to function as a cohesive project. The result of the development was a new four-story 68-unit apartment building that was developed in the Argus Mill parking area. The mill building was converted into six two-bedroom apartments, while the two houses were made into office spaces for local nonprofits. Mill Street Square was opened in 2023, offering 74 affordable apartments. Ten two-bedrooms and 12 one-bedrooms were restricted to households earning no more than 80% of the area median income. The other 52 units were for households earning no more than 50% of the area median income, targeting grandparents raising grandchildren. As of May 2024, the occupancy rate was at 90%, offering multigenerational families affordable housing (Office of Policy Development and Research, 2024).

Ethical Considerations

Environmental impact is a core consideration in adaptive reuse projects. Older buildings can contain hazardous materials such as asbestos and lead, which could need expensive, and possibly disruptive remediation approaches. There is a need to ensure a comprehensive assessment is conducted to ensure that an adaptive reuse initiative is feasible and sustainable.

Good Practice Three: Form-Based Code

Officials in South Salt Lake developed two form-based codes (Wood et al., 2020). The first code was focused on transit-oriented development that was to be done along the S-line streetcar between 500 East and State Street. The second was focused on State Street I-15, I-80, and 2,100 South. In the city between 2012 and 2015, more than 600 new dwellings along the Streetcar Corridor were approved for construction. In 2016 and 2017, two projects that contained 195 units, the majority of which were allocated for affordable housing, were approved. Later in 2019, a mixed-use project incorporating 150,000 square feet of housing and office units in a 10-story multifamily structure was approved. Accordingly, form-based codes promoted a significant redevelopment of the streetcar corridor and industrial area in South Salt Lake, promoting affordable housing (Wood et al., 2020).

Ethical Considerations

A possible ethical issue is the occurrence of unintended consequences such as gentrification, displacing existing residents, and inequity in accessing housing of not effectively implemented. Gentrification, displacing existing residents, and inequity hinder the creation of inclusive communities. If form-based codes are designed without considering affordability, it can result in redevelopment projects for higher-income residents, causing a displacement of existing communities in the neighborhood (Talen, 2021). Ineffectively designed, form-based codes can result in unintendedly barriers, hindering entry for certain housing types, and exacerbating the problem of housing segregation. The ethical issue emerges because of irresponsible planning, which hinders local government authorities from anticipating the unintended consequences.

GOOD PRACTICE EXAMPLES IN TRANSPORTATION AND ETHICAL CONSIDERATIONS

At the local level, mobility and accessibility are essential because it links people to employment, goods, and services. In this section, three best practices related to transport are provided. The best practices identified are related to complete streets and leveraging ridesharing.

Complete Streets

The City of Carson developed the Carson Area Metropolitan Planning Organization (CAMPO) to create complete streets within the downtown corridor (United States Department of Transportation, 2023). Carson enacted the complete streets policy, which was funded by the one-eight percent sales tax increase. The funds, in addition to two federal grants of $7.5 million and $9.3 million, respectively allowed the city to develop complete streets. The first project was the Carson Street Downtown Corridor, where an overbuilt and retired state highway was renovated with new travel lane configurations, for pedestrians and cyclists. The other project was Curry Street, which involved replacing aging water, storm drain, and sewer drain infrastructure; landscaping, street furnishings, and installation of energy-efficient streetlights. In 2020, the city began the South Carson Complete Streets project that included a road diet that decreased travel lanes, offered dedicated bicycle facilities, a shared-use path for cyclists and pedestrians, a multi-lane roundabout, upgraded utilities, improved business access, and aesthetic improvements.

Ethical Considerations

Complete streets have been supported to promote rights among citizens by ensuring that there is safe pedestrianism, walkable streets, and cycling lanes (Appleyard & Riggs, 2021; Wendler, 2024). Complete streets need to be designed with the needs of individuals living with disabilities in mind, to promote equity for those with auditory, visual, and mobility impairments. Although the development of complete streets can be dependent; their construction and maintenance could have an adverse environmental impact.

Leveraging Ridesharing

In Monrovia, California, the city in March 2018 launched the GoMonrovia program in partnership with Lyft and LimeBike to subsidize on-demand ride-hailing and bike-sharing services (National Transit Institute, 2019). The program offers residents access to Lyft rides to anywhere covered by the GoMonrovia service at $0.50. Through the program, residents can access over 200 LimeBikes for $1.00 per 30-minute use. Based on an evaluation, it was identified that the program costs approximately $1 million annually and facilitates more than 30,000 rides annually. Over 2,700 people have signed up for the LimeBike.

Ethical Considerations

The first possible ethical consideration related to leveraging ridesharing is that the significantly subsidized rides and bicycles could result in disproportionality benefiting higher-income residents who can afford smartphones and the ability to use on-demand services. The second ethical consideration is that the services might not be accessible to individuals with disabilities, who require specialized transportation options. The third ethical consideration is that the program's efficacy could vary based on the residents' location because it only covers specific areas of Monrovia. Fourth, that although the program could decrease car use, it could potentially increase traffic congestion if there is a significant shift of residents from walking or cycling to ride-hailing.

GOOD PRACTICE EXAMPLES IN WASTE MANAGEMENT AND ETHICAL CONSIDERATIONS

Local governments have a core role in waste management because they create and enforce related regulations. Good or best practices are essential to ensure that the implemented policies are feasible. The identified best practices include the mandatory recycling and composting ordinance and youth educational program.

Mandatory Recycling and Composting Ordinance

San Francisco has a mandatory recycling and compositing ordinance, which was enacted in 2009 requiring everyone in the city to have recyclables, compostables, and trash separated (San Francisco Environment Department, 2009). Recyclables such as cans, papers, and bottles are placed in blue bins. Compostables such as yard waste and food scraps are placed in green bins. Trash such as non-recyclable plastics and food-soiled paper is placed in black bins. The aim is to decrease the amount of waste that is sent to landfills. The benefits experienced include decreased greenhouse gas emissions, natural resources conservation, and environmental protection. The ordinance has supported San Francisco in achieving a 15% decrease in solid waste generation and a 50% reduction in disposal to incineration or landfills (San Francisco Environment Department, 2009).

Ethical Considerations

The mandatory recycling and composting ordinance results in some ethical considerations. The identified ethical consideration is that it can be argued that making recycling mandatory can infringe on individual freedom and people's right to dispose of property as they deem fit. As such, it is essential to determine whether infringing individual liberty supersedes promoting the collective good of environmental protection and resource conservation.

Youth Educational Program

In Portland, a comprehensive youth education program was introduced to provide free-of-charge education (Metro, n.d.). The program targets schools and young adult groups, to ensure the population becomes environmentally conscious citizens. In the comprehensive curriculum, the concepts covered include recycling, composting, climate change, and sustainability principles. The interactive program involves participants engaging in hands on activities, watching videos and presentations, and listening to experts from the recycling and waste management industry. The long-term goal is to make recycling a sustainable habit in families and communities, inspire young people to pursue careers in environmental-related fields and create a zero-waste culture.

Ethical Considerations

It is irrefutable that recycling and environmental issues are complex. The ethical consideration that could emerge because of the program is the oversimplification of the issues, which could result in a superficial understanding. The limited understanding could hinder meaningful engagement. The education program needs to focus on improving critical thinking among the population.

RECOMMENDATIONS

Most of the elected officials and government staff lack adequate training or background in policy and systems change. For this reason, policy transfer is essential because it can help local governments achieve change outcomes. Through policy transfer, local government officials can understand the suitable changes that can be implemented to address existing issues. Policy transfer ensures that policymaking has an evidence-based foundation. An evidence-based approach is essential because it assesses the root causes instead of simply addressing the perceived issues. Accordingly, the recommendation for policymakers is to always start with understanding the problem to identify the solution, instead of beginning with a proposed policy solution that could not impact the root cause.

Policymaking requires working in teams to create trust and connection, strengthening the government's capacity to identify the issue and implement a solution. Collaboration with internal and external partners ensures that the policy change is feasible and increases public support. The involvement of internal and external partners can result in better implementation and outcomes.

Monitoring land use is essential because it informs policies related to factors such as the environment. Local governments should aim to have compact, connected, and sustainable cities. Compact development is associated with numerous advantages such as reduced traffic congestion, which supports the need for local governments to take advantage of the best practice. Collaboration and partnership between developers and city officials are essential in creating an environment that allows the development of a vibrant neighborhood.

Another recommendation is the adoption of "by-right" development, which promotes housing affordability by decreasing the cost of development via a faster and more predictable approval procedure and increasing housing supply. The local government needs to ensure that "by-right" development is founded on a rule-based approval procedure to increase predictability, which could reduce the cost of obtaining development approvals. Effective "by-right" development is those that occur on a larger scale to achieve affordability. By-right development promotes affordability by increasing the supply of housing to fulfill the demand. Cities should not limit "By-right" multifamily development to a small area, because it hinders the policy's impact in addressing affordability challenges.

The mismatch between housing needs and products in the United States can partly be attributed to a lack of empathy among the decision-makers (Karki, 2023). A recommendation is for housing decision-makers to consider the needs of the intended users and engage them in dialogue, to promote the development of tailored solutions. Through cognitive empathy, decision-makers can understand others' perspectives, by being reasonable, analyzing, and applying critical thinking to understand others' behavior and circumstances. An application of emotional empathy can empale decision-makers perceive the affected individuals' fear, happiness, worries, and anger toward the situation.

Overlay zones should be introduced because they offer a flexible approach to increasing the supply of affordable housing. The zones offer flexibility because they can be modified to be site-specific and cover a larger area, ensuring development in targeted areas, consistent with local policy goals. Local governments could use adaptive reuse because the best practice offers an opportunity to supply new housing at a lower price within a shorter development timeline. Adaptive reuse can assist and facilitate the development of large, multifamily projects in areas where a similar new construction would have been challenging (Aydemir & Akın, 2024; Glumac & Islam, 2020; Terner Center, 2021).

Local jurisdictions should have zoning and planning ordinances that anticipate and promote adaptive reuse. The ordinances can include allowing "by-right" use changes discretionary or environmental approvals and not requiring the provision of net new parking, Notably, it is essential to be cognizant that architectural considerations, political and legislative constraints, and problems relating to economic feasibility should be considered.

The adoption of form-based codes can encourage revitalization and housing because the practice helps overcome the limitations imposed by zoning regulations. Local officials can collaborate with on-demand cab service providers to create a program that promotes ridesharing. Local governments can introduce youth educational awareness programs on waste management, which can promote creating a culture of sustainability and resource conservation. Overall, there is a need for collaboration between land use, housing, transportation, and waste-management policy makers. The policies should be thought of holistically, as opposed to individually, which can ensure better outcomes. The policies are intrinsically linked, which supports the need for policymakers to think about how one impacts the other to eliminate the occurrence of inequitable outcomes.

FUTURE RESEARCH WORKS

Additional research is needed on the ethical considerations of the identified best practices. There is a lack of adequate focus on the ethical aspects of the best practices, which limits a comprehensive understanding. Accordingly, future researchers need to explore more on the ethical aspects of policies, by interviewing decision-makers and citizens affected to understand the potential unintentional outcomes that could emerge because of the good practices implemented. Future researchers can conduct primary quantitative studies showing the impact of the identified best practices.

Longitudinal qualitative studies can be conducted over an extended period such as 10 years, to help understand the longevity of the intervention. The possibilities for future research are extensive, especially with the numerous good practices that continue to be implemented, and the population needs change.

CONCLUSION

The author provides a discussion of the good practice policies examples in America's local governments and their ethical considerations. The importance of good practices in land use, housing, transportation, and waste management cannot be understated. In land-use compact development promotes sustainable development, protects exurban areas, encourages people to drive less, and fosters connectedness. Conversely, it is essential to consider the possibility of outcomes such as gentrification and displacement. Affordable and diverse housing is a land-use good practice that promotes access to shelter, decreasing homelessness. It is important to promote input from different stakeholders in adorable and diverse housing construction projects, to mitigate overcrowding, pollution, and strain on existing infrastructure. Overlay zones can foster the development of affordable housing, but it is essential to ensure that the rents and sale prices do not reinforce prevailing social divisions. Adaptive reuse can increase the availability of affordable housing within a short period when compared to beginning construction from the ground up. However, it is essential to ensure that the buildings adapted for reuse are free from asbestos and lead. Form-based code can also promote affordable housing, but issues of gentrification inequality, and displacing existing residents should be addressed to prevent their occurrence. In transportation compact streets and leveraging ridesharing are good practices that can result in better outcomes. Better waste management can be achieved through mandatory recycling and composting, but the balance between individual freedom and collective good should be balanced to achieve better outcomes. Youth educational programs can promote in creation of environmentally conscious citizens, which can promote outcomes. Overall, land use, housing, transportation, and waste management are correlated concepts, which supports the need for policymakers to have a comprehensive understanding of how the four are correlated to ensure sustainability.

REFERENCES

American Planning Association. (2007). *Property topics and concepts.* APA. https://www.planning.org/divisions/planningandlaw/propertytopics.htm

American Planning Association. (2014). *Housing Act of 1949.* https://www.planning.org/awards/2014/1949housingact.htm

Appleyard, B., & Riggs, W. (2021). Human rights to the street: Ethical frameworks to guide planning, design, and engineering decisions toward livability, equity, and justice. *Journal of Transport and Land Use, 14*(1), 911–931. DOI: 10.5198/jtlu.2021.1918

Aydemir, A. Z., & Akın, T. (2024). Adaptive reuse of high-rise buildings for housing: A study of Istanbul Central Business District. *Urban Planning, 9*(2), 1–10. DOI: 10.17645/up.7698

Baker, P., & Critchlow, D. T. (2020). *The Oxford American political history.* Oxford University Press., DOI: 10.1093/oxfordhb/9780199341788.001.0001

Barrall, A., & Monkkonen, P. (2024). *The fair housing land use score in California: An evaluation of 199 municipal plans.* eScholarship. https://escholarship.org/uc/item/6fn5g105

Bibri, S. E., Krogstie, J., & Kärrholm, M. (2020). Compact city planning and development: Emerging practices and strategies for achieving the goals of sustainability. *Developments in the Built Environment, 4*, 100021. Advance online publication. DOI: 10.1016/j.dibe.2020.100021

Blake, O., Glaser, M., Bertolini, L., & te Brömmelstroet, M. (2021). How policies become best practices: A case study of best practice making in an EU knowledge sharing project. *European Planning Studies, 29*(7), 1251–1271. DOI: 10.1080/09654313.2020.1840523

Chakraborty, A., & McMillan, A. (2022). Is housing diversity good for community stability? Evidence from the housing crisis. *Journal of Planning Education and Research, 42*(2), 150–161. DOI: 10.1177/0739456X18810787

Colorado Department of Local Affairs. (2024a). *Compact development - case briefings.* DOLA. https://dlg.colorado.gov/compact-development-case-briefings

Colorado Department of Local Affairs. (2024b). *Affordable housing - case briefings.* DOLA. https://dlg.colorado.gov/affordable-housing-case-briefings

Deakin, E. (2021). *A brief history of transportation policies and institutions*. University of California. https://escholarship.org/content/qt2fs5w7jp/qt2fs5w7jp_noSplash_3b11338828fdc45c6b624dfd3da0110e.pdf?t=r7iai1

Flanagan, R. M. (1997). The Housing Act of 1954: The sea change in national urban policy. *Urban Affairs Review, 33*(2), 265–286. DOI: 10.1177/107808749703300207

Fraser. (1933). *Repeal of direct loan provision of Federal Home Loan Bank Act.* https://fraser.stlouisfed.org/files/docs/historical/congressional/hola1933_congress.pdf

Glumac, B., & Islam, N. (2020). Housing preferences for adaptive re-use of office and industrial buildings: Demand side. *Sustainable Cities and Society*, *62*, 102379. Advance online publication. DOI: 10.1016/j.scs.2020.102379

Govinfo. (2022). *[Public Law 89–272; Approved October 20, 1965] [As Amended Through P.L. 117–58, Enacted November 15, 2021]*. https://www.govinfo.gov/content/pkg/COMPS-893/pdf/COMPS-893.pdf

Govinfo. (n.d.a). *Chapter 11—Federal Home Loan Banks*. https://www.govinfo.gov/content/pkg/USCODE-2020-title12/html/USCODE-2020-title12-chap11.htm

Govinfo. (n.d.b). *United States Housing Act of 1937*. https://www.govinfo.gov/content/pkg/COMPS-10348/pdf/COMPS-10348.pdf

Griggs, T. (2024). *At long last, Portland's bike ridership is on the mend. What Now?* Portland Mercury. https://www.portlandmercury.com/news/2024/02/15/47036503/at-long-last-portlands-bike-ridership-is-on-the-mend-what-now

Hivo. (2023). *Exploring local government land use planning*. https://hivo.co/blog/exploring-local-government-land-use-planning

Iizuka, S., Xuan, Y., Takatori, C., Nakaura, H., & Hashizume, A. (2020). Environmental impact assessment of introducing compact city models by downscaling simulations. *Sustainable Cities and Society*, *63*, 102424. Advance online publication. DOI: 10.1016/j.scs.2020.102424

Jama, T., Tenkanen, H., Lönnqvist, H., & Joutsiniemi, A. (2024). Compact city and urban planning: Correlation between density and local amenities. *Environment and Planning. B, Urban Analytics and City Science*, *52*(1), 1–10. DOI: 10.1177/23998083241250264

Jay, N. (2010). *History of United States waste management.* https://www.researchgate.net/publication/258698791_History_of_United_States_Waste_Management Joint Center for Housing Studies. (2023). *The state of the nation's housing 2023.* https://www.jchs.harvard.edu/sites/default/files/reports/files/Harvard_JCHS_The_State_of_the_Nations_Housing_2023.pdf

Karki, T. (2023). Why public housing has been less successful in American history? https://papers.ssrn.com/sol3/Delivery.cfm/SSRN_ID4356830_code4921372.pdf?abstractid=4352289&mirid=1

Lark, T. J., Mueller, R. M., Johnson, D. M., & Gibbs, H. K. (2017). Measuring land-use and land-cover change using the US Department of Agriculture's cropland data layer: Cautions and recommendations. *International Journal of Applied Earth Observation and Geoinformation*, *62*, 224–235. DOI: 10.1016/j.jag.2017.06.007

Lowe, M., Adlakha, D., Sallis, J. F., Salvo, D., Cerin, E., Moudon, A. V., Higgs, C., Hinckson, E., Arundel, J., Boeing, G., Liu, S., Mansour, P., Gebel, K., Puig-Ribera, A., Mishar, P. B., Bozovic, T., Carson, J., Dygryan, J., Florindo, A. A., & Giles-Corti, B. (2022). City planning policies to support health and sustainability: An international comparison of policy indicators for 25 cities. *The Lancet. Global Health*, *10*(6), e882–e894. https://www.thelancet.com/pdfs/journals/langlo/PIIS2214-109X(22)00069-9.pdf. DOI: 10.1016/S2214-109X(22)00069-9 PMID: 35561723

Manville, M., Monkkonen, P., & Lens, M. (2020). It's time to end single-family zoning. *Journal of the American Planning Association*, *86*(1), 106–112. DOI: 10.1080/01944363.2019.1651216

Martin, C., McTarnaghan, S., & Williams, J. L. (2020). *Articulating a program for resilience*. Urban Institute. https://www.urban.org/sites/default/files/publication/102401/articulating-a-program-for-resilience.pdf

Metro. (n.d.). *Resource conservation and recycling education*. OregonMetro. https://www.oregonmetro.gov/tools-partners/education-resources/resource-conservation-and-recycling-education

Monkkonen, P., Barrall, A., & Echavarria, A. (2024). Meaningful action: Evaluating local government plans to affirmatively further fair housing in California. *Housing Policy Debate*, *1*(1), 1–25. DOI: 10.1080/10511482.2024.2337033

National Archives. (1933). *National Industrial Recovery Act (1933)*.https://www.archives.gov/milestone-documents/national-industrial-recovery-act

National Transit Institute. (2019). *Case study. City of Monrovia: Leveraging emerging ride-sharing services to expand mobility options.* Advancing Mobility Management. https://www.apta.com/wp-content/uploads/Resources/resources/mobility/Documents/GoMonrovia%20Case%20Study.pdf

Office of Policy Development and Research. (2020). *HUD's historical timeline.* https://www.huduser.gov/portal/hudtimeline_1930.html

Office of Policy Development and Research. (2024). *Adaptive reuse creates affordable housing for grandparents and grandchildren.* HUDUSER. https://www.huduser.gov/portal/pdredge/pdr-edge-inpractice-073024.html

Portland.Gov. (2018). *2035 Comprehensive Plan and supporting documents.* https://www.portland.gov/bps/planning/comp-plan-2035/about-comprehensive-plan/2035-comprehensive-plan-and-supporting#toc-2035-comprehensive-plan-as-amended-through-may-2023-

Ross, D. E., & Law, H. J. (2023). Evolution of municipal solid waste management in North America. *Waste Management & Research, 41*(7), 1177–1187. DOI: 10.1177/0734242X231173308 PMID: 37246621

Salt Lake City. (2020). *Affordable housing overlay.* SLC. hhttps://storymaps.arcgis.com/collections/026ff1b6235a436d85bcf87712ad5d19?item=1

San Francisco Environment Department. (2009). *The city's mandatory recycling and composting ordinance.* https://www.sfenvironment.org/sites/default/files/policy/sfe_zw_sf_mandatory_recycling_composting_ord_100-09.pdf

Scally, C. P., Schilling, J., Fedorowicz, M., Heinrichs, A., Aceves, L., & Pegna, S. W. (2023). *Developing a policy and systems change compass for local government.* https://www.urban.org/sites/default/files/2023-10/Developing%20a%20Policy%20and%20Systems%20Change%20Compass%20for%20Local%20Government.pdf

Steil, J. P., & Kelly, N. (2019). Survival of the fairest: Examining HUD reviews of assessments of fair housing. *Housing Policy Debate, 29*(5), 736–751. DOI: 10.1080/10511482.2018.1524444

Talen, E. (2021). The socio-economic context of form-based codes. *Landscape and Urban Planning, 214*, 104182. Advance online publication. DOI: 10.1016/j.landurbplan.2021.104182

Terner Center. (2019). *Affordable housing overlay zones: Oakley.* UC Berkeley. https://ternercenter.berkeley.edu/wp-content/uploads/2020/10/Affordable_Housing_Overlay_Zones_Oakley.pdf

Terner Center. (2021). *Adaptive reuse challenges and opportunities in California*. UC Berkeley. https://ternercenter.berkeley.edu/wp-content/uploads/2021/11/Adaptive-Reuse-November-2021.pdf

The Housing Agency. (2024). *Sustainable compact development international case study analysis*. https://www.housingagency.ie/sites/default/files/2024-11/Sustainable_Compact_Development_International_Case_Study_Analysis.pdf

The Transport Politic. (2019). *Travel mode shares in the U.S.* https://www.thetransportpolitic.com/databook/travel-mode-shares-in-the-u-s/

The White House. (2021). *Fact sheet: The bipartisan infrastructure deal*. https://www.whitehouse.gov/briefing-room/statements-releases/2021/11/06/fact-sheet-the-bipartisan-infrastructure-deal/

United States Department of Housing and Urban Development. (n.d.). *National Affordable Housing Act*. https://www.hud.gov/program_offices/administration/hudclips/acts/nah-act

United States Department of Transportation. (2023). *Case Study: Carson City, Nevada's multi-faceted approach to complete streets*. https://www.planning.dot.gov/documents/Carson_City_CompleteStreets_Case_Study_Final-021023.pdf

United States Environmental Protection Agency. (2024a). *EPA history: Resource Conservation and Recovery Act*. EPA. https://www.epa.gov/history/epa-history-resource-conservation-and-recovery-act

United States Environmental Protection Agency. (2024b). *Summary of the resource conservation and recovery Act*. https://www.epa.gov/laws-regulations/summary-resource-conservation-and-recovery-act

Wendler, K. (2024). Developing the road to nowhere: Ethical considerations of highway expansions. *Viterbi Conversations in Ethics*, *7*(3), 1-10. https://vce.usc.edu/volume-7-issue-3/developing-the-road-to-nowhere-ethical-considerations-of-highway-expansions/

Wood, J., Eskic, D., Benway, D. J., & Macdonald-Poelman, K. (2020). *Housing affordability: What are best practices and why are they important?* https://d36oiwf74r1rap.cloudfront.net/wp-content/uploads/Best-Practices-Dec2020.pdf?x71849#page=10.75

KEY TERMS AND DEFINITIONS

Adaptive reuse: A housing good practice that involves reusing existing structures that have economic and functional obsolescence as residentials.

Best practices: Best or good practices are the set standards that guide policy-makers in making their decision based on evidence-based strategies that have been supported to be effective.

By-right development: The by-right development is a land use designation where specific types of development are allowed without needing special approval from the local government. In essence, the by-right means that land is automatically allowed within a zoning district.

Compact development: A good practice strategy applied for building cities that utilize resources and land effectively.

Complete streets: A transportation best practice that involves designing streets to be operated to enable safe use and promote user mobility.

Form-based code: A housing good practice that promotes predictable bult outcomes and a high-quality public realm by applying physical form instead of separation of uses as the organizing principle.

Overlay zones: A housing best practice where a special zoning district is created on an already existing one to promote affordable housing.

Policy transfer: Policy transfer is the process of adopting ideas or practices from one government or jurisdiction.

Chapter 8
Innovation in Improving Local Refugee Integration Systems and the Roles of Lithuanian and Croatian Municipalities

Remigijus Civinskas
https://orcid.org/0000-0001-5570-1013
Vytautas Magnus University, Kaunas, Lithuania

Mirna Varga
https://orcid.org/0000-0002-9310-5287
University of Zagreb, Croatia

Jaroslav Dvorak
https://orcid.org/0000-0003-1052-8741
Klaipeda University, Lithuania

ABSTRACT

The current research will examine the innovative aspects of municipal services for refugees in Lithuania and Croatia.. The scientific literature constantly debates the most effective social refugee integration structure or systems. The central government provided social integration services for the local government. In some cases, municipalities took the initiative and started some services in partnership with NGOs. So not only was the process top-down, but often the local communities or local authorities were proactive. There have certainly been more proactive initiatives to welcome Ukrainians compared to refugees from other countries of origin. This would

DOI: 10.4018/979-8-3373-0452-6.ch008

allow us to discuss how a reactive response to crises allows for the improvement of municipal services and the transfer of impacts. On the other hand, it will allow us to ask why some successful solutions were short-lived and what factors (lack of resources, bureaucratic machinery, the logic of short-term crises) led to this.

INTRODUCTION

The response of local public policy makers to waves of migration has become a prominent research theme, bringing together scholars from different disciplines, cross-cutting themes and conceptual approaches (Caponio & Borkert, 2010; Glorius & Doomernik, 2020; Doomernik & Ardon, 2018; Homberger et al., 2022). Migration research scholars focus on the roles of local actors in asylum or refugee policies, as well as in the design and reform of municipal asylum scholars also illuminate the diverse roles played by large European cities, often referred to as 'solidarity cities', 'cities of refuge' or 'migrant-friendly' cities, and small municipalities in facilitating the inclusion and continued integration of asylum seekers (Homberger et al., 2022; Glorius & Doomernik, 2020; Meijer et al., 2023; Jonitz et al., 2024; Dimitriadis et al., 2023). 2023). The research revealed that local actors (local authorities, related NGOs, volunteers, etc.) have become the central agents of public policies, especially regarding to the migration crisis (Caponio & Jones-Correa, 2018; Darling, 2022). In European governance and multidimensional policies, this phenomenon is known as the 'local turn' or 'spatial turn.'

Migration research reveals that some European cities have adopted a range of innovations (related to governance, public service provision, social work, networking models, etc.) to the reception of asylum seekers and refugees (Oliver et al., 2020; Guzmán et al., 2023; Geuijen et al., 2020). The influx of asylum seekers, particularly in southern European cities, has shaped these innovations. The context of the migration crisis was important. New governance concepts related to collaborative governance, co-creation, and transformative politics were at work (Oliver et al., 2020; Guzmán et al., 2023). Some scholars have emphasised the innovative design of municipal policies, individual administration or service provision (Oliver et al., 2020; Guzmán et al., 2023). Meanwhile, other scholars address the innovativeness of the migration policy process and explore models (networking of NGOs, volunteers, activists and other actors) or the multiplicity of policy implementation (Geuijen et al., 2020; Holbrook, 2020; Campomori & Casula, 2023; Campomori et al., 2023). Thus, innovations in municipal migration policies (in design, strategies, service delivery, cooperation models, etc.) have potentially addressed the reception crises of asylum seekers and the longer-term challenges of refugee integration. The research on municipal policies or social innovations primarily focuses on Southern European municipalities during the period 2016–2020 for asylum seekers. These studies do not touch on the context of Ukrainian refugee reception in 2022–2024. The research centers on municipal responses to refugee integration, with particular attention to how local actors translate national frameworks into local innovations in small and mid-sized municipalities in Croatia and Lithuania.

The issue of the influx of Ukrainian refugees in European countries has also been discussed in the context of innovative and collaborative governance. There is limited research on this topic. Research reveals that some European municipalities have associated Ukrainian refugees with economic and demographic benefits, such as potential solutions to demographic problems and the ability to attract the necessary labour force. (Matuszczyk, 2023; Błaszczyk et al., 2024; Meijer et al., 2023; Pędziwiatr & Magdziarz, 2023; Gońda, 2021). In European cities, reception practices for asylum seekers are highly variable, ranging from passive (reactive but short-term) to long-term (long-term policies and the allocation of local resources to immigrants). For complex reasons, some studies reveal that sub-national entities face failures in policies for the reception and integration of Ukrainian refugees. (Campomori & Ambrosini, 2020). Other studies provide evidence of success due to the choice of appropriate objectives, the allocation of local resources, and the use of effective tools (Bielewska et al., 2024; Wach & Pachocka, 2022). The research on municipal and local integration policies, local networking, and assistance initiatives aimed at Ukrainian refugees is relatively underdeveloped. Many factors have influenced this situation. Scholars, on the one hand, have tended to analyse the complexity by focusing on the support provided by central governments. The paucity of such studies is because migration is a relatively new phenomenon and migration flows are not exceptionally high in some countries.

LITERATURE REVIEW

Academic discourses on public governance frequently emphasize innovation and change as key conceptual tools. These multidimensional 'umbrella' terms are introduced through diverse theoretical perspectives, often reflecting broader shifts in administrative paradigms, normative frameworks, or incremental policy instruments. In the context of refugee governance, the so-called 'local turn', which refers to a reorientation of responsibility toward subnational actors, has created favorable conditions for public and social policy innovation (Oliver et al., 2020). This shift has not followed a uniform trajectory across Europe, as it remains deeply embedded in national and regional contexts.

As research evidence shows, some reception and integration systems for asylum seekers and refugees are fragmented, too centralised, poorly coordinated and have major efficiency gaps (Pędziwiatr & Magdziarz, 2023). Indeed, this depends on the national or regional context and other factors (i.e., the country's governance structure, responsibilities for asylum and refugee policies, etc.). Central, regional, and local governments share the responsibility of welcoming asylum-seeker refugees. This includes different levels of policy measures, such as relocation, accommodation, the provision of certain social and educational services, and even employment. Local settings play an exceptionally important role here (Glorius & Doomernik, 2020; Kreichauf & Mayer, 2023; Oomen et al., 2021).

The academic literature debates whether centralizing and effectively coordinating refugee reception and integration policies is necessary. Scholars do not seem to be unanimous. Some argue that these policies must inevitably have hierarchical or other forms of coordination systems. Meanwhile, others argue that there needs to be a 'decoupling' of local policies for migrant integration to be effective (Homberger et al., 2022; Oomen et al., 2021). In essence, centralization advocates argue that a complex and large-scale problem requires appropriate coordination arrangements and adequate resources. Scholars who talk about the integrity and multidimensionality of refugee integration policies do not consider the importance of local actors (local politicians, local bureaucracies, NGOs, volunteers, etc.) and the arguments for flexibility and innovation. Also, the different local contexts of migration (number of migrants and their statuses, population, and business attitudes towards migrants, etc.), economy (nature of the labour market, economic situation) and social environment (population size, level of urbanisation, ethnic localism and its relation to migration, civic culture of the society, etc.) are important (Camponio, 2021; Oliver et al., 2020; Bauder, 2021). A variety of structural factors also play a significant role. It is thus crucial to take structural factors into account. For instance, the local economy is an important factor in refugee integration to the labour market (Wehrhahn & Hathat, 2022).

The role of municipalities is not straightforward, and their interests often change. Because of their crisis-responsive nature, local municipalities have played a much greater role in asylum policies, as the research shows. The role of municipalities and other local actors in integration policies has not been unambiguous. First, they have often been passive enforcers of policies in a 'top-down' manner (Oliver et al., 2020; Bauder, 2021; Özdemir, 2022). Second, some municipalities (mostly metropolitan cities) have shown solidarity with refugees and have become key supporting agents. Some municipalities have become 'Refugee Towns', depending on trends and context factors. Also, networks of pro-migrant 'open to refugees' cities have emerged (Doomernik & Ardon, 2018). Third, in some municipalities, particularly medium-sized or smaller ones, elites and a portion of the public have resisted welcoming asylum seekers, integrated refugees, or cooperating with refugees (Jonitz et al., 2024). Cities open to refugees and migrants have developed innovative ideas, strategies and tools relevant to them (Oliver et al., 2020). Municipalities have incrementally chosen and applied innovative measures to address the faced crises.

As the research shows, the involvement of different actors (from the NGO sector, individual public policy entrepreneurs, volunteers, etc.) in the design and implementation of local migration policies has had a significant impact on innovativeness (Campomori et al., 2023). Non-state local actors actively participate in the policy process to aid migrants, fostering a highly collaborative approach (Ataç et al., 2021; De Coninck & Solano, 2023; Matuszczyk, 2023; Goda, 2021). The local asylum-seeking and refugee policies enable the frameworks that integrate the different actors in co-development, co-design, co-provision of services, joint implementation of integration programmes, and networking initiatives (Kreichauf & Mayer, 2023). Thus, the complexity of the migration governance phenomenon and the high dynamics of change force actors to make unconventional policy choices.

The application of local migration and asylum policies is influenced not only by factors that drive innovation and creative solutions but also by constraints and barriers. As research reveals, these include constraints imposed by legal regimes (especially in asylum policies), limited discretion of local governments in decision-making (most decisions are taken at higher levels of government) and financial constraints (Oliver et al., 2020; Guzmán et al, 2023; Kanas & Kosyakova, 2023; Wehrhahn & Hathat, 2022). Some scholars argue that local policies face implementation gaps due to closedness, and under-inclusiveness of actors (encountering conflicts and resistance from groups) (Guzmán et al, 2023). Integration of refugees into the labour market is often negatively affected by unfavourable local economies that limit employability (Azlor et al., 2020).

UKRAINIAN REFUGEE GROUPS IN LITHUANIA AND CROATIA

The Russian invasion and annexation of Crimea (2014) have influenced the forced migration of Ukrainians to the EU and other countries. Thousands of Ukrainian refugees have moved to many European countries, including Croatia and Lithuania. The following data demonstrate the impact of this phenomenon. In May 2024, Ukrainians (beneficiaries of EU special status of temporary protection) received refugee status in Croatia (24,400) and Lithuania (78,110) (EUROSTAT, 2024a). Lithuania has attracted more refugees for complex reasons—geography, favourable cultural factors (cultural proximity, possibilities to communicate in Russian, etc.). Enthusiastic public support, refugee support (through volunteering and NGOs), and state asylum measures have driven refugee reception. In Croatia, the process followed a similar pattern.

Ukrainian refugee groups are similar across many demographic and socioeconomic criteria, as is the case in many European countries. In Lithuania and Croatia, their compositions are not exceptional. According to Eurostat statistics, the majority of refugees are female (67% in Lithuania, 66.4% in Croatia, and 62.2% in all EU countries; data analysed for January 2024) (Eurostat, 2024b). Also, a significant number of children under 18 years of age have arrived (31.1% in Lithuania and 33.8% in Croatia) (Eurostat, 2024b). Research data and reports by Tkachuk et al. (2023), UNHCR Croatia (2023) and IOM (2023) show that a significant proportion of Ukrainian refugees have higher education. In Lithuania, around 30 percent of refugees have higher education qualifications, while in Croatia, this figure reaches 48 percent. The resettlement of Ukrainian children has also encouraged the arrival of many teachers and education specialists, especially to Lithuania, where they have settled mainly in large cities. According to Deimantas and Şanlıtürk (2023), around 10–12 percent of Ukrainian refugees in Lithuania are highly qualified workers. However, most of them are in medium-skilled jobs, which indicates a certain underutilization of education or a mismatch of skills in the labour market.

Admittedly, there are some key differences. There are a number of Ukrainian men who arrived in Lithuania before 2022, and their status is legally uncertain, as some of them have permits while others have expired. Most of these men work as drivers, builders, shipbuilders, etc. Another notable aspect is the increased employment rate of Ukrainians in Lithuania, which stands at approximately 40% in 2023 and 51% in 2025 (OECD, 2023; Deimantas & Şanlıtürk, 2023). Ukrainian refugees benefit from a wide range of support policies in Croatia, Lithuania and most other European countries. As previously mentioned, many European countries have implemented crisis response policies in response to the Ukrainian refugee influx. Specifically, Lithuania and Croatia had relatively underdeveloped asylum reception and refugee integration policies (Dimitrov & Pavlov, 2023; Gregurović & Župarić-Iljić, 2023; Rijavec et al., 2021; Pandek & Župarić-Iljić, 2018). The asylum and refugee systems in Lithuania and Croatia have been underdeveloped (at least until 2019), focused on the state, lacking integration programs, and lacking good cross-sectoral coordination, among other things (Čepeliauskaitė, 2018; Wolffhardt et al, 2019; Kiralj & Ajduković, 2022; Rijavec et al., 2021; Pandek & Župarić-Iljić, 2018). The Migrant Integration Policy Index and its indicators covering the years 2013-2019 reveal a similar situation. Both countries have progressed in developing migrant integration policies, but their rankings in 2020 (Lithuania, -37/100; Croatia, -39/100) are comparatively low (MIPEX, 2020a; MIPEX, 2020b). The implementation of the policies was the responsibility of the centrist authorities (responsible ministries and subordinate institutions), while the involvement of NGOs was relatively limited. In summary, Lithuania and Croatia have progressively developed asylum, refugee and migration policies, but they have been restrictive, inefficiently coordinated and underdeveloped for a long time.

LOCAL SELF-GOVERNMENT SYSTEMS: ASPECTS OF REFUGEE INTEGRATION

Since 2022, municipalities in Lithuania and Croatia have become visible and, in the case of individual municipalities, innovative policy makers for refugee integration. In this section, we will provide a brief overview by assessing the municipalities' asylum powers and responsibilities related to refugee integration. Lithuania and Croatia are unitary states and have relatively centralised systems of self-government (see box). There are a number of similarities between them. Municipalities in both countries have relatively little autonomy and can exert limited influence on public policies (see Table 1). This is important in the context of refugee innovation, as these policies are the state's responsibility and municipalities are involved in their implementation. However, the municipal systems in the countries under consideration are different, given the slightly different structure, size of municipalities, functional responsibilities, etc.

Table 1. Comparison of features of local government systems

Characteristic	Croatia	Lithuania
Features of the local government systems	Croatia is a unitary and highly centralised state. The two-tier system: the first level consists of 428 rural municipalities and 128 urban municipalities (cities). 20 counties, totalling 576 units, make up the second level. Key characteristics of Croatia's local government system include a fragmented territorial structure.	Lithuania is a unitary, quite centralised state. 60 municipalities make up Lithuania's one tier of local government. Lithuania has relatively large municipalities (average number of permanent residents: 51,219 in 2024). The Lithuanian local government system is characterized by relatively large municipalities and a lower degree of fragmentation compared to the national government.
Municipalities' functions and policy scope	The municipal units are responsible for services directly benefiting local citizens, such as housing, childcare, social welfare, primary healthcare, and primary education. Most municipalities are small, with 80% having fewer than 5,000 inhabitants, resulting in weak administrative and fiscal capacities. This limits their ability to manage local affairs and services effectively, influencing the integration of migrants at the local level.	The legal framework separates the municipal functions into 1) independent areas such as infrastructure development, public transport, water supply-waste management, education, and social services provision, and 2) public health and primary health care, cultural and sports services, etc. 2) Allocated/state-delegated (implementation of national policies, social benefits administration, fire and public safety protection, etc.). The municipalities are executing state-delegated functions under the supervision of state institutions.
Relations between municipalities and central government and the autonomy of local government	The Croatian local government system has significant supervision and control by the central government. Sectoral legal frameworks often constrain the functions of local governments, limiting their discretion. They reinforce a top-down relationship between the central and local government levels.	Lithuania has high legal-administrative autonomy and increased functional autonomy over the last 15 years due to central government allocative tasks. However, municipalities have low financial autonomy based on fiscal autonomy, financial self-reliance, borrowing autonomy, and financial transfer systems. Municipalities are co-deciding in some matters of public policy and autonomous in others.

Source: Giljević and Lalić Novak, 2020; Ladner et al., 2019; Šaparnienė et al., 2021, Koprić et al., 2019.

Municipalities took advantage of local innovation ecosystems, NGO networks, and social economies. Research indicates that in Croatia, the city and region of Zagreb hold significant importance due to the hierarchical relations between local government units, while in Lithuania, there are three major metropolitan areas: Vilnius, Kaunas, and Klaipėda (Švaljek et al., 2019; Keser, 2023; Giljević, & Lalić Novak, 2020; Vitálišová & Dvořák, 2023; Szara & Ślusarczyk, 2020; Bučaitė-Vilkė & Lazauskienė, 2021). In general, the primary analysis indicates that Lithuania has been more advanced in developing migrant-inclusive policies. Zagreb's refugees' integration policy stands out due to its effectiveness in comparison to other municipalities. In Lithuania, there are no such significant differences between municipalities.

It is important to note that asylum and refugee policies are at the level of the central government and are the responsibility of several ministries and their subordinate departments and agencies (Burbulytė et. al., 2016; EMN, 2022; EMN, 2020; EC, 2024a; EC, 2024b; Koprić et al., 2021).

As already analysed, Croatia and Lithuania have developed centralised framework design policies in response to migration crises and the chosen response strategy. In this context, the integration of refugees has been a secondary issue, although there have been positive developments. From 2014 to 2020, we have strengthened the national refugee policies by improving policy coordination, improving asylum procedures and legal regimes, and developing several strategic documents that reflect the integration of refugees and other migrants (EC, 2024a; EC, 2024b; MIPEX, 2020a; MIPEX2020b). However, research and evaluations have shown that there are still a number of gaps in refugee policies and incomplete measures related to the socio-economic integration of refugees, due to complex reasons (Giljević, & Lalić Novak, 2020; Koprić et al., 2021; Wolffhardt et al., 2019; Žibas, 2015). Negative societal attitudes, insufficient allocation of resources, and ineffective coordination, among other factors, have negatively affected the development and application of refugee integration measures (Giljević & Lalić Novak, 2020; Blažytė et al, 2016).

Between 2018 and 2021, municipalities started to be involved in the implementation of refugee integration (or more broadly, assistance to migrants) policy measures. The crisis of Belarusian migrant arrivals prompted a growing number of municipalities in Lithuania to collaborate with refugee reception centres in welcoming asylum seekers and refugees, providing them with accommodation, essential services, and counselling, among other things (Wolffhardt et al., 2019). The Action Plan for 2018-2020 on the Integration of Foreigners into Society (Ministry of Social Security and Labour of the Republic of Lithuania, 2018) consolidated this cooperation. It foresaw the fact that municipalities are one of the most important links in helping foreigners integrate. Additionally, the policy document anticipated municipalities' involvement in several specific measures, such as offering various services and establishing integration centres for foreigners, with three such centres operating as one-stop shops in major cities. It is noteworthy that this policy document partially combined migration and refugee policies.

Similarly, during this period, Croatia also took steps to address the integration of migrants and refugees, focussing on the development at the local level. The Croatian Government's Office for Human Rights and Rights of National Minorities formulated a 'Framework for the Integration of Persons Who Have Received International Protection at the Local Level' between 2017 and 2020. The framework outlines strategic areas such as employment, social inclusion, housing, and social protection (Government's Office for Human Rights and the Rights of National Minorities, 2020). Koprić et al. (2021) identified weaknesses in public service provision, public governance, and coordination. Strong NGOs or networks, informally coordinated by them, have compensated for the weaknesses in refugee policies (Giljević & Lalić Novak, 2018). For example, NGO refugee centres in Lithuania ('InLT', the oldest operating Red Cross Migrant Integration Centre in Kaunas) and Croatia (the strongest, the Red Cross Integration House in Zagreb; the Jesuit Refugee Service) have provided services and support to aid in the integration of refugees (Giljević & Lalić Novak, 2018; Koprić et al., 2021; Pandek & Župarić-Iljić, 2018; Blažytė & Žibas, 2019).

In general, both Lithuania and Croatia lacked effective (adequately resourced, targeted, well-coordinated, inclusive, etc.) national and local measures for socio-economic integration of migrants and refugees. However, national policies have removed some of these measures, and municipalities and other local actors are now involved in their implementation. This shift in refugee and migration policies is due to the international migration crisis (2016-2020) and the need for integration of labour migrants (the case of Lithuania). Strong NGO centres working with refugees and migrants in Lithuanian and Croatian urban municipalities have compensated for the lack of local policymakers.

The mass flight of Ukrainian refugees from the war to Lithuania and Croatia, which started in 2022, has significantly transformed or initiated local policies for socio-economic integration of refugees (Blažytė et al., 2022; Lalić Novak & Giljević, 2023). Initial research reveals several significant issues: 1) Municipalities are not adequately prepared to receive refugees. Municipalities with more work with refugees relied on more acute practices, networking and cooperation with NGOs and national-level institutions (Blažytė et al., 2022). Metropolitan municipalities and individual cities had most of these experiences. 2) In 2022 and early 2023, municipal representatives prioritized short-term primary assistance (crisis response) over long-term integration. It is true that some of the Lithuanian municipal representatives saw Ukrainians as potential permanent residents and linked this to solving localised demographic problems. 3) The effects of integration depend on the practices of local NGOs and their cooperation. 4) There is a lack of both horizontal and vertical coordination, as well as an insufficient concentration of aid instruments, which could be attributed to the lack of refugee-centred access. The focus was on the lack of cooperation with the centre's authorities. 5) The attitudes and involvement of mayors and other municipal leaders (Blažytė et al., 2022).

Some municipalities assess the integration of Ukrainians through cultural proximity access (emphasis on the favourable attitude of the local population, the empathy generated by the war, the possibility of communicating with them, etc.) (Blažytė et al., 2022). In addition, the studies carried out reveal good practices related to the appropriate use of integration tools, which include horizontal coordination (Croatian case), informing Ukrainians (information sharing and counselling through portals for

Ukrainians (Lithuanian and Croatian municipalities cases), and registration centres for Ukrainians (Lithuanian municipality cases). Lithuania has established seven centres for refugee registration and service provision in its municipalities (refugee-focused approach), and has recruited Ukrainian specialists to work in its municipal service centres (Lalić Novak & Giljević, 2023; Blažytė et al, 2022). Zagreb city municipality has been exceptional in the integration of Ukrainians and other refugees, and its good practices have been linked to Croatia's exceptional clear refugee and migrant policy and its key document, Action Plan of the City of Zagreb, Akcijski Plan Grada Zagreba (adopted in 2022). The support for the Ukrainians was based on its instruments and the networking with NGOs that resulted from it (Zagreb concluded a cooperation agreement with eight organisations of civil society on the implementation (Lalić Novak & Giljević, 2023).

Since 2022, some municipalities in Lithuania and Croatia have increasingly played a visible role in Ukrainian refugee integration and introduced innovative approaches, creative programs etc. This innovative process was driven by many factors naming several like cultural proximity to Ukrainians, emotional effects of the war and the geopolitical situation, previous experiences of working with Ukrainians, etc. Other causal factors were also important. In both countries, refugee integration efforts have been driven by local innovation ecosystems (especially in larger cities), NGO networks, labour market needs for new employees, national asylum and refugees' policies focused on Ukrainian integration etc.

The integration of Ukrainian refugees in Lithuania and Croatia has revealed both systemic weaknesses and local adaptation potential. While both countries initially lacked well-coordinated and adequately resourced national and local integration measures, the migration crisis and the arrival of Ukrainian refugees since 2022 have prompted changes in policy implementation, especially at the municipal level. Local actors, in particular NGOs and metropolitan municipalities, have compensated for the inaction at the state level by adopting flexible responses, promoting horizontal and vertical cooperation and using cultural proximity as a facilitating factor.

METHODOLOGY

This study applies a qualitative research approach to explore innovation in refugee integration within Croatian and Lithuanian municipalities. Qualitative methods are well-suited to examining socio-economic integration and public service innovation but raise ethical concerns (Subramanian et al., 2022; Neergaard, 2007). The approach fits the selected theoretical frameworks (integration and public policy studies) and provides context-based insights (Morawska, 2018; Zapata-Barrero, 2018).

Fieldwork was conducted in 7 Lithuanian and 2 Croatian municipalities, targeting officials and civil servants responsible for migrant integration, alongside experts experienced in Ukrainian refugee policies. This two-group sampling reflected the multi-level nature of integration governance and innovative practices, aligning with established methods in migration research (Barglowski, 2018; Neergaard, 2007).

Interviews were supplemented with organisational communications and project reports to capture inclusive policy practices. Data, collected in late 2023 and 2024, were analysed using thematic and conceptual approaches focused on local government innovations, identifying causal drivers and barriers in Ukrainian refugee integration. Semi-structured interviews allowed for spontaneous narratives, guided by frameworks such as local integration, innovation in governance, and the three refugee work domains (Ager & Strang, 2008).

We conducted the interviews either in-person or remotely through video or telephone calls, initially reaching out to the informant over the phone before agreeing on a suitable interview format. Thus far, we have conducted a total of 20 interviews in Lithuania and Croatia.

Table 2. Characteristics of Respondents

	Municipal representatives*	**Refugee reception centres**	**State institutions representatives****	**Experts (NGO, trade union)**
Croatia	4	-	-	4
Lithuania	4	2	4	2

*Politico-administrative leaders, top municipal managers, coordinators.

** Ministerial officials and senior civil servants; representatives from state agencies.

The qualitative study had an uneven distribution of participants, depending on the countries selected. This was due to several reasons. Firstly, Lithuania's reception of refugees (both state and sub-national policies) is more developed than Croatia's. Thus, a much higher number of municipalities have applied innovative measures in the socio-economic integration of Ukrainian refugees. Similarly, state support through targeted programs and regulatory measures has been more extensive. Secondly, as already analysed, Croatia has a pronounced concentration of refugees in one city, which determines existing integration policies and practices.

It is noteworthy some of the informants represented the major cities of Lithuania and Croatia (Zagreb, Klaipėda, Kaunas, Telšiai), but they also included other municipalities with innovative practices in terms of the reception of refugees or volunteer centres, the existing innovative culture, and the individual entrepreneurialism of the municipality (e.g., Osijek, Biržai, Jonava). A total of 8 municipal informants participated in qualitative research.

We encouraged informants to express their opinions more openly and freely during the interviews, disregarding institutional policies, measures, etc. Thus, the interviews thematically deviated from the initial set of questions related to the social integration of Ukrainians and municipal innovations.

RESULTS

Drivers for Ukrainian refugee integration. As discussed above, researchers are looking at the causal mechanisms behind the integration of asylum seekers and refugees, which are often also the drivers of innovation in the provision of services or assistance. The qualitative research findings indicate a whole complex of causal factors was at work, which drove the aid factors. However, a few significant factors were mentioned particularly frequently. A higher proportion of informants shared personal experiences of feeling compassionate and moral solidarity towards Ukrainian refugees, and some even got involved in voluntary assistance themselves (Kaunas civil servant; Biržai civil servant; Vilnius top manager; Vilnius deputy minister). Strong positive emotions, therefore, influenced the assistance to the Ukrainians. The interviewees explained that they did not have similar emotions towards other refugee groups. Some shared that they even felt some hostility towards refugees (or so-called irregular migrants) from Belarus.

Informants explained their active involvement by referring to the unexpected effect of the Russo-Ukrainian war. They mentioned a certain emotional shock and cognitive dissonance (due to the unimaginable war and the violence during the war) that encouraged involvement already in the first days after the migrants arrived in their municipality. For example, one municipal employee spoke about how she got involved in coordinating support for Ukrainians on a volunteer basis, building a network of people (Biržai civil servant). As a result of her motivation and involvement, the municipality's management even changed her functions, and she became the coordinator of support for Ukrainians. Thus, an unexpected public policy event helped to initiate new municipal policies. It is important to note some informants shared their experiences of how the war, as a public policy event, contributed to the massive, active involvement of individual citizens and businesses in providing assistance to refugees in 2022.

In Croatia, interview-based insights indicate that there has existed a clear political will to accommodate and provide support to Ukrainian refugees, both at the state and municipal levels. Osijek Baranja County stands out as the only county in Croatia that drafted and implemented an action plan aimed solely at Ukrainian integration.

Some Croatian public institutions are recognised for their exceptional work in supporting the socio-economic integration of Ukrainian refugees. The analysis of the interview findings reveals that cultural proximity coupled with strong political will appears to have gone hand in hand in the process of establishing support mechanisms for Ukrainian refugees (Zagreb NGO worker; Osijek, municipal representative). In addition to these, strong NGO sectors in both Zagreb and Osijek supported the implementation of integration activities and served as drivers of many, if not most, innovative practices related to the integration processes. The Croatian data is notable for the vividness of the experience of the last war and the strong historical memory that influences some of the actors involved in refugee policy. In addition, this driver has a regional dimension. The interview results uncover that what stands out from the interviews, particularly reflected in conversations we had with informants from Osijek, is sympathy with the consequences of war. (Osijek, municipal representative)

Municipalities roles. However, senior officials expressed partial criticism towards municipal involvement, pointing out that the municipality lacks a refugee policy and does not consider migrants when providing services. One informant outlined the situation as follows: Additionally, municipalities lack a function dedicated to the integration of refugees and migrants. *They don't have someone working with migrants, and they don't have financial resources. So, the wave of Ukrainian refugees made them think about migrants and foreigners. This is a plus. [...] The Ministry intends to invest in the creation of municipal coordinators. We have set up pilot projects, and we plan to have continuity of refugee integration policies.* We aim to incorporate the work with refugees and migrants into the municipal function, a role that the Law on Local Government enshrines and regulates. *[...] Regarding employment, we are collaborating with the Employment Service on this matter. However, the municipal refugee coordinators should also manage economic integration by establishing a local network. Such a network should include state agencies (e.g., the Employment Service, the Labour Inspectorate) and the main providers of education and personal health services. This coordinator oversees specific services and collaborates with various services, including employment services.* (Vilnius, ministry top civil servant). This interview revealed several things. On the one hand, Lithuanian political and administrative elites were mixed about the municipalities' efforts to help Ukrainians. Their assessments were positive, emphasising excellent practices and success stories. Ministerial elites, on the other hand, saw the need to institutionalize refugee policy (in relation to Ukrainian integration) by creating a new design, allocating functions, and providing for appropriate regulation. The interviews particularly emphasised the need for horizontal coordination and the provision of services to refugees in a one-stop shop manner. Broad-based refugee inclusion projects have made progress towards implementing the visions presented in the interviews.

Lithuania municipal representatives were positive about the social integration policies and highlighted the fact that the state had made a significant contribution in the period 2023-2024 (Biržai civil servant; Kaunas civil servant; Vilnius, top manager; Telšiai, adviser to the mayor). In general, the positive assessments were because that one significant project ("Reception and early integration of refugees from Ukraine" financed by the Asylum, Migration and Integration Fund under the measure "Emergency Assistance") supported a significant number of initiatives, which were financed from municipal budgets, public support funds or covered through NGO activities. Thus, the EU and Lithuanian state have positively received the targeted support. However, individual measures (e.g., related to labour market integration, cultural socialisation, language training) were viewed more critically (Kaunas, civil servant). Furthermore, some informants were critical of the central government's desire to use the case of Ukrainian refugees to transfer responsibility for migrant and refugee policies to municipalities. The qualitative research revealed a significant involvement of municipalities in the implementation of Ukrainian refugee policies in the top-down approach. The new refugee influx crisis management involved a lot of intensive inter-institutional collaboration and alignment of objectives. On the other hand, Lithuanian political-administrative elites were developing new visions for the design of these policies, planning for institutionalisation, and wanting to harness the capacities of municipalities to work with Ukrainian refugees. Meanwhile, the municipalities were relatively reserved and cautious.

In Croatian case, the interview data reveals that municipalities have been major policy players in Ukrainian refugee social-economic integration (Zagreb, the City representative; Osijek, municipality representative). This is a serious issue, as already analysed, there are gaps in national migration and refugee policy, and the responsibilities of municipalities in the implementation of refugee policy are not well defined. Sub-national institutions, lacking a top-down policy process approach, initiated policies (some strategically and others incrementally) to help Ukrainian refugees. It is true that the nature and scale of the initiatives varied.

Zagreb is a unique case in Croatia since it holds two-level sub-national status, i.e., a county and a city. This makes coordination and policymaking more straightforward and less complicated. Osijek municipality, the largest city in Osijek Baranja County, has its own policy-making processes for integrating refugees. In the years prior to the onset of war in 2022, Osijek municipal actors took the lead in designing an action plan for the integration of persons under international protection. The process was initiated by the NGO Centre for Peace, nonviolence and Human Rights (this organisation has a long history of support for work with refugees and is strong player in municipal politics). The Centre for Peace started networking with all the relevant locals to help refugees, and it was impactful (Osijek, NGO manager)

In March 2022, the Osijek Baranja County developed another action plan, solely for the purpose of integrating Ukrainian refugees. Despite the fact that only one civil society organisation from Osijek holds the mandate to coordinate activities and receives all funding, other NGOs inform us that their activities complement the actions outlined in the action plan. Therefore, there seems to be a parallel process going on in Osijek Baranja County, albeit rather complementary (Osijek, NGO manager).

The interview data indicates that Croatian municipalities have been key players in the socio-economic integration of Ukrainian refugees, often stepping in to fill gaps left by unclear national policies, with Zagreb and Osijek (county and city) serving as notable examples of proactive local policymaking.

In summary, while Lithuania adopted a comprehensive, multi-actor approach with an evolving policy framework, Croatia's integration efforts were marked by fragmentation, slower progress, and reliance on local initiatives to compensate for national policy gaps. Both countries faced challenges, but Lithuania demonstrated a more coordinated, wider scope (focus on easing regulations, special programs to integrate Ukrainians) and dynamic integration strategy compared to Croatia's more ad hoc, municipality-led efforts. The three municipalities' initiatives on specific policies for Ukrainian integration and their successful implementation are based on cooperation with NGOs and other stakeholders.

Local networks are the driver for innovation. As discussed above, the roles of municipalities in the implementation of refugee policies differ between Lithuania and Croatia. Lithuania's centralized, top-down refugee policy has not been a major driver in Ukrainian integration. However, it was founded on a certain level of openness, flexibility, and the effective selection of measures. Furthermore, it was founded on the principles of multi-levelness and inclusion. Thus, its nature became one of the conditions for innovative initiatives to emerge in individual municipalities. However, we must take into account the causal complexity.

Local networking involving NGOs, business associations/foundations (or even individual businesses), municipal mayors with teams (or enterprising administrators), and municipal institutions (schools, social service centres, health clinics, and other organisations) has become an important basis for social innovation in refugee integration, as the interviews with municipal representatives show.

In the case of Croatian cases, the establishment of social support for Ukrainian refugees has centred around networks of NGOs with municipalities become involved as important secondary actors. In addition, the provision of support aimed at fostering social connections was less coordinated (than in the case of Lithuania) and more spontaneous and dynamic. This is reflected in the experiences of one informant:

Our idea to work on inclusive communities is to work with local people and build these bridges in parallel. Of course, some kind of solidarity practice is also important to us. What we were doing then was spontaneous, we didn't think much.

And in other cases as well we go for meeting a direct need, we don't wait. And where we contributed the most this time was precisely in the establishment of those community ties, where the people who came to us were able to really establish a circle of support for themselves for different things. (Osijek, NGO manager).

The resulting niches in the reception of aid and support have created preconditions for the functioning of self-help networks for Ukrainian refugees. Thus, in the case of Croatia, the role of Ukrainian social capital has become significant and partly compensates for the shortcomings of integration measures (in Lithuania, this was pronounced only in one municipality). Ukrainian networks have involved volunteers (engagement with Ukrainian communities and other forms of networking) who have provided significant services. The informants spoke of many individuals who volunteered to provide interpretation and translation services, accompaniment to doctors' or school appointments, connecting people and establishing relations with the community, but also creating their own NGOs and collaborating with already established stakeholders in the community. New NGOs were also set up and partnership networks established with other existing third sector organisations. (Zagreb, NGO worker; Osijek, NGO manager).

In Croatia, networks of NGOs, supported by volunteers and social capital, have played a key role in aiding Ukrainian refugees through spontaneous, dynamic efforts, partially compensating for less coordinated integration measures. However, there was less involvement of local government actors in these networks compared to Lithuania case.

Municipality as central actor in innovative networking. Interview data show that municipalities (Biržai, civil servant; Vilnius, civil servant) played a central role in the formation and operation of some networking (2022-2023). In these networking sites, the role of the municipality's political leadership (mayor, mayoral advisors, vice mayors, etc.) or active civil servants was prominent. They both managed the networks and played a coordinating role. NGOs, businesses, local community organizations, and activists complemented these broad networks and were active in 2022. The innovations that emerged in these networks primarily related to the markers and means domains (accommodating a portion of Ukrainians, providing health and social services), and also included some facilitator domains (e.g., cultural integration measures, ensuring stable access to services). Although the forms of innovative governance were short-lived, some remained and provided stability and service access for Ukrainians.

The City of Zagreb adopted the action plan for the integration of international protection seekers just before the influx of Ukrainian refugees. The plan encompassed numerous innovative measures and marked a significant advancement in collaborating with refugees and asylum seekers. Of course, the plan also included extensive municipal partnerships with third-sector stakeholders and did not focus on Ukrainians as an exclusive target group. Rather, it was aimed at integration of all persons under international and temporary protection, but also migrants in vulnerable position. One view mirror this: *I don't like to separate, but I don't see it that way; I see everything equally (integration of all persons in need of protection). That's why I spoke about everyone, not just Ukrainians. There is no doubt that their integration is important.* (Zagreb, the city representative)

The previous interview excerpt shows the professionalism and equality-based approach. Clearly, the interview reveals that the timing of the implementation of the plan was important as an opportunity to use individual activities for the integration of Ukrainians. This was successfully done.

Innovations in practice: addressing the most pressing issues. In our qualitative research, we analysed the most pressing issues related to the successful recruitment of Ukrainians and the resolution of their psychological problems, moving on to the next topic. We have targeted several municipalities in their efforts to assist Ukrainian refugees and tackle local issues.

The first social initiative focused on addressing the emotional problems of refugees and fostering social interactions among them. Several **Lithuanian** municipalities organised therapeutic meetings led by psychologists or held without a therapist, but with the participation of municipal staff through passive monitoring (Biržai, civil servant; Jonava, top manager; Telšiai, adviser to the mayor). The informants said that in the first half of the year, visitors needed these conversations to recover and share their experiences. The municipalities provided rooms for the meetings, as well as psychologists or observers. Indeed, this has proven to be a useful and valuable form of support, although the level of professionalism remains unclear. The innovativeness of these measures was doubled. As the expert interviews reveal, few authorities and NGOs (except for a few working professionally with refugees) were aware of refugees' emotional state and their possible differences from other Ukrainian labor migrants. Moreover, they did not always consider the needs of single women and the elderly. Secondly, there is a lack of professional psychotherapists, psychologists and psychiatrists in rural municipalities. Some of the younger mental health professionals are not fluent in Russian, and a language barrier would reduce the effectiveness of their service. Therefore, refugees may have limited access to mental health facilities. Innovative solutions to encourage and enable association have emerged as the foundation for social innovation. Remarkably, these groups were successful in 2022. Certain municipalities have heightened their focus on Ukrainian women with special needs. It is true that several informants were critical of this focus on target groups. They commented on the fact that such assistance is characterized by "positive discrimination" and suggested improving overall accessibility to services and creating non-discriminatory environments (Jonava, Top Manager).

Similar to the Lithuanian case, several **Croatian** municipalities have prioritized the social integration of Ukrainian refugees. Innovations in support include the creation of spaces in Osijek dedicated to providing psychosocial assistance to Ukrainian refugees and building connections with the local community. A local NGO quickly facilitated this, leveraging its existing resources to offer immediate support.

The Ukrainian social club we founded is also innovative. We did work for them. They also wanted an English-speaking club. So, our international volunteers worked with their young people and children in English because they wanted to, considering that some might have planned to go further, which was important to them. (Osijek, NGO manager)

Clearly, the English language instruction showed an unfocused but empathetic approach to Ukrainian integration. Key forms of support in both Osijek and Zagreb include legal assistance, language courses, cultural mediation, psychosocial services, as well as recreational and cultural activities. (Osijek, municipality representative; Zagreb, the City representative)

In Lithuania, Other municipal 'experiments' were related to the employment of qualified Ukrainians by helping them (temporary lifting of restrictions, assistance in learning Lithuanian, ...). For example, one municipality was notorious for assigning nurses to doctors who were employed in a municipal clinic (they had completed a basic Lithuanian language course), who assisted them and also translated as needed (Vilnius, Top manager). Other municipalities followed suit. Importantly, there was an enormous demand for doctors in this and other municipalities. Similar practices were used to recruit Ukrainian teachers for teaching foreign languages, among other roles. For example, they could work as teaching assistants. Thus, some municipalities have developed a supportive framework economic flexible integration approach. The contextual factor is also important, as municipalities have been interested in recruiting highly skilled professionals in their health and other institutions. On the other hand, the labour market context was favourable to Ukrainian recruitment, in the interest of local entrepreneurs and the majority of the population.

DISCUSSION

The analysis of Central European and Baltic local government responses to waves of migration, particularly focussing on asylum seekers and refugees, highlights the evolving role of municipalities and the emergence of innovative approaches to socio-economic integration. In the context of innovative European migration governance, the 'local turn' has become a defining characteristic, where local governments and associated non-state actors, such as NGOs, volunteers, policy entrepreneurship, and some business-related NPOs, take on vital roles in policy implementation (Caponio & Jones-Correa, 2018; Darling, 2022). This shift emphasises the importance of local authorities in crafting innovative responses, which may not always align with broader national policies. On the other hand, municipalities can participate in the implementation of national migration policies through various forms of decoupling from the central government. Local governments are becoming laboratories for policy experimentation, and adaptive governance structures are taking shape, as the Ukrainian adoption cases show.

The case studies of Lithuania and Croatia illustrate these dynamics well. Some Lithuanian municipalities (before 2022), benefiting from a more structured approach to refugee integration and significant involvement from NGOs, have shown relatively successful integration outcomes. On the other hand, some Croatian city municipalities, while also innovative, have faced more pronounced challenges due to a lack of prior experience with large-scale migration and more limited institutional capacity (Gregurović & Župarić-Iljić, 2023; Blažytė et al., 2022). These variations underscore the importance of context-specific factors, including historical migration patterns, socio-economic conditions, and existing local governance structures. As our research demonstrates, the Lithuanian government is willing to use innovative public policy tools, experiences, and networks of excellence and institutionalise them by transferring migration policy management to local governments. This is a complex manoeuvre aimed at altering refugee and migration policies, and it could potentially yield some success. It is noteworthy that attempts to transfer these functions to refugees from Asia and other regions coming from Belarus (in the case of Lithuania) or via the Balkans using the 'transit route' have not worked. On the other hand, the Russia-Ukraine war and the migration it has generated are exceptional events in refugee policy that should be seen in the unusual context of the crisis.

The empirical study revealed that a combination of several factors, including cultural proximity to Ukrainian refugees, war's emotional-cognitive effects on populations, the empathic relationship with refugees, and the local economic conjuncture (the need for suitable workers), are the main drivers for innovation. They have enabled the development and some successful application of innovative tools for the integration of Ukrainians in Lithuania and Croatia. This included all levels of integration domains: markers-means; social connections; facilitators; and dozens of operationalised measures. Indeed, the qualitative research confines itself to examining their efficacy, financial impacts, and indirect effects. It is also challenging to assess their universality in isolation from their context. This would require additional case studies.

CONCLUSION

Emotional, historical, social, and cultural factors drove both Lithuanian and Croatian approaches. In Lithuania, feelings of compassion, moral solidarity, and emotional shock in response to the Russo-Ukrainian war acted as key motivators for both individuals and municipal officials. Cultural proximity was another influential factor, with many Ukrainians already residing in Lithuanian municipalities.

Similarly, in Croatia, the historical memory of the Homeland War and political will at both national and municipal levels shaped a supportive environment for Ukrainian refugees. Cultural proximity and strong regional sentiments, especially in areas like Osijek, further fuelled support mechanisms. Croatian NGOs' experiences with wartime assistance and existing social support networks also drove the country's innovative practices in refugee integration.

Lithuanian municipalities implemented various innovative policies aimed at socio-economic integration. They introduced flexible labour market regulations, created employment programs, supported Lithuanian language learning, and provided temporary housing solutions. One notable measure involved employing nurses to assist Ukrainian doctors at municipal clinics, temporarily lifting restrictions and facilitating smoother integration into the health sector. Croatia's initiatives were more fragmented and community driven. Measures included legal assistance, cultural mediation, recreational activities, and language courses provided by NGOs. In Osijek, an innovative approach included establishing a Ukrainian social club and offering English-language learning opportunities, catering to those planning to migrate further, while in Zagreb there was an immediate establishment of a cultural program aimed at Ukrainians psychosocial relief and creation of connections with the local community.

In summary, the results demand a more nuanced view of municipalities' roles in the governance of migration, emphasising the necessity of funding, legal changes, and capacity-building for sustainable integration. Furthermore, encouraging cooperative frameworks that improve coordination between various sectors and governmental levels can aid in filling in the gaps in policy application and guarantee the scaling and sustainability of creative local practices. The success of local innovation in migration policy depends on removing structural barriers and promoting multi-level cooperation. As migration flows continue to shape European societies, building resilient, inclusive, and adaptable local governance frameworks will be critical for managing the complexities of migration and ensuring the successful integration of diverse migrant populations.

REFERENCES

Ajduković, D., Čorkalo Biruški, D., Gregurović, M., Matić Bojić, J., & Župarić-Iljić, D. (2019). Challenges of integrating refugees into Croatian society: attitudes of citizens and the readiness of local communities. Government of the Republic of Croatia, Office for Human Rights and Rights of National Minorities. 1-158

Ager, A., & Strang, A. (2008). Understanding integration: Conceptual framework. *Journal of Refugee Studies*, *21*(2), 166–191.

Ataç, I., Rygiel, K., & Stierl, M. (2021). Building transversal solidarities in European cities: Open harbours, safe communities, home. *Critical Sociology*, *47*(6), 923–939. DOI: 10.1177/0896920520980522

Azlor, L., Damm, A. P., & Schultz-Nielsen, M. L. (2020). Local labour demand and immigrant employment. *Labour Economics*, *63*, 101808. DOI: 10.1016/j.labeco.2020.101808

Barglowski, K. (2018). Where, what and whom to study? Principles, guidelines and empirical examples of case selection and sampling in migration research. *Qualitative research in European migration studies*, 151-168.

Bauder, H. (2021). Urban migrant and refugee solidarity beyond city limits. *Urban Studies (Edinburgh, Scotland)*, *58*(16), 3213–3229. DOI: 10.1177/0042098020976308

Bielewska, A., Ślęzak-Belowska, E., & Czeranowska, O. (2024). How Do Bigger and Smaller Cities Manage Migration? Ukrainian War Refugees in Polish Cities. *Eastern European Politics and Societies.*

Błaszczyk, M., Dolińska, K., Makaro, J., & Pluta, J. (2024). Governance agility in reception of war refugees from Ukraine: The case of Wrocław, Poland. *Social Policy and Administration*, *58*(1), 189–204. DOI: 10.1111/spol.12958

Blažytė, G., Bielevičiūtė, I., & Stoma, S. (2022). *Savivaldybių atsakas į karo pabėgėlių iš Ukrainos: iššūkiai ir gerosios patirtys, Tyrimo atsakaita*, VšĮ Diversity Develpoment Group, 1-50, https://sppd.lrv.lt/uploads/sppd/documents/files/Karo%20pabegeliu%20is%20Ukrainos%20priemimas_final.pdf

Blažytė, G., Sotirovič, V. P., & Žibas, K. (2016). Visuomenės nuostatos apie socialines ir etnines grupes Lietuvoje: nepakantumo ir socialinės distancijos stebėsena. *Lietuvos gyventojų grupių socialinė kaita*, 109-124.

Blažytė, G., & Žibas, K. (2019). Integration of beneficiaries of international protection in the Lithuanian labour market: Policies and practices. *Transfer: European Review of Labour and Research, 25*(1), 113–119. DOI: 10.1177/1024258918819981

Bučaitė-Vilkė, J., & Lazauskienė, A. (2021). Local state-society relations in Lithuania. *Close Ties in European Local Governance: Linking Local State and Society*, 243-257.

Burbulytė-Tsiskarishvili, G., Dvorak, J., & Žernytė, A. (2018). Savivaldybių funkcijų ir galių kaita Lietuvoje 1994-2016 metais. *Viešoji politika ir administravimas, 17*(3), 399-420.

Campomori, F., & Ambrosini, M. (2020). Multilevel governance in trouble: The implementation of asylum seekers' reception in Italy as a battleground. *Comparative Migration Studies, 8*(1), 22. DOI: 10.1186/s40878-020-00178-1

Campomori, F., & Casula, M. (2023). How to frame the governance dimension of social innovation: Theoretical considerations and empirical evidence. *Innovation (Abingdon), 36*(2), 171–189. DOI: 10.1080/13511610.2022.2036952

Caponio, T., & Borkert, M. (2010). *The local dimension of migration policymaking* (p. 204). Amsterdam University Press, 9-20.

Caponio, T., & Jones-Correa, M. (2018). Theorising migration policy in multilevel states: The multilevel governance perspective. *Journal of Ethnic and Migration Studies, 44*(12), 1995–2010. DOI: 10.1080/1369183X.2017.1341705

Čepeliauskaitė, G. (2018). The analysis of effective immigrant integration policy in Lithuania: Practice and problems. *Public Policy and Administration, 17*(3), 421–438. DOI: 10.5755/j01.ppaa.17.3.21956

Croatia, U. N. H. C. R. (2023). *Intentions and perspectives of refugees from Ukraine in Croatia*. https://www.unhcr.org/hr/wp-content/uploads/sites/19/2023/12/croatia intention survey-2023.pdf

Darling, J. (2022). The politics of discretion: Authority and influence in asylum dispersal. *Political Geography, 94*, 102560. DOI: 10.1016/j.polgeo.2021.102560

De Coninck, D., & Solano, G. (2023). Integration policies and migrants' labour market outcomes: A local perspective based on different regional configurations in the EU. *Comparative Migration Studies, 11*(1), 23. DOI: 10.1186/s40878-023-00347-y

Deimantas, V. J., & Şanlıtürk, A. E. (2023). Refugees from Ukraine in Lithuania and the Lithuanian labour market: A preliminary assessment. *Migration Research Series. IOM Migration*, (75), 1–22.

Dimitriadis, I., Hajer, M. H., Fontanari, E., & Ambrosini, M. (2023). Local "Battlegrounds". Relocating multi-level and multi-actor governance of immigration. *Revue européenne des migrations internationales, 37*(1 et 2), 251-275.

Dimitrov, A., & Pavlov, V. (2023). Economic Challenges to Ukrainian Refugee Integration in Central and Eastern Europe. *Journal of Liberty and International Affairs*, *9*(3), 98–118. DOI: 10.47305/JLIA2393089d

Doomernik, J., & Ardon, D. (2018). The city as an agent of refugee integration. *Urban Planning*, *3*(4), 91–100. DOI: 10.17645/up.v3i4.1646

EC. European Commission, (2024a), *Governance of migrant integration in Croatia*, https://migrant-integration.ec.europa.eu/country-governance/governance-migrant-integration-croatia_en

EC. (2024b), *Governance of migrant integration in Lithuania*, https://migrant-integration.ec.europa.eu/country-governance/governance-migrant-integration-lithuania_en

EMN. (2020). *Organisation of Migration and Asylum System in Croatia, Overview*, https://home-affairs.ec.europa.eu/system/files/2022-03/2020_EMN_Croatia_factsheet_organogram_EN.pdf

EMN. European Migration Network, (2022). Organisation of Migation and Asylum System in Lithuania, Orveview. https://www.emn.lt/uploads/Products/product_1542/Santrauka-EN2.pdf

EUROSTAT. (2024a). Beneficiaries of temporary protection at the end of the month by citizenship, age and sex - monthly, *Online data set, code 'migr_asytpsm'*, https://ec.europa.eu/eurostat/databrowser/view/MIGR_ASYTPSM__custom_7394287/default/table?lang=en

Eurostat. (2024b). *Beneficiaries of temporary protection at the end of the month by citizenship*, age and sex - monthly data, migr asytpsm, https://ec.europa.eu/eurostat/databrowser/view/migr_asytpsm__custom_12497557/default/table?lang=enDOI: 10.2908/migr_asytpsm

Geuijen, K., Oliver, C., & Dekker, R. (2020). Local innovation in the reception of asylum seekers in the Netherlands: Plan Einstein as an example of multi-level and multi-sector collaboration. *Geographies of asylum in Europe and the role of European localities*, 245-260.

Giljević, T., & Lalić Novak, G. (2020). Integration of migrants through a prism of specific sustainable development goals: A perspective of public administration. *Sustainable Development (Bradford)*, *28*(4), 1002–1009. DOI: 10.1002/sd.2052

Glorius, B., & Doomernik, J. (2020). *Introduction, Geographies of asylum in Europe and the role of European localities*. Springer Nature.

Gońda, M. (2021). Waiting for immigration to come. The case of Lodz. *Studia Migracyjne-Przegląd Polonijny*, *47*(3), 293–317. DOI: 10.4467/25444972SMPP.21.042.14462

Gregurović, M., & Župarić-Iljić, D. (2023). "At first it was not very pleasant... Now it is different": Experiences and Challenges of Refugee Integration in Croatia. Treatises and Documents, *Journal of Ethnic Studies/Razprave in Gradivo, Revija za narodnostna vprašanja*, 91(91), 157-177.

Guzmán, C., Santos, F. J., Valiente, L., & Santolaya, F. J. (2023). Social Innovation for the Socio-Labour Integration of Refugees in New Host Countries: The Spanish Case. *Journal of Social Entrepreneurship*, •••, 1–26. DOI: 10.1080/19420676.2023.2275132

Holbrook, C. (2020). Redesigning collaborative governance for refugee settlement services. *Australian Journal of Political Science*, *55*(1), 86–97. DOI: 10.1080/10361146.2019.1686116

Homberger, A., Kirchhoff, M., Mallet-Garcia, M., Ataç, I., Güntner, S., & Spencer, S. (2022). Local responses to migrants with precarious legal status: Negotiating inclusive practices in cities across Europe. *Zeitschrift für Migrationsforschung*, *2*(2), 93–116.

IOM (International Organization for Migration). (2023). *DTM Lithuania Surveys with refugees from Ukraine: needs, intentions and integration challenges*, Vilnius. June 2023, 1-19, https://lithuania.iom.int/sites/g/files/tmzbdl1336/files/inline-files/dtm_2023_lt_needs-intentions_ukraine_q3_corrected-4_1.pdf

Jonitz, E., Schiller, M., & Scholten, P. (2024). Are small towns a battleground for migration governance? Negotiating refugee integration in small towns in the Netherlands. *Local Government Studies*, •••, 1–24. DOI: 10.1080/03003930.2024.2357306

Kanas, A., & Kosyakova, Y. (2023). Greater local supply of language courses improves refugees' labor market integration. *European Societies*, *25*(1), 1–36. DOI: 10.1080/14616696.2022.2096915

Keser, I. (2023). Interdependence and Complementarity of a Multi-Dimensional Concept of Sustainable Development and the Integrated Approach to Urban Governance—Case Study City of Zagreb. *Sustainability (Basel)*, *15*(12), 9213. DOI: 10.3390/su15129213

Kiralj, J., & Ajduković, D. (2022). Integration of Refugees in Croatia–A Qualitative Study of the Integration Process and Intergroup Relations of Refugees from Syria. *Društvena istraživanja: časopis za opća društvena pitanja*, 31(4), 661-682.

Koprić, I., Lalić Novak, G., & Giljević, T. (2021). Local Integration Policy of Migrants in Croatia: In *Search of Coherence and Capacity. Local Integration of Migrants Policy: European Experiences and Challenges*, 215-230.

Koprić, I., Škarica, M., & Manojlović Tomań, R. (2019). Local public services and austerity measures in Croatia: Adaptations of the resilient social model through the central-local power and blame games. *Local public services in times of austerity across Mediterranean Europe*, 167-191.

Kreichauf, R., & Mayer, M. (2023). Negotiating urban solidarities: multiple agencies and contested meanings in the making of solidarity cities. In *Displacement, Asylum and the City* (pp. 111-134). Routledge. DOI: 10.4324/9781003381297-6

Ladner, A., Keuffer, N., Baldersheim, H., Hlepas, N., Swianiewicz, P., Steyvers, K., & Navarro, C. (2019). *Patterns of local autonomy in Europe* (Vol. 184). Palgrave Macmillan. DOI: 10.1007/978-3-319-95642-8

Lalić Novak, G., & Giljević, T. (2018). Integration of 'new' refugees in the non-immigrant countries along the Balkan route of migration-overview of legal framework and practices, *Ročenka uprchlického a cizineckého práva*. Brno: Veřejný ochránce práv, 2018, 453-470.

Lalić Novak, G., & Giljević, T. (2019). Legal and Institutional Framework of Integration of Migrants in Croatia–Towards a European Model. *Godišnjak Akademije pravnih znanosti Hrvatske*, 10(1), 163-184.

Lalić Novak, G., & Giljević, T. (2023). *Protokol postupanja prilikom integracije osoba kojima je odobrena međunarodna zaštita i pripadajući priručnik s primjerima dobre prakse*, https://pravamanjina.gov.hr/UserDocsImages/dokumenti/Protokol%20postupanja%20prilikom%20integracije%20osoba%20kojima%20je%20odobrena%20me%C4%91unarodna%20za%C5%A1tita.pdf

Matuszczyk, K. (2023). Immigrants, residents, employees. Refugees from Ukraine in local migration policy in Poland illustrated with the example of selected agglomerations. *Social Insurance.Theory into Practice*, *155*(4), 67–84.

Meijer, M., Popławska, J. Z., & Szytniewski, B. (2023). Spaces of Decoupling in the Netherlands and Poland: Emerging Local Governance Networks for Hosting Non-EU Migrants in Peripheral and Shrinking Areas. *Journal of International Migration and Integration*, *24*(S5, Suppl 5), 839–862. DOI: 10.1007/s12134-023-01057-1

MIPEX. (2020b). *Croatia*https://www.mipex.eu/croatia

MIPEX (Migrant Integration Policy Index). (2020a). *Lithuania*, 2019; https://www.mipex.eu/lithuania

Morawska, E. (2018). Qualitative migration research: Viable goals, open-ended questions, and multidimensional answers. *Qualitative research in European migration studies*, 113-131.

Neergaard, H. (2007). 10 Sampling in entrepreneurial settings. *Handbook of qualitative research methods in entrepreneurship*, 253-278.

OECD. (2023). *What we know about the skills and early labour market outcomes of refugees from Ukraine, OECD Policy Responses on the Impacts of the War in Ukraine*. OECD Publishing., DOI: 10.1787/c7e694aa-

Oliver, C., Dekker, R., Geuijen, K., & Broadhead, J. (2020). Innovative strategies for the reception of asylum seekers and refugees in European cities: Multi-level governance, multi-sector urban networks and local engagement. *Comparative Migration Studies*, *8*(1), 1–14. DOI: 10.1186/s40878-020-00189-y

Oomen, B., Baumgärtel, M., Miellet, S., Durmus, E., & Sabchev, T. (2021). Strategies of divergence: Local authorities, law, and discretionary spaces in migration governance. *Journal of Refugee Studies*, *34*(4), 3608–3628. DOI: 10.1093/jrs/feab062

Özdemir, G. Ş. (2022). Urban solidarity typology: A comparison of European cities since the crisis of refuge in 2015. *Cities (London, England)*, *130*, 103976. DOI: 10.1016/j.cities.2022.103976

Pandek, K., & Župarić-Iljić, D. (2018). Strengthening borders, managing centres: Reception conditions and provisions of services to asylum seekers in Croatia. *Migracijske i Etnicke Teme*, *34*(3), 217–249. DOI: 10.11567/met.34.3.1

Pędziwiatr, K., & Magdziarz, W. (2023). The reception and integration of refugees from Ukraine in Poland, Czechia, Slovakia and Hungary–the new immigration destinations of Central Europe. *Social Policy Issues*, *59*(4), 345–377. DOI: 10.31971/pps/162968

Rijavec, D., Štambuk, A., & Pevcin, P. (2021). Evidence-based assessment of readiness to solve wicked problems: The case of migration crisis in Croatia and Slovenia. *Social Sciences (Basel, Switzerland)*, *10*(6), 188. DOI: 10.3390/socsci10060188

Subramanian, I., Finsterwalder, J., & Hall, C. M. (2022). A systematic literature review of service-related research on refugees. *Journal of Services Marketing*, *36*(7), 908–939. DOI: 10.1108/JSM-09-2021-0312

Švaljek, S., Rašić Bakarić, I., & Sumpor, M. (2019). Citizens and the city: The case for participatory budgeting in the City of Zagreb. *Public Sector Economics*, *43*(1), 21–48. DOI: 10.3326/pse.43.1.4

Szara, K., & Ślusarczyk, B. (2020). Capacities for the development of creative capital in Lithuanian counties. *European Review (Chichester, England)*, *28*(4), 678–692. DOI: 10.1017/S1062798720000137

Tkachuk, A., Kostrykina, S., & Janeliūnas, T. (2023) *Adaptation and Integration of Ukrainian migrants in Lithuania, Research study*, Eastern Europe Studies Center, EESC, 1-19, https://www.eesc.lt/wp-content/uploads/2023/11/v01_Ukrainian-report_Janeliunas_EN_A4.pdf

Vitálišová, K., & Dvořák, J. (2023). Differences and Similarities in Local Participative Governance in Slovakia and Lithuania. In *Participatory and Digital Democracy at the Local Level: European Discourses and Practices* (pp. 125–146). Springer International Publishing. DOI: 10.1007/978-3-031-20943-7_8

Wach, D., & Pachocka, M. (2022). Polish Cities and Their Experience in Integration Activities-The Case of Warsaw. *Studia Europejskie-Studies in European Affairs*, *26*(2), 89–105. DOI: 10.33067/SE.2.2022.6

Wehrhahn, R., & Hathat, Z. E. (2022). Refugee Migration to Europe-Current Challenges and Potentials for Cities and Regions. *Comparative Population Studies*, *47*, 513–532. DOI: 10.12765/CPoS-2022-19

Wolffhardt, A., Conte, C., & Huddleston, T. (2019). *The European Benchmark for refugee integration: A comparative analysis of the national integration evaluation mechanism in 14 EU countries*. Baseline Report, https://ec.europa.eu/migrant-integration/system/files/2022-06/NIEM%20report%20second%20evaluation%202022.pdf

Zapata-Barrero, R. (2018). Applied political theory and qualitative research in migration studies. *Qualitative research in European migration studies*, 75-92.

Žibas, K. (2015). Immigration policies in Lithuania: institutional and legislative developments, challenges and opportunities. *Problemy Polityki Społecznej. Studia i dyskusje*, (31 (4)), 59-79.

Chapter 9
Maslikhats in Kazakhstan in the Context of Electoral Reforms and Governance Evolution

Amina Urpekova
https://orcid.org/0000-0002-8882-5562
Kazakhstan Institute for Strategic Studies, Astana, Kazakhstan

Zhanar Sankhayeva
https://orcid.org/0009-0003-2914-7954
Kazakhstan Institute for Strategic Studies, Astana, Kazakhstan

ABSTRACT

This study examines the evolution of maslikhats in Kazakhstan, focusing on their role in governance and recent electoral reforms. Maslikhats, established as local representative bodies, have undergone significant changes to enhance their authority and political participation. The 2022 constitutional amendments introduced a mixed electoral system, allowing for both party-affiliated and independent candidates, which aimed to increase political competition and local self-governance. However, challenges remain, including financial and structural limitations that restrict their autonomy. The findings highlight the impact of these reforms on political dynamics, representation, and the effectiveness of local governance, emphasizing the need for further decentralization and institutional strengthening.

DOI: 10.4018/979-8-3373-0452-6.ch009

INTRODUCTION

The political trajectory of Kazakhstan has undergone profound changes since the leadership transition in 2019, with the shift from Nursultan Nazarbayev to Kassym-Jomart Tokayev. This transition marked the beginning of a series of political reforms aimed at addressing the longstanding demand for political liberalization and systemic changes in governance. The January 2022 events further catalyzed these efforts, emphasizing the urgency of democratization and the transformation of governance structures, particularly at the local level. The 2022 constitutional referendum and subsequent amendments to electoral legislation introduced a wave of reforms that significantly expanded the role of various political actors, making the decision-making process more inclusive and participatory.

Central to this transformation has been the evolving role of maslikhats, Kazakhstan's representative bodies at the regional and local levels. Established in 1993 as part of the country's broader decentralization efforts, maslikhats have undergone significant changes over the decades.

Since the adoption of the first regulations governing the functioning of maslikhats in the 1990s, significant steps have been taken to strengthen and structurally modernize this representative body. In December 1993, the institution of maslikhats was established in Kazakhstan through the adoption of the Law "On Local Representative and Executive Bodies of the Republic of Kazakhstan." This legislative act laid the foundation for transferring local representative functions from oblast, city, and district councils to a new representative body – the maslikhats. This served as the basis for holding the first maslikhat elections on March 7, 1994.

Today, maslikhats operate at multiple levels, including regional maslikhats, maslikhats of cities of republican significance, as well as city and district maslikhats. Their activities are regulated by the Law of the Republic of Kazakhstan "On Local Public Administration and Self-Government in the Republic of Kazakhstan." Additionally, a standard maslikhat regulation establishes ethical norms for deputies, defining standards of conduct during maslikhat sessions, interactions with voters and the public, and relations with government bodies and officials, including engagement with the media (President of the Republic of Kazakhstan, 2013).

As a result of successive reforms, particularly those initiated under the constitutional reform framework, maslikhats have significantly expanded and strengthened their powers at the local level. They play a key role in the political system by carrying out essential functions such as electing deputies to the Senate of Parliament and approving the appointment of akims of oblasts or cities of republican significance. Thus, maslikhats serve as an integral part of Kazakhstan's governance system, ensuring representation and the effective functioning of both the executive and legislative branches of power.

Along with the need to strengthen the influence of maslikhats, President K.K. Tokayev, in his Address to the People of Kazakhstan, "New Kazakhstan: The Path of Renewal and Modernization," emphasized the importance of increasing public trust in representative authorities at the local level (Tokayev, 2022). This highlights the significance of improving mechanisms of interaction between voters and their elected representatives, ensuring greater accountability and transparency in decision-making at the regional level.

Therefore, the process of forming the composition of maslikhat deputies is crucial, as they represent the interests of local voters and influence the outcomes of elections to the Senate of Parliament and other government bodies. The importance of maslikhat elections lies in their ability to accurately reflect the diversity of opinions and interests within society at the regional level, thereby ensuring the legitimacy and transparency of decisions and legislation at both the local and national levels.

According to recent constitutional reforms, maslikhat elections have been transitioned to a mixed electoral system. The changes included the introduction of a mixed system for electing deputies of maslikhats in cities of republican significance, the implementation of a majoritarian system for electing deputies of district maslikhats and maslikhats of oblast-level cities, the establishment of a recall procedure for deputies, and the transformation of the position of maslikhat secretary into that of chairman.

Throughout the history of independent Kazakhstan, the mixed electoral system has been used twice in parliamentary elections. The first time was in the 1999 elections. This initial reform marked a departure from the majoritarian system, which had been used in the Kazakh SSR and the early years of independence. However, the majoritarian element continued to dominate, as only 10 out of 77 deputies in the second convocation of the Mazhilis were elected through the proportional system.

Later, a full transition to a proportional system was implemented, which was used in elections from 2007 to 2021. From this perspective, the mixed system of 1999–2007 can be seen as an intermediate stage in Kazakhstan's gradual transition from a majoritarian electoral system for the lower house of Parliament to a proportional one.

It is worth noting that the transition of Mazhilis elections to a mixed system in 1999 was not followed by a corresponding shift in the election process for maslikhat deputies. Moreover, no changes were made to the maslikhat electoral system even after the Mazhilis transitioned to elections based solely on the proportional system.

In 2018, a proportional electoral system was introduced for electing deputies to maslikhats. As a result, election by party lists was implemented for deputies at the local level. Deputies to maslikhats were elected under this system in 2021.

In 2022–2023, the second transition to a mixed electoral system occurred, and this time, the changes affected not only the Mazhilis but also the maslikhats of oblasts and cities of republican significance. It is important to note that the majoritarian component in the election of deputies progressively increased from the Mazhilis to the maslikhats. Thus, deputies in the lower house of Parliament are primarily elected through party lists: 70% of deputies are elected this way, while 30% are elected in 29 single-member districts. In the maslikhats of oblasts and cities of republican significance, 50% of deputies are elected through party lists, and the remaining 50% are elected in single-member districts, ensuring a balance between the proportional and majoritarian components. In contrast, all deputies to maslikhats of districts and cities of oblast-level significance are elected through the majoritarian system.

An important aspect of the 2022 reforms also included changes to party legislation, which lowered the vote threshold for political parties to enter elected bodies from 7% to 5%, as well as changes that facilitated the registration process for political parties. This led to the registration of two new political parties in 2022–2023 and an increase in party representation in maslikhats following the elections.

Thus, the most recent electoral campaign was marked by new electoral conditions, which significantly invigorated the election process at the local level. In this context, the study of maslikhat elections becomes particularly relevant, as it allows for an assessment of the effectiveness of the reforms being implemented, identification of challenges, and the exploration of prospects for the development of the local election system and its impact on the effectiveness of local self-governance.

Before the reforms, the political system of Kazakhstan was characterized by one-party dominance and the weakness of independent candidates. Changes in the electoral legislation now open new opportunities for civil society and independent political forces. This chapter aims to examine key aspects of local elections, using maslikhat election campaigns as a case study. The study will address the following questions:

- Has competition in elections really increased?
- How does the mixed electoral system (proportional and majoritarian) influence the composition of maslikhats? What is the level of representation of various social and political groups in maslikhats?
- What factors continue to limit political diversity? How successfully can independent candidates compete with party lists?
- What strategies are used by candidates in conducting election campaigns? How is electoral consulting developing at the local level, and what factors determine its effectiveness?

Thus, this chapter places particular emphasis on the updated procedure for electing local deputies, candidate nomination and registration procedures, as well as the analysis of voting results in order to assess their impact on political dynamics. Studying these issues helps to understand the specificities of election campaigns for maslikhat deputies and the development of electoral culture across regions. The empirical analysis of the most recent election campaigns will reveal how well the new mechanisms work in practice and which barriers still need to be addressed.

The study used a comprehensive methodology, enabling a multifaceted examination of the 2023 maslikhat elections at all levels. The primary data sources were statistical information obtained from both primary and secondary sources. For a comprehensive assessment of campaigns, and to identify the characteristics depending on the maslikhat level, an expert survey was conducted with the participation of 25 experts, political scientists, and public figures. The expert survey contained six key questions regarding the evaluation of the 2023 election campaign. The expert analysis provided qualitative data that supplemented the statistical findings.

STRUCTURE AND POWERS OF MASLIKHATS

Maslikhats in Kazakhstan operate at various levels, playing a crucial role in the country's governance by ensuring flexibility in decision-making and adapting policies to local needs. Broadly, maslikhats can be categorized into two tiers: the first level includes regional (oblast) maslikhats and the maslikhats of cities with republican significance (Astana, Almaty, and Shymkent), while the second level consists of district and city maslikhats.

The distinction between these levels is based on four key factors that shape their structure and functions. First, there is a difference in regional representation, meaning that the number of deputies and the geographical scope they cover vary depending on whether they serve at the oblast, city, or district level. Second, the number of deputies differs across levels, reflecting variations in population size. Third, election methods vary: regional maslikhat deputies are elected through a mixed system, whereas district-level representatives are chosen solely through a majoritarian system. Finally, each level of maslikhat has distinct areas of decision-making authority and influence, covering various aspects of social, economic, and cultural governance that require tailored approaches.

Another major factor influencing the activities of maslikhats is the size of the local budget, which is determined by the scale of the territory, population, and specific responsibilities of local self-governance bodies. Regional maslikhats typically manage larger budgets, as they oversee extensive social and economic programs and major infrastructure projects. While budgets at the district and city level are smaller, these maslikhats play a vital role in addressing local issues and implementing municipal programs. However, their financial autonomy is limited – they must approve local budgets in accordance with the national budget. For instance, the regulations of the Astana City Maslikhat stipulate that the capital's budget must be approved in a session no later than two weeks after the President of Kazakhstan signs the national budget into law.

As of the most recent elections in 2023, Kazakhstan has a total of 3,415 deputies across 223 maslikhats at various levels (Central Election Commission of Kazakhstan, 2023). This marks an increase from the previous count of 3,276 deputies in 216 maslikhats ("The CEC RK spoke about the upcoming elections", 2020). The rise in the number of deputies and maslikhats is primarily due to the administrative and territorial reorganization of the country between the 2021 and 2023 maslikhat elections, which saw the creation of three new regions – Abai, Zhetysu, and Ulytau.

According to the Law of the Republic of Kazakhstan "On Local Public Administration and Self-Governance," when new districts or regions are established, maslikhat deputies elected through party lists are redistributed proportionally based on the population of the newly divided areas, while also considering the positions of political parties. Similarly, deputies elected in single-mandate constituencies are reassigned according to the territorial jurisdiction of their electoral district. In cases where districts or regions are merged, the existing deputies retain their mandates and continue their work within the newly reorganized maslikhats until the next election cycle. This reorganization mechanism ensures the institutional continuity of maslikhats, allowing them to function effectively without disruptions, thereby maintaining stability and efficiency in local decision-making.

Legislation also stipulates that for a maslikhat to be considered legally constituted, at least three-quarters of its total seats must be filled. This requirement serves as a safeguard to ensure adequate representation of diverse voter interests. The number of deputies in each maslikhat is determined by the Central Election Commission of Kazakhstan at the time of election scheduling and varies by level:

- Up to 50 deputies in regional (oblast) maslikhats and maslikhats of cities with republican significance;
- Up to 30 deputies in city maslikhats;
- Up to 25 deputies in district maslikhats.

The number of maslikhat deputies is primarily determined based on population size. For example, in regional (oblast) maslikhats, the number of deputies ranges from 26 for populations up to 300,000, while in the maslikhats of cities with republican significance and the capital, the minimum is 30 deputies for populations up to 1.1 million. Notably, for every additional 200,000 residents, two more deputy mandates are added ("On Determining the Number of Elected Deputies of the Maslikhats," 2020). This system is applied not only in major cities but also at the district and municipal levels, ensuring electoral balance and allowing for flexible adjustments in response to demographic shifts.

Beyond population size, other factors must also be considered when determining the number of mandates, particularly in regional maslikhats. In addition to overall population figures, population density in the southern regions and the spatial distribution of settlements in the northern regions are crucial factors. This approach helps prevent underrepresentation of both densely populated areas and remote rural communities. As shown in Figure 1, the three regions with the highest population density – Turkestan (18.2 people per km^2), Almaty (14.3 people per km^2), and Zhambyl (8.4 people per km^2) – also lead in the number of deputies in regional maslikhats (Zholdybalina et al., 2024). However, failing to account for population density variations can create imbalances in the representation of voters from different districts and rural areas.

Figure 1. Population density and number of villages in Kazakhstan's regions as of early 2023

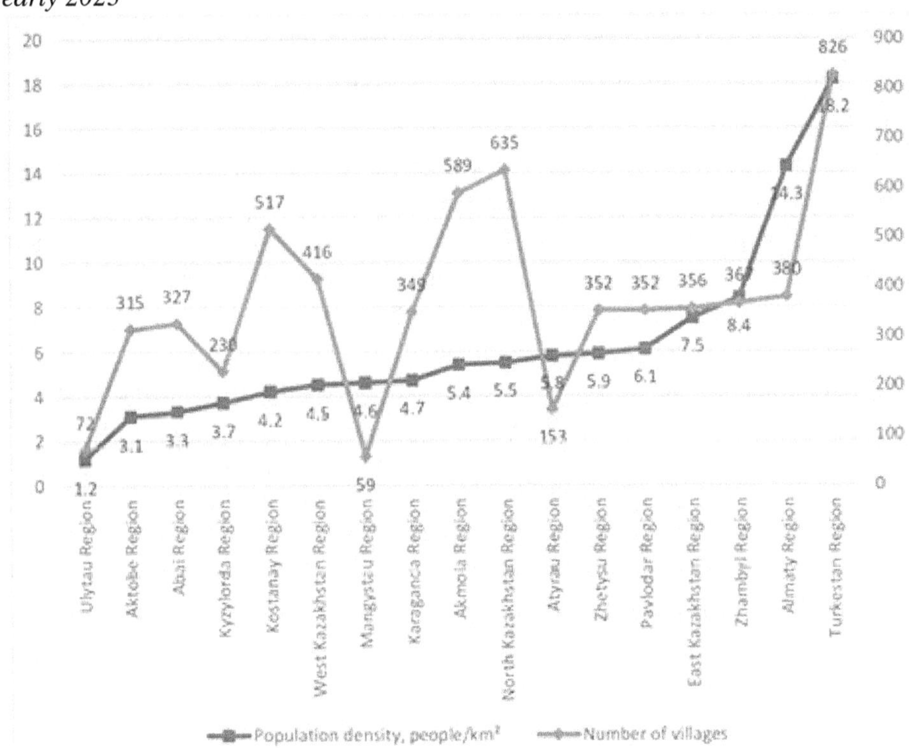

Source: Data from the National Statistical Bureau of the Agency for Strategic Planning and Reforms of the Republic of Kazakhstan

On one hand, high population density simplifies election campaign efforts, making it more cost-effective for parties and candidates to visit villages and hold meetings with voters compared to less densely populated districts and regions. On the other hand, the concentrated needs of residents in the densely populated southern regions necessitate a larger number of deputies to effectively address local issues. In contrast, the sparsely populated northern regions require consideration of distances and accessibility to ensure an equitable distribution of resources.

One of the defining characteristics of maslikhats is their authority and influence over local governance, which is shaped by both legal provisions and practical implementation mechanisms. The powers of maslikhats in Kazakhstan are established by the Law "On Local Public Administration and Self-Governance in the Republic of Kazakhstan," while broader policy directions for local self-governance and maslikhats are outlined in development concepts.

The 2012 Concept for the Development of Local Self-Governance in Kazakhstan aimed to strengthen the role of maslikhats by expanding their authority and enhancing oversight over the activities of akimats. It envisioned a gradual decentralization process, greater financial independence, and increased influence over personnel policy, including the appointment of akims. Additionally, the concept considered the professionalization of deputies by transitioning some of them to full-time roles. While some of these proposed reforms were implemented, particularly in terms of professionalization and influence over personnel decisions, others remained only partially realized.

The new 2021–2025 Concept places a strong emphasis on developing digital democracy mechanisms and enhancing public oversight, which also affects maslikhats. This shift is accompanied by a political neutralization of maslikhats: while they previously served as a counterbalance to akims, helping maintain equilibrium between representative and executive power, their role in personnel policy was significantly reduced following the introduction of direct elections for akims. A key issue in the ongoing development of local self-governance remains the financial independence of maslikhats and their ability to exercise real budgetary control.

When examining the competencies and powers of maslikhats, two main categories emerge: general competencies shared by maslikhats at all levels and specific powers assigned to different levels of maslikhats.

Overall, maslikhats have a broad range of responsibilities, particularly in budgetary and financial regulation, social policy, urban planning, and territorial development, as illustrated in Table 1. However, in practice, their role is largely limited to an approval function, where they mainly endorse documents drafted by executive bodies. This working format raises questions about their ability not only to oversee akimats but also to independently shape regional development agendas. At the same time, concerns remain regarding the professional expertise and qualifications of deputies, particularly their capacity to provide informed assessments or independently draft regional development strategies.

Despite the formal limitations on their authority, maslikhats still retain certain levers of influence over the executive branch, primarily in personnel decisions. They are responsible for approving the structure and composition of akimats, advisory and consultative bodies, and also participate in the appointment process of regional and city akims in cities of republican significance. In theory, this mechanism should help maintain a balance between executive and representative power. However, in a centralized decision-making system, the role of maslikhats in this process remains largely nominal.

Maslikhats also play a significant role in the electoral process. They not only elect senators representing their region in the Senate but also determine the composition of territorial and precinct election commissions. While this mechanism is officially positioned as a safeguard for the independence of electoral procedures, in practice, it creates an institutional feedback loop: the bodies responsible for organizing elections are formed by the very representative institutions that later undergo the election process themselves.

Table 1. Powers of maslikhats at all levels

Area	Powers
Budget and finance	Approval of development plans, economic and social programs, local budgets, and reports on their implementation, including the approval of budgetary programs. Submission of proposals on audit and financial oversight to revision commissions.
Supervision and oversight of the executive authority	Review of reports from heads of government bodies and initiation of accountability for officials, oversight of the execution of the local budget and territorial development programs, and review of the annual report on budget execution submitted by revision commissions.
Social policy	Approval of target indicators for family support and social assistance, as well as approval of measures aimed at the development and operation of healthcare organizations, including medical care within the penitentiary system.
Urban planning and territorial development	Approval of regulations for the preparation and implementation of the heating season, as well as approval of rules for urban landscaping, including the creation, maintenance, and protection of green spaces.
Personnel regulation	Approval of the akimat's structure and personnel composition based on the akim's proposal, approval of the personnel composition of advisory and consultative bodies under the akimat on interdepartmental issues upon the akim's recommendation, election of members of territorial and precinct election commissions through secret or open voting, a vote of no confidence in akims, and the election of Senate deputies.
Cultural and regional identity	Approval of regional symbols, honorary titles, and awards.

continued on following page

Table 1. Continued

Area	Powers
Land relations	Regulation of land relations in accordance with the legislation
Activities of the maslikhat	Establishment of permanent commissions and other bodies within the maslikhat, review of reports on their activities, and organizational support for the activities of the Public Council.

Source: The Law of the Republic of Kazakhstan "On Local Public Administration and Self-Governance"

As noted earlier, in addition to the general authorities granted to all levels of maslikhats, the law also defines competencies specific to certain maslikhats.

An analysis of the distribution of powers among different levels of maslikhats reveals significant disparities in their influence over decision-making and public governance. Regional maslikhats and those of cities with republican significance have the broadest range of powers, including strategic planning for territorial development, oversight of key social policies, and regulation of public affairs. Their jurisdiction includes approving regional planning schemes, appointing members of audit commissions, regulating migration, and making strategic decisions on matters such as the placement of nuclear facilities and the use of natural resources. This highlights their critical role in making long-term decisions that impact entire regions.

It is worth noting that, following a series of political reforms, district and city maslikhats lost their authority to approve the appointment of akims, while this function was retained by regional maslikhats and those of republican cities.

City maslikhats of oblast significance and district maslikhats have a more limited set of functions, reflecting the centralization of authority in favor of higher-level representative bodies. Their role is mainly focused on local issues, such as approving the list of housing certificate recipients, regulating social assistance, and making decisions on the potential resignation of an akim. However, they do not have jurisdiction over migration control, the appointment of audit commission members, or the regulation of utility tariffs, leaving them in a position of implementing rather than shaping policy.

Furthermore, the regulation of tourism fees, animal control, and social services falls under the jurisdiction of maslikhats of cities with republican significance and oblast centers, underscoring their greater role in urban governance and social policy. District maslikhats, despite their close proximity to local communities, lack similar tools of influence, which limits their ability to tailor policies to local needs.

Thus, the distribution of authorities among maslikhats of different levels reflects the persistence of a vertical power structure, where strategic and economically significant decisions are made at the oblast and major city level, while district maslikhats primarily perform administrative and supervisory functions. Their authority is largely constrained by decisions made at higher levels, reducing their capacity to respond swiftly to local needs.

As previously mentioned, the professionalization of maslikhats remains a key issue in discussions about improving their effectiveness. The structure of professional support for maslikhats is based on strict regulatory constraints governing the number of staff, the roles of chairpersons and deputies, as well as training and financial support. The staffing ratio of one employee per five deputies ensures a minimal administrative apparatus but does not account for variations in workload between large and small maslikhats.

Political balance within maslikhats is maintained by limiting the number of permanent commission chairpersons working on a full-time basis and prohibiting them from belonging to the same political party. While this measure is designed to prevent the dominance of a single political force, it may also complicate policy coordination and decision-making processes. Additionally, restrictions on deputies engaging in business or other paid activities (except in education, science, and the arts) help mitigate conflicts of interest but also deter professionals for whom serving in a maslikhat may be economically unfeasible. This factor could narrow the pool of candidates to professionals from select fields that are not involved in the private sector.

The centralized approach to deputy training through the Academy of Public Administration under the President of Kazakhstan ensures standardized preparation but limits the availability of alternative educational programs, potentially reducing deputies' adaptability to local realities. Financial support for deputies during their tenure allows them to retain their salaries, but the ceiling is tied to the salary of the head of the akim's office, which may not be a sufficient incentive to attract professionals.

Overall, the system of professional support for maslikhats is designed to regulate and control deputies' activities, but it also imposes strict administrative limitations that may reduce operational efficiency and flexibility in personnel policies.

ELECTION TO MASLIKHATS 2023: OPPORTUNITIES FOR INDEPENDENT CANDIDATES

The political reforms of 2019–2023 in Kazakhstan were a response to the challenges of modernizing the system of public administration and addressing society's demand for greater government transparency. A key trend in these reforms was the redistribution of powers across different levels of government, strengthening local self-governance institutions and enhancing their role in decision-making. These changes were accompanied by the liberalization of the political space, including lower barriers for party registration, the introduction of a majoritarian electoral system, and expanded public oversight. However, the central question is not only about the formal redistribution of authority but also about whether these reforms create real mechanisms for citizen participation in governance.

The transformation of the political system occurred alongside the development of human rights protections and the strengthening of public oversight. The re-establishment of the Constitutional Court, the enhanced role of the Ombudsman, the adoption of the Law "On Public Oversight," and the decriminalization of certain offenses were significant steps toward protecting citizens' rights. Recent political reforms represent an attempt to balance centralized control with providing society with new channels for political participation.

In the context of local self-governance, these political reforms affected the formation of maslikhats and the expansion of representation for local communities. The 2022–2023 reforms reinstated a mixed electoral system, strengthening the majoritarian component. As a result, 30% of the Mazhilis deputies are now elected from single-member districts, while in regional maslikhats, this share is 50%. In district and city maslikhats, deputies are elected exclusively through a majoritarian system.

These changes have important implications for the development of local self-governance. First, the stronger majoritarian component creates greater opportunities for independent candidates, enabling local community representatives to run in elections without relying on party lists. This makes maslikhats more diverse and responsive to public demands. Second, the simplification of political party registration and the reduction of the electoral threshold from 7% to 5% have increased political competition, leading to the registration of new parties and expanding their presence in maslikhats. In the long run, this could reduce the dominance of a single party at the local level, fostering greater debate and strengthening maslikhats' ability to influence executive power.

The return of single-member districts also enhances deputies' personal accountability to voters. However, several challenges remain: the dependence of local budgets on the central government, the limited authority of maslikhats, and ongoing administrative support for pro-government candidates may still hinder the full development of local self-governance. Nevertheless, these reforms create conditions for the gradual strengthening of maslikhats and greater citizen involvement in local governance.

Thus, the elections to the Mazhilis of the Parliament of Kazakhstan and maslikhats in March 2023 were the first conducted under the new electoral system, allowing citizens to nominate themselves as independent candidates.

This broadened opportunities for political participation, especially considering the relatively simple requirements for maslikhat candidates: Kazakhstani citizenship, active voting rights, and a minimum age of 20 – making maslikhats the elected bodies with the lowest age requirement for candidates.

An important eligibility criterion is the absence of a criminal record for corruption-related offenses, aligning with the state's broader anti-corruption policy. Unlike in the Mazhilis elections, candidates for maslikhats are not required to reside in the district where they are running. While this provides political parties with greater flexibility in nominating candidates and strengthens regional branches, it may also limit local residents' direct participation in elections.

The implementation of the new electoral system was particularly evident in the elections for deputies of regional maslikhats and those of cities with republican significance, where, for the first time, citizens were able to run for office without party affiliation.

As shown in Table 2, a total of 1,712 candidates contested 334 seats in single-member districts, of whom 1,081 (63.1%) were independent candidates. This reflects a high level of self-nomination at the candidacy stage, allowing more citizens to participate in regional governance without being tied to political parties. The highest number of independent candidates was observed in cities of republican significance: Almaty (163 candidates), Astana (151), and Shymkent (112). Together, candidates from these three cities accounted for 39.4% of all independent nominees in the country. In contrast, some regions, such as Ulytau (43 candidates), Atyrau (50), and Kyzylorda (58), exhibited lower levels of civic engagement.

However, the registration process proved to be a major challenge for independent candidates. Of the 1,449 candidates who successfully registered, the overall disqualification rate was 15.4%. The rejection rate for party-affiliated candidates was 7.4%, whereas for independent candidates, it was significantly higher at 20%. This indicates that self-nominated candidates faced greater difficulties in completing the registration process. The most common reasons for disqualification were voluntary withdrawal before registration (48.7%) and submission of incomplete documentation (39.4%). It appears that a lack of experience in elections, along with limited resources for conducting campaigns, were the main obstacles for independent candidates. As political analyst A. Chebotarev (2023) notes, many of these candidates were running for office for the first time, and some were unable to complete registration or conduct a full-fledged campaign.

The final election results revealed that despite strong engagement at the nomination stage, independent candidates faced significant challenges in securing seats. Out of 334 deputy mandates, only 37 (11%) were won by independent candidates, while party-affiliated candidates secured 297 seats (89%). Regionally, independent candidates failed to win in five regions, whereas their strongest performance was observed in the Abai, Akmola, and Mangystau regions, as well as in the cities of Almaty and Shymkent, where they secured four seats each.

Table 2. Nomination and election results of candidates for single-member districts in regional maslikhats, cities of republican significance

N°	Region	Number of seats	Nominated		Elected candidates	
			Party-affiliated	Independent Candidates	Party-affiliated	Independent Candidates
1.	Abai Region	15	21	36	11	4
2.	Akmola Region	16	24	40	12	4
3.	Aktobe Region	17	28	57	16	1
4.	Almaty Region	19	31	33	19	0
5.	Atyrau Region	15	25	25	14	1
6.	West Kazakhstan Region	15	23	41	15	0
7.	Zhambyl Region	18	33	53	16	2
8.	Zhetysu Region	16	25	38	14	2
9.	Karaganda Region	18	28	42	15	3
10.	Kostanay Region	16	19	40	14	2
11.	Kyzylorda Region	16	22	36	16	0
12.	Mangystau Region	16	19	59	12	4
13.	Pavlodar Region	16	39	32	15	1
14.	North Kazakhstan Region	15	44	18	15	0
15.	Turkestan Region	23	72	46	20	3
16.	Ulytau Region	13	32	11	11	2
17.	East Kazakhstan Region	16	23	48	16	0
18.	Astana	17	42	151	17	0
19.	Almaty	21	47	163	17	4
20.	Shymkent	16	34	112	12	4
Kazakhstan		**334**	**717**	**1 081**	**297**	**37**

Source: Data provided by territorial election commissions

The elections to city and district maslikhats showed lower participation rates for independent candidates compared to elections at the regional and republican city levels.

As shown in Table 3, in the elections for city maslikhats, 2,542 candidates contested 617 seats, with 1,463 (57.6%) being independent. This confirms the overall trend of increasing political participation outside party structures. However, in certain regions, party-affiliated candidates were more active, particularly in Pavlodar, Zhambyl, Atyrau, North Kazakhstan, and Ulytau regions. Meanwhile, the highest number of candidates was recorded in Karaganda (396 candidates) and Turkestan (233 candidates) regions.

Overall, at the city maslikhat level, 2,165 candidates were officially registered, with an overall disqualification rate of 14.8%. The primary reasons for disqualification were incomplete documentation (48.3%) and voluntary withdrawal before registration was completed (47.1%). Only 2.8% of candidates were removed due to late submission after registration, while 1.8% were disqualified for failing to meet eligibility requirements.

Similar trends were observed in the district maslikhat elections. A total of 7,512 candidates ran for 2,130 seats, with 4,458 (59.3%) being independent. In most regions, self-nominated candidates predominated, except in North Kazakhstan (342 party-affiliated candidates), Pavlodar (251), and Ulytau (47), where party candidates were more active. In some districts, party-affiliated candidates also had a strong presence, such as in Temir District of Aktobe Region (19 party candidates vs. 10 independents), Karasai District of Almaty Region (40 vs. 38), and Saryagash District of Turkestan Region (89 vs. 33).

In the district maslikhat elections, 6,589 candidates were registered, with a disqualification rate of 12.3%. The main reasons for candidate withdrawals were similar to those in city maslikhat elections: 60.9% withdrew before registration, 34.4% failed to submit a complete document package, 3.4% were disqualified after registration, and 1.3% were removed due to non-compliance with eligibility criteria.

Table 3. Nomination of candidates for city and district maslikhats in single-member districts

N°	Region	Number of seats	City maslikhats		District maslikhats	
			Party-affiliated	Independent Candidates	Party-affiliated	Independent Candidates
1.	Abai Region	128	53	67	108	185
2.	Akmola Region	133	70	87	237	437
3.	Aktobe Region	171	58	97	174	274
4.	Almaty Region	190	21	27	249	309
5.	Atyrau Region	110	44	40	112	162
6.	West Kazakhstan Region	158	45	59	167	271
7.	Zhambyl Region	174	53	52	214	386
8.	Zhetysu Region	136	37	62	128	223
9.	Karaganda Region	178	154	242	102	191
10.	Kostanay Region	232	61	125	184	362

continued on following page

Table 3. Continued

N°	Region	Number of seats	City maslikhats		District maslikhats	
			Party-affiliated	Independent Candidates	Party-affiliated	Independent Candidates
11.	Kyzylorda Region	120	37	60	110	240
12.	Mangystau Region	105	57	105	88	171
13.	Pavlodar Region	157	121	94	251	134
14.	North Kazakhstan Region	163	41	34	342	121
15.	Turkestan Region	292	61	172	399	780
16.	Ulytau Region	57	93	22	47	2
17.	East Kazakhstan Region	192	73	118	142	210
По РК		***631***	***1079***	***1 463***	***3054***	***4458***

Source: Data provided by territorial election commissions

According to the data in Table 4, the results of the elections for deputies of district and city maslikhats in single-member districts show that out of 2,746 seats, 2,428 (88.4%) were won by party-affiliated candidates, while 318 (11.6%) were secured by independent candidates.

At the regional level, the highest share of seats won by party-affiliated candidates was observed in Kostanay Region, where out of 232 seats, 225 (97%) were taken by party candidates. This was followed by Ulytau Region (96.5%) and North Kazakhstan Region (95%).

At the same time, in some regions, independent candidates managed to secure a relatively higher number of seats. In Almaty Region, for instance, out of 190 seats, 56 (29.5%) were won by independent candidates. In Zhambyl Region, independent candidates secured 35 out of 174 seats (20.1%), while in Mangystau Region, they won 17 out of 105 seats (16.2%).

From a macro-regional perspective, independent candidates gained the most support in the southern regions of the country. A particularly notable case was the elections for the Karasai district in Almaty Region, where independent candidates won 27 out of 30 seats.

Table 4. Election results for deputies of district and city maslikhats in single-member districts by region

Region	Number of district and city maslikhats	Number of seats in single-member districts	Elected candidates	
			Party-affiliated	Independent Candidates
Abai Region	10	128	95	**33**
Akmola Region	20	233	211	22
Aktobe Region	13	171	154	17
Almaty Region	10	190	134	**56**
Atyrau Region	8	110	97	13
West Kazakhstan Region	13	158	148	10
Zhambyl Region	11	174	139	**35**
Zhetysu Region	10	136	122	14
Karaganda Region	13	178	158	20
Kostanay Region	20	232	225	7
Kyzylorda Region	8	120	105	15
Mangystau Region	7	105	88	17
Pavlodar Region	13	157	149	8
North Kazakhstan Region	14	163	155	8
Turkestan Region	17	292	265	27
Ulytau Region	5	57	55	2
East Kazakhstan Region	11	142	128	14
Total	**203**	**2746**	**2428**	**318**

Source: Data provided by territorial election commissions

The elections of maslikhat deputies at various levels, conducted under the new electoral system, provided citizens with the opportunity to run as independent candidates, marking a significant step in enhancing political participation in Kazakhstan. However, an analysis of the final results reveals that despite a substantial number of independent candidates at the nomination stage, their representation among elected deputies remained limited. This raises several questions regarding political competition, barriers for independent candidates, and the overall balance between party-affiliated and independent representatives in local legislative bodies.

One of the key observations is the high level of independent candidates' participation at the nomination stage and their relatively low success rate in the elections. At the regional and republican city maslikhat levels, they accounted for over 60% of all nominees, yet only 11% of elected deputies were independents. A similar trend was observed in city and district maslikhats, where out of 2,746 seats, only 318 (11.6%) were won by self-nominated candidates. This indicates that mere participation in elections does not guarantee success, as party-affiliated candidates enjoy significant competitive advantages.

At the same time, the overall candidate disqualification rate during the registration stage was relatively low (11–15%). This suggests that most independent candidates successfully completed the registration process, but their main challenges arose during the campaign and voting stages. The primary reasons for candidate withdrawals were voluntary withdrawal (accounting for 47% to 60% of disqualified candidates) and incomplete document submission (ranging from 34% to 39%).

Despite the opportunity to participate in elections, independent candidates faced several obstacles that impacted their chances of success. Party-affiliated candidates had better organizational support, allowing them to conduct more effective campaigns. Given that the elections were held under a newly introduced system, many independent candidates lacked the experience needed to develop a winning electoral strategy. Voter preferences in several regions still leaned toward party-affiliated candidates. In regions where party structures have traditionally been strong – such as Kostanay, North Kazakhstan, and Ulytau – independent candidates secured less than 5% of the seats. Meanwhile, in the southern regions, independents received greater support, particularly in Almaty and Zhambyl regions, where they won 20–30% of the seats. Even among registered independent candidates, many lacked the financial and resource capacity to run a full-fledged campaign. Experts noted that a significant portion of independent candidates attempted to participate in elections with minimal expenditures, which negatively affected their competitiveness.

Although party-affiliated candidates continue to dominate maslikhats, the high level of independent candidates' engagement suggests positive shifts in the political system. In the future, the number of independent candidates may continue to grow, especially if measures are taken to simplify the registration process, improve electoral literacy, and introduce mechanisms to support independent candidates. It is also important to consider that the success of independent candidates in the southern regions may serve as a foundation for new electoral trends. If independent candidates can build sustainable support networks, their representation in local government bodies may gradually increase.

The election results for district and city maslikhats show that the majority of seats were won by candidates from the AMANAT party, reaffirming its dominant position in Kazakhstan's political landscape. Members of this party secured 1,963 seats, accounting for 71.5% of all maslikhat mandates. However, the party received the lowest number of seats in Zhambyl, Turkestan, Mangystau, and West Kazakhstan regions, where its support was relatively weaker.

Beyond its overall dominance, AMANAT also played the leading role in ensuring women's representation in maslikhats. Of the 642 female deputies elected, 543 were members of AMANAT, highlighting the party's significant contribution to gender inclusion. The highest number of female party members were elected in northern regions of the country.

The second-largest party in terms of maslikhat representation was "Auyl", which won 180 seats (6.5%), including 21 female deputies. The party's candidates received the most support in West Kazakhstan and Kyzylorda regions. The third-largest party was "Ak Zhol", whose representatives secured 128 mandates, including 23 female deputies. The highest number of "Ak Zhol" deputies was elected in Kostanay Region, while in Pavlodar Region, the party failed to win any seats. The People's Party of Kazakhstan secured 73 seats, including 14 female deputies. In three regions, the party did not gain any representation in maslikhats. The party with the fewest mandates was "Respublica", which won 34 seats, including 10 female deputies. The highest number of its candidates were elected in Kostanay Region, but in eight regions, the party failed to secure any seats.

The election results revealed several major trends related to party representation, political competition, and party strategies during the electoral process. One of the most notable issues was the uneven regional representation of parties. In some regions, such as Pavlodar, certain parties barely fielded candidates, directly affecting their election results. This suggests weaknesses in party recruitment strategies, inadequate election cycle preparation, and limited party activity in specific regions.

Beyond regional representation, the elections demonstrated imbalances in party competition. AMANAT secured 71.5% of district and city maslikhat seats, while other parties lagged far behind. This indicates a monopolized political landscape, despite formal steps toward a multi-party system. Under such conditions, the competitiveness of other parties remains low, raising questions about the need to strengthen their positions and voter engagement strategies.

Another key aspect of the elections was gender representation. Women accounted for 23.4% of all elected deputies, with the majority representing AMANAT. This confirms that female participation in politics heavily depends on party structures, while independent candidates and other parties provide limited support for female candidates. The low percentage of women elected outside AMANAT suggests the need for more active efforts to promote gender inclusion, especially at the regional level.

The elections also highlighted differences in party strategies. Some parties, such as "Auyl", focused their efforts on specific regions, such as West Kazakhstan and Kyzylorda, allowing them to achieve relatively strong results at the local level. Meanwhile, parties with less-defined regional strategies, such as "Respublica", performed inconsistently and failed to secure broad representation, indicating inadequate preparation and weak local networks.

Additionally, party mobilization played a crucial role in election outcomes. For example, "Ak Zhol"'s failure to win any seats in Pavlodar Region was due to the party fielding only one candidate there. This demonstrates that even parties with a stable electorate can lose influence if their mobilization efforts are weak.

Another important trend was the limited role of new parties. "Respublica", despite positioning itself as a promising, change-oriented political force, failed to secure a significant number of seats and remained unrepresented in eight regions. This underscores the challenges that new parties face in Kazakhstan's political system, where established parties maintain a stronghold over the electorate.

Finally, the election results highlighted the gap between party lists and single-member districts. Although the electoral system was reformed, parties still prioritize list-based nominations, while participation in single-member districts remains underdeveloped. As a result, voters predominantly cast their ballots for party-backed candidates, limiting competition and reinforcing the dominance of party structures in Kazakhstan's local governance system.

ELECTION CAMPAIGNING IN THE NEW CONDITIONS

The introduction of a mixed electoral system for regional maslikhats and a majoritarian system for district maslikhats brought significant changes to the election campaign process. The 2023 maslikhat elections differed from previous campaigns as, in addition to political parties, independent candidates also entered the political and electoral competition, increasing the level of contestation.

These electoral system changes affected not only the composition of participants but also the rules governing election campaigns. In response to the new conditions, the state developed mechanisms to regulate campaigning activities, ensuring transparency in the electoral process and equal opportunities for all candidates. According to election laws, each candidate, depending on the level of the representative body, received an equal amount of state funding for their campaign. However, candidates nominated through party lists were not provided with state financing.

One of the innovations in election campaigning was the introduction of online platforms as a medium for campaign activities, regulated similarly to mass media. Users of these platforms who wished to place campaign materials on a contractual basis were required to submit information regarding payment amounts and placement conditions to the Central Election Commission of the Republic of Kazakhstan. Additionally, any published campaign materials had to indicate the source of funding.

Thus, in accordance with legal regulations, election campaigning was conducted through the following channels: mass media; online platforms; the production and distribution of campaign materials; public campaign events; as well as personal meetings between candidates, their authorized representatives, and voters.

Beyond state regulation, the strategic organization of campaigns and their adaptation to modern information realities became key factors in determining their effectiveness. The ability to utilize existing tools efficiently largely influenced the competitiveness of election campaigns. A candidate's success depended on multiple factors: their motivation and determination, the strategic work of their campaign team, the availability of financial, time, and human resources, the thoughtfulness of the campaign, its creativity, its level of transparency, and other aspects affecting voter perception.

To assess the election campaigns and identify their key characteristics, an expert survey was conducted as part of a study on the 2023 maslikhat elections at all levels. The survey gathered insights from 25 experts across different fields. Evaluating the campaigns of candidates running for regional maslikhats and maslikhats of cities of republican significance in single-member districts on a 10-point scale, the majority of experts (43.6%, combined scores of 4–6) gave an average rating, as illustrated in Figure 2. A third of experts (34.8%, combined scores of 7–10) noted that the campaigns were quite engaging. Conversely, 21.6% (combined scores of 1–3) described the campaigns as weak.

Similar evaluations were recorded regarding the campaign efforts of political parties that nominated party lists for elections to regional maslikhats and maslikhats of cities of republican significance. A total of 39.0% of experts characterized the organization and visibility of the campaigns as average. A third of respondents gave high ratings to party-led campaign efforts. However, a quarter (26.0%) highlighted a low level of organization and engagement in party list campaigns.

Figure 2. Expert evaluation of election campaign effectiveness for deputies of oblast maslikhats and maslikhats of cities of republican significance on a 10-point scale (where 1 represents a poorly organized campaign, and 10 represents a bright, engaging, and dynamic campaign)

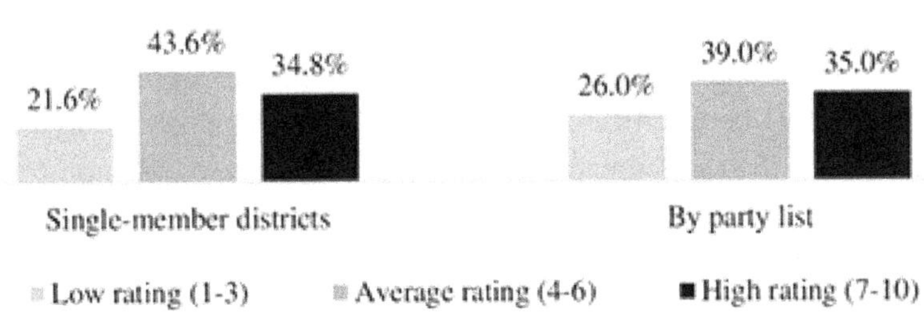

The monitoring of campaign activities by candidates and political parties revealed that election campaigns could be classified into two main approaches: traditional and technology-driven.

Overall, the election campaigns of maslikhat candidates at all levels primarily relied on traditional campaign techniques, including the distribution of flyers and brochures, publication of informational messages in the media, and in-person meetings with voters. This approach had several advantages. First, traditional campaign methods remained the simplest and most proven way to run a campaign within the limited one-month timeframe. Second, at the district maslikhat level, where a majoritarian electoral system was applied, direct meetings with the population and labor collectives proved to be the most effective strategy. The relatively small number of voters and the territorial compactness of electoral districts enabled candidates to establish direct communication with the electorate, increasing trust and name recognition.

Candidates adopted two primary approaches to organizing public events. Proactive activities included hosting sports competitions, meeting with labor collectives, and participating in expert discussions, which allowed candidates to promote their ideas and proposals. Meanwhile, in district maslikhat elections, candidates often employed a reactive approach by attending public gatherings in places such as markets, stores, and residential courtyards, directly engaging with citizens and collecting feedback.

Digital technologies also played an important role in election campaigns, providing candidates with additional tools for voter engagement and broad audience outreach. Candidates actively used social media, online platforms, and mobile applications to share information about their platforms, organize virtual meetings and surveys, and conduct online discussions and debates.

One of the most notable examples of digital technology use in election campaigns was the implementation of QR codes on campaign materials, allowing voters to easily access candidates' programs and objectives. Additionally, virtual offices were established during the campaigns, enabling citizens to submit inquiries and proposals, thereby creating additional channels for voter interaction. Some candidates for city maslikhats in regional centers also adopted modern promotional techniques, such as participating in podcasts and interviews on YouTube, which expanded their audience and improved voter awareness. Moreover, some candidates, on their own initiative and when technically feasible, organized debates on video-hosting platforms, arranging these events among themselves. An example of this was the live-streamed debate between candidates for the Ust-Kamenogorsk city maslikhat in the 9th electoral district, which attracted over 9,000 viewers, demonstrating the significant interest in online platforms as a tool for political communication ("Coming Out" of a Candidate, n.d.).

At the same time, alongside publications in the media, candidates actively leveraged social networks. The highest level of activity was observed on Instagram and Facebook, while TikTok and YouTube were used the least. The use of social media for campaign promotion was particularly common among candidates running in cities of republican significance and for regional maslikhats.

One of the distinctive features of the 2023 election campaign was the scale of the elections and the number of candidates across different maslikhat levels, which led to candidate coalitions during campaign meetings with the public. This approach was more common among party-list candidates and single-member district candidates affiliated with political parties. Candidates running for different levels of maslikhats within the same territorial electoral district often held joint campaign events.

Independent candidates also collaborated in organizing campaign activities. For example, in Almaty, a joint campaign rally was held with candidates for both the Mazhilis and the city maslikhat, allowing each participant to present their platform. Moreover, such rallies served as significant media events, helping to draw additional public attention to the candidates and organizers.

Despite the wide range of available campaign tools, not all candidates fully utilized them, limiting their ability to effectively reach diverse audiences and engage with voters through all available channels. According to expert survey results, at all levels, despite the use of social media and online messaging platforms, campaigns remained uniform and lacked creativity. Experts also highlighted the correlation between candidate activity and their official positions as well as the funding allocated for the campaign. In larger cities, election campaigns often appeared formal and uninspired.

When assessing the campaign efforts of candidates for city and district maslikhats, the majority of experts (43.5%) rated the organization and engagement levels as average, as shown in Figure 3. Meanwhile, 30.5% of experts gave high ratings to the election campaigns at the district and city maslikhat levels. However, a quarter (26.0%) of experts expressed the opinion that the campaigns were weak and unengaging.

Figure 3. Expert evaluation of election campaign effectiveness for deputies of district and city maslikhats on a 10-point scale (where 1 represents a poorly organized campaign, and 10 represents a bright, engaging, and dynamic campaign)

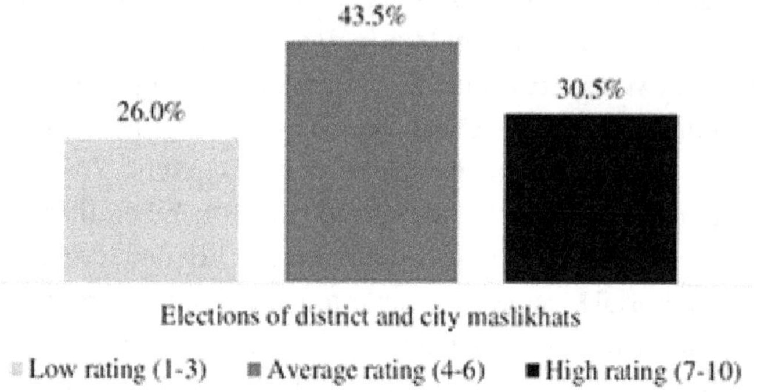

Experts highlight that the return of the majoritarian system was the primary factor influencing campaign dynamics, as it allowed citizens to run as independent candidates. Overall, it was noted that the large number of candidates energized the electoral process and increased competition to some extent. However, many of them struggled to mobilize voters and conducted weak campaign efforts, largely due to their lack of experience in public politics and the shortage of political strategists at the regional level.

Another important factor was election fatigue among the population, caused by the frequent electoral cycles in recent years, including the referendum, presidential, and parliamentary elections. This necessitated more creative approaches to campaigning to engage voters effectively.

Summarizing the key constraints in election campaigning, the following groups of limiting factors were identified:

- Short campaign period, placing significant pressure on candidates and their teams, who had to maximize the use of limited resources within tight deadlines.
- Increased competition for campaign-related services, such as venue rentals, distribution of promotional materials, and advertising, leading to higher campaign costs.
- Lack of experience in online campaigning among most independent maslikhat candidates, which negatively impacted voter outreach in an era where digital promotion plays an increasingly important role.

Given these challenges, political consulting and PR at the regional level are becoming increasingly important under the mixed electoral system. Some experts believe that the regional political consulting market could receive a boost in development due to the growing need for personalized voter engagement strategies and local-level political competition.

On the other hand, several factors may limit the development of this market. One of the main barriers is the long hiatus and lack of continuous political consulting practice in the regions. Many candidates are unwilling to invest heavily in their political careers as they do not see a clear path for advancement from the regional to the national level. Additionally, strict election regulations could act as a constraint on the political consulting industry. Furthermore, there is an acute shortage of professionals in regional political consulting and PR, which further complicates the situation.

Overall, the 2023 maslikhat elections demonstrated that developing a strategic campaign plan requires thorough preparation, taking into account risks and potential barriers. At the same time, the elections provided a valuable learning experience for a large number of citizens, allowing them to gain practical insights into political competition. This experience could serve as valuable training for future campaigns and elections, helping candidates and campaign teams develop strategic planning, voter communication, and adaptability skills.

Moreover, the need to stimulate the regional political consulting market has become increasingly relevant, especially considering the introduction of direct elections for rural and district akims, which will further increase demand for effective campaign strategies and political advisory services at the local level.

CONCLUSION

The maslikhats of Kazakhstan play a crucial role in the system of local governance, ensuring the representation of citizens' interests at various levels. Their structure and functions are shaped by the country's administrative-territorial organization, population size and density, and budgetary constraints. Differences in powers, election methods, and budget sizes define the specific functions of regional, city, and district maslikhats.

Moreover, as demonstrated by the 2023 elections, the evolution of the administrative-territorial structure leads to changes in the number of maslikhats and deputies, requiring flexible mechanisms for the redistribution of mandates. A key issue remains ensuring balanced representation in regions with varying population densities, as disparities can affect accessibility and governance efficiency. Therefore, further improvements in local self-government should consider both quantitative and qualitative factors to enhance stability and adaptability to the country's socio-economic developments.

One of the key challenges is the lack of autonomy in decision-making. Although the law grants maslikhats powers in budget regulation, social development, territorial planning, and oversight of akimats, their actual role is often limited to approving documents prepared by the executive branch. This raises doubts about their ability not only to control akimats but also to actively shape regional development agendas. This issue is particularly acute for district maslikhats, whose functions are largely administrative, rather than policy-oriented.

The professionalization of maslikhats also remains a pressing issue. The transition of some deputies to full-time positions is a positive step, but strict regulatory constraints limit the talent pool. The cap on staff numbers, the ban on combining deputy duties with business activities, and other regulatory barriers create obstacles for qualified specialists, ultimately affecting the quality of decision-making.

The 2019–2023 political reforms marked an important stage in the transformation of governance in Kazakhstan, aiming to increase openness and inclusivity in the political process. A key component of these changes was electoral system reform, including the introduction of the majoritarian system in maslikhat elections, lowering barriers for party registration, and expanding opportunities for independent candidates. However, election results indicate that despite formal changes, political competition remains limited, and party structures continue to dominate local representative bodies.

One of the key trends emerging from these reforms is the increased participation of citizens in politics, evident in the rise in independent candidates. The new election system allowed a greater number of independents to run for office, marking an important step toward pluralism. However, their actual chances of winning remained low, indicating the presence of barriers beyond legislative reforms. These challenges include unequal conditions in campaign financing and organizational support, where party-backed candidates enjoy clear advantages.

Another significant trend is the persistence of party dominance in maslikhats. Despite lowering the electoral threshold and simplifying party registration, the dominance of a single political force remains unchanged. This suggests that the political system is still structurally dependent on administrative resources, and while competition has increased, it has not led to a radical transformation of the political landscape. Even parties that expanded their presence largely complement the existing system rather than offering alternatives to the ruling power.

Independent candidates had little chance of success, highlighting the need for policies that ensure equal opportunities in the electoral process. This trend also underscores a broader issue – independents without party backing face greater difficulties in navigating the electoral process.

The reforms also revealed imbalances between party politics and electoral processes at the local level. In some regions, political parties failed to mobilize effectively, not fielding enough candidates, reflecting weak organizational structures at the regional level. Meanwhile, voter preferences remained conservative, indicating electoral inertia and low trust in new parties and independent candidates.

Another key issue was the difficulty of implementing new political competition mechanisms. Despite creating conditions for independent candidacy, many self-nominated candidates faced challenges in both registration and campaigning. Limited financial resources, lack of experience, and low voter recognition contributed to their poor performance.

The 2023 maslikhat elections also highlighted changes in campaign strategies, influenced by the introduction of mixed and majoritarian electoral systems. The increased participation of independent candidates and greater competition stimulated electoral engagement but also exposed issues such as limited resources, lack of experience, and repetitive campaign strategies.

Despite these challenges, the 2023 elections provided valuable political experience for many candidates, laying the groundwork for more competitive elections in the future. Moving forward, fostering independent political institutions, strengthening local self-governance, and ensuring equal electoral conditions will be essential to developing a more democratic and pluralistic system in Kazakhstan.

REFERENCES

Chebotarev, A. (2023). Выборы-2023: уроки для основных участников. [Elections-2023: Lessons for Key Participants]. [Electronic resource]. https://search.app/rZWW8xqTnqFSQVX59

President of the Republic of Kazakhstan. (2013, December 3). *Decree of the President of the Republic of Kazakhstan No. 704 On the approval of Model regulations for a maslikhat.* Official legal resource of the Republic of Kazakhstan. https://adilet.zan.kz/eng/docs/U1300000704/history

Tokayev, K. K. (2022, March 16). *New Kazakhstan: the path of renewal and modernisation.* Official website of the President of the Republic of Kazakhstan. https://www.akorda.kz/en/state-of-the-nation-address-by-president-of-the-republic-of-kazakhstan-kassym-jomart-tokayev-17293

Zholdybalina, A. S., Sankhaeva, Zh. M., Urpekova, A. G., Sailau, Q. S., Oteghali, D. B., & Yqylas, Q. E. (2024). Выборы депутатов маслихатов-2023: особенности и тенденции. К 30-летию образования маслихатов. [Elections of Maslikhat Deputies-2023: Features and Trends. On the 30th Anniversary of the Establishment of Maslikhats] (Collective monograph). Astana: Kazakhstan Institute for Strategic Studies under the President of the Republic of Kazakhstan.

KEY TERMS AND DEFINITIONS

Maslikhat: elected body, elected by population of region, city of republican significance and a capital city or district (city of regional significance), expressing will of population and in accordance with legislation of the Republic of Kazakhstan determined actions, necessary for its realization, and controlling its execution

Local government: the administrative system responsible for managing public affairs and services at the local level, including regional, district, and city governments.

Local self-government: the system where local authorities, such as maslikhats, have the power to manage and govern their own territories, ensuring representation and decision-making within the local community.

Election: the formal process in which citizens vote to elect representatives, such as deputies, to local and national offices, including maslikhats and the Parliament.

Mixed electoral system: an electoral system that combines proportional and majoritarian elements, used for elections to maslikhats and other political bodies, with candidates being elected both from party lists and single-member districts.

Independent candidate: a candidate who runs for election without affiliation to any political party, aiming to represent the interests of their constituents without party-based influence.

Maslikhat's powers: the legal powers and functions held by maslikhats at various levels, including the approval of budgets, policies, and appointments, as well as overseeing local governance.

Election campaign: the organized efforts by candidates and political parties to communicate their policies and persuade voters to support them in the elections.

Political reforms: changes made to the political system or electoral laws, intended to enhance democracy, increase transparency, and promote greater participation in the political process.

Chapter 10
Sustainable Food Policies in Cities Milan Urban Food Policy Pact and Practices from Türkiye

Elif Yucebas
https://orcid.org/0000-0002-2544-1318
Dokuz Eylul University, Izmir, Turkey

ABSTRACT

This study examines the role of urban areas in developing sustainable food systems. Current global challenges, including the rapid increase in urban populations, climate change, food security issues, and food waste, involve the development of sustainable food policies by local governments. This paper analyzes the Milan Urban Food Policy Pact (MUFPP) as a key initiative in the development of sustainable food systems and policies and evaluates the suggested approaches created at both global and local levels. It investigates the actions taken by the member cities of MUFPP concerning sustainable food production, distribution, and consumption and examines the impact of these actions. This study analyzes Türkiye's sustainable food policies, national strategies, and MUFPP member municipalities' projects. By examining Mezitli, Istanbul, Nilufer, Balıkesir, Efeler, Eregli, and Muratpasa it reveals the current state of sustainable food policies. The study highlights local government efforts, successful practices, and future improvement plans.

DOI: 10.4018/979-8-3373-0452-6.ch010

INTRODUCTION

Climate change and the negative impacts it brings with it are becoming more evident at the urban level. The rapid growth of cities and population increases make them more vulnerable to the effects of climate change. In this context, food security, sustainable production and consumption, and access to food in cities have become more important than ever. National strategies and policies and international cooperation play an important role in mitigating the impacts of climate change at the urban level. National governments determine road maps for food systems, and global collaboration supports this process. Local administration is one of the key actors in implementing policies related to food systems.

Local governments are the first-line management units that provide services in line with the needs of the society. In particular, they can develop policies that directly affect the basic processes of the food system, such as food production, distribution, consumption, and waste management. In addition, they can offer locally specific solutions for environmental sustainability, food safety, and healthy nutrition. As the main actors of the food system, local governments implement a wide range of practices, such as supporting local producers, reducing food waste and loss, promoting healthy nutrition, increasing food access for disadvantaged groups, and promoting environmentally friendly agricultural methods.

Climate change affects all levels, from local to global. International cooperation that unites cities and local governments is increasingly essential to mitigate these effects. Cities facing analogous challenges exchange the strategies they have formulated with other municipalities and local authorities through these cooperation, facilitating the dissemination of advantageous methods. The Milan Urban Food Policy Pact (MUFPP) is a significant international organization established to enhance sustainable food policies in urban areas. Initiated in 2015, this program seeks to enable local governments to establish shared objectives and exchange implementation experiences to improve sustainable food systems. It guides local governments' policy formulation in crucial areas involving food governance, sustainable nutrition and food equity, food production, supply and distribution, and food waste management. Currently, numerous cities participate in the MUFPP, enacting sustainable food policies and cultivating creative, locally customized approaches for improving the adaptability of their food systems. In this context, it separates itself from other international organizations by providing accessible and practical alternatives for urban food policies, encouraging collaboration among cities, and connecting with sustainable development goals. This study includes it because it provides relevant policy tools adapted for local government circumstances rather than a global context.

This study analyzes the role of local governments in creating sustainable food systems and specifically evaluates the policies developed within the Milan Urban Food Policy Pact (MUFPP) framework. The study analyzes the policies and actions implemented by local governments that signed the Milan Urban Food Pact (MUFPP) in Türkiye to support healthy and environmentally sustainable food. In this context, the Milan Urban Food Pact and national and international reports, legal regulations regarding local governments, strategic plans, and activity reports have been evaluated in detail.

The study consists of four basic sections. In the first part, sustainable food systems and the role of local methods are discussed, and the literature on this field is included. The second part examines examples of food policies and good practices implemented globally within the framework of MUFPP. The third section evaluates national policies and strategies for creating sustainable food systems in Türkiye. The last section includes the projects, practices, and strategies implemented by the municipalities that signed the MUFPP in Türkiye to create sustainable food systems.

LITERATURE REVIEW

Sustainable Food Systems and the Role of Local Governments

Local governments play a crucial role in supporting social, economic, and environmental sustainability. They are an essential component, especially for developing healthy and sustainable food systems. Local governments are the units closest to the local community and develop food policies appropriate to their needs. Thanekar et al. (2024) emphasizes the importance of policy coherence in aligning climate change actions with healthy eating behaviors at the municipal level. This coherence is crucial for developing an integrated approach to food systems that simultaneously addresses multiple issues. The research shows how local governments can use their distinct positions to establish policies that improve public health and minimize the effects of climate change, thus supporting a sustainable food environment.

In addition, the development of tools such as the Local Food Systems Policy Index (Local Food-EPI+) emphasize the importance of local governments thoroughly assessing their food policies. Ruffini et. al. (2024) evaluates how this tool improves the involvement of local governments with various departments and stakeholders in the development of policies, thus promoting collaboration and knowledge sharing. By evaluating local regulations against best practices, policymakers can identify gaps and opportunities for improvement, ultimately resulting in improved and equitable food systems. Cohen (2022) defined the roles of local governments in developing urban food policy as in Table 1.

Table 1. Urban Food Policy Types by Municipal Agency

City Agencies	Types of food policies
Economic development	Subsidies for food retail Ownership of public food markets Food sector business development
Education	K-12 food education (wellness education, school gardens) School feeding programs Higher education culinary training
Government operations	Food procurement Public feeding programs Food marketing restrictions
Parks and recreation	Sites and resources for urban agriculture
Public health	Food safety regulations Nutrition regulations and ingredient bans Informational regulations to promote healthy eating Healthy food discounts and promotions
Sanitation	Organic (food) waste management Food packaging regulations
Social services	Support for emergency feeding programs/congregate meals Management of federal food benefit programs
Transportation	Food transportation infrastructure planning and development
Urban planning	Planning and zoning to support food systems Resilience planning for food distribution infrastructure

Source: (Cohen, 2022)

This table shows how city agencies contribute to food systems (Cohen, 2022, p. 422). Food policies are addressed across a wide range, from economic development to education and social services, public health to urban planning. The aim is to create a healthy and sustainable food system, ensure food security, and improve public access to food.

The role of local governments in promoting urban food resilience is also underscored in the literature. Kamil and Romadhan (2020) explore how local governments can harness geographical and political conditions to establish food security initiatives, such as food security villages and urban farming programs. These programs develop resilience and community involvement and provide food access. Local governments may create strategies that address specific issues their populations face by relating local policy to community needs.

Barbour et al. (2021) offer that the requirement for local governments to promote sustainable development and healthy diets. Their research points out a variety of initiatives that, particularly in urban settings, have the potential to transform the food system. They propose that regulations that reduce the consumption of foods derived from animals and encourage plant-based diets, which have been demonstrated to have significant beneficial impacts both on the environment and human health, should be assigned top priority by local governments. Consequently, this is in line with the more general objective of reaching an environment that is beneficial for environmental sustainability and public health.

According to Galli et al. (2020), European municipalities should reduce obstacles to sustainable food systems. They argue that communities can support sustainable ecosystems by supporting market access, assisting regional producers, and furthering research on sustainable food practices. By such governance processes, municipalities may establish a more pluralistic food system that reflects (Galli et al., 2020).This kind of involvement is crucial for maintaining fair and sustainable food policies.

Incorporating food policies into entire sustainability frameworks is shown by projects in cities such as New York and those participating in the Milan Urban Food Policy Pact. Issac et al. (2022) show that New York City has built food policies into its sustainability framework, promoting urban agriculture and improving food access with community gardens and farms. The Milan Urban Food Policy Pact also supports cities in creating food policies that focus on social justice and food equity, showing the potential of municipal governments to effect reform in food systems (Barbour et al., 2023).

Candel's assessment of food strategies in MUFPP signatory cities indicates that local food policies often focus on sustainable diets, social equity, and food production (Candel, 2020). However, food production and distribution receive insufficient attention, which results in a lack of ensuring that all community members access sustainable food practices. This emphasizes the importance of local governments executing a comprehensive plan that involves every aspect of the food system, from production to consumption.

Thomas et al. (2020) argue that community-based organizations (CBOs) may be vital platforms to encourage collective impact and promote systemic change in food production and consumption layouts. Local governance structures are vital in assisting these groups, fostering and ensuring that food policies align with local needs and goals.

The literature underlines that stakeholders' participation has an important role in developing sustainable food systems. Ulug et al. (2021) suggest that efficient food security approaches require collaboration among many stakeholders, including municipal governments, community organizations, and citizens. This cooperative approach is essential for solving the complex problems associated with food systems and ensuring that policies adapt to the local environment.

The literature additionally investigates the concept of resilience in local food systems, focusing on the principles and criteria that promote sustainable food practices. Campbell et al. (2022) offer an audit tool for local governments to assess the resilience of their food systems, including issues such as agricultural sustainability, community health, and fair food supply. Accordingly, local governments may identify areas for improvement and adopt policies that support the overall resilience of their food systems (Campbell et al., 2022).

In conclusion, the literature indicates that local governments play many roles in making food systems more sustainable. However, it is important that these efforts expand beyond the local level, encouraging broader impact through partnership and the sharing of experiences between cities. The success of sustainable food policy increases when towns facing similar social, economic, and environmental difficulties formulate shared solutions and exchange best practices. The Milan Urban Food Policy Pact (MUFPP), which supports international cooperation among cities, is a important project that helps local governments in achieving sustainability objectives (Barbour et al., 2023).

MILAN URBAN FOOD POLICY PACT (MUFPP): A GLOBAL APPROACH FOR SUSTAINABLE FOOD SYSTEMS

Globalization encourages cities and local governments to develop relationships within their regions or countries and globally. This process empowers local governments from various locations to work together and design global policies that focus on solving climate change (UN-HABITAT, 2024). Although their distinct economic, social, and environmental features, cities have similar challenges (FAO et al., 2024) . Thus, networking between cities is generally seen as the most effective way to strengthen cities' capacity to solve major environmental and social problems, deliver urban services to its residents, and develop effective urban governance and management structures (Keiner & Kim, 2007, p. 1371). In this context, there are various city networks (Resilience cities, ICLEI-Local Governments for Sustainability, URBACT, etc.) that encompass cities/local governments, civil society organizations, scientific institutions/universities, companies/private sector, and individual memberships (Keiner & Kim, 2007, p. 1381). The Milan Urban Food Policy Pact is a global agreement signed on October 15, 2015, during the Expo 2015: Feeding the Planet, Energy for Life event in Milan (MUFPP, 2023, p. 16). The pact focuses on cities that play an important role in creating sustainable food systems. Accordingly, it is important to encourage local governments to adopt healthy, accessible, and environmentally friendly food policies. This pact has further encouraged local authorities to identify and implement public actions and regulatory mechanisms to increase people's Access to food such as, for example, the harmonization of urban development with the development of small local food producers, with particular emphasis on the joint venture of the food supply system with agro-food production (Nicolescu et al., 2017, p. 349). In this context, the Pact, which was opened for signature in 2015, has been signed by 290 cities today. The Pact is structured within the framework of 6 categories and 37 action policies. (MUFPP, 2015).

- Governance
- Sustainable Diets and Nutrition
- Social and Economic Equity
- Food Production
- Food Supply and Distribution
- Food Waste

There are six action proposals in the governance category. These are: collaboration among actors in urban governance and stakeholder participation; identification and mapping of local initiatives; development of urban food policies and plans; creation of data for the urban food system, establishment of an information system for institutions to share data; and the creation of a disaster risk reduction strategy to enhance the resilience of the urban food system. (MUFPP, 2015).

There are seven action proposals in the category of sustainable diets and nutrition. These include promoting sustainable nutrition; addressing diseases caused by malnutrition and obesity; creating sustainable nutrition guidelines; establishing standards related to sustainable nutrition and access to clean water; increasing the participation of the private sector and public institutions to promote sustainable nutrition; encouraging the health and food sectors to spread healthy eating habits; and investing in access to clean and safe drinking water (MUFPP, 2015).

There are six proposals for action in the Social and Economic Equity category. This includes promoting sustainable nutritional practices by considering various community beliefs, cultures, traditions, and dietary habits; integrating healthy, seasonal, and sustainable food production and consumption into school nutrition efforts, thus using local and regional resources; focusing on the employment of women within the food and agriculture sectors; executing programs that encourage sustainable livelihoods and guarantee food accessibility in both urban and rural environments; improving access to nutritious food for disadvantaged populations and improving social solidarity; and promoting for education, vocational training, and research to ensure universal access to healthy food (MUFPP, 2015).

Seven action plans exist within the Food Production area. Promoting food production within the city and its surrounds, highlighting small-scale producers and family-owned businesses to improve and maintain the relationship between urban and rural food systems; creating comprehensive and integrated land use strategies aimed at biodiversity safeguarding; creating policies and plans that support agricultural production by local governments for sustainable food production in urban and nearby areas; providing financial and technical support to producers to promote sustainable food production in the city and its surroundings; strengthening the food supply chain between urban and rural regions to promote local and sustainable food production; facilitating the reuse of wastewater in agriculture and food production; and reorganizing public procurement and trade policies to improve access to healthy and sustainable food (MUFPP, 2015).

There are 7 action proposals in the Food Supply and Distribution category. These include increasing access to healthy and affordable food in low-income neighborhoods and creating an environmentally friendly food supply system; supporting infrastructure that connects urban areas with nearby rural areas through improved food storage, processing, transportation, and distribution technologies to reduce food waste; strengthening food control systems by implementing local food safety legislation and regulations; supporting various market systems to strengthen the food supply chain by local governments and developing solutions suitable for the economic, social, and cultural conditions of different cities; improving and expanding the infrastructure of market systems to establish a stronger connection between urban consumers and producers in rural and semi-urban areas; and recognizing and supporting the informal sector (street vendors, small-scale producers, etc.) that plays a significant role in urban food systems (MUFPP, 2015).

Four action proposals are included in the Food Waste category. These are ensuring the reduction of food loss and waste at all stages of the food supply chain and making holistic plans; organizing events and campaigns to raise awareness about food loss and waste; developing municipal policies and regulations to prevent waste and ensure the sustainability of food; and creating redistribution mechanisms for sustainable food production and consumption (MUFPP, 2015).

One of MUFPP's main objectives is to share best practices and experiences among the cities that have signed the pact and to promote cooperation. The learning between cities has become a primary legacy of the Milan Pact in three ways (FAO, 2018, p. 5):

1. Through national, regional and international city networks use of the Milan Pact as a framework for city-to-city exchanges and collaborations;
2. Through developing indicators to measure progress of cities' food practices implementing the Framework of action; and
3. Through submissions of food policy and practice in the Milan Pact Awards.

Cities that fulfill the commitments of the Pact and implement creative practices are being rewarded. Thus, it promotes sustainable food production and consumption at the local level and contributes to its feasibility. With the award program launched 2016, 621 applications have been collected in 290 cities across 84 countries.

The 6th Milan Pact Awards, held in 2022, saw participation from 251 initiatives across 133 cities (MUFPP, 2023). The six cities that scored the highest in each category of the Milan Pact were awarded. The table includes the categories and examples of practices for the cities.

Table 2. Milan Pact Awards 2022 city practice and category

Category	Country	City	Title Of Practice
Governance	US	New York	A New York City framework for good food purchasing
Sustainable Diets&Nutrition	Ethiopia	Addis Ababa	Addis Ababa school feeding programme
Socıal&Economic Equity	India	Rourkela	E-Cool Mandi
Food Production	Argentina	Rosario	Agro-ecological food production in Rosaio
Food Supply&Distribution	South Korea	Yeosu	Strategy for securing our talents and small farms
Food Waste	UK	London	London's food waste reduction programme

Source: MUPFF, 2023.

The "A New York City framework for good purchasing" project of New York City, selected in the Governance category, has been implemented since 2017. The project aims to create a fair and sustainable food system with public resources. In this context, the project has been associated with reducing inequalities, partnerships for goals, responsible production and consumption, and sustainable development goals. It is developing innovative methods to support small producers, reduce the carbon footprint, and enhance social value criteria in public procurement (Milan Pact Awards 2022 New York, 2022). The actors participating in the project include 15 municipal departments, 24 NGOs, a research center, and the private sector.

The "Addis Ababa school feeding programme," selected in the Sustainable Diets and Nutrition category, was launched as a pilot project in 2019 in Addis Ababa, Ethiopia. The project focuses on the issues of poverty and food insecurity in the city. The main objective of the project is to combat hunger, ensure continuity in education, improve the quality of nutrition, and reduce the financial burden on families. In this context, free breakfast and lunch are provided to schools in 255 primary schools. The participating actors are municipal departments (3), public institutions (6), and a research center. The city administration has integrated school gardens into the nutrition program by promoting vegetable and fruit cultivation in schools; organic fertilizer has been produced from food waste. (Milan Pact Awards 2022 Addis Abba, 2022). It has been pointed out that budget constraints are an obstacle to the program's sustainability.

The "E-Cool Mandi" initiative, started in Rourkela, India in 2021, aims to reduce food waste, improve the financial circumstances of small-scale farmers and vendors, and enhance women's possibilities for employment (Milan Pact Awards 2022 Rourkela, 2022). In India, many fruits and vegetables are wasted due to the lack of proper cold chain infrastructure. The Rourkela Municipality has established solar-powered cold storage facilities in response to this issue. This program promotes sustainable agriculture, energy use, and women's employment.

The project "Agro-ecological food production in Rosario," selected in the food production category, has been implemented in Rosario, Argentina, since 2002 (Milan Pact Awards 2022 Rosaio, 2022). The project aims to promote sustainable food production by utilizing agricultural areas in the city and its surroundings. In this context, seven vegetable gardens were established on 30 hectares of land in the city, providing agricultural production opportunities for 450 poor families. The project is being carried out in collaboration with local governments, universities, research centers, small producers, and non-governmental organizations. In addition, with the "Rosario Green Belt Project" launch in 2016, 800 hectares of rural land have been opened to agroecological production; 286 hectares have completed this transformation. Thanks to agroecological production, carbon emissions are being reduced, and resilience against natural disasters is increasing.

The "Strategy for Securing Our Talents and Small Farms" project, chosen in the food supply and distribution category, was carried out between 2020 – 2022. This project addressed the food supply chain issues encountered during the pandemic. The project participants are municipal departments, public institutions, and the private sector. In the project's first phase, the city administration distributed food packages of ecological agricultural products to all students from kindergarten to high school. In the second phase, families were given online shopping vouchers, allowing small farmers to reach consumers through digital platforms. This project created a sustainable model supporting the local economy and ecological farming during the pandemic. The success of this project has led to similar projects being implemented in eight metropolitan cities and provinces in South Korea (Milan Pact Awards 2022 Yeosu, 2022).

The "London's food waste reduction programme," selected in the food waste category, was implemented in London between 2019 and 2024. The program aimed to reduce food waste and carbon emissions across the city. It aims to minimize waste by intervening at every stage of the food supply chain. The program is being carried out in cooperation with local governments, the private sector, academic institutions, and non-governmental organizations. The municipality aims to reduce losses in the supply chain and promote a circular economy by collaborating with large food companies. The size and demographic diversity of the city of London are restrictive in terms of reducing food waste and financial sustainability. The program has the potential to develop innovative projects aimed at reducing food waste and to serve as a model for other cities (Milan Pact Awards 2022 London, 2022). In conclusion, the Milan Urban Food Policy Pact promotes the cooperation of local governments globally in building sustainable food systems. Turkey has implemented various policies and practices in line with the United Nations' 2030 Sustainable Development Goals. These policies are transferred to the local level, especially through national development plans and strategic documents. Turkey has given important responsibilities to local governments in the development of sustainable food systems.

ESTABLISHING SUSTAINABLE FOOD SYSTEMS: POLICIES AND PRACTICES IN TÜRKIYE

Various policies and practices have been developed in Türkiye in accordance with the UN's 2030 Agenda for Sustainable Development Goals. As a result, sustainable development goals were specifically included in the 11th Development Plan (2019-2023). In this context, it has been stated that the sustainable development goals will be reflected in sectoral and thematic policy documents in line with national priorities and conditions (Presidency of The Republic of Türkiye Presidency of Strategy and Budget, p. 212). In implementing sustainable development goals, local governments have been designated as stakeholders in the national-level committee to be established. The regulatory changes by the Ministry of Environment, Urbanization, and Climate Change, which enable the establishment of zero waste and climate change-related units in metropolitan, provincial, and district municipalities, are an important step. The 11th Development Plan outlines goals related to ensuring food security, implementing effective stock management, reducing losses in the supply chain, and preventing waste within the framework of creating sustainable food systems (Presidency of The Republic of Türkiye Presidency of Strategy and Budget, p. 98). In addition, the "National Strategy Document and Action Plan on the Prevention, Reduction, and Management of Food Losses and Waste (2021-2023)" has been prepared in collaboration with the Ministry of Agriculture and Forestry and the Food and Agriculture Organization (FAO) of the United Nations (FAO, 2020).

Table 3. The Role of Local Governments in Türkiye's National Strategy for Food Loss and Waste Prevention, Reduction, and Management

Strategic Objectives	Actions	Role of Local Governments
Preventing and reducing food loss and waste	- Raising awareness and conducting consumer education campaigns - Establishing systems for measuring, monitoring, and evaluating food loss and waste - Optimizing packaging use and strengthening cold chain management	- Organizing training and awareness campaigns to educate the local population - Developing waste prevention initiatives in local food markets - Contributing to monitoring and reporting food losses through waste management systems
Recovering and redistributing food for direct human consumption	- Developing food donation mechanisms - Expanding food banking systems - Ensuring that safe and nutritious food reaches those in need	- Collaborating with food banks and social assistance organizations to distribute surplus food - Coordinating with markets, restaurants, and hotels to encourage food donations - Providing logistical support for food donations
Redirecting food waste to alternative uses (animal feed, fertilizer, etc.)	- Utilizing food unfit for human consumption as animal feed - Recovering energy from organic food waste	- Facilitating the use of organic waste in biogas and compost facilities - Collaborating with municipal animal shelters to repurpose appropriate food waste
Ensuring the recycling of food loss and waste	- Separating organic waste and processing it with appropriate Technologies - Promoting compost and biogas production - Strengthening waste management systems	- Implementing organic waste separation and composting systems as part of Zero Waste projects - Supporting biogas production facilities and enhancing waste management policies at the metropolitan level

Source: (FAO, 2020)

Table 3 summarizes the strategic areas, actions, and responsibilities local governments should undertake as outlined in Türkiye's National Strategy Document and Action Plan for the Prevention, Reduction, and Management of Food Losses and Waste. Local governments directly contribute to areas such as the widespread implementation of zero-waste practices, the reduction of food losses and waste, the establishment of sustainable supply chains, and food banking. In Türkiye, local governments have various duties and responsibilities in implementing sustainable food policies.

Municipalities Law No. 5393 and Metropolitan Municipality Law No. 5216 determine municipalities' authorities and responsibilities regarding sustainable food systems. These laws encompass the duties of local administrations to protect public health, support agriculture and livestock, protect the environment, and ensure food safety (Municipality Law No.5393, 2005). Metropolitan municipalities are especially obliged to develop effective food production and distribution policies (Metropolitan Municipality Law No.5216, 2004). In this context, they are carrying out various projects to promote organic farming, spread urban agriculture practices, and improve the quality of agricultural production.

In order to ensure environmental sustainability, the 2872 Environmental Law imposes significant obligations on local governments regarding waste management and the prevention of air, water, and soil pollution (Environment Law No. 2872, 1983). Regarding the sustainability of agricultural production, Law No. 5957 on the Trade of Vegetables and Fruits and the Wholesale Market Registration System covers producer support, the regulation of vegetable and fruit trade, and the provision of healthy food to consumers (Law on the Regulation of Trade in Vegetables and Fruits and Other Goods with Sufficient Supply and Demand Depth No.5957, 2010). In this context, local markets ensure food safety.

The management of food waste is one of the fundamental components of sustainable food systems. The Waste Management Regulation and the Regulation on the Regular Storage of Waste regulate separating, recovering, and disposing of food waste at the source. These regulations impose an obligation on municipalities to ensure the sustainable management of biodegradable food waste and evaluate it for producing organic fertilizer or biogas. (Waste Management Regulation, 2015) (Regulation on Landfill of Waste, 2010). The Zero-Waste Regulation imposes various responsibilities on municipalities regarding the efficient use of natural resources, the prevention of waste generation, and the establishment of recycling systems. In this context, municipalities must implement zero-waste management systems to reduce food waste, collect it at the source through separation, and manage the recycling processes. (Zero Waste Regulation, 2019). Municipalities must also ensure that food waste is minimized by introducing regulations to prevent food waste in markets, restaurants, and hotels.

MUNICIPALITIES IN TÜRKIYE PARTICIPATING IN THE MILAN URBAN FOOD POLICY PACT AND THEIR PRACTICES

To create sustainable food systems in Türkiye, local governments must act by the strategies and regulations determined at the national level and participate in international collaborations. In this context, some municipalities are joining international platforms that shape food policies within the framework of sustainable development goals and are carrying out projects on sustainable food production and consumption, food waste, sustainable agriculture, etc.

Table 4. Türkiye's MUFPP Member Municipalities

Municipality	Signature Year
Mezitli Municipality (Mersin)	2019
Istanbul Metropolitan Municipality	2022
Nilufer Municipality (Bursa)	2022
Efeler Municipality (Aydın)	2022
Balıkesir Metropolitan Municipality	2024
Eregli Municipality (Konya)	2024
Muratpasa Municipality (Antalya)	2024

In Türkiye, seven municipalities, including two metropolitan municipalities, have signed the Milan Urban Food Policy Pact (Table 4). The first municipality in Türkiye to sign the MUFPP was Mezitli Municipality. In the following years, Istanbul Metropolitan Municipality, Nilufer Municipality, Efeler Municipality, Balıkesir Metropolitan Municipality, Eregli Municipality, and Muratpasa Municipality became members of MUFPP. In this context, municipalities are carrying out projects and sharing best practices on sustainable food production, consumption, supporting local producers, reducing food waste, and access to healthy food etc. Within the framework of these national policies and legal regulations, some municipalities in Turkey are taking an active role in sustainable food systems not only at the local and national level but also through international cooperation. The next section includes the practices of municipalities that are members of MUFPP, focusing on sustainable food policies and award-winning initiatives.

Mezitli Municipality Practices

Mezitli is a district in the Mersin province of Türkiye, located on the Mediterranean coast in the country's south. Mezitli Municipality is one of the district municipalities of Mersin Metropolitan Municipality, with a population of 223,424 (Mezitli Municipality, 2023, p. 4). Agriculture, tourism, and trade are prominent in the district, with a rapidly developing urban structure. Mezitli Municipality promotes local production through sustainable agricultural practices, urban agriculture projects, and food security efforts. In this context, Mezitli Municipality, which supports and implements sustainable development projects, is Türkiye's first municipality to sign the MUFPP. In addition to MUFPP, Mezitli Municipality is a signatory to various international partnerships (Mezitli Municipality, 2025):

- EUROCITIES (European Cities Organization)
- UCLG (United Cities and Local Governments)

- UCLG-MEWA (United Cities and Local Governments Middle East and West Asia Section)
- World Health Organization Regions for Health Network
- World Health Organization Cities Network
- UN Global Compact
- Global Covenant of Mayors for Climate and Energy

The Mezitli Municipality engages in various projects related to sustainable food production, consumption, and agriculture. "The Excess Food Project" collects products from supermarkets and distributes them to a soup kitchen, serving them as meals to needy individuals. In 2022, the scheme facilitated the provision of around 1 million TL in donated food (Mezitli Municipality, 2022, p. 176). The Biodegradable Waste Management Project involves collecting rotten and bruised fruits and vegetables from marketplaces at closing hours, setting them aside for compost production, and delivering those still in a consumable condition to those in need. Another municipality's project aims to support local women producers and ensure their participation in economic life. In this context, women's producer markets have been established, and various activities have been carried out. Mezitli Female Producers' Market is one of the projects that received an award in the social and economic equity category from MUFPP in 2019. Mezitli Women's Producers' Market is an important project in Türkiye because it is entirely operated by women producers. To strengthen the local market, no fees are charged to female producers for opening sales stands, and only female producers are allowed to sell at the market. Organic vegetables obtained from small gardens and handmade products are offered for sale (MUFPP, Milan Pact Awards 2019 Mezitli, 2019).

The "Urban Applications for Sustainable Agriculture" project is being carried out to support sustainable agriculture and encourage citizens' participation in local food production. With this project, the municipality has applied for the "Healthy Cities Best Practice Competition" in the "Climate-Friendly City" category (Mezitli Municipality, p. 200). In addition, the municipality is continuing its international collaborations and sustainability efforts by applying to the NetZeroCities Pilot Cities Program.

Istanbul Metropolitan Municipality Practices

With a population of 16 million, Istanbul is Türkiye's largest metropolis and economic center. While a global city with a rich historical and cultural heritage, it also plays an important role in many sectors, such as industry, trade, and agriculture. In line with sustainable development goals, it carries out various activities and projects on issues such as combating climate change, food security, and supporting agricultural production. In this context, Istanbul's food security and sustainability policies are shaped under international norms and are part of various global networks. The Istanbul Metropolitan Municipality (IBB) has memberships in different international organizations that operate in areas such as environment, food policies, healthy urbanization, cultural heritage preservation, and social services (Istanbul Metropolitan Municipality, 2023, p. 63):

- Organization of Islamic Capitals and Cities (OICC)
- United Cities and Local Governments World Organization (UCLG)
- World Union of Great Metropolises (METROPOLIS)
- European Cities Against Drugs Organization (ECAD)
- Union of Historical Cities (LHC)
- European Cities Organization (EUROCITIES)
- Organization of World Heritage Cities (OWHC)
- Earthquakes and Megacities Initiative (EMI)
- World Halls Union (WUWM)
- World Health Organization (WHO) Healthy Cities Network
- Turkish World Municipalities Union (TDBB)
- Asia Mayors Forum (AMF)
- European Social Network (ESN)
- International Committee of Historic House Museums (DEMHIST)
- Urban Mobility European Institute of Innovation and Technology (EIT)
- CIVITAS Forum Network
- C40 Cities Climate Leadership Group
- B40 Balkan Cities Network
- International Lighting Association (LUCI)
- Milan Urban Food Policy Pact (MUFPP)
- Global Sustainable Tourism Council (GSTC)

The Istanbul Metropolitan Municipality became a member of MUFPP in 2022. The "Istanbul Food Strategy Document" was implemented in 2021 to establish a sustainable food system in Istanbul. The scope of this document includes protecting local producers in the short, medium, and long term, combating hunger, ensuring food access, social security, healthy food and nutrition policies, food safety, water security, preventing food waste, loss, and spoilage, and making the city resilient to crises and disasters (Istanbul Metropolitan Municipality, 2021). This document aims to transition to a food system considering economic, social, and ecological priorities, ensuring everyone can access healthy and good food (Istanbul Metropolitan Municipality, 2021).

Various activities are being carried out to ensure that Istanbul can access healthy and affordable food. The IBB Public Market e-commerce project supports the marketing of products through cooperatives in which farmers are partners. At Public Market, producers' products within the provincial borders and the regional products produced by all producers and women's cooperatives across Türkiye are offered for sale. At the İBB Public Market, more than 800 products from 57 cooperatives are offered for sale (Istanbul Metropolitan Municipality, 2023, p. 259). Various activities are being carried out within the borders of Istanbul to support urban agriculture and ensure the reuse of agricultural land (Istanbul Metropolitan Municipality, 2023).

- "The Kemerburgaz Biometanization Facility" produces fertilizer from food and kitchen waste.
- As part of the domestic seed research begun in 2021, experimental plantings and harvests were conducted in Silivri and Catalca.
- To reintroduce agricultural areas in Istanbul to production and support farmers, vegetable seedlings, oilseed sunflower seeds, and fodder plants are being distributed.
- Farmers are provided with various trainings on food safety, quality, vegetable training, and digital marketing.
- The "From Soil to Shelf Food Monitoring Model," supported by the Istanbul Development Agency, has been a national project since 2021.
- Practical agricultural education and training on healthy food consumption are being provided to students.

In addition to these activities, the Istanbul Metropolitan Municipality is making various efforts to meet citizens' food needs within the framework of the right to food.

- "Istanbul Public Bread Project" produces bread to meet the local community's need for healthy, high-quality flour and baked goods.
- "The Public Milk Project" has been implemented since 2019, providing free milk to children.
- Food parcel support, which includes essential consumption products, is provided to ensure that households facing social and economic difficulties can access food. (Istanbul Metropolitan Municipality, 2023, p. 266).
- Mobile support is provided to the areas in need with mobile buffet vehicles to meet basic food needs in situations where direct supply of food and beverages is difficult 7/24.

Istanbul Metropolitan Municipality, in the interest of creating a sustainable food system, encourages producers and implements various initiatives that guarantee inhabitants access to nutritious and economical food. These actions, ranging from promoting local agriculture to mitigating food waste, as well as social assistance and educational initiatives, seek to establish a more resilient, equitable, and sustainable food ecosystem in Istanbul's future. Given the city's magnitude and dynamic framework, such extensive policies and initiatives are crucial for Istanbul and Türkiye's food security and sustainable development objectivesand sustainable development objectives in Istanbul and Türkiye.

Nilufer Municipality Practices

Nilufer is a Bursa province settlement and one of the city's most important central districts. As of 2023, the total population of Nilufer has reached 543,934 (Nilufer Municipality, 2023, p. 9). It is a developed region with industry, commerce, education, social, and cultural opportunities. Nilufer Municipality engages in international collaborations and is a member of many organizations within the environmental and social sustainability framework. The municipality, which became a member of MUFPP in 2022, is a member of many international organizations (Nilufer Municipality, 2023, s. 9):

- UCLG-MEWA (United Cities and Local Governments Middle East and West Asia Section)
- World Health Organization (WHO) Healthy Cities Network
- European Network of Local Authorities in Energy Transition (ENERGYCITIES)
- Global Fund for Cities Development (FMDV)

In 2023, the "Nilufer Food Living Lab and Nilufer Social Entrepreneurship Center projects" were awarded in the "Exemplary Initiatives" category of the VI. Guangzhou International Urban Innovation Award, supported by the United Nations and Local Governments (UCLG), the World Association of Major Metropolises (Metropolis), and Guangzhou. By being included in the publicly accessible "Urban Innovation Database," both projects contribute to knowledge exchange and mutual learning on urban innovation and sustainable development (Nilufer Municipality, 2023, p. 108).

Nilufer Municipality is conducting various projects on sustainable food systems and agricultural development. "Hasanaga Food Center" is a project established to support local producers and ensure sustainable agricultural products meet consumers directly (Nilufer Municipality, 2023, p. 214). Hasanaga Food Center supports producers, cooperatives, and women's associations in the Hasanaga neighborhood in producing, processing, and storing food products; it encourages reliable and high-quality food production (Nilufer Municipality, 2023, p. 398).

Within the scope of the "Nilufer Garden Project," sales points have been established in the city to encourage the consumption of healthy and natural food. These points allow local producers to offer their products directly to the public. With the opening of the sixth branch in 2023, agricultural products such as figs, wheat, corn, and sunflowers are offered to the local public at these sales points (Nilufer Municipality, 2023, p. 400).

Another project aimed at supporting sustainable agriculture is the "Agricultural Analysis Laboratory." Within the scope of this project, soil, plant, and irrigation water analyses are conducted to ensure that farmers engage in more conscious production and to provide guidance on plant nutrition; the scientific data obtained are shared over the internet (Nilufer Municipality, 2023, p. 401). The "Compost Production" project has encouraged compost production to ensure the recycling of organic waste, thereby reducing food waste and increasing agricultural sustainability. 3.3 tons of compost were produced in 2023 as a result of this project. (Nilufer Municipality, 2023, p. 398).

Efeler Municipality Practices

Efeler Municipality is an Aegean Region district affiliated with Aydın Province. According to 2023 data, the district's population is 308,039. The city, influenced by the Mediterranean climate, is rich in agricultural products; olives, figs, chestnuts, cotton, tobacco, and citrus fruits are among the main agricultural products. (Efeler Municipality, 2024, p. 12).

Efeler Municipality has strategic goals such as developing agriculture and increasing employment, establishing facilities where agricultural and livestock products can be processed and marketed, supporting productive women, and functionally using municipal lands. (Efeler Municipality, 2024, p. 65). In line with these goals, the "100% Women's Labor Agricultural Products Factory" project is one of the important projects contributing to the city's sustainable food production and consumption. In 2022, it was awarded in the "Food Production" category at the Milan Pact Awards (MUFPP, 2023). Products grown on agricultural lands belonging to the municipality (artichokes, black wheat, cauliflower, cabbage) are processed at the "Women's Labor Agricultural Products Factory" and offered to the public. The food products produced in the factory are sold through Efe Bakkallar. However, the sale of the produced food products is not limited to the city; they are delivered to every part of Türkiye through various chain stores and online sales platforms (Efeler Municipality, 2024). This project contributes to the creation of sustainable food systems, the use of local resources, the involvement of women's labor in the production process, and the delivery of healthy foods to the public.

Balıkesir Metropolitan Municipality Practices

Balıkesir is a province in the Marmara Region with a population of 1,273,519 according to 2023 data. Within the borders of Balıkesir Metropolitan Municipality, there are 20 district municipalities. Becoming a member of MUFPP in 2024, Balıkesir Metropolitan Municipality conducts various activities and projects to enhance the local population's social and economic welfare by supporting rural development and sustainable agriculture within the framework of sustainable development goals. Balıkesir Metropolitan Municipality carries out its activities in this field through the companies it has established. BATAS (Balıkesir Agricultural Products Joint Stock Company); established in 2017, operates in production and marketing in the agriculture and livestock sectors throughout the province. On the other hand, BAGYAS (Balıkesir Real Estate Investment and Food Joint Stock Company) produces bread and its varieties in its bread factory and sells them at bread sales booths to ensure that the public consume healthy and high-quality bread (Balıkesir Metropolitan Municipality, 2023).

The municipality's principal objectives are to raise plant production within the provincial boundaries and improve agricultural output's effectiveness, efficiency, and sustainability. The activities carried out by the Balıkesir Metropolitan Municipality are as follows (Balıkesir Metropolitan Municipality, 2023):

- The "Heirloom Seed Village Project" aims to preserve, spread, and distribute local seeds at risk of extinction to producers.
- The "Honey Forest Project" has introduced many kinds of plants, including both medicinal and fragrant species, to improve beekeeping efforts and enrich the flora present in honey wood.
- "Agriculture Camps" are being organized to enhance farmers' agricultural knowledge.
- Making agricultural production agreements with producers provides seedling support to producers for 3 years.
- Einlorn wheat provides support to producers who want to cultivate einkorn wheat.
- It provides material support to fig and olive producers.

Agricultural training programs are being organized to increase farmers' knowledge and awareness levels. Olive Cultivation, a Practical Gardening course, and a Practical Plant Tissue Culture Course can be given as examples. Food assistance is provided to disadvantaged groups to increase the social and economic welfare of the local population and ensure their access to healthy food. In this context, Balıkesir Metropolitan Municipality provides “Food Card” support to those in need, which can be used in chain supermarkets (Balıkesir Metropolitan Municipality, 2023). Furthermore, food packs and hot meals are being disseminated.

Eregli Municipality Practices

Eregli, affiliated with Konya province, has a population of 150,978 (Eregli Municipality, 2025). As of 2024, the Eregli Municipality, which joined MUFPP, is carrying out various projects in sustainable agriculture and food production. These projects promote environmentally friendly production, local development, and healthy food consumption.

The Adabag Organic Agriculture Project has carried out seedling planting within the scope of the Adabag Neighborhood Organic Agriculture Zone, and vegetables have been grown there. Some harvested tomatoes were sent to sales points as paste and vegetables, while some were gifted to the municipal staff (Eregli Municipality, 2023, p. 92). This project aims to establish Eregli as a leading city in organic agriculture. (Eregli Ajans, 2022).

The Eregli Municipality Agricultural Services Directorate aims to prevent soil and water pollution by monitoring agricultural activities and to protect human health. The activities to be carried out within this scope are as follows (Eregli Municipality, 2025, p. 100):

- Conducting inspections of the long zucchini, black carrot, sheep yogurt, and white cherry with geographical indications
- Increasing activities aimed at promoting regional and geographically marked products
- Supporting and promoting environmentally friendly practices within the scope of environmental protection and combating climate change
- Supporting good agricultural practices and organic farming to increase product reliability and contribute to the sustainable use of natural resources
- Implementation of agricultural support and training for farmers

Eregli Municipality conducts various programs to ensure healthy nutrition and access to food for disadvantaged groups. As part of the “Soup Kitchen Meal Assistance” project, it delivers daily hot meals to those in need (Eregli Municipality, 2023, p. 61). Another service is the distribution of food aid packages consisting of essential food items at regular intervals (Eregli Municipality, 2023, p. 70). In 2025, the municipality aims to provide at least one meal daily to high school students studying in the district (Eregli Municipality, 2025, p. 118). These projects are being carried out to ensure food security, increase social solidarity, and support disadvantaged groups.

Muratpasa Municipality Practices

Muratpasa is a district in the Mediterranean Region affiliated with Antalya province. Its population is 512,700. Muratpasa Municipality became a member of MUFPP in 2024. The Muratpasa Municipality Climate Change and Zero Waste Department is working on establishing natural farming methods, ecological balance, biodiversity, safe food production, and a fair food distribution system (Muratpasa Municapility, 2023, p. 50). Additionally, various activities and projects are being carried out in these areas to ensure sustainable development.

The Muratpasa Municipality participated in the "Food Trails Cascade" learning program, a Horizon 2020 program funded by the European Union (EU) in 2023. This program aims to spread knowledge and best practices throughout cities to redesign, develop, and implement sustainable, healthy, and inclusive food policies (Food Trails, 2025). Within the project's scope, Muratpasa Municipality has been paired with Roeselare from Belgium and Thessaloniki from Greece, one of the 11 project partners. The "Muratpasa Food Policy Guide" is being prepared as part of this project (Muratpasa Municapility, 2023, p. 158).

Muratpasa Municipality has initiatives to increase the local population's economic and social welfare through food aid and social support projects. In this context, it provides disadvantaged groups hot meals and dry food aid. To raise awareness among the local population about issues such as healthy eating and food safety, a project titled "There is Life in the Garden" is being carried out. Discussions and workshops are being held on environmental issues, crises of climate change, food, and consumption patterns (Muratpasa Municipality, 2023, p. 157). In 2023, a seminar on healthy eating, including safe food consumption, label meaning, illness caused by food, and conscious consumption, was organized within the project's framework in collaboration with the Antalya Olimpos Rotary Club (Muratpasa Municipality, 2023, p. 158).

Workplace and school cafeterias within the municipal limits are routinely inspected to guarantee safe food consumption. The inspections performed in school canteens assess the appropriateness of the food offered, adherence to general hygiene regulations, and preservation standards. The initiatives of the Muratpasa Municipality in food safety, sustainable production, and mindful consumption play a pivotal role in formulating local urban food policy.

CONCLUSION

Local governments are essential in implementing the Sustainable Development Goals as the entities closest to the population. They are a primary institution that provides services to meet community needs and formulates policy. In areas such as sustainable urban development, responsible production and consumption, and health and well-being, they develop and advance policies and practices tailored to local needs.

Sustainable food systems are directly connected to the economic, social, and environmental dynamics of cities, and the role of local governments in this area is becoming increasingly important. Cities are actively taking responsibility in many areas, such as developing policies that promote healthy eating, preventing food waste, supporting local producers, and combating climate change. In this context, international platforms such as the Milan Urban Food Policy Pact (MUFPP) provide an important framework that guides cities in creating sustainable food systems.

The literature and case studies examined in the study demonstrate that political coherence, stakeholder collaboration, and community participation are critical for local governments to implement sustainable food policies successfully. Following good practices on a global scale is important for enhancing the capacities of local governments. The examples of cities that are members of MUFPP show that city administrations can effectively implement sustainable food policies through good governance and strategic planning.

Within the framework of sustainable food policies in Türkiye, the participation of the municipalities of Istanbul, Mezitli, Nilufer, Efeler, Eregli, Balıkesir, and Muratpasa in the MUFPP demonstrates the local government's efforts to integrate into the global transformation in this field. Upon examining the initiatives and practices of the member municipalities, it is obvious that they take an active role in diverse domains, involving sustainable food production and consumption, reducing food waste and loss, ensuring access to healthy food for those who are disadvantaged, rural development, organic farming, and strengthening local producers. For example, Mezitli Municipality contributes directly to women's employment by supporting female producers. In this respect, a municipality in Türkiye is a member of MUFPP and has received an award for the first time as a good practice example. Nilufer Municipality has developed projects on sustainable agriculture and establishing direct producer-consumer connections. Eregli Municipality has taken significant steps to promote organic farming. Balıkesir Metropolitan Municipality has tried to protect local seeds and increase agricultural production. Muratpasa Municipality, on the other hand, contributes to the development of sustainable food policies by improving the sharing of knowledge and experience through international projects.

The food strategy document implemented by the Istanbul Metropolitan Municipality indicates that sustainable food systems can be applied locally.

When the practices of municipalities such as Mezitli, Nilüfer, and Istanbul are analyzed, it is seen that the implementation of sustainable food policies in Turkey is not equal among local governments. While some municipalities have developed strategies aligned with the MUFPP, others are still in the planning or implementation phase. Moreover, systematic monitoring and evaluation mechanisms are needed, even though many initiatives aim to address food waste, support local producers, or increase access to healthy food.

Sustainable food systems are an environmental policy and a multidimensional process that includes social and economic development. For sustainable food systems at the local level to be successful, it is necessary to strengthen the financial and technical capacities of local governments, promote inter-city information sharing, and ensure that local governments are more integrated into national and international food policies. In this context, monitoring and sharing successful practices in combating climate change in Türkiye and around the world guide local governments in developing sustainable food policies while increasing the resilience of cities. Thus, city administrations can implement these policies more efficiently, building sustainable and resilient food systems in the long term.

REFERENCES

Balıkesir Metropolitan Municipality. (2023). *Balıkesir Metropalitan Municipality Annual Report 2023.*https://balikesir.bel.tr/Dosyalar/DosyaListe/AF_btr_DosyaListeDetay_file_Dosya_b7a99056-e8eb-4230-b55d-c698d2e722f1/bbb_fr_2023.pdf

Barbour, L., Lindberg, R., Woods, J., Charlton, K., & Brimblecombe, J. (2021). Local urban government policies to facilite healthy and environmentally sustainable diet-related practices: A scoping review. *Public Health Nutrition*, *25*(2), 471–487. DOI: 10.1017/S1368980021004432 PMID: 34693899

Barbour, L. R., Woods, J. L., & Brimblecombe, J. K. (2023). Local government policy to facilitate healthy and sustainable diets and the broader policy hierarchy: Insights from Milan Urban Food Policy Pact cities. *Health Research Policy and Systems*, *21*(35), 1–9. DOI: 10.1186/s12961-023-00988-6 PMID: 37226248

Campbell, C. G., Papanek, A., DeLong, A., Diaz, J., Gusto, C., & Tropp, D. (2022). Community food systems resilience: Values, benefits, and indicators. *Journal of Agriculture, Food Systems, and Community Development*, *11*(4), 89–113. DOI: 10.5304/jafscd.2022.114.006

Candel, J. J. (2020). What's on the menu? A global assessment of MUFPP signotary cities' food strategies. *Agroecology and Sustainable Food Systems*, *44*(7), 919–946. DOI: 10.1080/21683565.2019.1648357

Cohen, N. (2022). Roles of cities in creating healthful food systems. *Annual Review of Public Health*, *43*(1), 419–437. DOI: 10.1146/annurev-publhealth-052220-021059 PMID: 34936824

Efeler Municipality. (2024). *Efeler Municipality Strategic Plan 2025-2029.*https://www.efeler.bel.tr/upload/content/2025-2029-stratejik-plan.pdf

Efeler Municipality. (2024). https://www.efeler.bel.tr/guncel/haberler/kadin-emegiyle-uretilen-dogal-urunler-simdi-marketlerde

Environment Law No. 2872. (1983). https://www.mevzuat.gov.tr/MevzuatMetin/1.5.2872.pdf

Eregli Ajans. (2022). (2025, January 02) https://eregliajans.net/eregli-belediyesi-adabagda-baslattigi-projede-organik-tarim-alaninda-hasata-hazirlaniyor

Eregli Municipality. (2023). *Eregli Municipality Annual Report 2023.*https://eregli.bel.tr/upload/other/2023%20y%C4%B1l%C4%B1%20Ere%C4%9Fli%20Belediyesi%20Faaliyet%20Raporu-1_1714136689.pdf

Eregli Municipality. (2025). *Eregli Municipality Performance Report 2025.* https://eregli.bel.tr/upload/other/2025%20PERFORMANS%20PROGRAMI-1_1736142313.pdf

Eregli Municipality. (2025). (2025, February 02) https://www.eregli.bel.tr/sayfalar/ilcemiz

FAO. (2018). *The role of cities in the transformation of food systems: Sharing lessons from Milan Pact cities.*https://www.milanurbanfoodpolicypact.org/wp-content/uploads/2022/01/The-Role-Of-Cities-In-The-Transformation-Of-Food-Systems-Sharing-Lessons-From-Milan-Pact-Cities.pdf

FAO. (2020). *Türkiye's National Strategy Document and Action Plan for the Prevention, Reduction, and Management of Food Losses and Waste.* Ankara. https://faolex.fao.org/docs/pdf/tur209489.pdf

FAO, CIRAD & RUAF. 2024. *Building resilience of city region food systems: a comparative study of eleven city perspectives*. Rome. https://doi.org/DOI: 10.4060/cd2836en

Food Trails. (2025). (2025, January 02).https://foodtrails.milanurbanfoodpolicypact.org/consortium/

Galli, F., Prosperi, P., Favili, E., D'Amico, S., Bartolini, F., & Brunori, G. (2020). How can policy processes remove barriers to sustainable food systems in Europe? Contributing to a policy framework for agrifood transitions. *Food Policy*, *96*, 1–15. DOI: 10.1016/j.foodpol.2020.101871

Issac, J., Newell, R., Dring, C., White, C., Ghadiri, M., Pizzirani, S., & Newman, L. (2022). Integrated sustainability planning and local food systems: Examining areas of and gaps in food systems integration in community sustainability plans for municipalities across British Columbia. *Sustainability (Basel)*, *14*(6724), 1–17. DOI: 10.3390/su14116724

Istanbul Metropolitan Municipality. (2021). *The Istanbul Food Strategy Document.* https://ipa.istanbul/wp-content/uploads/2021/10/Istanbul-Gida-Strateji-Belgesi.pdf

Istanbul Metropolitan Municipality. (2023). *Istanbul Metropalitan Municipality Annual Report 2023.*https://uploads.ibb.istanbul/uploads/2023_ANNUAL_REPORT_56373f7718.pdf

Kamil, M., & Romadhan, A. (2020). Local geo-politics of urban food resilience to achieve sustainable city development in Malang, Indonesia. *Advances in Social Science, Education and Humanities Research*, *436*, 782–785. DOI: 10.2991/assehr.k.200529.165

Keiner, M., & Kim, A. (2007). Transnational City Networks for Sustainability. *European Planning Studies*, *15*(10), 1369–1395. DOI: 10.1080/09654310701550843

Mezitli Municipality. (2022). *Mezitli Municipality Annual Report 2022.*https://mezitli.bel.tr/wp-content/uploads/2023/05/faaliyet-raporu-2022.pdf

Mezitli Municipality. (2023). *Mezitli Municipality Annual Report 2023.*https://mezitli.bel.tr/faaliyet-raporu/

Mezitli Municipality. (2025). (2025, February 03) https://mezitli.bel.tr/uluslararasi-uyelikler/

Milan Pact Awards 2022 Addis Abba. (2022). (2025, February 02) https://www.milanurbanfoodpolicypact.org/projects/addis-ababa-school-feeding-program/

Milan Pact Awards 2022 London. (2022). (2025, February 02) https://www.milanurbanfoodpolicypact.org/projects/londons-food-waste-reduction-programme

Milan Pact Awards 2022 New York. (2022). (2025, February 02) https://www.milanurbanfoodpolicypact.org/projects/a-new-york-city-framework-for-good-food-purchasing

Milan Pact Awards 2022 Rosaio. (2022). (2025, February 02) https://www.milanurbanfoodpolicypact.org/projects/agro-ecological-food-production-in-rosario/

Milan Pact Awards 2022 Rourkela. (2022). (2025, February 02) https://www.milanurbanfoodpolicypact.org/projects/e-cool-mandi-decentralized-cold-room-run-by-women-preventing-vendor-distress

Milan Pact Awards 2022 Yeosu. (2022). (2025, February 02) https://www.milanurbanfoodpolicypact.org/projects/strategy-for-securing-our-talents-and-small-farms

MUFPP. (2015). Milan Urban Food Policy Pact._https://www.milanurbanfoodpolicypact.org/the-milan-pact/

MUFPP. (2019). *Milan Pact Awards 2019 Mezitli.* (2025, February 01) https://www.milanurbanfoodpolicypact.org/milan-pact-awards/milan-pact-awards-2019

MUFPP. (2022). Milan Pact Awards 2022. (2025, February 02) https://www.milanurbanfoodpolicypact.org/milan-pact-awards/milan-pact-awards-2022

MUFPP. (2023). *Milan Pact Awards 2022*. Milano. https://www.milanurbanfood policypact.org/award/

Municipality Law No. 5393. (2005). https://www.mevzuat.gov.tr/MevzuatMetin/ 1.5.5393.pdf

Muratpasa Municipality. (2023). *Muratpasa Municipality Annual Report 2023.* https://muratpasa-bld.gov.tr/raporlar

Nicolescu, C. E., Bitoiu, I. T., & Radulescu, C. R. (2017). Good Practices for Sustainable Urban Food Policies. *SEA-Practical Application of Science, 15*(3), 347-352. https://ideas.repec.org/a/cmj/seapas/y2017i15p347-352.html

Nilufer Municipality. (2023). *Nilufer Municipality Annual Report.*https://www .nilufer.bel.tr/i/pdf/101.pdf

Presidency of The Republic of Türkiye Presidency of Strategy and Budget. *The Eleventh Development Plan (2019-2023).*https://www.sbb.gov.tr/wp-content/uploads/ 2022/07/On_Birinci_Kalkinma_Plani-2019-2023.pdf

Regulation on Landfill of Waste. (2010). https://www.mevzuat.gov.tr/MevzuatMetin/ yonetmelik/7.5.13887.pdf

Ruffini, O., Relf, C., Mann, D., Blake, M. R., Carrad, A., Reeve, B., Barbour, L., Vanderlee, L., Vandevijvere, S., & Sacks, G. (2024). Development of the local food systems policy index (Local Food-EPI+) tool and assessment process to benchmark the implementation of local government policies for creating healthy, equitable and environmentally sustainable food systems. *Public Health Nutrition*, *27*(1), 1–15. DOI: 10.1017/S136898002400140X PMID: 39354657

Thanekar, U., Sacks, G., Ruffini, O., Reeve, B., & Blake, M. R. (2024). Local government stakeholders' perceptions of potential policy actions to influence both climate change and healthy eating in Victoria: A qualitative study. *Health Promotion Journal of Australia*, *35*(4), 1158-1173. https://doi.org/DOI: 10.1002/hpja.848

Thomas, T., Gunden, C., & Legesse, B. (2020). Accounting for the impact of sustainable agriculture: The role of community based organization and local governance structures in promoting sustainable agriculture. *Multifunctionality and impacts of organix and conventioanl agriculture*.https://doi.org/DOI: 10.5772/intechopen.84385

Ulug, C., Trell, E.-M., & Horlings, L. (2021). Ecovillage foodscapes: Zooming in and out of sustainable food practices. *Agriculture and Human Values*, *38*(4), 1041–1015. DOI: 10.1007/s10460-021-10213-1

UN-HABITAT. (2024)., *World Cities Report 2024 Cities And Climate Action Case Study Annex*. https://unhabitat.org/sites/default/files/2024/11/wcr2024_-_full_report.pdf

Waste Management Regulation. (2015). https://www.mevzuat.gov.tr/File/GeneratePdf?mevzuatNo=20644&mevzuatTur=KurumVeKurulusYonetmeligi&mevzuatTertip=5

Zero Waste Regulation. (2019). https://www.mevzuat.gov.tr/mevzuat?MevzuatNo=32659&MevzuatTur=7&MevzuatTertip=5

Chapter 11
Municipalities and Disability Policies in Türkiye:
Roles, Challenges, and Social Municipalism

Emrah Atar
https://orcid.org/0000-0003-1221-5415
Reccep Tayyip Erdogan University, Merkez, Turkey

Sena Yıldırım
https://orcid.org/0009-0002-4010-8625
Recep Tayyip Erdoğan University, Rize, Turkey

ABSTRACT

Laws ensuring equal access to rights for individuals with disabilities are a crucial component of social policy. While central governments are responsible for policy formulation, local governments, particularly municipalities, play a key role in implementing these policies effectively. By creating more accessible physical and social environments, municipalities contribute significantly to improving the quality of life for individuals with disabilities. Within the framework of "social municipalism," they develop and enforce inclusive policies that promote social integration. This study examines the role and effectiveness of municipalities in Turkey in developing and implementing social policies for individuals with disabilities. It explores the challenges they encounter in this process and the strategies they employ to overcome them. Through a comprehensive analysis, the study assesses municipalities' contributions, the difficulties they face, and potential solutions to enhance the inclusion of individuals with disabilities in society.

DOI: 10.4018/979-8-3373-0452-6.ch011

1. INTRODUCTION

Recognizing individuals with disabilities as an integral part of social life and ensuring the protection of their rights are among the primary objectives of contemporary societies. Disability should not be viewed solely as a physical or mental condition but also as a domain requiring efforts to combat social inequalities. In this context, ensuring equal opportunities for individuals with disabilities in all areas, from education to employment and from healthcare services to social life, necessitates a sustainable social policy approach. Although significant progress has been made in Türkiye in recent years through legal and institutional regulations to achieve these goals, the effectiveness of these policies largely depends on the efficiency of local governments.

According to Keskin (2014:1-2), municipalities play a critical role in providing services that facilitate the daily lives of individuals with disabilities and in implementing social policies. Local-level initiatives not only encourage the active participation of individuals with disabilities in society but also directly influence their access to social and economic rights. Municipal services, which span a wide range from transportation and urban transformation projects to cultural activities and social assistance policies, have the potential to enhance the quality of life for individuals with disabilities. However, the scope and effectiveness of these services vary depending on multiple factors, including municipalities' financial resources, institutional capacity, and local awareness.

Establishing a sustainable social structure for individuals with disabilities is not merely a matter of individual rights advocacy; it is also a necessary step toward improving overall societal well-being. In this regard, municipalities' responsibilities in the field of social policies require a responsive approach that addresses individual needs and upholds the principles of social equality.

This study aims to analyze the services provided by municipalities for individuals with disabilities and to explore how a more inclusive social policy framework can be constructed at the local level.This paper examines the role and effectiveness of municipalities in the development and implementation of social policies for individuals with disabilities in Türkiye. While evaluating municipal services aimed at facilitating the lives of individuals with disabilities, it highlights the challenges encountered in this field and identifies gaps in existing policies. Furthermore, recommendations are presented to assist local governments in developing a more inclusive and sustainable policy approach (Atar and Usta, 2023).As a literature review-based study, qualitative data has been utilized. The first section discusses the concepts of disability, causes of disability, classification of disability, models explaining disability, perspectives on disability in Türkiye, and the challenges individuals with disabilities face in social participation. The second section focuses on the development of social policies for individuals with disabilities in Türkiye, fundamental principles of social policies for individuals with disabilities, the role of local governments in the field of social policy, the concept of social municipalism, and municipal services for individuals with disabilities. In the third section, the obstacles municipalities encounter in providing social services for individuals with disabilities are examined, followed by recommendations and conclusions.

2. THE CONCEPT OF DISABILITY

Understanding the concept of disability is essential for developing effective social policies and fostering an inclusive society. According to Arı (2022:590), the concept of disability generally refers to an individual's inability to fully perform the roles required in social life. In a way, it represents a state of deficiency. Although the term "disability" is often used interchangeably with "impairment" in social contexts, the latter is predominantly preferred in medical and legal frameworks.

Disability, as a concept, has existed since the beginning of humanity and will continue to persist as long as human existence endures. There are various definitions explaining this concept. The most general definition is provided by the United Nations Convention on the Rights of Persons with Disabilities (2009), which describes individuals with sensory, psychological, physical, or intellectual impairments as having limited participation in society compared to other individuals living in the same conditions (Uzunoğlu, 2019:237). Disability has been conceptualized in varied ways across medical, social, and rights-based discourses. The World Health Organization (WHO) has contributed to this debate through three key frameworks:

ICIDH (1980) – The International Classification of Impairments, Disabilities, and Handicaps (WHO, 1980) framed disability as an individual consequence of disease, emphasizing functional limitations. This model was later critiqued for its medicalized approach (Oliver, 1990; Shakespeare, 2006). ICF (2001) – The International Classification of Functioning, Disability and Health (WHO, 2001) introduced a biopsychosocial model, integrating environmental barriers. While more inclusive, it has been challenged for retaining residual medicalization (Barnes & Mercer, 2010). World Report on Disability (2011) – This report aligned with the social-ecological model, emphasizing societal barriers and rights, reflecting the UN Convention on the Rights of Persons with Disabilities (CRPD, 2006).

Personal, environmental, and health-related challenges significantly affect the lives of individuals with disabilities. When discussing disability, people often first think of individuals with visual or hearing impairments or those who have lost a limb. However, the concept of disability is not this narrow; on the contrary, it encompasses a broad spectrum. Just as an individual who loses a leg in an accident is categorized as disabled, a baby born with a disability also falls within the same category. The only distinction in such cases is the degree and type of disability. Despite this diversity, the common factor among all individuals with disabilities is the feeling of inadequacy and social exclusion.

a. Causes of Disability

In his study, Baran (2011) categorizes the factors leading to disability into three groups: prenatal, perinatal, and postnatal factors. Newborn children are influenced by genetic and environmental factors, which shape their lives from birth onward. It is important to recognize that many genetic and environmental factors can either be prevented through proper measures or mitigated to minimize their impact.

- **Prenatal Causes:** Factors affecting the unborn child include the mother's nutritional habits, mental health, medication use, alcohol and tobacco consumption, accidents, work routine, and Rh incompatibility between parents.
- **Perinatal Causes:** Conditions such as oxygen deprivation, excessive pressure on the baby's head during birth, and improper use of medical instruments during delivery can significantly affect a child's development.
- **Postnatal Causes:** Factors such as nutrition, accidents, illnesses, family environment, peer interactions, mass media exposure, and the passage of time are considered postnatal causes of disability.

b. Classification of Disability

Globally and in Türkiye, disabilities are classified into eight categories: intellectual, hearing, visual, speech and language, orthopaedic, psychological and emotional disorders, attention deficit and hyperactivity disorder (ADHD), and chronic illnesses (Kızıltaş, 2012: 30-38).

- **Intellectual Disabilities:** Individuals with varying degrees of cognitive impairment, including those with Down syndrome and intellectual developmental delays.
- **Hearing Impairments:** Individuals with complete or partial hearing loss in one or both ears, including those who require hearing aids.
- **Visual Impairments:** Individuals with complete or partial vision loss or impairment in one or both eyes. This category also includes those with colour blindness, night blindness, or those using ocular prostheses.
- **Orthopedic Disabilities:** Individuals with deficiencies, impairments, or functional losses in the musculoskeletal system.
- **Speech and Language Disorders:** Individuals with speech impairments, speech-related disorders, or voice disorders due to various causes.

- **Psychological and Emotional Disorders:** Individuals experiencing abnormalities in emotions, thoughts, and behaviours that hinder daily life and social relationships. This category includes conditions such as depression and schizophrenia.
- **Chronic Illnesses:** Long-term conditions requiring continuous medical care and treatment, which hinder an individual's daily functionality.
- **Attention Deficit and Hyperactivity Disorder (ADHD):** A disorder that manifests before the age of seven and is characterized by inattention, excessive activity, and hyperactive behaviour inconsistent with age and developmental level.

c. Models Explaining Disability

Disability has existed throughout human history, evolving according to the perspectives and ideologies of different periods. These perspectives have shaped various approaches to disability, which are collectively referred to as disability models. The dominant economic and political understanding of a given era largely determines the prevailing model of disability. In this context, four primary models of disability can be identified: the traditional model, the medical model, the social model, and the human rights model (Aköğretmen, 2023: 131-132).

- **Traditional Model (Feudal Era):** This model is shaped by the dominant religious and cultural values of society. During this period, mental and psychological disorders were believed to be caused by supernatural forces. Influenced by prevailing societal beliefs, individuals born with disabilities or those who later became disabled were often perceived as witches and considered dangerous. As a result, disabled individuals were frequently stigmatized and, in extreme cases, executed until the late Middle Ages (Aköğretmen, 2023: 132-133).
- **Medical Model (Industrial Revolution):** This model follows the broader developments occurring worldwide. Disability is regarded as a medical problem that requires treatment, and disabled individuals are seen as patients in need of medical intervention. In this approach, disability is equated with deficiency, and disabled individuals are often dependent on healthcare professionals to sustain their lives (Ünal, 2021: 238).
- **Social Model (Welfare State Era):** This model shifts the focus to the social, cultural, and physical environment of individuals with disabilities. According to this perspective, the greatest barrier faced by disabled individuals is social exclusion. Unlike the medical model, which perceives disability as a deficiency, the social model views it as a difference. It emphasizes that disabled individuals should not be seen as dependent on others but rather as individu-

als who can lead independent lives and participate actively in society (Ünal, 2018: 1464).

- **Human Rights Model (Contemporary Era):** This model is based on the principle that disabled individuals have equal rights with other members of society and should enjoy the same legal protections. It actively opposes social injustice, discrimination, and inequality. Under this model, the state has a duty to protect and uphold the rights of disabled individuals, ensuring their full participation in all aspects of life (Çoban, 2017: 255).

This classification highlights the evolving perceptions of disability throughout history, demonstrating the shift from exclusionary and medicalized views toward a more inclusive and rights-based approach.

d. Disability in Türkiye

The societal perspective on disability in Türkiye has undergone significant transformation over time. Historically, disability was often seen as an individual's fate, with disabled people regarded not as active members of society but as individuals who needed to be protected. Recent years have witnessed a paradigm shift in understandings of disability, as discussed later in this work.. Societal prejudices and implementation gaps remain ongoing issues although legal regulations have been introduced in areas such as education, healthcare, employment, and accessibility. To build a truly egalitarian society, it is necessary not only to create policies but also to raise societal awareness that focuses on supporting people with disabilities. This is particularly crucial given the significant proportion of disabled individuals within Türkiye's total population.

Table 1. Proportion of Disabled Individuals by Gender and Age Group in Total Population

DISABLED INDIVIDUAL	POPULATION PERCENTAGE (%)	MALE (%)	FEMALE (%)
ALL AGE GROUPS	6.9	5.9	7.39
3-9	2.3	2.5	2.1
10-14	2.1	2.4	1.8
15-19	2.3	2.6	2.0
20-24	2.7	3.4	2.0
25-29	2.6	3.0	2.3
30-34	3.2	3.4	3.0
35-39	4.0	4.0	4.1
40-44	5.1	4.7	5.6

continued on following page

Table 1. Continued

DISABLED INDIVIDUAL	POPULATION PERCENTAGE (%)	MALE (%)	FEMALE (%)
45-49	6.9	5.9	7.8
50-54	8.8	7.1	10.7
55-59	12.1	9.2	15.0
60-64	16.5	12.3	20.4
65-69	23.0	18.3	27.2
70-74	31.9	26.3	36.3
75+	46.5	40.9	50.3

Source: Disabled Statistics 2021, Ministry of Family and Social Services (2021)

As shown in Table 1, according to the statistics from 2021, the proportion of disabled individuals within Türkiye's total population is 6.9%, with 5.9% being male and 7.39% being female. It is also observed that the age group with the highest disability rate is 75 years and above, where the percentage of disabled women surpasses that of disabled men.

According to Ünal (2021:239), approaches to disability in Türkiye have varied over time, influenced by the different political frameworks of each period. These periods can be categorized into three distinct phases. The first phase, covering the years 1920-1980, was a time when disability was seen as entirely the responsibility of the individual and their family. This period is referred to as the medical phase. The second phase, from 1980 to 2005, marked a shift towards viewing disabled individuals as part of society, with the recognition that society also had responsibilities. This phase combined both the medical and social models of disability. The third and most recent phase, from 2005 onwards, is characterized by the adoption of the human rights model, where disability is understood through the lens of human rights, leading to the creation and implementation of policies aligned with these principles.

e. Participation of Disabled Individuals in Social Life and the Challenges They Face

According to Genç (2016: 83-84), the challenges faced by individuals living with disability are not limited to the concept of disability itself but are accompanied by a range of other issues. Disabled individuals not only struggle with these challenges themselves but their family members are also forced to deal with these difficulties. Research findings have identified key issues, including difficulty with care (22%), psychological problems (11%), and social adaptation issues due to physical disabilities (8.2%). Additionally, families of disabled individuals reported challenges such as the need for rehabilitation services (7.2%), problems with home healthcare (3.8%), lack of access to services from public institutions (3.4%), and environmental difficulties faced by families of children with intellectual disabilities (3.4%). In general, the primary issues faced by disabled individuals are economic problems, care difficulties, and psychological concerns. A large portion of disabled individuals who are unable to work also experience significant economic hardship. This issue is partially alleviated through government assistance programs. However, societal pressure and indifference towards disabled individuals and their families remain a significant ongoing problem. As a result of social exclusion, disabled individuals may feel isolated and unhappy, which could lead them to be pushed to the margins of society.

The challenges faced by disabled individuals in participating in social life are frequently observed. According to data from the Turkish Statistical Institute (TÜİK, 2024), individuals with disabilities in Türkiye face a range of structural and social challenges that hinder their full participation in society. The most frequently reported issue is the inadequacy of facilities provided by the state, followed closely by the inability to use public transportation—problems that particularly affect women more than men. Other significant difficulties include the lack of access to technologically appropriate tools, the absence of environmental regulations, and society's general failure to offer adequate support. Gender disparities are evident across several categories, with women more frequently reporting barriers related to entering public buildings and participating in social and cultural activities. These findings underline the need for comprehensive and inclusive public policies that address the specific needs of disabled individuals, with particular attention to the intersection of disability and gender.

The participation of individuals with disabilities in social life is influenced not only by personal limitations but also by environmental and structural barriers. According to the World Report on Disability published by the World Health Organization and the World Bank, the majority of the nearly one billion individuals with disabilities worldwide face significant challenges in accessing education, employment, healthcare services, and social activities (WHO & World Bank, 2011: 263). These challenges are further exacerbated by the inadequate physical accessibility of public buildings, digital inequality in access to information, incompatibility of transportation infrastructure, and the persistence of discriminatory attitudes within society. The report highlights that especially in low- and middle-income countries, municipalities often fail to adequately address these issues due to limitations in infrastructure and resources. In this context, it is emphasized that local governments should not only act as service providers but also play an active role in fostering social awareness and participation regarding disability. Similarly, municipalities in Turkey are encouraged to go beyond physical modifications and develop inclusive social strategies, which is crucial for aligning with global approaches in the field (Wu and Atar, 2023).

3. THE DEVELOPMENT OF SOCIAL POLICIES FOR DISABLED INDIVIDUALS IN TÜRKIYE

Observations, research, statistics, and reports related to the relationship between individuals with disabilities and other members of society, as well as the challenges they face in social life, indicate that people with disabilities encounter numerous distinct issues. Solving, eliminating, or minimizing these problems requires a significant responsibility from every member of society. This responsibility is not merely a social duty, but an ethical one. As members of society, the primary responsibility lies in removing the obstacles faced by individuals with disabilities and providing support and motivation for their participation in social life. Furthermore, this responsibility should be expanded through policies and services developed in sectors such as health, economy, and education.

In Türkiye, the development of a comprehensive social policy approach for individuals with disabilities, who face multiple disadvantages in individual, economic, and social spheres, dates back to the late 1990s. Prior to this period, despite some initiatives and regulations, it was not possible to address policies for individuals with disabilities in a holistic manner (Metin, 2017: 328).

The introduction of special education in Türkiye began with a law enacted in 1950, with the Ministry of National Education assigned as the implementing authority. This marked a shift, as the issue of disability moved beyond its health aspect and the focus shifted toward education. With the adoption of the principle of the social state in the 1961 Constitution, articles related to special education (especially for the visually impaired) were included, and in 1971, the Employment Law introduced regulations for the employment of individuals with disabilities (quota) (Özgökçeler & Alper, 2010: 41).

In 1981, the United Nations General Assembly declared the year as the International Year of Disabled Persons, with one of the goals being the establishment of an institution responsible for coordinating services for individuals with disabilities worldwide. In response, Türkiye's Ministry of Labour and Social Security created the National Coordination Committee for the Protection of Disabled Persons in 1981. Although various services such as treatment, rehabilitation, education, employment, and social assistance were provided for individuals with disabilities in Türkiye, it was not until the 1990s that these issues began to be comprehensively discussed and gained traction among policymakers. In 1997, a decree law established the Prime Ministry's Disabled People Administration. One of the most significant developments for people with disabilities occurred with the enactment of the Law on Disabled Persons in 2005 (Law No. 5378), which brought substantial regulations for the disabled (Metin, 2017: 329-330).

After the 2000s, the approach to disability in terms of legal frameworks and policy objectives shifted from a medical model to a social model. The 1961 Constitution explicitly included provisions on enhancing the productivity of persons with disabilities and their special education, while the Primary Education and Training Law incorporated regulations on special education, leading to the first "Special Education Regulation" based on this legislation. During this period, the rehabilitation of persons with disabilities was also addressed (Özgökçeler & Alper, 2010). In 1971, an amendment to Labor Law No. 1475 introduced a 2% employment quota for persons with disabilities, and in 1976, Law No. 2022 was enacted to provide a basic income for unemployed persons with disabilities and those over 62 years of age. Thus, by the 1980s, partial progress had been made in education, rehabilitation, employment, and income security for persons with disabilities who could not be employed. The 1982 Constitution further guaranteed that "Everyone is equal before the law without distinction based on language, race, color, sex, political opinion, philosophical belief, religion, sect, or similar grounds" (Article 10). The most significant indicator of these changes were the increase in public expenditures for individuals with disabilities. A study on expenditures for individuals with disabilities between 2006 and 2015 revealed an increase in spending, with the share of annual public expenditures in GDP rising from 0.25% in 2006 to 0.70% in 2015 (Yılmaz & Yentürk, 2017:70).

In Türkiye, both legally and in terms of policy goals, the emphasis on a holistic approach to disability has grown, with public expenditures largely focusing on needs assessment and cash support. In addition, social policies for individuals with disabilities are closely linked with poverty. It is well-known that individuals with disabilities are more likely to experience poverty compared to non-disabled individuals. In this sense, individuals with disabilities in need play a significant role in public expenditures. Today, public services for individuals with disabilities have gone beyond cash assistance, encompassing all areas of social life through inclusive practices and services (Metin, 2017: 333).

3.1. Fundamental Principles of Social Policies for Individuals with Disabilities

According to Şen (2023:50-55), the level of development in societies can be measured not only by economic indicators but also by the social policies that improve the quality of life of individuals. In this context, the social policies created for individuals with disabilities aim to ensure their full participation in social life and provide an equal life within the framework of human rights. Disability is not merely a physical condition; it is also an experience shaped by environmental, social, and cultural barriers. In this regard, certain fundamental principles (like equality, accessibility, inclusion, empowerment and reasonable accommodation) should be adopted to overcome the challenges faced by individuals with disabilities and improve their quality of life. These principles are of critical importance in advocating for the rights of individuals with disabilities and offering equal opportunities in society.

3.2. Social Equality and Participation

According to Genç and Çat (2014: 365-366), benefiting from social equality is a fundamental principle for ensuring that individuals with disabilities not only participate in social life but also have access to the opportunities they deserve. Social equality requires individuals with disabilities to have the same rights as others in areas such as education, health, and employment. Individuals with disabilities should participate in social life not only physically but also socially, culturally, and psychologically. This participation enables the thoughts, desires, and potentials of individuals with disabilities to be acknowledged within society.

Individuals with disabilities must have equal opportunities not only in terms of physical accessibility but also in education, work life, and social relations. This ensures that individuals with disabilities can integrate into society without exclusion or prejudice. Moreover, the establishment of a sense of social equality allows individuals with disabilities to feel valued and provides them with greater opportunities to contribute to society.

3.3. Accessibility

As discussed by Şen (2023: 70-71), accessibility is an essential principle for enabling individuals with disabilities to participate in social life. Individuals with disabilities must be able to use the physical environment, transportation, public services, and social spaces with ease. This is not limited to ramps at building entrances but should also encompass access to schools, hospitals, public transportation, and digital services.

Accessibility involves not only the removal of physical barriers but also the adaptation of information and technological infrastructure to meet the needs of individuals with disabilities. Municipalities and other local authorities should eliminate transportation barriers for individuals with disabilities by building accessible roads, disability-friendly public transport vehicles, and buildings. Such infrastructure projects ensure that individuals with disabilities can live independently and participate in all aspects of social life.

3.4. Independence and Freedom

Supporting the independent living of individuals with disabilities is one of the fundamental principles of social policies. Independence refers to the ability of individuals with disabilities to organize their lives according to their desires and needs. Social policies must provide the necessary infrastructure for individuals with disabilities to lead an independent life. For example, special housing for individuals with disabilities, home care services, and daily life support services play an important role in this regard.

Independence is not only about the physical environment but also a mental and emotional process. Individuals with disabilities should be able to make decisions freely, live under their control, and enjoy equal rights regardless of factors such as gender, age, or ethnicity. Independence allows individuals with disabilities to respect themselves and play a more active role in society.

3.5. Equal Opportunity

In their work, Çaha (2016: 129) states that equal opportunity allows individuals with disabilities to have the same conditions as others in social life. This ensures that individuals with disabilities have equal opportunities in education, workforce participation, healthcare, and social rights. Equal opportunity enables individuals with disabilities to be part of social and economic life without facing discrimination.

Ensuring equal opportunities in education, employment, and social services improves not only the lives of individuals with disabilities but also the overall welfare of society. Special education programs for individuals with disabilities, accessibility arrangements in workplaces, and disability-friendly employment opportunities contribute to achieving equal opportunity. Additionally, social programs that allow individuals with disabilities to develop their potential are also a part of the equal opportunity principle.

3.6. Combating Discrimination and Raising Awareness

Discrimination is one of the biggest barriers faced by individuals with disabilities. Misconceptions, prejudices, and stigmatization regarding disability in society can make it difficult for individuals with disabilities to participate in social life. Individuals with disabilities must be protected against such discrimination in all areas, from education to employment.

Awareness-raising efforts are crucial in increasing sensitivity in society regarding the rights, needs, and potential of individuals with disabilities. Awareness campaigns conducted in educational institutions and through the media can show society ways to combat discrimination against individuals with disabilities. This is a significant step in facilitating the acceptance of individuals with disabilities and promoting societal integration.

4. THE ROLE OF LOCAL GOVERNMENTS IN SOCIAL POLICY

Social policies play a crucial role in ensuring the welfare of society, particularly for vulnerable groups, and are an essential element of a well-functioning community. These policies not only address the needs of disadvantaged individuals but also contribute to broader societal development. Local governments, which are elected by the community, play a key role in the implementation of social policies, as they are closest to the people they serve and better understand local needs. In Türkiye, as in other countries, local governments—especially municipalities—are tasked with a significant role in the execution of social policies alongside the central government.

According to Tiyek (2016:56), all the problems encountered in daily social life fall within the scope of social policy. In this context, social policy, especially for disadvantaged individuals who require protection, plays a crucial role in ensuring justice, equality, and the empowerment of individuals. While policies related to the working conditions of individuals have only recently been developed, social policies, in a broad sense, are as old as human history. Conceptually, social policy addresses the fulfilment of social needs and deals with the relationship between policy and society in ensuring social welfare.

Local governments, especially municipalities, play a significant role in the implementation of social policies in Türkiye, alongside the central government. Local governments are elected by the local population, and these governing bodies, chosen by the people, are responsible for meeting the common needs of the local community (Tekeli, 1983: 3).

In Türkiye, local government units consist of municipalities, provincial special administrations, and villages. Particularly with the intensification of urbanization, the role of municipalities, which are responsible for cities and towns, has been growing in importance. Therefore, within the context of the role of local governments in social policy, the services carried out by municipalities have become increasingly significant and continue to develop.

Local governments are primarily responsible for providing public services in areas related to social policy within their jurisdiction, which is a task also undertaken by central governments. Although local governments are obliged to carry out the same duties as central governments, their role and effectiveness in the field of social policy are broader. For example, measures regulating the working environment (narrowly defined as the subject of social policy) are carried out by central governments (Metin, 2017: 334).

The emergence and development of local governments in Türkiye occurred at a later stage compared to some European countries like United Kingdom (UK). In addition, in European countries, municipalities not only have the duty to meet local needs but also play an important role in acting as civil society entities in relation to the central government (Tekeli, 1983: 6). In UK, social policies implemented by local governments in response to poverty continued until World War II, and the role and effectiveness of local governments in this area significantly increased. This situation continued until the 1970s, during which local governments became a key component of social programs, gaining substantial authority and responsibilities (Ersöz, 2011: 70-74).

Municipal services in the Ottoman Empire were initially delivered through religious foundations (waqfs) and guilds (Keleş, 2016:155–157). The first formal municipality was established in Istanbul in 1855, headed by a şehir emin (city mayor) and a 12-member council. The 1869 Municipal Regulation codified these efforts, expanding municipalities to other cities and laying the groundwork for village and provincial administrations by the century's end.

Following the empire's collapse, the Republic of Turkey inherited a fragmented municipal system. Limited resources forced municipalities to prioritize urban infrastructure (e.g., roads, water supply) over social services. Social welfare remained largely state-driven, with municipalities playing a marginal role (Keskin, 2012:74–76).

By the late 1970s, municipalities began institutionalizing social municipalism—addressing local needs of disadvantaged groups through housing, healthcare, and cultural services. This shift reflected growing urbanization and political demands for participatory governance.

The 1980s marked a turning point, as liberalization policies emphasized decentralization and private-sector partnerships (Keskin, 2012:74–76). Municipalities expanded their social policy roles, outsourcing services while adopting a welfare-oriented approach (e.g., subsidies for low-income groups). Today, they balance infrastructure management with social equity goals, though challenges like funding disparities persist.The understanding of social municipalism in Türkiye has developed and continues to grow as a result of local municipalities. One of the most important factors in the rise of social municipalism as a mandatory mission is the pressure from impoverished voters. In short, the understanding of social municipalism feeds from the needs of society (Keskin, 2012: 198). Additionally, through laws enacted for municipalities, local governments have been assigned important duties, and with the support of these laws, social assistance and services are provided for vulnerable groups, such as individuals with disabilities, in Türkiye. Therefore, local governments are tasked with carrying out all services in accordance with the needs of disadvantaged groups in society (Ersöz, 2011: 131).

The "Law on Persons with Disabilities" that came into force in Türkiye in 2005 assigns responsibilities to municipalities regarding accessibility and vocational rehabilitation. According to the relevant provisions, it is stated that the environment should comply with construction, design, and manufacturing standards for individuals with disabilities to live an accessible life (Art. 7/1). Furthermore, the law also stipulates that public and private transportation vehicles should be accessible to individuals with disabilities (Art. 7/2). Municipalities and metropolitan municipalities were given a deadline of July 7, 2018, to implement the necessary measures in these areas (Transitory Article 3). In addition, eight years were defined for municipalities to ensure that areas such as roads, pedestrian crossings, open and green spaces, and sports areas are accessible to individuals with disabilities. Municipalities that fail to meet these obligations are subject to administrative fines ranging from 5,000 to 25,000 Turkish Lira for each violation (Additional Clause 4). Moreover, although the responsibility for providing vocational training for the employment of individuals with disabilities lies with the Ministry of National Education and the Ministry of Labor and Social Security, these training services are provided by municipalities (Art. 13/2).

4.1. The Concept of Social Municipalism

The concept of social municipalism is not merely a model of local service delivery, but rather a holistic approach aimed at constructing social justice and societal equality at the local level. In this context, the previously discussed notions of disability, principles of social policy concerning persons with disabilities, and the roles of municipalities within the realm of social policy converge within the framework of social municipalism. This approach, which prioritizes the effective participation of disadvantaged groups—especially individuals with disabilities—in social life, transforms theoretical foundations into practical service models by encompassing practices such as social assistance, accessibility, care services, and employment support. Therefore, this section demonstrates that the notion of social municipalism is not only a theoretical construct, but also directly linked to local policies that contribute to the social integration of persons with disabilities, thereby establishing a functional connection to the overall coherence of the study.

Social municipalism is a concept that has gained significant attention in Türkiye in recent decades. Local government units in Türkiye are composed of provincial special administrations, municipalities, and village administrations. While social policy activities aimed at disadvantaged individuals are the responsibility of all local government units in Türkiye, the concept of "social municipalism" is more prominent. This is because, when referring to local governments in Turkish society, municipalities are typically the first units that come to mind. Municipalities generally have greater resources and serve a broader segment of the population. As a result, municipalities play a critical role in the planning, implementation, and evaluation of social policy programs. The primary purpose of establishing local governments is to identify local problems and find solutions, thereby ensuring the satisfaction of the community. Social municipalism, as an approach, assigns municipalities the task of planning and implementing social policies, thus incorporating areas like health, education, and housing into public spending with a focus on social objectives.

Koç and Ökmen (2015: 71) argue that services within the framework of social municipalism began to be offered in Türkiye after the 1970s, and by the 1990s, the social activities of municipalities became more prominent. By the 2000s, societal and administrative changes began to be reflected in the legal structure, marking a significant shift. Municipalities serve as a buffer to address unemployment and poverty in society, continuing these efforts until these issues are resolved. However, the success of municipalities in fulfilling this role has been questioned. Research has shown that there is a lack of a comprehensive social municipalism approach in Türkiye, particularly regarding social and economic rights. Instead, local policies in social services and social assistance are limited and do not fully meet the needs of the population. According to TÜİK statistics (2024), only 50% of individuals expressed satisfaction with the services provided by municipalities in Türkiye.

4.2. Services Provided by Municipalities for People with Disabilities

In Türkiye, provincial, district, and metropolitan municipalities are obligated to provide social services to the community, including services for individuals with disabilities and their families. The legal basis for these obligations comes from various laws. The Municipalities Law No. 5393 (1982) and the Metropolitan Municipality Law No. 5216 (2004) have included individuals with disabilities in the responsibilities of municipalities and mayors while delivering local public services. These services can generally be categorized as follows:

4.2.1. Establishing Centers for People with Disabilities

Municipalities in Türkiye have been actively working to provide services for individuals with disabilities. These services are often delivered through specialized centres that cater to various needs. For example, the Municipality of Yenimahalle in Ankara stands out with the establishment of its "Employment and Life Center for Individuals with Intellectual Disabilities." This center promotes the economic participation of individuals with intellectual disabilities and also plays a supportive role in areas such as housing, rehabilitation, and social integration. The center aims to enable these individuals to lead independent lives, offering vocational training opportunities to enhance their employability. Additionally, it ensures that individuals with disabilities can continue to live in a safe environment in cases where their families pass away or are no longer able to provide care (Fırat, 2008: 91). Through this initiative, employment opportunities have been created specifically for individuals with disabilities, and the center provides a space where they can continue their lives after the loss of their caregivers (Fırat, 2008: 91).

Similarly, the Izmir Metropolitan Municipality implements the "Disability Service Centers" initiative, which consolidates a wide range of services under one roof to support the full social participation of individuals with disabilities. These centers offer psychological counseling, vocational skill development courses, rehabilitation services, and opportunities for participation in social activities. The İzmir case is particularly significant as it illustrates how the concept of social municipalism has become institutionalized—transforming services from being solely charity-based to focusing on the social integration of individuals (Alimanoğlu Yemişçi & Sarı Gerşil, 2021: 130).

These centers alleviate not only the psycho-social burden on individuals with disabilities but also that of their families, while simultaneously contributing to the creation of societal awareness around disability issues. These practices, which prioritize the participation of persons with disabilities as equal members of society, can be regarded as concrete implementations of the principles of social municipalism in the field.

4.2.2. Care and Support Services

Individuals in need of care require assistance from others to carry out daily activities. These needs go beyond physical support to include financial assistance, healthcare, therapy, protection, and social support. For example, home care services allow individuals with disabilities to continue their lives at home for a certain fee. Institutional care services, on the other hand, involve the care of individuals who are unable to live independently, provided at official or private care centres based on the family's request. In Türkiye, there are 159 private care centres, serving 13,843 individuals in need of care (Öztürk et al., 2017: 53-54).

Care and support services play a crucial role in enabling individuals with disabilities to maintain their daily lives and participate in social life. Municipalities are developing supportive practices in this field, offering both in-home care and services through day or residential care facilities. These services not only address individual needs but also contribute to overall societal welfare by alleviating the caregiving burden on family members.

The Istanbul Metropolitan Municipality provides care and support services for individuals with disabilities under its "Home-Based Health and Social Support Services" program. Within this framework, bedridden individuals with disabilities receive in-home medical services, as well as personal care, cleaning, and psycho-social support. These services are delivered by multidisciplinary teams and allocated based on the outcomes of social assessments. The initiative aims to support individuals with disabilities in living independently in their own environments for as long as possible (Istanbul Metropolitan Municipality Directorate for Disability Services, 2018).

The Bursa Metropolitan Municipality offers similar support under the umbrella of its "Live Without Barriers Center" (Engelsiz Yaşa Merkezi), which provides essential services to individuals with disabilities in need of care. The center addresses basic needs, encourages participation in social activities, and contributes to the psycho-social development of its users. Additionally, the municipality organizes courses designed to enhance daily living skills among individuals with disabilities. These services aim to enable individuals to live more independently (Bursa Metropolitan Municipality, n.d.).

These practices, as reflections of the social municipalism approach, represent a multidimensional support mechanism that goes beyond physical care to include social participation and psychological well-being. In this respect, the care and support services provided by municipalities significantly contribute to the visibility and active involvement of individuals with disabilities in society.

4.2.3. Providing Transportation Accessibility

Like all individuals, people with disabilities have the right to move about independently. This right is fundamental to their participation in society, yet access to transportation can be a significant challenge for them. Physical and infrastructure limitations are key barriers to accessible transportation. Municipalities in Türkiye address this issue by offering services or privileges to individuals with disabilities: they can travel for free or at a discounted rate. For example, intercity travel offers a 50% discount, and airlines provide up to a 25% discount for individuals with disabilities, depending on the severity of their condition. Additionally, those with a special driver's license can purchase modified vehicles to drive themselves (Sarı, 2022: 1). Several municipalities have implemented projects to address these transportation challenges. For instance, Denizli Metropolitan Municipality provides specialized transportation for people with disabilities to hospitals and rehabilitation centres free of charge, and aims to make all public transportation fully accessible

(Denizli Metropolitan Municipality, n.d.). Mersin Metropolitan Municipality has updated its bus fleet with accessible vehicles to facilitate public transportation for individuals with disabilities and introduced the "Accessible Taxi" project for personal transportation needs (Mersin Metropolitan Municipality, n.d.). The Altınordu Municipality (Ordu) provides free transportation for individuals with disabilities to attend appointments or personal errands through its "Accessible Transportation Vehicle" service, which is especially helpful in rural areas (Altınordu Municipality, n.d.). Additionally, the Istanbul Metropolitan Municipality has implemented voice guidance systems and prioritized services for individuals with disabilities on Metrobus and tram lines to improve urban mobility (Istanbul Metropolitan Municipality Disability Directorate, 2018).

These practices demonstrate that municipalities are not limited to merely organizing the physical environment; they also support the right of individuals with disabilities to move independently by providing personalized transportation solutions. In this context, the expansion of services that facilitate accessible transportation is critically important for ensuring the social participation of individuals with disabilities and promoting equal opportunities.

4.2.4. Urban Planning and Accessibility

People with disabilities often face accessibility issues in urban environments. The solution to this challenge is the concept of an "accessible city," which ensures that individuals with disabilities can move freely and access all the services they need. The concept of an accessible city is not limited to the existence of physical structures for people with disabilities but encompasses a broader planning approach that considers the needs of all disabled individuals. However, it is necessary to provide additional support to enable individuals with disabilities to fully exercise their rights (Erten & Aktel, 2020: 899).

Full participation of individuals with disabilities in urban life is not only dependent on access to services but also on the accessibility of the physical environment. Sidewalks, transportation stops, public buildings, parks, walkways, pedestrian crossings, and social facilities are among the key elements that directly affect the mobility of individuals with disabilities. Accordingly, municipalities are implementing urban planning interventions to make public spaces accessible to all.

As part of its "Accessible Istanbul" initiative, the Istanbul Metropolitan Municipality has installed wheelchair ramps along sidewalks, introduced audible traffic signals to assist visually impaired individuals in crossing streets, and conducted accessibility audits in public buildings. Furthermore, accessibility standards have been made mandatory in all new urban development projects. Elevators, escalators, and warning systems for persons with disabilities have been integrated into metro and metrobüs stations (Istanbul Metropolitan Municipality Directorate for Disability Services, 2018).

The Konya Metropolitan Municipality, under the slogan "Barrier-Free City Konya," has equipped sidewalks and crossings with tactile surfaces, installed accessible toilets in public spaces, and created barrier-free entrances in social facilities. Additionally, the municipality has developed smart city applications adapted for individuals with disabilities. Smart stop systems across the city now feature audio announcements and visual screens to improve access to information for individuals with visual and hearing impairments (Konya Metropolitan Municipality, n.d.).

The Eskişehir Metropolitan Municipality is also among those prioritizing accessibility in urban planning processes. Particularly along tram lines, improvements such as ramp systems, wide sidewalks, and low-floor vehicles have been implemented to eliminate physical barriers. Furthermore, the municipality has built dedicated walking paths and playgrounds in public parks for individuals with disabilities (Eskişehir Metropolitan Municipality, n.d.).

Since 2013, the Izmir Metropolitan Municipality has been implementing the "Engelsizmir" (Barrier-Free Izmir) project to enhance physical accessibility in urban spaces. As part of this initiative, tools such as an accessible building inspection unit, an accessibility guide, and impact assessment mechanisms have been developed. All new public buildings in Izmir are inspected for accessibility compliance, and necessary modifications are mandated if requirements are not met. The municipality has also introduced mobile applications and mapping tools to facilitate access for individuals with disabilities to public transport stops and recreational areas (Alimanoğlu Yemişçi & Sarı Gerşil, 2021: 138).

These practices illustrate that municipalities embracing the principle of accessibility in urban planning enable individuals with disabilities to move independently in public spaces, thereby reducing the risk of social exclusion and fostering social inclusion. Transforming the physical environment is as crucial as effective service provision, and municipal efforts in this area contribute significantly to the realization of sustainable social policy goals.

4.2.5. Vocational Training Programs for People with Disabilities

Municipalities organize vocational training courses for people with disabilities to help develop their skills and increase their employability. These courses are part of a broader improvement process that aims to reduce dependency and increase opportunities for individuals with disabilities to acquire professions and find jobs. Article 24 of the UN Convention on the Rights of Persons with Disabilities states that parties to the Convention recognize the right to education for persons with disabilities, and the Convention has been signed by 164 countries and ratified by 191 (Aver, 2019: 331).

The "Disability Employment Workshop" initiative carried out by the Fatih Municipality (Istanbul) serves as a notable example in this field. In collaboration with the Fatih Public Education Center, the municipality offers free vocational training courses for literate individuals with disabilities aged 14 and above. These courses cover a wide range of areas, including decorative wood painting, leather accessory production, jewelry design, felt-making, computer literacy, marbling art (ebru), and sign language. Held at the Dervişali Community Center, the courses aim to foster personal development and equip participants with skills in handicraft-based production (Fatih Municipality, 2024).

The Erzurum Metropolitan Municipality also conducts vocational training activities for individuals with disabilities through its Women and Disability Services Coordination Center. The municipality offers courses in fields such as hair care and styling, traditional cloth weaving, and decorative home accessory production. This initiative not only encourages the participation of individuals with disabilities in the production process but also enables them to generate income and contribute to economic life (Erzurum Metropolitan Municipality, 2023).

In conclusion, many municipalities in Turkey are actively supporting the social inclusion of individuals with disabilities through vocational training programs. These courses contribute not only to professional development but also to increased self-confidence, expanded social networks, and the capacity to lead independent lives. Municipal practices in this domain represent a concrete embodiment of social policy at the local level and promote the support of individuals with disabilities based on the principle of equal opportunity.

4.2.6. Sports Teams and Cultural Activities for People with Disabilities

Sports and cultural activities implemented by municipalities to promote the social participation of individuals with disabilities constitute a significant component of local-level social inclusion policies. Through these activities, both the physical and psychosocial development of individuals with disabilities are supported, while their processes of integration into society are also reinforced.

Municipalities and metropolitan municipalities in Türkiye support the participation of individuals with disabilities in social life by providing support for sports clubs and facilitating access to sporting activities. For instance, in the 2015 Türkiye Paraplegic Cup, six athletes with disabilities won medals. Additionally, seminars on combating obesity have been organized for people with disabilities and their families. Malatya Metropolitan Municipality's "Accessible Life Fair" features booths from public and private institutions offering services for individuals with disabilities. The fair also hosts performances, art exhibitions, and awareness-raising activities about disability, contributing to the integration of people with disabilities into society (Kalaycı & Akin, 2019: 670). Looking at some municipalities' initiatives for disabled individuals, Istanbul Metropolitan Municipality has established specialized sports facilities such as wheelchair basketball courts, swimming pools, and tennis areas. The municipality has also established professional teams for individuals with disabilities in national leagues, thereby promoting physical health and social participation (Istanbul Metropolitan Municipality, n.d.). Bursa Metropolitan Municipality has also created teams for wheelchair basketball and other sports and ensures that its facilities are accessible to people with disabilities, leading to success at national and international levels (Bursa Metropolitan Municipality, n.d.).

Similarly, the Ankara Metropolitan Municipality supports the empowerment of individuals with disabilities in the field of sports. The Ankara Disabled Sports Club contributes to both sporting success and social visibility by forming professional teams in disciplines such as deaf football and wheelchair basketball. Additionally, workshops in areas like handicrafts, music, and painting are organized for individuals with disabilities at the BELMEK courses within the municipality; through these courses, disabled individuals can actively participate in production processes. In Ankara, supportive initiatives such as accessible cinema screenings and free transportation to cultural events are also implemented (Ankara Metropolitan Municipality, n.d.).

As can be understood from these examples, municipalities are important institutions that support the participation of individuals with disabilities in sports and cultural activities. These types of social inclusion policies established at the local level are among the essential tools for ensuring the full and active participation of individuals with disabilities in social life.

4.2.7. Social Activities

Social and cultural activities are another significant factor in promoting the social inclusion of people with disabilities. Local governments organize various social and cultural events to provide opportunities for people with disabilities and their families to enjoy healthy and happy times together, enhancing their social interaction. Additionally, some metropolitan municipalities organize cultural events such as festivals, theatre performances, museum visits, and excursions during the annual Disabilities Week (Uzunoğlu, 2019: 253). For example, Ankara Metropolitan Municipality organizes social events during Disabilities Week, such as concerts, theatre shows, and awareness walks, to encourage the participation of people with disabilities in social life (Ankara Metropolitan Municipality, n.d.).

The Eskişehir Metropolitan Municipality carries out exemplary initiatives to enable individuals with disabilities to play an active role in the art and cultural life through inclusive cultural policies. Accessible theater performances and creative drama workshops are organized within the municipality to support the participation of individuals with disabilities in the performing arts. For instance, as part of the 2024 International Day of Persons with Disabilities, a theater play in which individuals with disabilities participated after nearly a year of preparation was staged at the city theater and received praise from a wide audience. Such initiatives provide an opportunity for disabled participants to engage in artistic production. The Eskişehir Municipality also facilitates access to the city's cultural venues for disabled citizens by organizing cultural trips (museum and city tours). Mixed exhibitions organized to introduce the artworks of individuals with disabilities to the public are also notable activities. Indeed, a "Painting and Handicrafts Exhibition" featuring paintings, ceramics, and handicrafts produced by individuals served at the Municipal Mental Disability Daycare Center was opened to the public during disability day events and attracted great attention from the community (Eskişehir Metropolitan Municipality, 2024). These events increase the participation of individuals with disabilities in cultural life as both audience members and producers, and strengthen social awareness.

In Turkey, municipalities implement various cultural and artistic activities to support the equal participation of individuals with disabilities in social life. As seen in the examples of Ankara and Eskişehir municipalities, these activities, ranging from concerts and theater workshops to exhibitions and tours, help individuals with disabilities develop their skills, provide them with opportunities for self-expression, and facilitate their integration into society. Such inclusive cultural and artistic programs at the local level make a significant contribution to the social inclusion process of individuals with disabilities and help create a more equitable and sensitive societal structure.

4.3. Barriers Faced by Municipalities in Providing Social Services for People with Disabilities

Municipalities in Türkiye provide various social services (including accessible urban ınfrastructure, free public transport for persons with disabilities, vocational training, cultural activities) aimed at facilitating the participation of people with disabilities in social life, improving their quality of life, and offering them equal opportunities (Yıldırım, 2021: 100-110). However, it is a reality that local governments face numerous challenges in effectively delivering these services. The main barriers faced by municipalities in providing social services for people with disabilities stem from structural, financial, legal, and cultural factors. Overcoming these obstacles will ease the integration of individuals with disabilities into society and contribute to the creation of a more inclusive community.

The success of local governments in providing services to individuals with disabilities is directly related not only to legal obligations but also to administrative capacity, financial adequacy, and the quality of institutional collaborations. According to a report published by the OECD in 2020, one of the biggest barriers to municipalities providing effective and inclusive services for individuals with disabilities is staff shortages and a lack of financial resources. The report particularly emphasizes that small and medium-sized local governments face significant capacity issues in planning and implementing services tailored to the needs of individuals with disabilities (OECD, 2020: 14).

4.3.1. Resource and Financial Issues

According to Yemişçi, A. and Gergil, S. (2021: 149-150), municipalities may not always have sufficient financial resources to enhance the effectiveness of the services they offer to individuals with disabilities. Many municipalities face budget constraints when implementing projects for people with disabilities, and they struggle to ensure that resources are used efficiently. Larger metropolitan municipalities often overcome this issue with bigger budgets and more resources, whereas smaller and medium-sized municipalities find it challenging to provide these services due to limited financial capacity.

4.3.2. Lack of Trained Personnel

As Boztepe and Mecek (2023: 128) note, the quality of services provided to individuals with disabilities depends on specialized personnel. However, especially many normal municipalities lack trained staff who can understand the needs of individuals with disabilities and provide suitable services. To ensure that services are more effectively delivered, significant emphasis must be placed on training staff to meet the specific requirements of people with disabilities.

4.3.3. Lack of Social Awareness

According to Çaha (2015: 141-142), increasing social awareness is essential for the effectiveness of the services offered by municipalities. Unfortunately, the level of social awareness regarding disabilities in Türkiye remains inadequate. To allow individuals with disabilities to participate more fully in social life, raising awareness and changing perceptions about disability is crucial. Municipalities should not only provide services but also organize awareness campaigns to change societal perceptions and promote the integration of people with disabilities into society.

4.3.4. Bureaucratic Barriers and Coordination Deficiencies

Boztepe and Mecek (2023: 125) explain that municipalities must coordinate with the central government to enhance the effectiveness of services provided to individuals with disabilities. However, bureaucratic barriers and legal and policy conflicts between local governments and the central government can cause delays and disruptions in the implementation of services. Deficiencies in legal regulations or conflicts with central government policies can negatively impact the quality of services offered by municipalities.

5. CONCLUSION

In Türkiye, the participation of individuals with disabilities in social life is facilitated not only through legal regulations but also through local-level practices including public policies and public service deliveries. Municipalities play a crucial role in enhancing the quality of life for individuals with disabilities, providing equal opportunities, and facilitating their social integration. This article has thoroughly examined the effectiveness of the social policies created by municipalities for people with disabilities and the challenges they face.

Municipalities serve as an important institutional mechanism in ensuring that individuals with disabilities can access their fundamental rights. Services such as transportation, education, healthcare, and employment provided by local governments offer a significant opportunity for the integration of individuals with disabilities into society. However, the quality and scope of services provided by municipalities vary. Limited budgets, infrastructure and capacity deficiencies, and the diverse needs of individuals with disabilities can hinder the effectiveness of these services. Additionally, social and cultural barriers that prevent the participation of people with disabilities in social life sometimes limit the effectiveness of the services municipalities provide.

The challenges faced by municipalities in delivering these services are related not only to financial resources but also to administrative capacity. Many municipalities experience difficulties in accurately identifying the needs of individuals with disabilities and developing appropriate solutions to address them. Local governments should not only focus on providing physical accessibility but also on developing projects aimed at raising social awareness. Changing societal perceptions of disability and promoting the active participation of individuals with disabilities in social life should be a priority for local governments.

To provide more inclusive and sustainable services for individuals with disabilities, it is essential to enhance the capacity of local governments. In this context, increasing the budgets allocated to municipalities, investing more in services for people with disabilities, and strengthening the central government's support for local governments is crucial. Moreover, collaborating with civil society organizations and experts will ensure that municipalities develop more effective policies that are sensitive to the rights of people with disabilities.

The role of municipalities in improving the lives of individuals with disabilities goes beyond merely providing services. This process involves ensuring that people with disabilities have an equal place in society, eliminating discrimination, and promoting social equality of opportunity. By producing policies that respect the rights of individuals with disabilities and support their contributions to social life, municipalities will contribute to the creation of a more inclusive society in the long term. In conclusion, municipalities can strengthen the integration of individuals with disabilities into social life in Türkiye by developing more effective, responsive, and inclusive policies, ultimately improving the lives of people with disabilities.

REFERENCES

Aköğretmen, M. (2023). Batıda Engelli Emeğinin Kısa Tarihi: Engellilik Modelleri Bağlamında Bir Değerlendirme. *Hak İş Uluslararası Emek Ve Toplum Dergisi, 12*(32), 129–144. DOI: 10.31199/hakisderg.1209599

Alimanoğlu Yemişci, D., & Sarı Gerşil, G. (2021). Sosyal Belediyecilik Kapsamında Engelli Bireylerin Entegrasyonu: İzmir İli Örneği. *Çalışma İlişkileri Dergisi, 12*(2), 125-153.

Altınordu Belediyesi. (t.y.). *Altınordu'nun Engelsiz Ulaşım Aracı Engel Tanımıyor.* https://www.altinordu.bel.tr/

Ankara Büyükşehir Belediyesi. (t.y.). *Sosyal ve Kültürel Etkinliklerimiz.* https://www.ankara.bel.tr/sosyal-hizmetler/engelli-hizmetleri/sosyal-ve-kulturel-etkinliklerimiz

Arı, A. (2022). Türkiye'de Engellilik ve Engellilerin Eğitimi Üzerine Bir Derleme. *Humanistic Perspective, 4*(3), 589–605. DOI: 10.47793/hp.1117918

Atar, E., & Usta, Y. (2023). Merkezileşme -yerelleşme bağlamında 6360 sayılı kanun üzerine bir analiz. *Turkish Studies - Economics, Finance. Politics, 18*(1), 1–15. DOI: 10.7827/TurkishStudies.66442

Aver, Ö. F. (2019). Engellilerin Mesleki Eğitimi ve İstihdamı. *Uluslararası Sağlık Yönetimi Ve Stratejileri Araştırma Dergisi, 5*(3), 327–354.

Balcılar, A. N., & Çınarlı, S. (2020). Türkiye'de Sosyal Belediyecilik Uygulamaları ve Bornova Belediyesi Örneği. *Cumhuriyet Üniversitesi İktisadi Ve İdari Bilimler Dergisi, 21*(2), 122–156. DOI: 10.37880/cumuiibf.614314

Baran, G. (2011). Çocuk Gelişimine Giriş. *Çocuk Gelişimi,* (Edit: N. Aral ve G. Baran),17-51, İstanbul: Ya-Pa Yayınları.

Barnes, C., & Mercer, G. (2010). *Exploring Disability* (2nd ed.). Polity.

Boztepe, Ö., & Mecek, M. (2023). Belediye Çalışanlarının Engelli Bireylere Yönelik Hizmet Sunumunda Bireysel Tutumlarının İncelenmesi: Afyonkarahisar Belediyesi Çalışanları Örneği. *İktisadi Ve İdari Yaklaşımlar Dergisi, 5*(2), 123-146. https://doi.org/DOI: 10.47138/jeaa.1386087

Bursa Büyükşehir Belediyesi. (t.y.). *Engelli Hizmetleri.* https://www.bursa.bel.tr/hizmetler/engelli-hizmetleri-115

Çaha, H. (2015). Engellilerin Toplumsal Hayata Katılmasına Yönelik Politikalar: Türkiye, ABD ve Japonya Örnekleri. *İnsan Ve Toplum, 5*(10), 123-150.

Çoban, R. (2017). Sosyal Adalet, Eşitlik ve Sosyal Hizmet. *Gümüşhane Üniversitesi Sağlık Bilimleri Dergisi, 6*(4), 252–260.

Denizli Büyükşehir Belediyesi. (t.y.). *Engellilere Ulaşım Hizmetleri.*https://www.denizli.bel.tr/

Ersöz, H. Y. (2011). *Sosyal Politikada Yerelleşme.* İstanbul Ticaret Odası Yayınları. Yayın No.

Erten, Ş., & Aktel, M. (2020). Engellilerin Erişebilirlik Hakkı: Engelsiz Kent Yaklaşımı Çerçevesinde Bir Değerlendirme. *Süleyman Demirel Üniversitesi Vizyoner Dergisi, 11*(28), 898–912. DOI: 10.21076/vizyoner.691690

Erzurum Büyükşehir Belediyesi. (2023). Büyükşehir'den Engelliler Yönelik Mesleki Eğitim Kursu. https://www.erzurum.bel.tr/ebb-engelli/3.html

Fatih Belediyesi. (2024). Engelliler İş Atölyesi Yeni Dönem Kurs Kayıtları. https://www.fatih.bel.tr/tr/main/news/engelliler-is-atolyesi-yeni-donem-kurs-kayitl/20

Fırat, S. (2008). Belediyelerin engellilere dönük sosyal hizmet projeleri. *Toplum ve Sosyal Hizmet, 19*(1), 89–100.

Genç, D. D. Y. (2016). Engellilerin Sosyal Sorunları ve Beklentileri. *Sosyal Politika Çalışmaları Dergisi, 35*(2), 65–92. DOI: 10.21560/spcd.77043

Genç, Y., & Çat, G. (2014). Engellilerin İstihdamı ve Sosyal İçerme İlişkisi. *Akademik İncelemeler Dergisi, 8*(1), 363–394.

Kalaycı, S., & Akin, A. (2019). Engellilere Yönelik Yerel Sosyal Hizmetlerde Belediyelerin Yeri: Malatya Büyükşehir Belediyesi. *Selçuk Üniversitesi Sosyal Bilimler Meslek Yüksekokulu Dergisi, 22*(2), 663–674. DOI: 10.29249/selcuksbmyd.633505

Kızıltaş, M. (2012). *Engellilerle 360° İletişim.* Elma Yayınevi.

Koç, N., & Ökmen, M. (2015). Sosyal belediyecilik anlayışı çerçevesinde seçilmiş belediyelerin sosyal bütçelerinin değerlendirilmesi. *Maliye Dergisi, 168*, 69–84.

Metin, B. (2017). Engellilere Yönelik Sosyal Politikalarda Yerel Yönetimlerin Rolü: Keçiören Belediyesi Örneği. *Gazi Üniversitesi İktisadi Ve İdari Bilimler Fakültesi Dergisi, 19*(1), 320–344.

OECD. (2020). The role of local governments in supporting people with disabilities. OECD Publishing. https://www.oecd.org/inclusive-growth/resources/people-with-disabilities/

Oliver, M. (1990). *The Politics of Disablement.* Macmillan. DOI: 10.1007/978-1-349-20895-1

Özgökçeler, S., & Alper, Y. (2010). Özürlüler Kanunu'nun sosyal model açısından değerlendirilmesi. İşletme ve Ekonomi Araştırmaları Dergisi, 1(1), 33-54.

Öztürk, Y. E., Şentürk, Ş., & Macit, Y. (2017). Evde Bakım Hizmeti Alan Engelli Bireye Sahip Ailelerin Bakım Verme Yüklerinin Belirlenmesi: Amasya Örneği. *Türkiye Sosyal Hizmet Araştırmaları Dergisi, 1*(1), 48–67.

Sarı, A. (2022), "Engellilere Toplu Taşımada, Toplu Konut İdaresi'nde ve Belediye Hizmetlerinde Uygulanan İndirimli Tarifeler", https://www.engelsizkariyer.com/

Şen, M. (2023). *Türkiye'de Engelliler ve Sosyal Politikalar.* Efe Akademi Yayınları.

Shakespeare, T. (2006). *Disability Rights and Wrongs.* Routledge. DOI: 10.4324/9780203640098

Tekeli, İ. (1983). Yerel Yönetimlerde Demokrasi ve Türkiye'de Belediyelerin Gelişimi. *Amme Idaresi Dergisi, 16*(2), 3–22.

Tiyek, Y. (2016). Yerel Yönetimlerin Sosyal Politika Uygulamalarındaki Rolü: İstanbul Büyükşehir Belediyesi Sosyal Yardım Birimi Örneği. *Yerel Politikalar,* (2), 53–84.

TÜİK. (2024). Yaşam Memnuniyeti Araştırması https://data.tuik.gov.tr/Bulten/Index?p=Yasam-Memnuniyeti-Arastirmasi-2024-53785

Türkiye İstatistik Kurumu. (2002). Türkiye Özürlüler Araştırması Raporu. https://evam.tuik.gov.tr/dataset/detail/16

Ünal, V. (2018). Engellilerin Engelliliğe Bakışı Ve Dine Yaklaşımları. *Cumhuriyet İlahiyat Dergisi, 22*(3), 1457–1482. DOI: 10.18505/cuid.440470

Ünal, V. (2021). Türkiye'de Engellilik Yaklaşımlarının Sosyal Politika Açısından Değerlendirilmesi. *Cumhuriyet Üniversitesi Fen-Edebiyat Fakültesi Sosyal Bilimler Dergisi, 45*(2), 235–258.

Uzunoğlu, E. (2019). Engelli Bireylerin Toplumsal Yaşama Katılımında Yerel Yönetimlerin İşlevleri: Sakarya Büyükşehir Belediyesi Örneği. *The Journal of Academic Social Science, 7*(91), 236–258. DOI: 10.16992/ASOS.14888

WHO. (2001). International Classification of Functioning, Disability and Health (ICF). https://www.who.int/standards/classifications/international-classification-of-functioning-disability-and-health

Wu, H., & Atar, E. (2023). The Application of Self-directed Learning in the Local Level Workplace. *ASR: CMU Journal of Social Sciences and Humanities, 10*(1), e2023013. DOI: 10.12982/CMUJASR.2023.013

Yıldırım, Y. Z. (2021). *Dezavantajlı Bir Grup Olarak Engelliler ve Engellilere Yönelik Yerel Yönetim Faaliyetleri*. Filiz Kitabevi.

Yılmaz, V., & Yentürk, N. (2017). Türkiye'de Engellilere Yönelik Kamu Harcamalarının On Yıllık Seyri. *Çalışma Ve Toplum, 1*(52), 59-74.

Compilation of References

Ager, A., & Strang, A. (2008). Understanding integration: Conceptual framework. *Journal of Refugee Studies, 21*(2), 166–191.

Ajduković, D., Čorkalo Biruški, D., Gregurović, M., Matić Bojić, J., & Župarić-Iljić, D. (2019). Challenges of integrating refugees into Croatian society: attitudes of citizens and the readiness of local communities. Government of the Republic of Croatia, Office for Human Rights and Rights of National Minorities. 1-158

Aköğretmen, M. (2023). Batıda Engelli Emeğinin Kısa Tarihi: Engellilik Modelleri Bağlamında Bir Değerlendirme. *Hak İş Uluslararası Emek Ve Toplum Dergisi, 12*(32), 129–144. DOI: 10.31199/hakisderg.1209599

Alimanoğlu Yemişci, D., & Sarı Gerşil, G. (2021). Sosyal Belediyecilik Kapsamında Engelli Bireylerin Entegrasyonu: İzmir İli Örneği. *Çalışma İlişkileri Dergisi, 12*(2), 125-153.

Al-Kodmany, K. (2000). Public Participation: Technology and Democracy. *Urban Studies (Edinburgh, Scotland), 37*(2), 224.

Alrashedi, R., Persaud, A., & Kindra, G. (2015). Drivers of e-participation: Case of Saudi Arabia. *Journal of Business Inquiry, 14*(1), 1–22.

Altınordu Belediyesi. (t.y.). *Altınordu'nun Engelsiz Ulaşım Aracı Engel Tanımıyor.* https://www.altinordu.bel.tr/

Altman, D. (2011). *Direct Democracy Worldwide*. Cambridge University Press.

American Planning Association. (2007). *Property topics and concepts*. APA. https://www.planning.org/divisions/planningandlaw/propertytopics.htm

American Planning Association. (2014). *Housing Act of 1949*. https://www.planning.org/awards/2014/1949housingact.htm

Ankara Büyükşehir Belediyesi. (t.y.). *Sosyal ve Kültürel Etkinliklerimiz*. https://www.ankara.bel.tr/sosyal-hizmetler/engelli-hizmetleri/sosyal-ve-kulturel-etkinliklerimiz

Appleyard, B., & Riggs, W. (2021). Human rights to the street: Ethical frameworks to guide planning, design, and engineering decisions toward livability, equity, and justice. *Journal of Transport and Land Use*, *14*(1), 911–931. DOI: 10.5198/jtlu.2021.1918

Arblaster, A. (1994). Democracy. Open University Press, 136.

Arceneaux, K., & Vander Wielen, R. J. (2023). Do voters prefer educated candidates? How candidate education influences vote choice in congressional elections. *Electoral Studies*, *82*, 102596. https://doi.org/https://doi.org/10.1016/j.electstud.2023.102596. DOI: 10.1016/j.electstud.2023.102596

Arı, A. (2022). Türkiye'de Engellilik ve Engellilerin Eğitimi Üzerine Bir Derleme. *Humanistic Perspective*, *4*(3), 589–605. DOI: 10.47793/hp.1117918

Arnstein, S. R. (1969). A ladder of citizen participation. *Journal of the American Institute of Planners*, *35*(4), 216–224. DOI: 10.1080/01944366908977225

Asis, M. M. (Ed.). (2011). *Minding the gap: Migration, development and governance in the Philippines*. Scalabrini Migration Center.

Ataç, I., Rygiel, K., & Stierl, M. (2021). Building transversal solidarities in European cities: Open harbours, safe communities, home. *Critical Sociology*, *47*(6), 923–939. DOI: 10.1177/0896920520980522

Atar, E., & Usta, Y. (2023). Merkezileşme -yerelleşme bağlamında 6360 sayılı kanun üzerine bir analiz. Turkish Studies - Economics, Finance. *Politics*, *18*(1), 1–15. DOI: 10.7827/TurkishStudies.66442

Aubakirova, Z., & Aimagambetov, E. (2020). Problems of local self-government development in Kazakhstan. *Central Asian Economic Review*, *6*(135), 46-57. https://caer.narxoz.kz/jour/article/view/272/275

Aver, Ö. F. (2019). Engellilerin Mesleki Eğitimi ve İstihdamı. *Uluslararası Sağlık Yönetimi Ve Stratejileri Araştırma Dergisi*, *5*(3), 327–354.

Aydemir, A. Z., & Akın, T. (2024). Adaptive reuse of high-rise buildings for housing: A study of Istanbul Central Business District. *Urban Planning*, *9*(2), 1–10. DOI: 10.17645/up.7698

Azlor, L., Damm, A. P., & Schultz-Nielsen, M. L. (2020). Local labour demand and immigrant employment. *Labour Economics*, *63*, 101808. DOI: 10.1016/j.labeco.2020.101808

Babaoğlu, C., & Akman, E. (2022). "Participation with social media: The case of Turkish metropolitan municipalities in facebook", in *Research Anthology on Citizen Engagement and Activism for Social Change* (Edt: Mehdi Khosrow-Pour, Steve Clarke, Murray E. Jennex & Ari-Veikko Anttiroiko), Hersey: IGI, 77-95. DOI: 10.4018/978-1-6684-3706-3.ch006

Babaoğlu, C., & Leblebici, D. N. (2021). "Public participation in disability policy: The case of metropolitan Ankara", in *The Handbook of Global Challenges to Improving Public Services and Government Operations*, (Edt. C. Babaoğlu, O. Kulaç & E. Akman), Hersey: IGI, 506-524.

Bachtiar, P. P. (2011) The governance of Indonesian overseas employment in the context of decentralisation. Discussion Papers Series 2011-25, December 2011. Philippine Institute of Development Studies (PIDS). Retrieved from https://www.pids.gov.ph/publication/discussion-papers/the-governance-of-indonesian-overseas-employment-in-the-context-of-decentralization

Bailey, A., & Ngwenyama, O. (2011). The challenge of e-participation in the digital city: Exploring generational influences among community telecentre users. *Telematics and Informatics*, *28*(3), 204–214. DOI: 10.1016/j.tele.2010.09.004

Baker, P., & Critchlow, D. T. (2020). *The Oxford American political history*. Oxford University Press., DOI: 10.1093/oxfordhb/9780199341788.001.0001

Balabiev, K. (2014). Questions development of local government in the Republic of Kazakhstan and the role of international experience in its improvement. *Austrian Journal of Humanities and Social Sciences*, *2*(1-2), 181–189.

Balaguer-Coll, M. T., Prior, D., & Tortosa-Ausina, E. (2010). Decentralization and efficiency of local government. *The Annals of Regional Science*, *45*(3), 571–601. DOI: 10.1007/s00168-009-0286-7

Balcılar, A. N., & Çınarlı, S. (2020). Türkiye'de Sosyal Belediyecilik Uygulamaları ve Bornova Belediyesi Örneği. *Cumhuriyet Üniversitesi İktisadi Ve İdari Bilimler Dergisi*, *21*(2), 122–156. DOI: 10.37880/cumuiibf.614314

Baldwin-Edwards, M., & Kraler, A. (2009). *REGINE: Regularisations in Europe*. ICMPD. DOI: 10.5117/9789085550082

Balıkesir Metropolitan Municipality. (2023). *Balıkesir Metropalitan Municipality Annual Report 2023*.https://balikesir.bel.tr/Dosyalar/DosyaListe/AF_btr_DosyaListeDetay_file_Dosya_b7a99056-e8eb-4230-b55d-c698d2e722f1/bbb_fr_2023.pdf

Bannister, F., & Connolly, R. (2012). Defining e-governance. *e-Service Journal: A Journal of Electronic Services in the Public and Private Sectors, 8*(2), 3-25.

Baran, G. (2011). Çocuk Gelişimine Giriş. *Çocuk Gelişimi,* (Edit: N. Aral ve G. Baran),17-51, İstanbul: Ya-Pa Yayınları.

Barber, B. R. (1995). Strong Democracy: Participatory Politics for a New Age. University of California Press, 288-295.

Barbour, L. R., Woods, J. L., & Brimblecombe, J. K. (2023). Local government policy to facilitate healthy and sustainable diets and the broader policy hierarchy: Insights from Milan Urban Food Policy Pact cities. *Health Research Policy and Systems, 21*(35), 1–9. DOI: 10.1186/s12961-023-00988-6 PMID: 37226248

Barbour, L., Lindberg, R., Woods, J., Charlton, K., & Brimblecombe, J. (2021). Local urban government policies to facilite healthy and environmentally sustainable diet-related practices: A scoping review. *Public Health Nutrition, 25*(2), 471–487. DOI: 10.1017/S1368980021004432 PMID: 34693899

Bardhan, P. K., & Mookherjee, D. (Eds.). (2006). *Decentralization and Local Governance in Developing Countries: A Comparative Perspective.* The MIT Press., https://doi.org/https://doi.org/10.7551/mitpress/2297.001.0001 DOI: 10.7551/mit-press/2297.001.0001

Barglowski, K. (2018). Where, what and whom to study? Principles, guidelines and empirical examples of case selection and sampling in migration research. *Qualitative research in European migration studies*, 151-168.

Barnes, C., & Mercer, G. (2010). *Exploring Disability* (2nd ed.). Polity.

Barou, J. (2009). Immigration et intégration en France: État des lieux. *Regards Sociologiques, 37*, 25–45.

Barrall, A., & Monkkonen, P. (2024). *The fair housing land use score in California: An evaluation of 199 municipal plans.* eScholarship. https://escholarship.org/uc/item/6fn5g105

Basa, C., & Villamil, L. (2009) Migration, local development and governance in two small towns: Two examples from the Philippines. Working Paper Series on Rural-Urban Interactions and Livelihood Strategies (no. 17), September 2009. International Institute for Environment and Development (IIED). Retrieved from https://www.iied.org/10576iied

Bauder, H. (2021). Urban migrant and refugee solidarity beyond city limits. *Urban Studies (Edinburgh, Scotland), 58*(16), 3213–3229. DOI: 10.1177/0042098020976308

Beckley, T. M., Parkins, J. R., & Stedman, R. C. (2005). *Public Participation in Sustainable Forest Management: A Reference Guide*. Sustainable Forest Management Network.

Beisembayeva, G., Mussina, A., & Sartova, R. (2014). Development of local government in the Republic of Kazakhstan at the present stage. *Journal of Economic Research & Business Administration, 104*(4), 32–39. https://be.kaznu.kz/index.php/math/article/view/436

Bernt, M. (2019). Migration and Urban Governance in Berlin. *Urban Research & Practice*.

Berry, F., & Berry, W. (1990). State lottery adoptions as policy innovations: An event history analysis. *The American Political Science Review, 84*(2), 395–415. DOI: 10.2307/1963526

Betts, A. (2011). *Global Migration Governance*. Oxford University Press. DOI: 10.1093/acprof:oso/9780199600458.001.0001

Betts, A., & Collier, P. (2017). *Refuge: Transforming a Broken Refugee System*. Penguin Books.

Bibri, S. E., Krogstie, J., & Kärrholm, M. (2020). Compact city planning and development: Emerging practices and strategies for achieving the goals of sustainability. *Developments in the Built Environment, 4*, 100021. Advance online publication. DOI: 10.1016/j.dibe.2020.100021

Bielewska, A., Ślęzak-Belowska, E., & Czeranowska, O. (2024). How Do Bigger and Smaller Cities Manage Migration? Ukrainian War Refugees in Polish Cities. *Eastern European Politics and Societies*.

Bingöl, S. E. (2022). ''Kamu yönetiminde katılım üzerine geleneksel ve güncel tartışmalara ilişkin genel bir çerçeve'', in *Kamu Yönetiminde Katılım Üzerine Güncel Tartışmalar* (Edt: Ezgi Seçkiner Bingöl), Ankara; Gazi Kitapevi.

Blake, O., Glaser, M., Bertolini, L., & te Brömmelstroet, M. (2021). How policies become best practices: A case study of best practice making in an EU knowledge sharing project. *European Planning Studies, 29*(7), 1251–1271. DOI: 10.1080/09654313.2020.1840523

Błaszczyk, M., Dolińska, K., Makaro, J., & Pluta, J. (2024). Governance agility in reception of war refugees from Ukraine: The case of Wrocław, Poland. *Social Policy and Administration, 58*(1), 189–204. DOI: 10.1111/spol.12958

Blažytė, G., Bielevičiūtė, I., & Stoma, S. (2022). *Savivaldybių atsakas į karo pabėgėlių iš Ukrainos: iššūkiai ir gerosios patirtys, Tyrimo atsakaita*, VšĮ Diversity Develpoment Group, 1-50, https://sppd.lrv.lt/uploads/sppd/documents/files/Karo %20pabegeliu%20is%20Ukrainos%20priemimas_final.pdf

Blažytė, G., Sotirovič, V. P., & Žibas, K. (2016). Visuomenės nuostatos apie socialines ir etnines grupes Lietuvoje: nepakantumo ir socialinės distancijos stebėsena. *Lietuvos gyventojų grupių socialinė kaita*, 109-124.

Blažytė, G., & Žibas, K. (2019). Integration of beneficiaries of international protection in the Lithuanian labour market: Policies and practices. *Transfer: European Review of Labour and Research, 25*(1), 113–119. DOI: 10.1177/1024258918819981

Boon, L. S., Malek, J. A., Hussain, M. Y., & Tahir, Z. (2020). Participation in e-government services and smart city programs: A case study of Malaysian local authority. *Planning Malaysia*, (18), 300–312.

Bozec, G., & Simoulin, V. (2018). Les politiques publiques locales de l'immigration. *Revue française d'administration publique*, 167(3), 599–616.

Boztepe, Ö., & Mecek, M. (2023). Belediye Çalışanlarının Engelli Bireylere Yönelik Hizmet Sunumunda Bireysel Tutumlarının İncelenmesi: Afyonkarahisar Belediyesi Çalışanları Örneği. *İktisadi Ve İdari Yaklaşımlar Dergisi, 5*(2), 123-146. https://doi.org/DOI: 10.47138/jeaa.1386087

Brubaker, R. (2001). The return of assimilation? Changing perspectives on immigration and its sequels in France, Germany, and the United States. *Ethnic and Racial Studies, 24*(4), 531–548. DOI: 10.1080/01419870120049770

Brubaker, R. (2020). *Laïcité, Integration and Citizenship in Contemporary France. Ethnic and Racial Studies, 43*(3), 405–424.

Bučaitė-Vilkė, J., & Lazauskienė, A. (2021). Local state-society relations in Lithuania. *Close Ties in European Local Governance: Linking Local State and Society*, 243-257.

Buhr, K., Federley, M., & Karlsson, A. (2016). Urban Living Labs for Sustainability in Suburbs in Need of Modernization and Social Uplift. *Technology Innovation Management Review, 6*(1), 27–34. DOI: 10.22215/timreview/958

Bulut, MA, Birgili, B., Koçoğlu, M., & Gülünay, O., Et. (2024). Contributions of Technology and Science Centers to the National Technology Move and the Example of T3 Foundation. *Babur Research, 3*(2), 117–132.

Burbulytė-Tsiskarishvili, G., Dvorak, J., & Žernytė, A. (2018). Savivaldybių funkcijų ir galių kaita Lietuvoje 1994-2016 metais. *Viešoji politika ir administravimas, 17*(3), 399-420.

Bursa Büyükşehir Belediyesi. (t.y.). *Engelli Hizmetleri.*https://www.bursa.bel.tr/hizmetler/engelli-hizmetleri-115

Çaha, H. (2015). Engellilerin Toplumsal Hayata Katılmasına Yönelik Politikalar: Türkiye, ABD ve Japonya Örnekleri. *İnsan Ve Toplum, 5*(10), 123-150.

Campbell, C. G., Papanek, A., DeLong, A., Diaz, J., Gusto, C., & Tropp, D. (2022). Community food systems resilience: Values, benefits, and indicators. *Journal of Agriculture, Food Systems, and Community Development, 11*(4), 89–113. DOI: 10.5304/jafscd.2022.114.006

Campomori, F., & Ambrosini, M. (2020). Multilevel governance in trouble: The implementation of asylum seekers' reception in Italy as a battleground. *Comparative Migration Studies, 8*(1), 22. DOI: 10.1186/s40878-020-00178-1

Campomori, F., & Casula, M. (2023). How to frame the governance dimension of social innovation: Theoretical considerations and empirical evidence. *Innovation (Abingdon), 36*(2), 171–189. DOI: 10.1080/13511610.2022.2036952

Candel, J. J. (2020). What's on the menu? A global assessment of MUFPP signotary cities' food strategies. *Agroecology and Sustainable Food Systems, 44*(7), 919–946. DOI: 10.1080/21683565.2019.1648357

Caponio, T., & Borkert, M. (2010). *The local dimension of migration policymaking* (p. 204). Amsterdam University Press, 9-20.

Caponio, T., & Borkert, M. (2010). *The Local Dimension of Migration Policymaking*. Amsterdam University Press. DOI: 10.5117/9789089642325

Caponio, T., & Jones-Correa, M. (2018). Theorising migration policy in multilevel states: The multilevel governance perspective. *Journal of Ethnic and Migration Studies, 44*(12), 1995–2010. DOI: 10.1080/1369183X.2017.1341705

Castles, S., de Haas, H., & Miller, M. J. (2014). *The Age of Migration: International Population Movements in the Modern World.* Palgrave Macmillan. DOI: 10.1007/978-0-230-36639-8

Çeliksoy, E., & Akça, A. (2024). Digital Transformation Process in Public Administration in Türkiye. Çankırı Karatekin University Journal of Social Sciences Institute, 15(2), 445-486. Https://Doi.Org/10.54558/Jiss.1426480

Čepeliauskaitė, G. (2018). The analysis of effective immigrant integration policy in Lithuania: Practice and problems. *Public Policy and Administration, 17*(3), 421–438. DOI: 10.5755/j01.ppaa.17.3.21956

Chakraborty, A., & McMillan, A. (2022). Is housing diversity good for community stability? Evidence from the housing crisis. *Journal of Planning Education and Research, 42*(2), 150–161. DOI: 10.1177/0739456X18810787

Chebotarev, A. (2023). Выборы-2023: уроки для основных участников. [Elections-2023: Lessons for Key Participants]. [Electronic resource]. https://search.app/rZWW8xqTnqFSQVX59

Chirwa, G. C., Petro, M. L., Michael, C., Anthony, G., Boniface, D., Happy, K., & Chinsinga, B. (2023). Assessing the relationship between digital divide and citizens' political participation in Africa. *Development Southern Africa, 40*(6), 1258–1276. DOI: 10.1080/0376835X.2023.2224363

Choi, J. C., & Song, C. (2020). Factors explaining why some citizens engage in E-participation, while others do not. *Government Information Quarterly, 37*(4), 101524. DOI: 10.1016/j.giq.2020.101524

Çoban, R. (2017). Sosyal Adalet, Eşitlik ve Sosyal Hizmet. *Gümüşhane Üniversitesi Sağlık Bilimleri Dergisi, 6*(4), 252–260.

Cohen, N. (2022). Roles of cities in creating healthful food systems. *Annual Review of Public Health, 43*(1), 419–437. DOI: 10.1146/annurev-publhealth-052220-021059 PMID: 34936824

Çolak, Ç. (2021). Kamu yönetimi, katılımcılık ve vatandaşın değişen rolü: Seçmenden ortak üretici vatandaşa. *Memleket Siyaset Yönetim, 16*(35), 37–72.

Colorado Department of Local Affairs. (2024a). *Compact development - case briefings*. DOLA. https://dlg.colorado.gov/compact-development-case-briefings

Colorado Department of Local Affairs. (2024b). *Affordable housing - case briefings*. DOLA. https://dlg.colorado.gov/affordable-housing-case-briefings

Coulibaly, H., & Lima, S. (2018). Decentralisation and territorialisation of migratory resources in Mali: Towards which local and transnational governance? In Lacroix, T., & Desille, A. (Eds.), *International Migrations and Local Governance: A Global Perspective* (pp. 97–110). Palgrave MacMillan. DOI: 10.1007/978-3-319-65996-1_6

Criado, J. I., & Carmen Ramilo, M. (2003). E-government in practice: An analysis of Web site orientation to the citizens in Spanish municipalities. *International Journal of Public Sector Management, 16*(3), 191–218. DOI: 10.1108/09513550310472320

Croatia, U. N. H. C. R. (2023). *Intentions and perspectives of refugees from Ukraine in Croatia*. https://www.unhcr.org/hr/wp-content/uploads/sites/19/2023/12/croatia_intention_survey-2023.pdf

Crosby, N., Kelly, J. M., & Schaefer, P. (1986). Citizens panels: A new approach to citizen participation. *Public Administration Review*, *46*(2), 266–278. DOI: 10.2307/976169

CSB. (2025, February 7). Republic of Türkiye Ministry of Environment, Urbanization and Climate Change, General Directorate of Local Administrations. Ministry Circular on the Use of Local Information System Published, https://Yerelyonetimler.Csb.Gov.Tr/Yerelbilgi-Sisteminin- Kullanilmasina-İliskin-Bakanlik-Genelgesi-Yayimlanmistir-Haber-266965

Darling, J. (2022). The politics of discretion: Authority and influence in asylum dispersal. *Political Geography*, *94*, 102560. DOI: 10.1016/j.polgeo.2021.102560

De Coninck, D., & Solano, G. (2023). Integration policies and migrants' labour market outcomes: A local perspective based on different regional configurations in the EU. *Comparative Migration Studies*, *11*(1), 23. DOI: 10.1186/s40878-023-00347-y

Deakin, E. (2021). *A brief history of transportation policies and institutions*. University of California. https://escholarship.org/content/qt2fs5w7jp/qt2fs5w7jp_noSplash_3b11338828fdc45c6b624dfd3da0110e.pdf?t=r7iai1

Debela, K. W. (2020). Local governance in Switzerland: Adequate municipal autonomy cumintergovernmental cooperation? *Cogent Social Sciences*, *6*(1), 1763889. Advance online publication. DOI: 10.1080/23311886.2020.1763889

Deimantas, V. J., & Şanlıtürk, A. E. (2023). Refugees from Ukraine in Lithuania and the Lithuanian labour market: A preliminary assessment. *Migration Research Series. IOM Migration*, (75), 1–22.

Deniz, A., Akarçay, P., & Karakaş, A. (2017). Development of Municipality in the Ottoman Empire and Modernization Efforts. *Academic Perspective International Refereed Journal of Social Sciences*, (64), 314–325.

Denizli Büyükşehir Belediyesi. (t.y.). *Engellilere Ulaşım Hizmetleri*.https://www.denizli.bel.tr/

Department of Migrant Workers. (n.d.). About DMW. Agency website. https://dmw.gov.ph/about-dmw

Dimitriadis, I., Hajer, M. H., Fontanari, E., & Ambrosini, M. (2023). Local "Battlegrounds". Relocating multi-level and multi-actor governance of immigration. *Revue européenne des migrations internationales, 37*(1 et 2), 251-275.

Dimitrov, A., & Pavlov, V. (2023). Economic Challenges to Ukrainian Refugee Integration in Central and Eastern Europe. *Journal of Liberty and International Affairs*, *9*(3), 98–118. DOI: 10.47305/JLIA2393089d

Dipoppa, G., & Grossman, G. (2020). The effect of election proximity on government responsiveness and citizens' participation: Evidence from English local elections. *Comparative Political Studies*, *53*(14), 2183–2212. DOI: 10.1177/0010414020912290

Doomernik, J., & Ardon, D. (2018). The city as an agent of refugee integration. *Urban Planning*, *3*(4), 91–100. DOI: 10.17645/up.v3i4.1646

Ducanes, G. (2012). *Situation Analysis of Outbound and Return Migration and Local Institutional Mechanisms to Support Migrants in La Union, Ilocos Sur and Nueva Ecija*. International Labor Organization.

Dunleavy, P., & Margetts, H. Z. (2010). The second wave of digital era governance. In APSA 2010 Annual Meeting Paper, Available at *SSRN*: https://ssrn.com/abstract=1643850

Dunleavy, P., Margetts, H., Bastow, S., & Tinkler, J. (2006). New public management is dead-long live digital-era governance. *Journal of Public Administration: Research and Theory*, *16*(3), 467–494. DOI: 10.1093/jopart/mui057

EC. (2024b), *Governance of migrant integration in Lithuania*, https://migrant-integration.ec.europa.eu/country-governance/governance-migrant-integration-lithuania_en

EC. European Commission, (2024a), *Governance of migrant integration in Croatia*, https://migrant-integration.ec.europa.eu/country-governance/governance-migrant-integration-croatia_en

Ecevit Satı, Z. (2023). *Yeni dijital teknolojiler ve dijital inovasyon yönetimi*. Der Yayınları.

ECHO. (2018). *Development of local self-government in Kazakhstan*. P. U. ECHO. https://echo.kz/images/reports/msu_echo.pdf

EDA. (2022). https://www.eda.admin.ch/aboutswitzerland/en/home/politik-geschichte/politischessystem/direktedemokratie.html#:~:text=In%20Switzerland%20the%20people%20play,average%20of%20fifteen%20such%20issues

Efeler Municipality. (2024). *Efeler Municipality Strategic Plan 2025-2029.*https://www.efeler.bel.tr/upload/content/2025-2029-stratejik-plan.pdf

Efeler Municipality. (2024). https://www.efeler.bel.tr/guncel/haberler/kadin-emegiyle-uretilen-dogal-urunler-simdi-marketlerde

EMN. (2020). *Organisation of Migration and Asylum System in Croatia, Overview,* https://home-affairs.ec.europa.eu/system/files/2022-03/2020_EMN_Croatia_factsheet_organogram_EN.pdf

EMN. European Migration Network, (2022). Organisation of Migation and Asylum System in Lithuania, Orveview. https://www.emn.lt/uploads/Products/product_1542/Santrauka-EN2.pdf

Environment Law No. 2872. (1983). https://www.mevzuat.gov.tr/MevzuatMetin/1.5.2872.pdf

Erdoğan, O. (2019). E-Municipality Applications in Local Governments: Ministry of Internal Affairs E-Municipality Information System. *Süleyman Demirel University Journal of Faculty of Economics and Administrative Sciences, 24*(3), 551–566.

Eregli Ajans. (2022). (2025, January 02) https://eregliajans.net/eregli-belediyesi-adabagda-baslattigi-projede-organik-tarim-alaninda-hasata-hazirlaniyor

Eregli Municipality. (2023). *Eregli Municipality Annual Report 2023.*https://eregli.bel.tr/upload/other/2023%20y%C4%B1l%C4%B1%20Ere%C4%9Fli%20Belediyesi%20Faaliyet%20Raporu-1_1714136689.pdf

Eregli Municipality. (2025). (2025, February 02) https://www.eregli.bel.tr/sayfalar/ilcemiz

Eregli Municipality. (2025). *Eregli Municipality Performance Report 2025.* https://eregli.bel.tr/upload/other/2025%20PERFORMANS%20PROGRAMI-1_1736142313.pdf

Ergin, O. N. (1995). Mecelle-I Umur-I Municipality. Istanbul Metropolitan Municipality Culture Inc. *Publications, 2*(2).

Ersöz, H. Y. (2011). *Sosyal Politikada Yerelleşme.* İstanbul Ticaret Odası Yayınları. Yayın No.

Erten, Ş., & Aktel, M. (2020). Engellilerin Erişebilirlik Hakkı: Engelsiz Kent Yaklaşımı Çerçevesinde Bir Değerlendirme. *Süleyman Demirel Üniversitesi Vizyoner Dergisi, 11*(28), 898–912. DOI: 10.21076/vizyoner.691690

Eryılmaz, B. (2013). Kamu Yönetimi: Düşünceler Yapılar Fonksiyonlar ve Politikalar.

Erzurum Büyükşehir Belediyesi. (2023). Büyükşehir'den Engelliler Yönelik Mesleki Eğitim Kursu. https://www.erzurum.bel.tr/ebb-engelli/3.html

Es, M. (2008). Local Administrations in the Ottoman Empire. *Local Politics Journal*, (27), 29–38.

EUROSTAT. (2024a). Beneficiaries of temporary protection at the end of the month by citizenship, age and sex - monthly, *Online data set, code 'migr_asytpsm'*, https://ec.europa.eu/eurostat/databrowser/view/MIGR_ASYTPSM__custom_7394287/default/table?lang=en

Eurostat. (2024b). *Beneficiaries of temporary protection at the end of the month by citizenship*, age and sex - monthly data, migr_asytpsm, https://ec.europa.eu/eurostat/databrowser/view/migr_asytpsm__custom_12497557/default/table?lang=enDOI: 10.2908/migr_asytpsm

Fadziso, T., Yerram, S. R., & Mallipeddi, S. R. (2022). Analyzing the progression from digital production to digital society: Industry 4.0 to industry 5.0 transition evaluation. *Journal of Fareast International University*, *5*(1), 11–22.

Faguet, J.-P. (2012). *Decentralization and popular democracy: governance from below in Bolivia*. University of Michigan Press. DOI: 10.3998/mpub.175269

Faist, T. (2000). *The Volume and Dynamics of International Migration and Transnational Social Spaces*. Oxford University Press. DOI: 10.1093/acprof:oso/9780198293910.001.0001

Falleti, T. G. (2010). *Decentralization and Subnational Politics in Latin America*. Cambridge University Press. DOI: 10.1017/CBO9780511777813

FAO, CIRAD & RUAF. 2024. *Building resilience of city region food systems: a comparative study of eleven city perspectives*. Rome. https://doi.org/DOI: 10.4060/cd2836en

FAO. (2018). *The role of cities in the transformation of food systems: Sharing lessons from Milan Pact cities*. https://www.milanurbanfoodpolicypact.org/wp-content/uploads/2022/01/The-Role-Of-Cities-In-The-Transformation-Of-Food-Systems-Sharing-Lessons-From-Milan-Pact-Cities.pdf

FAO. (2020). *Türkiye's National Strategy Document and Action Plan for the Prevention, Reduction, and Management of Food Losses and Waste*. Ankara. https://faolex.fao.org/docs/pdf/tur209489.pdf

Fassin, D. (2011). *Humanitarian Reason: A Moral History of the Present*. University of California Press.

Fatih Belediyesi. (2024). Engelliler İş Atölyesi Yeni Dönem Kurs Kayıtları. https://www.fatih.bel.tr/tr/main/news/engelliler-is-atolyesi-yeni-donem-kurs-kayitl/20

Federal Chancellery. (2013). *The Swiss Confederation: A Brief Guide*. SFBL.

Figueredo, J. C. (2005). Publıc partıcıpatıon ın transportatıon: an emperıcal test for authentıc partıcıpatıon. In: TheDepartment of Public Afairs in the College of Health and Public Afairs at the University of Central Florida Orlando, Florida, pp. 17–20

Fırat, S. (2008). Belediyelerin engellilere dönük sosyal hizmet projeleri. *Toplum ve Sosyal Hizmet*, *19*(1), 89–100.

Flanagan, R. M. (1997). The Housing Act of 1954: The sea change in national urban policy. *Urban Affairs Review*, *33*(2), 265–286. DOI: 10.1177/107808749703300207

Fleiner, T., & Misic, A. (2005). Swiss constitutional law.

Food Trails. (2025). (2025, January 02) https://foodtrails.milanurbanfoodpolicypact.org/consortium/

Fragomen (2024). France: New Comprehensive Immigration Law Introduccd. https://www.fragomen.com/insights/france-new-comprehensive-immigration-law-introduced.html?utm_source=chatgpt.com, Erişim tarihi: 10.03.2025.

Fraser. (1933). *Repeal of direct loan provision of Federal Home Loan Bank Act.* https://fraser.stlouisfed.org/files/docs/historical/congressional/hola1933_congress.pdf

Fung, A. (2006). Varieties of Participation in Complex Governance, Public Administration Review, vol. 66, Special Issue: Collaborative. *Public Management*, •••, 66–75.

Galli, F., Prosperi, P., Favili, E., D'Amico, S., Bartolini, F., & Brunori, G. (2020). How can policy processes remove barriers to sustainable food systems in Europe? Contributing to a policy framework for agrifood transitions. *Food Policy*, *96*, 1–15. DOI: 10.1016/j.foodpol.2020.101871

Garabiles, M., Gagni, E. M., Corpuz, A. M. F., Alonzo, V., & Opiniano, J. (2024). Mapping and evaluating the localized migrant assistance services in Ilocos Norte, Philippines: An asset-based and multi-stakeholder approach. *Journal of Social Service Research*, *50*(6), 1058–1074. DOI: 10.1080/01488376.2024.2393411

Garbaye, R. (2005). *Getting Into Local Power: The Politics of Ethnic Minorities in British and French Cities*. Blackwell Publishing. DOI: 10.1002/9780470761625

Gazzotti, L. (2018). Local governance, civil society and migrants' support to local development: Perspectives from Morocco. In Lacroix, T., & Desille, A. (Eds.), *International migrations and local governance: A global perspective* (pp. 79–96). Palgrave MacMillan. DOI: 10.1007/978-3-319-65996-1_5

Geddes, A., & Scholten, P. (2016). The politics of migration and immigration in Europe. *Sage (Atlanta, Ga.)*. Advance online publication. DOI: 10.4135/9781473982703

Genç, D. D. Y. (2016). Engellilerin Sosyal Sorunları ve Beklentileri. *Sosyal Politika Çalışmaları Dergisi, 35*(2), 65–92. DOI: 10.21560/spcd.77043

Genç, Y., & Çat, G. (2014). Engellilerin İstihdamı ve Sosyal İçerme İlişkisi. *Akademik İncelemeler Dergisi, 8*(1), 363–394.

Geser, H. (2004). The communes in Switzerland. Klöti, U. et al., Handbook of Swiss Politics, Neue Zürcher Zeitung Publishing, 349-391.

Geuijen, K., Oliver, C., & Dekker, R. (2020). Local innovation in the reception of asylum seekers in the Netherlands: Plan Einstein as an example of multi-level and multi-sector collaboration. *Geographies of asylum in Europe and the role of European localities*, 245-260.

Giljević, T., & Lalić Novak, G. (2020). Integration of migrants through a prism of specific sustainable development goals: A perspective of public administration. *Sustainable Development (Bradford), 28*(4), 1002–1009. DOI: 10.1002/sd.2052

Glorius, B., & Doomernik, J. (2020). *Introduction, Geographies of asylum in Europe and the role of European localities*. Springer Nature.

Glumac, B., & Islam, N. (2020). Housing preferences for adaptive re-use of office and industrial buildings: Demand side. *Sustainable Cities and Society, 62*, 102379. Advance online publication. DOI: 10.1016/j.scs.2020.102379

Goldfrank, B. (2007). The Politics of Deepening Local Democracy: Decentralization, Party Institutionalization, and Participation. *Comparative Politics, 39*(2), 147–168. https://www.jstor.org/stable/20434031

Gonda, M. (2021). Waiting for immigration to come. The case of Lodz. *Studia Migracyjne-Przegląd Polonijny, 47*(3), 293–317. DOI: 10.4467/25444972SMPP.21.042.14462

Govinfo. (2022). *[Public Law 89–272; Approved October 20, 1965] [As Amended Through P.L. 117–58, Enacted November 15, 2021]*. https://www.govinfo.gov/content/pkg/COMPS-893/pdf/COMPS-893.pdf

Govinfo. (n.d.a). *Chapter 11—Federal Home Loan Banks.* https://www.govinfo.gov/content/pkg/USCODE-2020-title12/html/USCODE-2020-title12-chap11.htm

Govinfo. (n.d.b). *United States Housing Act of 1937.* https://www.govinfo.gov/content/pkg/COMPS-10348/pdf/COMPS-10348.pdf

Gregorio, M.C.C. & Opiniano, J. (2011). Harvests and hardships: Analyzing overseas migration and Philippine rural development. Institute for Migration and Development Issues (IMDI) and the Philippine Partnerships for the Development of Human Resources in Rural Areas (PhilDHRRA).

Gregurović, M., & Župarić-Iljić, D. (2023). "At first it was not very pleasant... Now it is different": Experiences and Challenges of Refugee Integration in Croatia. Treatises and Documents, *Journal of Ethnic Studies/Razprave in Gradivo, Revija za narodnostna vprašanja*, 91(91), 157-177.

Griggs, T. (2024). *At long last, Portland's bike ridership is on the mend. What Now?* Portland Mercury. https://www.portlandmercury.com/news/2024/02/15/47036503/at-long-last-portlands-bike-ridership-is-on-the-mend-what-now

Grimmelikhuijsen, S., Porumbescu, G., Hong, B., & Im, T. (2013). The effect of transparency on trust in government: A cross-national comparative experiment. *Public Administration Review, 73*(4), 575–586. DOI: 10.1111/puar.12047

Grindle, M. S. (2007). *Going Local Decentralization, Democratization, and the Promise of Good Governance.* Princeton University Press., https://www.jstor.org/stable/j.ctt4cgd2m

Groupe URD. (2020). *L'accès au logement des personnes réfugiées en France.*

Guild, E. (2009). *Security and Migration in the 21st Century.* Polity Press.

Güler, B. A. (2003). Governance: All Power to Capital. *Praxis (Bern), 9*, 93–116.

Gül, H., Kiriş, H., Negiz, N., & Gökdayı, İ. (2014). *Türkiye'de Yerel Yönetimler ve Yerel Siyaset.* DetayYayıncılık.

Güven, A., (2022). "Provincial Administrations in Türkiye Within the Context of E-Municipality Applications

Guzmán, C., Santos, F. J., Valiente, L., & Santolaya, F. J. (2023). Social Innovation for the Socio-Labour Integration of Refugees in New Host Countries: The Spanish Case. *Journal of Social Entrepreneurship*, •••, 1–26. DOI: 10.1080/19420676.2023.2275132

Habermas, J. (1996). Between Facts and Norms: Contributions to a Discourse Theory of Law and Democracy. MIT Press, 17-18.

Harris, J. R., & Todaro, M. P. (1970). Migration, Unemployment and Development: A Two-Sector Analysis. *The American Economic Review*, *60*(1), 126–142.

Henden, H. B., & Henden, R. (2005). Changes in Service Provision of Local Governments and E-Municipality. *Electronic Journal of Social Sciences*, *4*(14), 48–66.

Hivo. (2023). *Exploring local government land use planning*. https://hivo.co/blog/exploring-local-government-land-use-planning

Holbrook, C. (2020). Redesigning collaborative governance for refugee settlement services. *Australian Journal of Political Science*, *55*(1), 86–97. DOI: 10.1080/10361146.2019.1686116

Holdar, G. G., & Zakharchenko, O. (2002). Citizen Participation Handbook: People's Voice Project. International Centre for Policy Studies, 12-17.

Homberger, A., Kirchhoff, M., Mallet-Garcia, M., Ataç, I., Güntner, S., & Spencer, S. (2022). Local responses to migrants with precarious legal status: Negotiating inclusive practices in cities across Europe. *Zeitschrift für Migrationsforschung*, *2*(2), 93–116.

Hooghe, L., & Marks, G. (2003). Unraveling the Central State, but How? Types of Multi-level Governance. *The American Political Science Review*, *97*(2), 233–243.

Ibadildin, N., & Pisareva, D. (2020). Central Asia in Transition: Social Contract Transformation in Nazarbayev and Post-Nazarbayev Kazakhstan. In Mihr, A. (Ed.), *Transformation and Development: Studies in the Organization for Security and Cooperation in Europe (OSCE) Member States* (pp. 101–116). Springer., DOI: 10.1007/978-3-030-42775-7_7

Ichou, M. (2013). Différences d'origine et performances scolaires. *Revue Française de Sociologie*, *54*(3), 463–498.

Iizuka, S., Xuan, Y., Takatori, C., Nakaura, H., & Hashizume, A. (2020). Environmental impact assessment of introducing compact city models by downscaling simulations. *Sustainable Cities and Society*, *63*, 102424. Advance online publication. DOI: 10.1016/j.scs.2020.102424

Ileuova, G., Serazhieva, S. H., & Aljani, J. K. (2002). Analiz rezul'tatov eksperimental'nykh vyborov akimov sel'skikh okrugov. *Analytical review*(1), 15-32.

International Organization for Migration IOM. (2004). *Glossary on Migration*. International Organization for Migration.

International Organization for Migration. (2005). [Costs and benefits of international migration. IOM.]. *World Migration Report*, •••, 2005.

IOM (International Organization for Migration). (2023). *DTM Lithuania Surveys with refugees from Ukraine: needs, intentions and integration challenges*, Vilnius. June 2023, 1-19, https://lithuania.iom.int/sites/g/files/tmzbdl1336/files/inline-files/dtm_2023_lt_needs-intentions_ukraine_q3_corrected-4_1.pdf

IOM. (2024). *The Migration Governance Indicators success stories 2024*. IOM.

Issac, J., Newell, R., Dring, C., White, C., Ghadiri, M., Pizzirani, S., & Newman, L. (2022). Integrated sustainability planning and local food systems: Examining areas of and gaps in food systems integration in community sustainability plans for municipalities across British Columbia. *Sustainability (Basel)*, *14*(6724), 1–17. DOI: 10.3390/su14116724

Istanbul Metropolitan Municipality. (2021). *The Istanbul Food Strategy Document.* https://ipa.istanbul/wp-content/uploads/2021/10/Istanbul-Gida-Strateji-Belgesi.pdf

Istanbul Metropolitan Municipality. (2023). *Istanbul Metropalitan Municipality Annual Report 2023*. https://uploads.ibb.istanbul/uploads/2023_ANNUAL_REPORT_56373f7718.pdf

İzci, F. (2014). Katılımcı Yerel Yönetime Genel Bakış. Göymen ve diğerleri (Ed.). Katılımcı Yerel Yönetim içinde. Kalkedon Yayınları: İstanbul, s.19-39.

Jama, T., Tenkanen, H., Lönnqvist, H., & Joutsiniemi, A. (2024). Compact city and urban planning: Correlation between density and local amenities. *Environment and Planning. B, Urban Analytics and City Science*, *52*(1), 1–10. DOI: 10.1177/23998083241250264

Jay, N. (2010). *History of United States waste management*. https://www.researchgate.net/publication/258698791_History_of_United_States_Waste_Management Joint Center for Housing Studies. (2023). *The state of the nation's housing 2023*. https://www.jchs.harvard.edu/sites/default/files/reports/files/Harvard_JCHS_The_State_of_the_Nations_Housing_2023.pdf

Joint Migration and Development Initiative. (2012). *Mapping local authorities' practices in the area of migration and development: A territorial approach to local strategies, initiatives and needs*. JMDI. https://www.local2030.org/library/190/Mapping-Local-Authorities-Practices-in-Migration-and-Development-Report.pdf

Joly, D. (2005). *L'intégration des immigrés en France: Entre assimilation et multiculturalisme.Revue Européenne des Migrations Internationales*, *21*(2), 39–59.

Jonitz, E., Schiller, M., & Scholten, P. (2024). Are small towns a battleground for migration governance? Negotiating refugee integration in small towns in the Netherlands. *Local Government Studies*, •••, 1–24. DOI: 10.1080/03003930.2024.2357306

Kalaycı, S., & Akin, A. (2019). Engellilere Yönelik Yerel Sosyal Hizmetlerde Belediyelerin Yeri: Malatya Büyükşehir Belediyesi. *Selçuk Üniversitesi Sosyal Bilimler Meslek Yüksekokulu Dergisi*, *22*(2), 663–674. DOI: 10.29249/selcuksbmyd.633505

Kamil, M., & Romadhan, A. (2020). Local geo-politics of urban food resilience to achieve sustainable city development in Malang, Indonesia. *Advances in Social Science, Education and Humanities Research*, *436*, 782–785. DOI: 10.2991/assehr.k.200529.165

Kanas, A., & Kosyakova, Y. (2023). Greater local supply of language courses improves refugees' labor market integration. *European Societies*, *25*(1), 1–36. DOI: 10.1080/14616696.2022.2096915

Karabulak, S. (2013), "Municipal History in Turkish Public Administration" Istanbul Aydın University, Institute of Social Sciences, Department of Political Science and International Relations, Master's Thesis, Istanbul.

Karkın, N. (2021). ''Elektronik vatandaş katılımına (E-katılım) ilişkin teorik çerçeve'', in *Kamu Yönetiminde Elektronik Vatandaş Katılımı* (Edt: Ayşegül Saylam), Ankara: Gazi Kitapevi.

Karkın, N. (2022). ''Kamu hizmetlerinde kitle kaynak kullanımı, yönetişim ve vatandaş katılımı'', in *Kamu Yönetiminde Katılım Üzerine Güncel Tartışmalar* (Edt: Ezgi Seçkiner Bingöl), Ankara: Gazi Kitapevi.

Karkın, N., & Janssen, M. (2014). Evaluating websites from a public value perspective: A review of Turkish local government websites. *International Journal of Information Management*, *34*(3), 351–363. DOI: 10.1016/j.ijinfomgt.2013.11.004

Karki, T. (2023). Why public housing has been less successful in American history? https://papers.ssrn.com/sol3/Delivery.cfm/SSRN_ID4356830_code4921372.pdf?abstractid=4352289&mirid=1

Kazakhstan, S. (2021). *Elections of 700 rural akims will be held on July 25 – Karin*. Sputnik Kazakhstan. https://ru.sputnik.kz/20210625/Vybory-700-selskikh-akimov-proydut-25-iyulya---Karin-17453504.html

Keiner, M., & Kim, A. (2007). Transnational City Networks for Sustainability. *European Planning Studies*, *15*(10), 1369–1395. DOI: 10.1080/09654310701550843

Kepel, G. (2012). *Banlieue de la R"publique*. Gallimard.

Keser, I. (2023). Interdependence and Complementarity of a Multi-Dimensional Concept of Sustainable Development and the Integrated Approach to Urban Governance—Case Study City of Zagreb. *Sustainability (Basel), 15*(12), 9213. DOI: 10.3390/su15129213

Kettl, D. F. (2005). The Global Public Management Revolution. Brookings Institution Press, 5-7.

Khishtovani, G. (2020). *Reviewing migration and development: The role of local authorities in Central Asia*. CAREC Institute., Retrieved from https://www.carecinstitute.org/wp-content/uploads/2020/09/VFP-2020-migration-in-Central-Asia.pdf

Kim, S., & Lee, J. (2012). E-participation, transparency, and trust in local government. *Public Administration Review, 72*(6), 819–828. DOI: 10.1111/j.1540-6210.2012.02593.x

King, D. & Stoker, G. (1996). Rethinking Local Democracy. Palgrave Macmillan, 50-56.

Kiralj, J., & Ajduković, D. (2022). Integration of Refugees in Croatia–A Qualitative Study of the Integration Process and Intergroup Relations of Refugees from Syria. *Društvena istraživanja: časopis za opća društvena pitanja*, 31(4), 661-682.

Kızıltaş, M. (2012). *Engellilerle 360° İletişim*. Elma Yayınevi.

Knell, M. (2021). The digital revolution and digitalized network society. *Review of Evolutionary Political Economy, 2*(1), 9–25. DOI: 10.1007/s43253-021-00037-4

Koç, N., & Ökmen, M. (2015). Sosyal belediyecilik anlayışı çerçevesinde seçilmiş belediyelerin sosyal bütçelerinin değerlendirilmesi. *Maliye Dergisi, 168*, 69–84.

Koprić, I., Lalić Novak, G., & Giljević, T. (2021). Local Integration Policy of Migrants in Croatia: In *Search of Coherence and Capacity. Local Integration of Migrants Policy: European Experiences and Challenges*, 215-230.

Koprić, I., Škarica, M., & Manojlović Tomań, R. (2019). Local public services and austerity measures in Croatia: Adaptations of the resilient social model through the central-local power and blame games. *Local public services in times of austerity across Mediterranean Europe*, 167-191.

Kosec, K., & Mogues, T. (2020). Decentralization Without Democracy. *World Politics, 72*(2), 165–213. DOI: 10.1017/S0043887120000027

Kosenov, A. (2013, August 28). 370 million tenge spent in Kazakhstan on rural akim elections. *Tengrinews*. https://tengrinews.kz/kazakhstan_news/370-millionov-tenge-potratili-kazahstane-vyiboryi-selskih-240627/

Kreichauf, R., & Mayer, M. (2023). Negotiating urban solidarities: multiple agencies and contested meanings in the making of solidarity cities. In *Displacement, Asylum and the City* (pp. 111-134). Routledge. DOI: 10.4324/9781003381297-6

Kübler, D. (2024). Citizen participation through direct legislation: A road to success? A perspective from Switzerland. *Global Public Policy and Governance*, *4*(2), 184–196.

Kussainova, M., & Ekberova, E. (2021). Kazakhstan hosts first direct elections of akims. *Anadolu Ajansı*. https://www.aa.com.tr/ru/мир/в-казахстане-проходят-первые-прямые-выборы-акимов/2313288

Ladner, A., Keuffer, N., Baldersheim, H., Hlepas, N., Swianiewicz, P., Steyvers, K., & Navarro, C. (2019). *Patterns of local autonomy in Europe* (Vol. 184). Palgrave Macmillan. DOI: 10.1007/978-3-319-95642-8

Lalić Novak, G., & Giljević, T. (2018). Integration of 'new' refugees in the non-immigrant countries along the Balkan route of migration-overview of legal framework and practices, *Ročenka uprchlického a cizineckého práva*. Brno: Veřejný ochránce práv, 2018, 453-470.

Lalić Novak, G., & Giljević, T. (2019). Legal and Institutional Framework of Integration of Migrants in Croatia–Towards a European Model. *Godišnjak Akademije pravnih znanosti Hrvatske*, 10(1), 163-184.

Lalić Novak, G., & Giljević, T. (2023). *Protokol postupanja prilikom integracije osoba kojima je odobrena međunarodna zaštita i pripadajući priručnik s primjerima dobre prakse*, https://pravamanjina.gov.hr/UserDocsImages/dokumenti/Protokol%20postupanja%20prilikom%20integracije%20osoba%20kojima%20je%20odobrena%20me%C4%91unarodna%20za%C5%A1tita.pdf

Lameck, W. U. (2023). Political decentralisation and political-administrative relation in the local councils in Tanzania. *Public Administration and Policy*, *26*(3), 335–344. DOI: 10.1108/PAP 07 2022 0077

Lao, M. E. (2013). Are local governments ready for migration? In Tigno, J. (Ed.), *Interrogating Migration: New Questions and Emerging Trends in the Philippines* (pp. 28–41). Philippine Social Science Council.

Lark, T. J., Mueller, R. M., Johnson, D. M., & Gibbs, H. K. (2017). Measuring land-use and land-cover change using the US Department of Agriculture's cropland data layer: Cautions and recommendations. *International Journal of Applied Earth Observation and Geoinformation*, *62*, 224–235. DOI: 10.1016/j.jag.2017.06.007

Larreguy, H., & Liu, S. X. (2024). When does education increase political participation? Evidence from Senegal. *Political Science Research and Methods, 12*(2), 354–371. DOI: 10.1017/psrm.2023.37

Le Blanc, D. (2020). E-participation: a quick overview of recent qualitative trends. DESA Working Paper No. 163. https://www.un.org/sites/un2.un.org/files/2020/08/1597341830.3171.pdf

Le Galès, P. (2002). *Gouverner par les instruments*. Presses de Sciences Po.

Leblebici, N. D. (2021). ''Kamu yönetiminde elektronik vatandaş katılımının sağladığı yararlar ve e-katılıma uyumun önündeki engeller'', in *Kamu Yönetiminde Elektronik Vatandaş Katılımı* (Edt: Ayşegül Saylam), Ankara: Gazi Kitapevi, 137-155.

Lee, E. S. (1966). A Theory of Migration. *Demography*, *3*(1), 47–57. DOI: 10.2307/2060063

Levitsky, S., & Way, L. A. (2010). *Competitive Authoritarianism: Hybrid Regimes after the Cold War*. Cambridge University Press., https://doi.org/DOI, DOI: 10.1017/CBO9780511781353

Lierl, M. M. (2017). Elections and embezzlement: experimental evidence from Burkina Faso. *World Bank Policy Research Working Paper*(8067).

Lironi, E. (2006). Lironi, E.: Potentıal and challenges of E-participation. In: The European Unıon, European Parliament's Policy Department for Citizens' Rights and Constitutional Afairs European Parliament B-1047 Brussels

Lowe, M., Adlakha, D., Sallis, J. F., Salvo, D., Cerin, E., Moudon, A. V., Higgs, C., Hinckson, E., Arundel, J., Boeing, G., Liu, S., Mansour, P., Gebel, K., Puig-Ribera, A., Mishar, P. B., Bozovic, T., Carson, J., Dygryan, J., Florindo, A. A., & Giles-Corti, B. (2022). City planning policies to support health and sustainability: An international comparison of policy indicators for 25 cities. *The Lancet. Global Health, 10*(6), e882–e894. https://www.thelancet.com/pdfs/journals/langlo/PIIS2214-109X(22)00069-9.pdf. DOI: 10.1016/S2214-109X(22)00069-9 PMID: 35561723

Macintosh, A. (2004). Characterizing e-participation in policy-making. *In37th Annual Hawaii International Conference on System Sciences,* 1 -10.

Makse, T., & Volden, C. (2011). The role of policy attributes in the diffusion of innovations. *The Journal of Politics, 73*(1), 108–124. DOI: 10.1017/S0022381610000903

Manor, J. (1999). *The political economy of democratic decentralization*. The World Bank. DOI: 10.1596/0-8213-4470-6

Manville, M., Monkkonen, P., & Lens, M. (2020). It's time to end single-family zoning. *Journal of the American Planning Association, 86*(1), 106–112. DOI: 10.1080/01944363.2019.1651216

Mapuva, J. (2015). Enhancing Citizen Participation in Local Governance through Participation Mechanisms. *Journal of Public Administration, 50*(3), 408.

Martin, C., McTarnaghan, S., & Williams, J. L. (2020). *Articulating a program for resilience.* Urban Institute. https://www.urban.org/sites/default/files/publication/102401/articulating-a-program-for-resilience.pdf

Martinez-Bravo, M., Padró i Miquel, G., Qian, N., & Yao, Y. (2022). The Rise and Fall of Local Elections in China. *The American Economic Review, 112*(9), 2921–2958. DOI: 10.1257/aer.20181249

Martin, P., Abella, M., & Midgley, E. (2004). Best practices to manage migration: The Philippines. *The International Migration Review, 38*(4), 1544–1559. DOI: 10.1111/j.1747-7379.2004.tb00247.x

Massey, D. S., Arango, J., Hugo, G., Kouaouci, A., Pellegrino, A., & Taylor, J. E. (1993). Theories of International Migration: A Review and Appraisal. *Population and Development Review, 19*(3), 431–466. DOI: 10.2307/2938462

Matuszczyk, K. (2023). Immigrants, residents, employees. Refugees from Ukraine in local migration policy in Poland illustrated with the example of selected agglomerations. *Social Insurance.Theory into Practice, 155*(4), 67–84.

Mauletbai, S. (2021). Hope, intrigue, apathy. How were the first elections of rural akims in Kazakhstan. *Informburo.* https://informburo.kz/stati/kak-prosli-vybory-selskix-akimov

Mecek, M. (2017). E-Government and E-Municipality: Conceptual Framework and Review of Studies on Municipality Websites in Türkiye. Süleyman Demirel University Journal of Faculty of Economics and Administrative Sciences, 22 (Kayfor 15 Special Issue), 1815-1851.

Medaglia, R. (2012). E-Participation research: Moving characterization forward (2006–2011). *Government Information Quarterly, 29*(3), 346–360. DOI: 10.1016/j.giq.2012.02.010

Meijer, M., Popławska, J. Z., & Szytniewski, B. (2023). Spaces of Decoupling in the Netherlands and Poland: Emerging Local Governance Networks for Hosting Non-EU Migrants in Peripheral and Shrinking Areas. *Journal of International Migration and Integration, 24*(S5, Suppl 5), 839–862. DOI: 10.1007/s12134-023-01057-1

Metin, B. (2017). Engellilere Yönelik Sosyal Politikalarda Yerel Yönetimlerin Rolü: Keçiören Belediyesi Örneği. *Gazi Üniversitesi İktisadi Ve İdari Bilimler Fakültesi Dergisi*, *19*(1), 320–344.

Metro. (n.d.). *Resource conservation and recycling education*. OregonMetro. https://www.oregonmetro.gov/tools-partners/education-resources/resource-conservation-and-recycling-education

Mezitli Municipality. (2022). *Mezitli Municipality Annual Report 2022*.https://mezitli.bel.tr/wp-content/uploads/2023/05/faaliyet-raporu-2022.pdf

Mezitli Municipality. (2023). *Mezitli Municipality Annual Report 2023*.https://mezitli.bel.tr/faaliyet-raporu/

Mezitli Municipality. (2025). (2025, February 03) https://mezitli.bel.tr/uluslararasi-uyelikler/

Milan Pact Awards 2022 Addis Abba. (2022). (2025, February 02) https://www.milanurbanfoodpolicypact.org/projects/addis-ababa-school-feeding-program/

Milan Pact Awards 2022 London. (2022). (2025, February 02) https://www.milanurbanfoodpolicypact.org/projects/londons-food-waste-reduction-programme

Milan Pact Awards 2022 New York. (2022). (2025, February 02) https://www.milanurbanfoodpolicypact.org/projects/a-new-york-city-framework-for-good-food-purchasing

Milan Pact Awards 2022 Rosaio. (2022). (2025, February 02) https://www.milanurbanfoodpolicypact.org/projects/agro-ecological-food-production-in-rosario/

Milan Pact Awards 2022 Rourkela. (2022). (2025, February 02) https://www.milanurbanfoodpolicypact.org/projects/e-cool-mandi-decentralized-cold-room-run-by-women-preventing-vendor-distress

Milan Pact Awards 2022 Yeosu. (2022). (2025, February 02) https://www.milanurbanfoodpolicypact.org/projects/strategy-for-securing-our-talents-and-small-farms

Ministère de l'Intérieur. (2023). *Rapport annuel sur l'immigration*.

MIPEX (Migrant Integration Policy Index). (2020a). *Lithuania*, 2019; https://www.mipex.eu/lithuania

MIPEX. (2020b). *Croatia*https://www.mipex.eu/croatia

Mishra, M. K. (2009). Democratisation Process in Kazakhstan: Gauging the Indicators. *India Quarterly*, *65*(3), 313–327. DOI: 10.1177/097492840906500306

Monde, L. (2023). *What's in France's controversial immigration law?*https://www.lemonde.fr/en/france/article/2023/12/20/what-s-in-france-s-controversial-immigration-law_6361995_7.html?utm_source=chatgpt.com#, Erişim tarihi: 10.03.2025.

Monkkonen, P., Barrall, A., & Echavarria, A. (2024). Meaningful action: Evaluating local government plans to affirmatively further fair housing in California. *Housing Policy Debate*, *1*(1), 1–25. DOI: 10.1080/10511482.2024.2337033

Moon, J., & Norris, D. (2005). Does Managerial Orientation Matter? The Adoption Of Reinventing Government And E-Government At The Municipal Level January. *Information Systems Journal*, *15*(1), 43–60. Https://Doi.Org/10.1111/J.1365-2575.2005.00185.X. DOI: 10.1111/j.1365-2575.2005.00185.x

Morawska, E. (2018). Qualitative migration research: Viable goals, open-ended questions, and multidimensional answers. *Qualitative research in European migration studies*, 113-131.

MUFPP. (2015). Milan Urban Food Policy Pact. https://www.milanurbanfoodpolicypact.org/the-milan-pact/

MUFPP. (2019). *Milan Pact Awards 2019 Mezitli.* (2025, February 01) https://www.milanurbanfoodpolicypact.org/milan-pact-awards/milan-pact-awards-2019

MUFPP. (2022). Milan Pact Awards 2022. (2025, February 02) https://www.milanurbanfoodpolicypact.org/milan-pact-awards/milan-pact-awards-2022

MUFPP. (2023). *Milan Pact Awards 2022.* Milano. https://www.milanurbanfoodpolicypact.org/award/

Municipality Law No. 5393. (2005). https://www.mevzuat.gov.tr/MevzuatMetin/1.5.5393.pdf

Muratpasa Municipality. (2023). *Muratpasa Municipality Annual Report 2023.* https://muratpasa-bld.gov.tr/raporlar

Nabatchi, T., & Amsler, L. B. (2014). Direct public engagement in local government. *American Review of Public Administration*, •••, 44.

National Archives. (1933). *National Industrial Recovery Act (1933).*https://www.archives.gov/milestone-documents/national-industrial-recovery-act

National Transit Institute. (2019). *Case study. City of Monrovia: Leveraging emerging ride-sharing services to expand mobility options.* Advancing Mobility Management. https://www.apta.com/wp-content/uploads/Resources/resources/mobility/Documents/GoMonrovia%20Case%20Study.pdf

Neergaard, H. (2007). 10 Sampling in entrepreneurial settings. *Handbook of qualitative research methods in entrepreneurship*, 253-278.

Nicolescu, C. E., Bitoiu, I. T., & Radulescu, C. R. (2017). Good Practices for Sustainable Urban Food Policies. *SEA-Practical Application of Science, 15*(3), 347-352. https://ideas.repec.org/a/cmj/seapas/y2017i15p347-352.html

Nijenhuis, G. (2009). Embedding international migration: The response of Bolivian local governments and NGOs to international migration. *Environment and Urbanization, 22*(1), 1–12.

Nilufer Municipality. (2023). *Nilufer Municipality Annual Report.*https://www.nilufer.bel.tr/i/pdf/101.pdf

Noiriel, G. (1991). *La tyrannie du national: le droit d'asile en Europe, 1793–1993*. Calmann-Lévy.

Norton, A. (1994). *International Handbook of Local and Regional Government. A Comparative Analysis of Advanced Democracies*. Edward Elgar Publishing. DOI: 10.4337/9781781954225

OECD. (2001). Citiziens as partners: OECD handbook on information, consultation and public participation in policy-making. OECD Publishing, Paris. https://www.oecd-ilibrary.org/governance/citizens-as-partners_9789264195561-en

OECD. (2018). *Working Together for Local Integration of Migrants and Refugees*. OECD Publishing.

OECD. (2020). The role of local governments in supporting people with disabilities. OECD Publishing. https://www.oecd.org/inclusive-growth/resources/people-with-disabilities/

OECD. (2022). *OECD guidelines for citizen participation processes, OECD public governance reviews*. OECD Publishing., DOI: 10.1787/f765caf6-

OECD. (2023). *What we know about the skills and early labour market outcomes of refugees from Ukraine, OECD Policy Responses on the Impacts of the War in Ukraine*. OECD Publishing., DOI: 10.1787/c7e694aa-

Office of Policy Development and Research. (2020). *HUD's historical timeline*. https://www.huduser.gov/portal/hudtimeline_1930.html

Office of Policy Development and Research. (2024). *Adaptive reuse creates affordable housing for grandparents and grandchildren*. HUDUSER. https://www.huduser.gov/portal/pdredge/pdr-edge-inpractice-073024.html

OFII (Office Français de l'Immigration et de l'Intégration). (2022). *Bilan annuel.*

Oliver, C., Dekker, R., Geuijen, K., & Broadhead, J. (2020). Innovative strategies for the reception of asylum seekers and refugees in European cities: Multi-level governance, multi-sector urban networks and local engagement. *Comparative Migration Studies*, *8*(1), 1–14. DOI: 10.1186/s40878-020-00189-y

Oliver, M. (1990). *The Politics of Disablement.* Macmillan. DOI: 10.1007/978-1-349-20895-1

Ölmez, M. (2021). Digital Transformation and E-Commerce in Public Policies in Türkiye: A Model Proposal. *Journal of Public Administration and Technology*, *3*(1), 9–33.

Onalbaiuly, S. (2019). *Democratisation of local government and local governance in Kazakhstan.* University of Cambridge.

Oni, A. A., Oni, S., Mbarika, V., & Ayo, C. K. (2017). Empirical study of user acceptance of online political participation: Integrating civic voluntarism model and theory of reasoned action. *Government Information Quarterly*, *34*(2), 317–328. DOI: 10.1016/j.giq.2017.02.003

Önver, Ş. B. (2019). Sixth Department-I Municipality and Comparison with Today's Municipal Services. *Takvim-I Vekayi*, *7*(1), 37–72.

Oomen, B., Baumgärtel, M., Miellet, S., Durmus, E., & Sabchev, T. (2021). Strategies of divergence: Local authorities, law, and discretionary spaces in migration governance. *Journal of Refugee Studies*, *34*(4), 3608–3628. DOI: 10.1093/jrs/feab062

Opiniano, J. (2021). *A reset for overseas migration? Recent developments in Filipinos' migration in the context of the COVID-19 pandemic (Migration Research Series no. 69).* International Organization for Migration.

Opiniano, J., & Ang, A. (2016). *Remittance Investment Climate Analysis in Rural Hometowns (RICART): Piloting a tool on rural hometown investing by overseas migrants. University of Santo Tomas - Research Center on Culture, Education and Social Issues.* UST - RCCESI.

Opiniano, J., & Ang, A. (2024). Remittance investment climate analysis: Ascertaining the local development potential of overseas remittances in Philippine rural hometowns. *Asian and Pacific Migration Journal*, *33*(3), 525–553. DOI: 10.1177/01171968241288259

Özdemir, G. Ş. (2022). Urban solidarity typology: A comparison of European cities since the crisis of refuge in 2015. *Cities (London, England)*, *130*, 103976. DOI: 10.1016/j.cities.2022.103976

Özgökçeler, S., & Alper, Y. (2010). Özürlüler Kanunu'nun sosyal model açısından değerlendirilmesi. İşletme ve Ekonomi Araştırmaları Dergisi, 1(1), 33-54.

Özgökçeler, S. (2014). An Effective Concept in Local Development: "Local Governance" [Bursa City Council Example]. İş, Güç. *Journal of Industrial Relations and Human Resources*, *16*(1), 67–82.

Öztürk, Y. E., Şentürk, Ş., & Macit, Y. (2017). Evde Bakım Hizmeti Alan Engelli Bireye Sahip Ailelerin Bakım Verme Yüklerinin Belirlenmesi: Amasya Örneği. *Türkiye Sosyal Hizmet Araştırmaları Dergisi*, *1*(1), 48–67.

Pandek, K., & Župarić-Iljić, D. (2018). Strengthening borders, managing centres: Reception conditions and provisions of services to asylum seekers in Croatia. *Migracijske i Etnicke Teme*, *34*(3), 217–249. DOI: 10.11567/met.34.3.1

Papademetriou, D. (2005). *The Global Struggle with Illegal Migration: No End in Sight*. Migration Policy Institute.

Pappel, I., Tsap, V., Pappel, I., & Draheim, D. (2018). ''Exploring e-services development in local government authorities by means of electronic document management systems'', in *International Conference on Electronic Governance and Open Society: Challenges in Eurasia*, Cham: Springer International Publishing, 223-234.

Pędziwiatr, K., & Magdziarz, W. (2023). The reception and integration of refugees from Ukraine in Poland, Czechia, Slovakia and Hungary–the new immigration destinations of Central Europe. *Social Policy Issues*, *59*(4), 345–377. DOI: 10.31971/pps/162968

Penninx, R. (2009). Decentralising Integration Policies: Managing Migration in Cities, Regions and Localities. *International Migration (Geneva, Switzerland)*, *47*(5), 1–19.

Pertierra, R. (1992). *Remittances and Returnees: The Cultural Economy of Migration in Ilocos*. New Day Publishers.

Phang, C. W., & Kankanhalli, A. (2008). A framework of ICT exploitation for e-participation initiatives. *Communications of the ACM*, *51*(12), 128–132. DOI: 10.1145/1409360.1409385

Philippine Statistics Authority. (2020, January 28). 12 Percent of Filipino Households Have an OFW Member (Results from the 2018 National Migration Survey). PSA website, https://psa.gov.ph/statistics/national-migration-survey/node/1684064156

POEA. (1991). *POEA Annual Report 1990*.https://dmw.gov.ph/archives/annualreports/1990.htm

POEA. (1995). *POEA Annual Report 1995*.https://dmw.gov.ph/archives/annualreports/1995.htm

POEA. (2012). *POEA Annual Report 2011*.https://dmw.gov.ph/archives/annualreports/2011.htm

POEA. (n.d. – b) MOUs with local government units." A project document by POEA's Workers Education Division. (Unpublished)

Portes, A., & Walton, J. (1981). *Labor, Class, and the International System*. Academic Press.

Portland.Gov. (2018). *2035 Comprehensive Plan and supporting documents*. https://www.portland.gov/bps/planning/comp-plan-2035/about-comprehensive-plan/2035-comprehensive-plan-and-supporting#toc-2035-comprehensive-plan-as-amended-through-may-2023-

Presidency of The Republic of Türkiye Presidency of Strategy and Budget. *The Eleventh Development Plan (2019-2023)*.https://www.sbb.gov.tr/wp-content/uploads/2022/07/On_Birinci_Kalkinma_Plani-2019-2023.pdf

President of the Republic of Kazakhstan. (2013, December 3). *Decree of the President of the Republic of Kazakhstan No. 704 On the approval of Model regulations for a maslikhat*. Official legal resource of the Republic of Kazakhstan. https://adilet.zan.kz/eng/docs/U1300000704/history

Primbetova, S., & Tlesova, A. (2015). Participation of the citizens in the decision making process at the local level as the priority of the reforming and foundation of legal capacity of the local authorities. *Actual Issues of Modern Science and Society*, (4), 13–17.

Putnam, R. D. (2000). *Bowling Alone: The Collapse and Revival of American Community*. Simon & Schuster.

Regulation on Landfill of Waste. (2010). https://www.mevzuat.gov.tr/MevzuatMetin/yonetmelik/7.5.13887.pdf

Republic of the Philippines. (1991). Republic Act 7160. https://lawphil.net/statutes/repacts/ra1991/ra_7160_1991.html

Republic of the Philippines. (1995). Republic Act 8042. https://library.laborlaw.ph/r-a-8042-migrant-workers-and-overseas-filipinos-act-of-1995/

Republic of the Philippines. (2011). Republic Act 10022. https://lawphil.net/statutes/repacts/ra2010/ra_10022_2010.html

Republic of the Philippines. (2021). Republic Act 11641. https://lawphil.net/statutes/repacts/ra2021/ra_11641_2021.html

Reuters. (2025). From France to Mali, a deportee's struggle far from home. https://www.reuters.com/investigates/special-report/migration-europe-africa/, Erişim Tarihi: 10.03.2025.

Riallant, C. (2017, January 10). Migration: An overlooked tool for local development. *OECD Development Matters*, https://oecd-development-matters.org/2017/01/10/migration-an-overlooked-tool-for-local-development/

Rijavec, D., Štambuk, A., & Pevcin, P. (2021). Evidence-based assessment of readiness to solve wicked problems: The case of migration crisis in Croatia and Slovenia. *Social Sciences (Basel, Switzerland)*, *10*(6), 188. DOI: 10.3390/socsci10060188

Robinson, C. (2020). Measuring 'well-governed' migration: The IOM's migration governance indicators. In *The International Organization for Migration: The New 'UN Migration Agency' in Critical Perspective* (pp. 123-143). Springer.

Rogers, E. (1995). *Diffusion of Innovations* (4th ed.). New Free Press.

Ross, D. E., & Law, H. J. (2023). Evolution of municipal solid waste management in North America. *Waste Management & Research*, *41*(7), 1177–1187. DOI: 10.1177/0734242X231173308 PMID: 37246621

Ruffini, O., Relf, C., Mann, D., Blake, M. R., Carrad, A., Reeve, B., Barbour, L., Vanderlee, L., Vandevijvere, S., & Sacks, G. (2024). Development of the local food systems policy index (Local Food-EPI+) tool and assessment process to benchmark the implementation of local government policies for creating healthy, equitable and environmentally sustainable food systems. *Public Health Nutrition*, *27*(1), 1–15. DOI: 10.1017/S136898002400140X PMID: 39354657

Ruhs, M. (2013). *The Price of Rights: Regulating International Labor Migration*. Princeton University Press.

Sæbø, Ø., Rose, J., & Flak, L. S. (2008). The shape of eParticipation: Characterizing an emerging research area. *Government Information Quarterly*, *25*(3), 400–428. DOI: 10.1016/j.giq.2007.04.007

Saka, E. (Ed.). (2019). *Internet History of Türkiye (New Media Studies V)*. Alternative Informatics Association., https://ekitap.alternatifbilisim.org/ymc5_turkiye_internet_tarihi.html

Salt Lake City. (2020). *Affordable housing overlay*. SLC. hhttps://storymaps.arcgis.com/collections/026ff1b6235a436d85bcf87712ad5d19?item=1

San Francisco Environment Department. (2009). *The city's mandatory recycling and composting ordinance*. https://www.sfenvironment.org/sites/default/files/policy/sfe_zw_sf_mandatory_recycling_composting_ord_100-09.pdf

Sanford, C., & Rose, J. (2007). Characterizing e-participation. *International Journal of Information Management*, *27*(6), 406–421. DOI: 10.1016/j.ijinfomgt.2007.08.002

Sankhayeva, Z., & Arzikulov, A. (2021). Elections in the system of local self-government: International practices and experience of Kazakhstan. *Kazakhstan Spectrum, 97*(1), 89-99. https://doi.org/https://doi.org/10.52536/KS/vol_97_issue_1_A6

Santamaría-Philco, A., Cerdá, J. H. C., & Gramaje, M. C. P. (2019). Advances in e-Participation: A perspective of Last Years. *IEEE Access : Practical Innovations, Open Solutions*, *7*, 155894–155916. DOI: 10.1109/ACCESS.2019.2948810

Sarı, A. (2022), "Engellilere Toplu Taşımada, Toplu Konut İdaresi'nde ve Belediye Hizmetlerinde Uygulanan İndirimli Tarifeler", https://www.engelsizkariyer.com/

Sari, A. M., Hidayanto, A. N., Purwandari, B., Budi, N. F. A., & Kosandi, M. (2018). Challenges and issues of E-participation implementation: A case study of e-complaint Indonesia. *In2018 Third International Conference on Informatics and Computing*, 1-6. DOI: 10.1109/IAC.2018.8780467

Sayım, F., & Aydın, V. (2015). A Theoretical Study on the Interaction of Service Sector Characteristics and Unsystematic Risks with Sector Securities. *Dumlupınar University Journal of Social Sciences*, (29), 245–262.

Saylam, A. (2021). Kamu yönetiminde elektronik vatandaş katılımını etkileyen faktörler ekseninde türk kamu yönetimi için bir ortak yapım portal önerisi: Millet-inkarari. gov. tr. *Kamu Yönetimi ve Teknoloji Dergisi*, *3*(1), 81–101.

Scally, C. P., Schilling, J., Fedorowicz, M., Heinrichs, A., Aceves, L., & Pegna, S. W. (2023). *Developing a policy and systems change compass for local government*. https://www.urban.org/sites/default/files/2023-10/Developing%20a%20Policy%20and%20Systems%20Change%20Compass%20for%20Local%20Government.pdf

Schmidthuber, L., Hilgers, D., Gegenhuber, T., & Etzelstorfer, S. (2017). The emergence of local open government: Determinants of citizen participation in online service reporting. *Government Information Quarterly*, *34*(3), 457–469. DOI: 10.1016/j.giq.2017.07.001

Schnapper, D. (1991). *La France de l'intégration*. Gallimard.

Scholten, P., & Penninx, R. (2016). The Multilevel Governance of Migration and Integration. In Zapata-Barrero, R., & Triandafyllidou, A. (Eds.), *Addressing Tolerance and Diversity Discourses in Europe*. Palgrave Macmillan. DOI: 10.1007/978-3-319-21674-4_6

Schwester, R. W. (2009). Examining the barriers to e government adoption. *Electronic Journal of E-Government*, *7*(1), 113–122.

Şen, A. F. (2022). Evaluating the role of media during elections: The case of local elections of 31st March 2019 in Turkey. *Advances in Applied Sociology*, *12*(4), 112–126. DOI: 10.4236/aasoci.2022.124011

Şen, M. (2023). *Türkiye'de Engelliler ve Sosyal Politikalar*. Efe Akademi Yayınları.

Şentürk, H. (2008). Demokratik Katılım ve Sivil Toplum Kuruluşları. İstanbul Üniversitesi Yayınları, 288.

Sewell, W. D., & Phillips, S. D. (1979). Models for the evaluation of public participation programmes. *Natural Resources Journal*, *19*(2), 337–358.

Shakespeare, T. (2006). *Disability Rights and Wrongs*. Routledge. DOI: 10.4324/9780203640098

Siegel, D. (2022). Decentralization, legitimacy, and democracy in post-Soviet Central Asia. *Journal of Eurasian Studies*, *13*(1), 66–81. DOI: 10.1177/18793665211068525

Smajlović, H., & Čolakhodžić, F. (2023). *How Does Media Coverage Affect the Outcomes of the Elections?* MAP Social Sciences. DOI: 10.53880/2744-2454.2023.4.109

Stark, O., & Bloom, D. E. (1985). The New Economics of Labor Migration. *The American Economic Review*, *75*(2), 173–178.

Steil, J. P., & Kelly, N. (2019). Survival of the fairest: Examining HUD reviews of assessments of fair housing. *Housing Policy Debate*, *29*(5), 736–751. DOI: 10.1080/10511482.2018.1524444

Strasbourg Ville et Eurométropole. (2023). *Rapport d'activit"s sur l'int"gration.*

Subramanian, I., Finsterwalder, J., & Hall, C. M. (2022). A systematic literature review of service-related research on refugees. *Journal of Services Marketing*, *36*(7), 908–939. DOI: 10.1108/JSM-09-2021-0312

Švaljek, S., Rašić Bakarić, I., & Sumpor, M. (2019). Citizens and the city: The case for participatory budgeting in the City of Zagreb. *Public Sector Economics*, *43*(1), 21–48. DOI: 10.3326/pse.43.1.4

Szara, K., & Ślusarczyk, B. (2020). Capacities for the development of creative capital in Lithuanian counties. *European Review (Chichester, England)*, *28*(4), 678–692. DOI: 10.1017/S1062798720000137

Tacoli, C. (2010). Editorial: Governance, migration and local development. *Environment and Urbanization*, *22*(1), 5–11. DOI: 10.1177/0956247810364111

Talen, E. (2021). The socio-economic context of form-based codes. *Landscape and Urban Planning*, *214*, 104182. Advance online publication. DOI: 10.1016/j.landurbplan.2021.104182

Tambouris, E., Liotas, N., & Tarabanis, K. (2007). ''A framework for assessing eParticipation projects and tools'', in *2007 40th Annual Hawaii International Conference on System Sciences (HICSS'07)*, IEEE. DOI: 10.1109/HICSS.2007.13

Tambouris, E., Macintosh, A., Smith, S., Panopoulou, E., Tarabanis, K., & Millard, J. (2012). Understanding eParticipation state of play in Europe. *Information Systems Management*, *29*(4), 321–330. DOI: 10.1080/10580530.2012.716994

Tana, J. (2004). Enhancing the performance of the Philippine public employment service office: Drawing lessons from Japan's public employment security office. Paper for the Japan Institute for Labor Policy and Training, https://www.jil.go.jp/profile/documents/Tana.pdf

Taylor, J. E., Arango, J., Hugo, G., Kouaouci, A., Masset, D., & Peregrino, A. (1996). International migration and community development. *Population Index*, *62*(3), 397–418. DOI: 10.2307/3645924

Tebayev, D. (2020). Returning to academician G. Sapargaliyev's scientific publication on self-government in the Republic of Kazakhstan. *Scientific and legal journal. Bulletin of the Institute of Legislation and Legal Information of the Republic of Kazakhstan*, *4*(62), 177–179. Advance online publication. DOI: 10.52026/1994-408X_2020_62_4_177

Tekeli, İ. (1983). Yerel Yönetimlerde Demokrasi ve Türkiye'de Belediyelerin Gelişimi. *Amme Idaresi Dergisi*, *16*(2), 3–22.

Temime, E. (1999). *Histoire de l'immigration en France*. Paris: La D"couverte.

Terner Center. (2019). *Affordable housing overlay zones: Oakley*. UC Berkeley. https://ternercenter.berkeley.edu/wp-content/uploads/2020/10/Affordable_Housing_Overlay_Zones_Oakley.pdf

Terner Center. (2021). *Adaptive reuse challenges and opportunities in California.* UC Berkeley. https://ternercenter.berkeley.edu/wp-content/uploads/2021/11/Adaptive-Reuse-November-2021.pdf

Thanekar, U., Sacks, G., Ruffini, O., Reeve, B., & Blake, M. R. (2024). Local government stakeholders' perceptions of potential policy actions to influence both climate change and healthy eating in Victoria: A qualitative study. *Health Promotion Journal of Australia, 35*(4), 1158-1173. https://doi.org/DOI: 10.1002/hpja.848

The Housing Agency. (2024). *Sustainable compact development international case study analysis.* https://www.housingagency.ie/sites/default/files/2024-11/Sustainable_Compact_Development_International_Case_Study_Analysis.pdf

The Transport Politic. (2019). *Travel mode shares in the U.S.* https://www.thetransportpolitic.com/databook/travel-mode-shares-in-the-u-s/

The White House. (2021). *Fact sheet: The bipartisan infrastructure deal.* https://www.whitehouse.gov/briefing-room/statements-releases/2021/11/06/fact-sheet-the-bipartisan-infrastructure-deal/

Thibault, H., & Insebayeva, S. (2024). The Political System of Kazakhstan. In Lempp, J., & Mayer, S. (Eds.), *Central Asia in a Multipolar World: Internal Change, External Actors, Regional Cooperation* (pp. 39–55). Springer International Publishing., DOI: 10.1007/978-3-031-63727-8_3

Thomas, T., Gunden, C., & Legesse, B. (2020). Accounting for the impact of sustainable agriculture: The role of community based organization and local governance structures in promoting sustainable agriculture. *Multifunctionality and impacts of organix and conventioanl agriculture.* https://doi.org/DOI: 10.5772/intechopen.84385

Tiyek, Y. (2016). Yerel Yönetimlerin Sosyal Politika Uygulamalarındaki Rolü: İstanbul Büyükşehir Belediyesi Sosyal Yardım Birimi Örneği. *Yerel Politikalar,* (2), 53–84.

Tkachuk, A., Kostrykina, S., & Janeliunas, T. (2023) *Adaptation and Integration of Ukrainian migrants in Lithuania, Research study*, Eastern Europe Studies Center, EESC, 1-19, https://www.eesc.lt/wp-content/uploads/2023/11/v01_Ukrainian-report_Janeliunas_EN_A4.pdf

Todaro, M. P. (1969). A Model of Labor Migration and Urban Unemployment in Less Developed Countries. *The American Economic Review.*

Tokayev, K. K. (2022, March 16). *New Kazakhstan: the path of renewal and modernisation.* Official website of the President of the Republic of Kazakhstan. https://www.akorda.kz/en/state-of-the-nation-address-by-president-of-the-republic-of-kazakhstan-kassym-jomart-tokayev-17293

Treisman, D. (2007). *The Architecture of Government: Rethinking Political Decentralization.* Cambridge University Press., https://doi.org/DOI, DOI: 10.1017/CBO9780511619151

TÜİK. (2024). Yaşam Memnuniyeti Araştırması https://data.tuik.gov.tr/Bulten/Index?p=Yasam-Memnuniyeti-Arastirmasi-2024-53785

Türkiye İstatistik Kurumu. (2002). Türkiye Özürlüler Araştırması Raporu. https://evam.tuik.gov.tr/dataset/detail/16

Ulceluse, M. (2021, December). The local turn in the governance of emigration and its effects. Dossier, Nederlandse Vereniging voon der Verenigde Naties (NVVN). https://nvvn.nl/the-local-turn-in-the-governance-of-emigration-and-its-effects/

Ulug, C., Trell, E.-M., & Horlings, L. (2021). Ecovillage foodscapes: Zooming in and out of sustainable food practices. *Agriculture and Human Values, 38*(4), 1041–1015. DOI: 10.1007/s10460-021-10213-1

Ulusoy, A., & Akdemir, T. (2010). *Local Administrations Theory - Application - Finance.* Seçkin Bookstore.

UN - United Nations. (2016). United Nations e-government survey 2016: E-Government in support of sustainable development. Sales No. E.16.II.H.2 https://publicadministration.un.org/en/research/un-e-governmentsurveys

UN. (2020). E-government survey 2020: Digital government in the decade of action for sustainable development. https://publicadministration.un.org/egovkb/Portals/egovkb/Documents/un/2020-Survey/2020%20UN%20E-Government%20Survey%20(Full%20Report).pdf

UN. (2024a). UN E-government knowledgebase. https://publicadministration.un.org/egovkb/Data-Center

UN. (2024b). E-Government survey 2024: Accelerating digital transformation for sustainable development. https://publicadministration.un.org/egovkb/en-us/

Ünal, V. (2018). Engellilerin Engelliliğe Bakışı Ve Dine Yaklaşımları. *Cumhuriyet İlahiyat Dergisi, 22*(3), 1457–1482. DOI: 10.18505/cuid.440470

Ünal, V. (2021). Türkiye'de Engellilik Yaklaşımlarının Sosyal Politika Açısından Değerlendirilmesi. *Cumhuriyet Üniversitesi Fen-Edebiyat Fakültesi Sosyal Bilimler Dergisi*, *45*(2), 235–258.

UN-HABITAT. (2024)., *World Cities Report 2024 Cities And Climate Action Case Study Annex*. https://unhabitat.org/sites/default/files/2024/11/wcr2024_-_full_report.pdf

UNHCR. (2022). *Global Trends: Forced Displacement in 2022*.

United Nations Economic Commission for Latin America and the Caribbean (UN ECLAC). (2020). The impact of COVID-19: an opportunity to reaffirm the central role of migrants' human rights in sustainable development. https://www.cepal.org/sites/default/files/publication/files/46354/S2000617_en.pdf

United States Department of Housing and Urban Development. (n.d.). *National Affordable Housing Act*. https://www.hud.gov/program_offices/administration/hudclips/acts/nah-act

United States Department of Transportation. (2023). *Case Study: Carson City, Nevada's multi-faceted approach to complete streets*. https://www.planning.dot.gov/documents/Carson_City_CompleteStreets_Case_Study_Final-021023.pdf

United States Environmental Protection Agency. (2024a). *EPA history: Resource Conservation and Recovery Act*. EPA. https://www.epa.gov/history/epa-history-resource-conservation-and-recovery-act

United States Environmental Protection Agency. (2024b). *Summary of the resource conservation and recovery Act*. https://www.epa.gov/laws-regulations/summary-resource-conservation-and-recovery-act

Utibaev, B., & Utibaeva, G. (2022). Improvement of the local self-government system in the Republic of Kazakhstan. *Problems of AgriMarket, 1*(1), 67-74. https://doi.org/https://doi.org/10.46666/2022-1.2708-9991.07

Uzunoğlu, E. (2019). Engelli Bireylerin Toplumsal Yaşama Katılımında Yerel Yönetimlerin İşlevleri: Sakarya Büyükşehir Belediyesi Örneği. *The Journal of Academic Social Science*, *7*(91), 236 258. DOI: 10.16992/ASOS.14888

Varnalı, T. (2025). E-Municipality in Türkiye: Digitalization Path of Local Governments and Application Analysis. *International Anatolia Academic Online Journal Social Sciences Journal*, *11*(1), 237–259.

Vigoda, E. (2002). From responsiveness to collaboration: Governance, citizens, and the next generation of public administration. *Public Administration Review*, *62*(5), 527–540. DOI: 10.1111/1540-6210.00235

Ville de Lyon. (2021). *Lyon Ville Refuge: un engagement de solidarit".*

Ville de Paris. (2022). *Maison des Réfugi"s – Rapport annuel.*

Vitálišová, K., & Dvořák, J. (2023). Differences and Similarities in Local Participative Governance in Slovakia and Lithuania. In *Participatory and Digital Democracy at the Local Level: European Discourses and Practices* (pp. 125–146). Springer International Publishing. DOI: 10.1007/978-3-031-20943-7_8

Wach, D., & Pachocka, M. (2022). Polish Cities and Their Experience in Integration Activities-The Case of Warsaw. *Studia Europejskie-Studies in European Affairs*, *26*(2), 89–105. DOI: 10.33067/SE.2.2022.6

Walker, R., Avellaneda, C., & Berry, F. (2011). Exploring the diffusion of innovation among high and low innovative localities: A test of the Berry and Berry model. *Public Management Review*, *13*(1), 95–125. DOI: 10.1080/14719037.2010.501616

Wallerstein, I. (1974). *The Modern World-System.* Academic Press.

Walsh, K. (1997). Citizenship and Welfare: Rediscovering a Lost Dimension. *Journal of Social Policy*, *26*(4), 4.

Waste Management Regulation. (2015). https://www.mevzuat.gov.tr/File/GeneratePdf?mevzuatNo=20644&mevzuatTur=KurumVeKurulusYonetmeligi&mevzuatTertip=5

Wehrhahn, R., & Hathat, Z. E. (2022). Refugee Migration to Europe-Current Challenges and Potentials for Cities and Regions. *Comparative Population Studies*, *47*, 513–532. DOI: 10.12765/CPoS-2022-19

Weil, P. (2005). *La France et ses étrangers: l'aventure d'une politique de l'immigration de 1938 à nos jours*. Gallimard.

Weil, P. (2005a). *La République et sa diversité: immigration, intégration, discrimination.* Seuil.

Wendler, K. (2024). Developing the road to nowhere: Ethical considerations of highway expansions. *Viterbi Conversations in Ethics, 7*(3), 1-10. https://vce.usc.edu/volume-7-issue-3/developing-the-road-to-nowhere-ethical-considerations-of-highway-expansions/

WHO. (2001). International Classification of Functioning, Disability and Health (ICF). https://www.who.int/standards/classifications/international-classification-of-functioning-disability-and-health

Wilson, J. (2000). Exploring the limits of public participation in local government, Oxford university press, s 247-259.

Wimmer, M. A. (2007). Ontology for an e-participation virtual resource centre. In *Proceedings of the 1st international conference on Theory and practice of electronic governance*. P: 89-98. DOI: 10.1145/1328057.1328079

Wirtz, B. W., Daiser, P., & Binkowska, B. (2018). E-participation: A strategic framework. *International Journal of Public Administration, 41*(1), 1–12. DOI: 10.1080/01900692.2016.1242620

Wirtz, B. W., Daiser, P., & Binkowska, B. (2018). E-Participation: The Role of Social Media in Citizen Engagement. *Government Information Quarterly, 35*(4), 2–3.

Wolffhardt, A., Conte, C., & Huddleston, T. (2019). *The European Benchmark for refugee integration: A comparative analysis of the national integration evaluation mechanism in 14 EU countries*. Baseline Report, https://ec.europa.eu/migrant-integration/system/files/2022-06/NIEM%20report%20second%20evaluation%20 2022.pdf

Wood, J., Eskic, D., Benway, D. J., & Macdonald-Poelman, K. (2020). *Housing affordability: What are best practices and why are they important?*https://d36oiwf74r1rap.cloudfront.net/wp-content/uploads/Best-Practices-Dec2020.pdf?x71849#page=10.75

Wray, H. (2021). *Migration and Local Governance*. Palgrave Macmillan.

Wu, H., & Atar, E. (2023). The Application of Self-directed Learning in the Local Level Workplace. *ASR: CMU Journal of Social Sciences and Humanities, 10*(1), e2023013. DOI: 10.12982/CMUJASR.2023.013

Yaman, K., Aşgın, S., Yetişken, Y., & Aksoy, E. (2013). Comparative Analysis Of The E-Municipality Applications In Türkiye: The Case Of Western Black Sea Region. *Celal Bayar University Journal of Management and Economics., 20*(1), 207–220.

Yavuz, N. (2015). ''Dijital çağ yönetişimi: Kamu yönetiminde ihtiyaç temelli bütünleşme çabası'', in *Kamu Yönetiminde Paradigma Arayışlar: Yeni Kamu İşletmeciliği ve Ötesi*, (Edt: Özer Köseoğlu & M. Zahid Sobacı), Dora Yayınları. 273-293.

Yavuz, N. (2021). ''Yerel yönetimlerde elektronik vatandaş katılımı'', in *Kamu Yönetiminde Elektronik Vatandaş Katılımı* (Edt: Ayşegül Saylam), Ankara: Gazi Kitapevi, 137-155.

Yavuz, N. (2022). ''Yerel yönetimlerde vatandaş katılımının etkinliği: Bursa Nilüfer Belediyesi üzerinden bir değerlendirme'', in *Kamu Yönetiminde Katılım Üzerine Güncel Tartışmalar* (Edt: Ezgi Seçkiner Bingöl), Ankara: Gazi Kitapevi.

Yeo, J., & Huang, X. (2020). Migration in public administration research: A systematic review and future directions. *International Journal of Public Administration, 43*(2), 176–187. DOI: 10.1080/01900692.2019.1672731

Yıldırım, Y. Z. (2021). *Dezavantajlı Bir Grup Olarak Engelliler ve Engellilere Yönelik Yerel Yönetim Faaliyetleri*. Filiz Kitabevi.

Yilmaz, D. (2008). The Concept and Criteria of Public Service in Turkish Law. Gazi University Faculty of Law Journal, XII(1-2).

Yılmaz, V., & Yentürk, N. (2017). Türkiye'de Engellilere Yönelik Kamu Harcamalarının On Yıllık Seyri. *Çalışma Ve Toplum, 1*(52), 59-74.

Yuvitsa, N. (2019). Local government in Kazakhstan: An attempt to create a national model. *Management, 7*(1), 26–34. https://doi.org/https://doi.org/10.26425/2309-3633-2019-1-26-34

Zapata-Barrero, R. (2018). Applied political theory and qualitative research in migration studies. *Qualitative research in European migration studies*, 75-92.

Zapata-Barrero, R., Caponio, T., & Scholten, P. (2017). Theorizing the 'Local Turn' in Immigration Policies. *International Review of Administrative Sciences, 83*(2), 241–260. DOI: 10.1177/0020852316688426

Zero Waste Regulation. (2019). https://www.mevzuat.gov.tr/mevzuat?MevzuatNo=32659&MevzuatTur=7&MevzuatTertip=5

Zhanuzakova, L. (2013). Elections of akims is a real step towards the formation of the system of local self-government in the Republic of Kazakhstan. *Bulletin of the Institute of Legislation of the Republic of Kazakhstan, 31*(3), 14–18. https://cyberleninka.ru/article/n/vybory-akimov-realnyy-shag-k-formirovaniyu-sistemy-mestnogo-samoupravleniya-v-respublike-kazahstan

Zheng, Y. (2017). Explaining citizens' E-participation usage: Functionality of E-participation applications. *Administration & Society, 49*(3), 423–442. DOI: 10.1177/0095399715593313

Zholdybalina, A. S., Sankhaeva, Zh. M., Urpekova, A. G., Sailau, Q. S., Oteghali, D. B., & Yqylas, Q. E. (2024). Выборы депутатов маслихатов-2023: особенности и тенденции. К 30-летию образования маслихатов. [Elections of Maslikhat Deputies-2023: Features and Trends. On the 30th Anniversary of the Establishment of Maslikhats] (Collective monograph). Astana: Kazakhstan Institute for Strategic Studies under the President of the Republic of Kazakhstan.

Žibas, K. (2015). Immigration policies in Lithuania: institutional and legislative developments, challenges and opportunities. *Problemy Polityki Społecznej. Studia i dyskusje*, (31 (4)), 59-79.

About The Contributors

Onur Kulaç is an Associate Professor in the Department of Political Science and Public Administration at Pamukkale University in Denizli, Turkey. He earned his Ph.D. in Politics and Public Administration from Pamukkale University in December 2016. He also holds a Master of Public Administration (MPA) from the University of York, UK, completed in 2011, and a bachelor's degree in International Relations from Ege University, Turkey. Currently serving as the Vice Dean of the Faculty of Economics and Administrative Sciences and the Director of the Social, Economic, and Political Research and Application Center at Pamukkale University, Dr. Kulaç has a significant role in the university's administrative and international relations efforts. His academic contributions are marked by postdoctoral research at prestigious institutions such as the University of Southern California and Pardubice University. Dr. Kulaç has made substantial contributions to public policy, higher education policy, and public administration education through numerous peer-reviewed publications and conference presentations. His research spans areas such as decision-making processes, climate change policy, and the role of think tanks in policy-making. Additionally, he has been involved in various international research projects, including studies on the impact of COVID-19 on public administration.

Çiğdem Akman graduated from Suleyman Demirel University, Department of Public Administration. She completed her master's degree at Sakarya University at the Institute of Social Sciences, Program of Public Administration. She completed her doctorate education at Suleyman Demirel University Institute of Social Sciences Program of Public Finance in 2015. She worked as a Lecturer at the Egirdir Vocational School between 2010-2015. In 2016, she has been appointed as an assistant professor at the Department of Public Administration at Suleyman Demirel University. Since 2020, she is working at Suleyman Demirel University, Department of Political Science and Public Administration as an associate professor. The author has books, many book chapters, and articles on Local Governments,

Local Government Finance, E-government, Artificial Intelligence, Government Systems, Policy Boards, Twinning City, and Cittaslow.

***

Violeta B. Alonzo is an associate instructor at the Department of Social Sciences, Mariano Marcos State University (MMSU) in Batac City, Ilocos Norte province, The Philippines.

Emrah Atar is Associate Professor of Political Science and Public Administration in the Faculty of Economics and Administrative Sciences at Recep Tayyip Erdoğan University, Turkey. He is also the Head of the Department of Political Science and Public Administration and the Department of Urbanization and Environmental Issues. Additionally, he serves as Deputy Director of the Climate Change and Environmental Issues Application and Research Center at the same university. In addition to his academic work, Atar serves as Book Review Editor for the International Migration Review, Assistant Editor for the Journal of Academic Value Studies, and Field Editor for the Uluslararası Ekonomi İşletme ve Politika Dergisi (International Journal of Economics, Business, and Politics).

Cenay Babaoğlu graduated from Hacettepe University, department of Political Science and Public Administration. He completed his graduate studies at the same university, at the Institute of Social Sciences, Program of Political Science and Public Administration and worked as research assistant at the same department between 2009-2015. During this period, he had academic visits to Bremen University/ Germany for one year, to Berlin/Germany for four months and to Skopje/ Macedonia for six months. After receiving his PhD in 2015, he began his career at the Grand National Assembly of Turkey. In 2017, he has been appointed as assistant professor at the Department of Public Administration at Ömer Halisdemir University. He is working as associate professor at Selcuk University, since 2019. The author has many books, book chapters and articles on public policy practices and civic engagement, social policies, public administration and technology. He is the Editor of Journal of Public Administration and Policy and assistant editor of the Journal of Public Administration and Technology.

Remigijus Civinskas is an Associate Professor of Public Policy and Management in the Department of Public Administration, and a Senior Research Fellow at the Vytautas Kavolis Transdisciplinary Research Institute, Vytautas Magnus University (Lithuania). His research interests lie in the fields of public policy studies and public service delivery. With over 15 years of experience in public policy research, Dr

Civinskas specialises in the analysis of evidence-based and participatory policy-making processes, with a particular focus on national government practices.

Ana Marie Faith Corpuz is an instructor at the Department of Social Sciences, Mariano Marcos State University

Hasret Duman completed her undergraduate studies in the Department of Political Science and Public Administration at Gazi University. She obtained her master's degree from Hacettepe University, Department of Public Administration, with a thesis titled "Comparative Analysis of Public Policies on Vaccination Worldwide: The Case of COVID-19." She is currently pursuing her doctoral studies in the Department of Public Administration at Hacettepe University and working as a research assistant at Hatay Mustafa Kemal University. Her research interests include public administration, public policy, and digital technologies in public administration.

Jaroslav Dvorak, born in 1974, Ph.D. in Political Sciences in 2011. He was visiting researcher at Uppsala University (2017), Institute of Russian and Eurasian Studies, Sweden, and visiting professor at Bialystok Technical University (2017), Poland. Jaroslav Dvorak is involved in the editorial board of international scientific journals. Jaroslav Dvorak is a professor and head of the Department of Public Administration and Political Sciences at Klaipeda University, Lithuania. He has executive and expert experience in national and international institutions. He was the Klaipeda University representative on the Klaipeda regional development council (2019-2021). He is a member of the Research Board at People Powered.

Oğuzhan Erdoğan was born in Trabzon in 1985. In 2007, he graduated from Hacettepe University, Faculty of Economics and Administrative Sciences, Department of Political Science and Public Administration. In 2010, he completed his master's degree at Karadeniz Technical University, Department of Public Administration and in 2018, he completed his PhD at Aksaray University, Department of Public Administration. In 2012, he worked as a lecturer at Trabzon Eurasia University. Oğuzhan Erdoğan has been continuing his academic life as a faculty member at Mehmet Akif Ersoy University since 2012. In addition to these duties, Mr. Erdoğan served as Chief Advisor at the Ombudsman's Office of the Grand National Assembly of Turkey, Chairman of the Supervisory Board at the Turkish Rugby Federation, Deputy Director at Çavdır Vocational School, Advisor and Deputy Mayor at Bucak Municipality, and member of the 12th Development Plan Local Governments Specialized Commission of the Presidency Strategy and Budget Presidency.

Elizabeth Marfel F. Gagni is associate professor at the Department of Social Sciences, Mariano Marcos State University (MMSU) in Batac City, Ilocos Norte province, The Philippines. She also heads MMSU's undergraduate Psychology program.

Melissa R. Garabiles is associate professor and graduate program coordinator at the Department of Psychology, De La Salle University (DLSU) in Manila, The Philippines.

Gulmira T. Ileuova is a sociologist and the President of the Public Foundation Center for Social and Political Studies "Strategy" in Almaty, Kazakhstan. She holds a Candidate of Sciences (Sociology) degree and has extensive experience in conducting research on political processes, governance, and civil society development in Kazakhstan and Central Asia. Her research interests include public administration, democratic governance, and social transformation in post-Soviet states.

Nurlan Muminov, Ph.D., is a Research Associate at the Eurasian Research Institute, Khoja Akhmet Yassawi International Kazakh–Turkish University, Turkistan, Kazakhstan. His research focuses on identity politics, ontological security, public administration, and political reforms in Central Asia. His academic interests include comparative politics and regional governance structures in post-Soviet states.

Raushan Nurbekova is a PhD candidate at the Department of Political Science and Political Technologies at Al-Farabi Kazakh National University in Almaty, Kazakhstan. Her research focuses on local governance and public administration reforms in Kazakhstan and the broader Central Asian region. Her academic interests include comparative politics, electoral systems, and regional governance structures.

Jeremaiah M. Opiniano is professor at the Department of Journalism, University of Santo Tomas (UST) in the Philippines.

Miray Özden works as an associate professor at Tekirdağ Namık Kemal University in Tekirdağ. She completed her doctorate in Marmara University, Department of Local Administrations and received her doctorate in 2020. Her research areas are local governments, local participation, local politics, governance, citizen participation methods and urban politics. At the same time, she has studies on participatory methods in the strategic planning process in local governments and a master's thesis that she directed.

Çiğdem Pank Yildirim started working as a Research Assistant at Muğla Sıtkı Koçman University in 2011. She completed her master's degree at Muğla Sıtkı Koçman University, Institute of Social Sciences in 2012. She started her doctorate education at Muğla Sıtkı Koçman University, Institute of Social Sciences, Department of Public Administration in September 2012. She completed her doctorate education at Muğla Sıtkı Koçman University, Institute of Social Sciences, Department of Public Administration in 2024. She currently works as a Research Assistant Doctor in the Department of Public Administration, Faculty of Economics and Administrative Sciences, Muğla Sıtkı Koçman University. She has numerous academic studies published on management sciences, local governments, constitutional institutions, and environmental management.

Ossama Ramadan, I have a bachelor's degree in Political Science from Egypt, and I am currently pursuing a master's degree in Turkey. I have experience in political research and writing, and I have published several political papers and articles in think tanks and magazines.

Zhanar Sankayeva, Author of more than a dozen scientific publications in academic publications and collections of materials of republican and international conferences. Including: "Prospects for inter-parliamentary cooperation of women deputies: Central Asia and Afghanistan"// Collection of materials on the results of a regional seminar, UN Regional Center UNRCCA – p. 105-111 I have experience in lecturing on topics of electoral politics, as well as on the activities of Kazakhstan's "think tanks"

Serdar Selman, He currently serves as the Deputy Secretary General at Pamukkale University. Prior to this role, he held various administrative positions within different departments of local government, where he gained substantial experience in public administration. His research interests primarily focus on local governments, public personnel management, and contemporary human resources management and processes.

Daniel U. Scott, PhD, JD, MPA, is an Administrative Law Judge and adjunct professor in the fields of management and law with over three decades of experience. He has served in the military and participated in various civil projects. He is a member of the Honor Society of Omega Nu Lambda, and The Society for Collegiate Leadership & Achievement. He has conducted in-depth academic research across disciplines and contributed to scholarly publications including significant contributions to the field of ethics.

Mirna Varga is an assistant and doctoral researcher at the Chair for Social Policy, which is part of the Faculty of Law, Department of Social Work, at the University of Zagreb. Her research focuses on migration and integration policies, particularly family reunification processes for non-EU nationals. She has also published work on parenting leaves, with a particular emphasis on fathers' involvement in early childcare. She is engaged in international research collaborations, including COST Action Sustainability@Leave, and actively contributes to policy work within the local community.

Sena Yıldırım began her professional career at the Trabzon Courthouse and currently serves as a civil servant at the Directorate of Judicial Support and Victim Services in the Rize Courthouse. Her knowledge and experience in public administration, social services, and justice enable her to perform her duties effectively. With a strong sense of social responsibility, Sena Yıldırım aims to continue playing a significant role in victim rights and public service.

Elif Yucebas completed her doctorate at Dokuz Eylul University, Institute of Social Sciences, Department of Public Administration in 2014. She is a lecturer in the Local Administrations Program at Dokuz Eylul University İzmir Vocational School. She currently works as a lecturer of Local Governments at Izmir Vocational School, Dokuz Eylul University. She continues to study in the field of local administrations and urbanization policies.

Index

I

K

L

M

O

P

S

T

www.ingramcontent.com/pod-product-compliance
Lightning Source LLC
LaVergne TN
LVHW080603300926
849162LV00005B/1035